WellSpring

— 365 devotional readings —

Well Spring

— *365 devotional readings* —

Ralph I. Tilley

LITS Books
PO Box 405
Sellersburg, Indiana 47172

This volume is affectionately dedicated to the memory of
Dr. S. I. Emery (1895-1977) —
a remarkable man of God, theologian,
preacher, teacher, mentor, and valued friend

Awake, Our Souls
by Isaac Watts

Awake, our souls; away, our fears;
Let every trembling thought be gone;
Awake and run the heavenly race,
And put a cheerful courage on.

True, 'tis a strait and thorny road,
And mortal spirits tire and faint;
But they forget the mighty God
That feeds the strength of every saint:

The mighty God, whose matchless power
Is ever new and ever young,
And firm endures, while endless years
Their everlasting circles run.

*From thee, the **overflowing Spring,***
***Our souls shall drink a fresh supply**,*
While such as trust their native strength
Shall melt away, and droop, and die.

Swift as an eagle cuts the air,
We'll mount aloft to thine abode;
On wings of love our souls shall fly,
Nor tire amidst the heavenly road.

Preface

The title of these devotional readings is *WellSpring*. A "wellspring" is the head of a spring, stream, or river. When used metaphorically, it means "a continuous, seemingly inexhaustible source or supply of something."

Our Father in heaven is the Christian's ultimate and infinite Wellspring: "Every good gift and every perfect gift is from above, coming down from the Father of lights, with whom there is no variation or shadow due to change" (James 1:17). God is our source and plentitude of salvation, mercy, grace, hope, love, goodness, fruitfulness, help, power, fruitfulness, and so much more.

The *WellSpring* you hold in your hand is merely a finite (except for the Bible texts) expression of my own understanding of the works and ways of our Sovereign God, drawn from my own *well* and includes many contributions from others. While we can know God and his Son, the Lord Jesus Christ, our capacity to know God will always be limited in this world: "For we know in part and we prophesy in part" (1 Cor. 13:9). But as limited as we are, we still strain to know God and his ways better: "I stretch out my hands to you; my soul thirsts for you like a parched land" (Ps. 143:6). This book will hopefully help the reader do some soul-stretching.

Each day's reading consists of four parts: A Bible text (*The Word*); an insightful quotation from an author (*Voice from the Church*); a brief comment from this writer (*Reflection*); and a verse of poetry (*Verse*). The verses without attribution are my own composition. Furthermore, readings for Holy Week begin on March 31.

A word of appreciation is due to my dear wife, Emily, who carefully pored over each page of this volume. However, she is not responsible for any errors, since my eyes were the last ones reviewing each page before it went to the printer.

I joyfully give glory to my Father in heaven, for any help his children may receive from this these readings. Now, may "the grace of the Lord Jesus Christ and the love of God and the fellowship of the Holy Spirit be with you all" (2 Cor. 13:14).

Ralph I. Tilley
Soli Deo Gloria

Scripture

Isaiah 12:3
*"With joy you will draw **water** from the wells of salvation."*

John 4:7-13
*[7] A woman from Samaria came to draw **water**. Jesus said to her, "Give me a drink."*
[8] (For his disciples had gone away into the city to buy food.)
[9] The Samaritan woman said to him, "How is it that you, a Jew, ask for a drink from me, a woman of Samaria?" (For Jews have no dealings with Samaritans.)
*[10] Jesus answered her, "If you knew the gift of God, and who it is that is saying to you, 'Give me a drink,' you would have asked him, and he would have given you living **water**."*
*[11] The woman said to him, "Sir, you have nothing to draw **water** with, and the well is deep. Where do you get that living **water**?*
[12] Are you greater than our father Jacob? He gave us the well and drank from it himself, as did his sons and his livestock."
*[13] Jesus said to her, "Everyone who drinks of this **water** will be thirsty again, [14] but whoever drinks of the **water** that I will give him will never be thirsty again. The **water** that I will give him will become in him a spring of **water** welling up to eternal life."*

John 7:37-39
[37] On the last day of the feast, the great day, Jesus stood up and cried out, "If anyone thirsts, let him come to me and drink.
*[38] Whoever believes in me, as the Scripture has said, 'Out of his heart will flow rivers of living **water**.'"*
[39] Now this he said about the Spirit, whom those who believed in him were to receive, for as yet the Spirit had not been given, because Jesus was not yet glorified.

Revelation 22:17
*The Spirit and the Bride say, "Come." And let the one who hears say, "Come." And let the one who is thirsty come; let the one who desires take the **water** of life without price.*

Wells of Salvation (1)

The Word
"With joy you will draw water from the wells of salvation."
Isaiah 12:3

Voice from the Church
Isaiah 12 is a hymn, praising God for His faithfulness in keeping His promises, especially the promise of salvation. Isaiah encouraged the people that deep in God's "wells of salvation" they would experience the cool water of God's grace, strength, and joy. This would refresh and strengthen their hearts and cause praise and gratitude to God." *(Our Daily Bread)**

Reflection
What the prophet prophesied under the Old Covenant is now fully realized under the New. Though the saints of old experienced a foretaste of God's saving grace, it was only through the gift of Messiah and his finished work and the poured-out Spirit, that God's refreshing salvation is enjoyed in its fulness.

The land of the prophets was essentially a land with little supply of water. Because of this lack, it became a region populated with wells of water. The men of old dug wells wherever they journeyed. These wells became a metaphor and symbol for God's gift of salvation for spiritually thirsty souls. What water and wells meant to physically needy people in an arid land, so God's saving grace means so much more to spiritually dehydrated creatures made in the image of God. "Wells" is in the plural, signifying there is an abundance of ever-flowing saving grace to all who will "draw" by faith through the Lord Jesus Christ.

Are you joyfully and refreshingly experiencing the benefits of God's "wells of salvation" today?

Verse
My soul was parched and thirsty; I was dry and dead deep within.
I saw a Well afar but was helpless because of my sin.
Then Wind I felt gently blowing; to the Well I came at last.
I drank with joy from its Waters; my thirst was relieved so fast.

Jesus at a Well (2)

The Word

> *Jesus answered her, "If you knew the gift of God, and who it is that is saying to you, 'Give me a drink,' you would have asked him, and he would have given you living water."*
> John 4:10

Voice from the Church

"It seemed to me that all that Heaven is or all that Heaven means broke in on my soul, and I was flooded with light and glory and was in a new world.... Well, glory to God forever. It never grows old, and is always fresh." (Bud Robinson, 1860-1942)*

Reflection

Thirsty-hearted souls sooner or later find their way to Jesus. Without always realizing what or Who is drawing them to the living water, the Spirit of God has been at work stirring within them an insatiable thirst for a satisfying and soul-quenching drink. The emptied-hearted sinner will never be truly satisfied in this world, until his inner longing brings him face to face with the Fountain of the water of life.

Man's greatest need is salvation—salvation from sin and sinning, salvation from eternal death and Hell, salvation from self-centeredness, salvation from the inevitable wrath of God poured out upon sinners.

The Good News is that "Christ Jesus came into the world to save sinners" (1 Tim. 1:15). This takes us all in, just as it did the Samaritan woman, who providentially encountered the Savior that one eventful and life-changing day at Jacob's well.

What the parched soul often settles for is nothing but a dry well. But if the truly thirsty will not be satisfied with anything less than real water, living water, their thirst will eventually be quenched by the Lord Jesus.

Verse

Well of water, ever springing,
Bread of life so rich and free,
Untold wealth that never faileth,
My Redeemer is to me. (Clara T. Williams, 1858-1937)**

Rivers of Living Water (3)

The Word

> *³⁷On the last day of the feast, the great day, Jesus stood up and cried out, "If anyone thirsts, let him come to me and drink. ³⁸Whoever believes in me, as the Scripture has said, 'Out of his heart will flow rivers of living water.'" ³⁹Now this he said about the Spirit, whom those who believed in him were to receive, for as yet the Spirit had not been given, because Jesus was not yet glorified.*
> John 7:37-39

Voice from the Church

"As the manger of Bethlehem was the cradle of the Son of God, so was the upper room the cradle of the Spirit of God." (A. J. Gordon, 1836-1895)*

Reflection

Before the Age of the Spirit could be ushered in, the Lord Jesus must first be "glorified" (crucified, resurrected, ascended to the Father's right hand). Ten days following Christ's ascension into Heaven, he and the Father poured out the Holy Spirit upon the waiting host gathered in a Jerusalem room. On that occasion, there was a baptism and infilling of the Holy Spirit—a mighty empowerment. Such a manifestation of the Spirit was unprecedented.

The Lord Jesus had promised the Spirit's coming: "I will ask the Father, and he will give you another Helper, to be with you forever" (John 14:16). On the great day of the feast, recorded in the above text, Jesus said the gift of the Spirit would be given to the thirsty-hearted: "If anyone thirsts, let him come to me and drink." To those receiving this promised gift, Jesus said "rivers of living water" would result—a life that refreshes and blesses others, a life of fruitfulness.

Are you thirsty?

Verse

Do you wish to be used of God,
Given entirely to His will?
Bring your thirsty heart to Jesus;
With His Spirit let Him now fill.

God's Gracious Invitation (4)

The Word

The Spirit and the Bride say, "Come." And let the one who
hears say, "Come." And let the one who is thirsty come;
let the one who is willing take the water of life without price.
Revelation 22:17

Voice from the Church

"Are you willing now to be saved—are you willing to forsake sin—willing to take Christ to be your Master from this day forth and for ever? Strange that it should be necessary to ask such questions, but still it is. Are you willing? Then remember that whatever may be against you—whatever may have defiled you—however black, however filthy, however worthless you may be, you are invited this day to take of the fountain of the water of life freely, for you are willing, and it is said, 'Whosoever will, let him come.'" (Charles Spurgeon, 1834-1892)*

Reflection

The events and provisions of salvation—the death, resurrection, ascension, intercessions of Christ, and the descent of the Spirit—were given by a loving God to rescue sinners from sin and themselves. It was God's love for fallen man that moved him to send his one and only Son into the world to purchase our salvation. The Bible makes this clear.

The Holy Spirit and the Bride of Christ have been engaged since the first century in graciously offering salvation to lost people: "Come." To all who will hear, to all who are thirsty, to each one who desires and is willing to receive God's gracious offer, they may "take of the water of life without price." Yes, salvation is free; it is the gift of God. But it is also costly. We must leave all our sin to receive the water of life.

Have you come? Are you inviting others to come?

Verse

Ho! every one that is thirsty in spirit,
Ho! every one that is weary and sad;
Come to the fountain, there's fullness in Jesus,
All that you're longing for: come and be glad! (Lucy J. Meyer, 1849-1922)**

The Wonders of the Spirit

The Word

> *"The wind blows where it wishes, and you hear its sound,*
> *but you do not know where it comes from or where it goes.*
> *So it is with everyone who is born of the Spirit."*
> John 3:8

Voice from the Church

"I know very well when, but hardly how, the final step was taken. I was driven to Whipsnade one sunny morning. When we set out I did not believe that Jesus Christ is the Son of God, and when we reached the zoo I did." (C. S. Lewis, 1898-1963)*

Reflection

Who can fully explain the wonders of the wind? Who among us can demystify the mysteries surrounding the mind and ways of God involved in one's spiritual birth. Though one possessed the intellectual knowledge of an Einstein, though one was schooled in the ways of Scripture as a Nicodemus, yet how and when the Spirit of God descends upon the soul bringing life out of death, no one completely understands nor can fully explain.

Because we cannot totally understand the workings of the Spirit of God does not mean that we cannot enjoy his marvelous new creation and testify to the same. We are simply told, "Repent and believe the gospel" (Mark 1:15); God will take care of the mysteries.

Have you experienced God's wonderful *birthing* grace? Have you ever told another person how God mercifully gave you new life in Christ? Don't allow yourself to keep quiet about God's mercy given to you just because you can't fully explain how it occurred. Your story must be told. Be bold!

Verse

I cannot tell thee whence it came,
This peace within my breast;
But this I know, there fills my soul
A strange and tranquil rest. (John S. Brown, (1899-?)**

Spirit Illumination

The Word
Now we have received not the spirit of the world, but the Spirit who is from God, that we might understand the things freely given us by God.
1 Corinthians 2:12

Voice from the Church
"Since it is the Holy Spirit who gives us the ability rightly to understand Scripture, we need to realize that the proper thing to do, particularly when we are unable to understand some passage or some doctrine of Scripture, is to pray for God's help. Often what we need is not more data but more insight into the data we already have. This insight is given only by the Holy Spirit." (Wayne Grudem, b. 1948)*

Reflection
God will give to each of his genuine followers everything, in his time, that is necessary for that person's sanctification and maturation. God is not obligated to disclose to any of us his hidden mysteries. However, he reveals to each one of his thirsty-hearted disciples what is required for one's fruitful and effective walk with him.

God has given us his Word and the Holy Spirit. We need the Holy Spirit to illuminate our minds to properly understand what the Word of God means and how to apply it to our lives. This was a primary concern of the apostles: "We have not ceased to pray for you, asking that you may be filled with the knowledge of his will in all spiritual wisdom and understanding, [10]so as to walk in a manner worthy of the Lord, fully pleasing to him: bearing fruit in every good work and increasing in the knowledge of God." (Col. 1:9-10).

It is not enough to read the Word of God; we need the Spirit's illumination so that we may live a God-glorifying fruitful life.

Verse
Silently now I wait for Thee,
Ready my God, Thy will to see,
Open my eyes, illumine me,
Spirit divine! (Clara H. Scott, 1841-1897)**

He Walked with God

The Word
Enoch walked with God, and he was not, for God took him.
Genesis 5:24

Voice from the Church
"We have many strong featured characters drawn in history. Some shine in all the brilliancy of martial achievements, and are renowned for the conquest of kingdoms. Others have gathered laurels in the paths of science and illumined the world with the flashes of their genius. Others by their counsels have swayed the fate of empires. And the deeds of these have been loudly sounded by the trumpet of fame. But more is said in praise of this man of God [Enoch] in the few short words of our text, than is said of them all. A greater character is given him in four words, than is ascribed to the most renowned warriors and statesmen by the whole voice of history and poetry." (Edward Griffin, 1770-1837)*

Reflection
What greater epitaph could be given to a man or woman than to say he or she simply "walked with God"? We are not told that Enoch performed any miracles. There is no record that he experienced phenomenal dreams or visions. It was not reported that he was a man of wealth and prosperity. He wrote no books, to our knowledge, nor left an earthly monument to honor his feats. But there was One in heaven who observed his life and conduct and took notice. "Enoch walked with God."

For the last few years I have texted my grandson, Luke, five days each week during the school year. I include in each text a verse of Scripture and a brief note. I frequently exhort him: "Walk with God today, Luke." That's precisely what Enoch did; he walked with God for 300 years. God's grace will enable you to walk with him today.

Verse
His face was fixed, his gait was steady;
Undeterred, he travelled fresh sod.
Though others chose a familiar path,
Enoch always walked with his God.

A Pure Heart

The Word
Draw near to God, and he will draw near to you. Cleanse your
hands, you sinners, and purify your hearts, you doubleminded.
James 4:8

Voice from the Church
"Christ's atoning blood and the inner working of the Holy Spirit have power to cleanse the heart of the believer to its innermost depths and bring the believer to the place where Christ is the supreme and reigning love of his or her life. So why are the history of the Church and the lives of most Christian believers full of strife and division? Is it not because the possibility of a heart controlled by the pure love of Christ has been largely inconceivable?" (Dennis F. Kinlaw, 1992-2017)*

Reflection
The atoning blood of Christ removes the guilt and condemnation of the repentant sinner, who has placed his trust in the Lord Jesus; the fiery cleansing of the Holy Spirit cures the trusting believer of his double-mindedness.

Many Christians need of a "second touch." These have a blessed assurance that "Jesus is mine"; however, their walk is an admixture: there is a love for Christ, but there remains some love for the world. Like the pre-Pentecost Simon Peter, such believers blow hot one moment and cold the next. One day they carry their cross, the next day they drop it. They have confessed Christ, but they fail to abide in Christ. In the morning they overcome their besetting sin; in the evening they suffer defeat.

Do not let any man tell you that God cannot give you a pure heart, removing your doublemindedness. If you are willing, God will cleanse your *inside*; you must cleanse the *outside*.

Verse
Breathe on me, breath of God,
Until my heart is pure,
Until with Thee I will one will,
To do and to endure. (Edwin Hatch, 1835-1889)**

Little Flock

The Word

"Fear not, little flock, for it is your Father's
good pleasure to give you the kingdom."
Luke 12:32

Voice from the Church

"I am a little shepherd, and preside over a tiny flock, and I am among the least of the servants of the Spirit. But Grace is not narrow, or circumscribed by place. Wherefore let freedom of speech be given even to the small—especially when the subject matter is of such great importance." (Gregory Nazianzen, 329-390)*

Reflection

The word "little" is a term used to describe something in comparison to something else that is larger. Jesus often spoke of "little children" and he rebuked his disciples for their "little faith." He addressed those who loved him "little" because they perceived they had been forgiven "little." At least on one occasion, our Lord referred to his chosen followers as a "little flock"; they were merely twelve men among the vast multitudes.

The world without Christ is huge in numbers as compared to the followers of Christ; Christians are destined to be in the minority in this present age. But more particularly, across this world, there are *little* Bible classes and groups, *little* ministries. and *little* churches. What does our Lord say to such diminutive groups? "Fear not, little flock, for it is your Father's good pleasure to give you the kingdom."

In the kingdom of God, "little" can mean *much* if God is in it. Bethlehem was a "little" town and Galilee was a "little" region. However, God Almighty accomplished *big* things in both locations.

Verse

Fear not, little flock, whatever your lot,
He enters all rooms, "the doors being shut,"
He never forsakes; He never is gone,
So count on His presence in darkness and dawn. (Paul Rader, 1878-1938)**

Touching the World through Prayer

The Word

¹First of all, then, I urge that supplications, prayers, intercessions, and thanksgivings be made for all people, ²for kings and all who are in high positions, that we may lead a peaceful and quiet life, godly and dignified in every way. ³This is good, and it is pleasing in the sight of God our Savior, ⁴who desires all people to be saved and to come to the knowledge of the truth.

1 Timothy 2:1-4

Voice from the Church

"I have heard that, in long after-years, the worst woman in the village of Torthorwald, [Scotland] then leading an immoral life, but since changed by the grace of God, was known to declare, that the only thing that kept her from despair and from the Hell of suicide, was when in the dark winter nights she crept close up underneath my father's window, and heard him pleading in Family Worship that God would convert 'the sinner from the error of wicked ways, and polish him as a jewel for the Redeemer's crown.'" (John Paton, 1824-1907)*

Reflection

Doubtless no one ever comes to faith in Christ apart from the intercessions of one or more of God's people. The Spirit says God "desires all people to be saved and come to the knowledge of the truth." The same Spirit (through the apostle) urges us to pray "for all people"—including those whom God "desires ... to be saved."

I am an answer to prayer. If you are a Christian, so are you. Often, I pray for the salvation of people I do not personally know. God hears; God answers. In the words of a friend (Dr. Wesley Duewel) who is now with the Lord, let us engage in "touching the world through prayer."

Verse

O Lord, increase our faith and love,
That we may all Thy goodness prove,
And gain from Thy exhaustless store
The fruits of prayer for evermore. (William Cowper, 1731-1800)**

Word and Spirit

The Word

> ¹²*Now we have received not the spirit of the world,*
> *but the Spirit who is from God, that we might understand*
> *the things freely given us by God.* ¹³*And we impart this in*
> *words not taught by human wisdom but taught by the Spirit,*
> *interpreting spiritual truths to those who are spiritual.*
> 1 Corinthians 2:12-13

Voice from the Church

"However, above everything else, this thesis remains absolute and certain: the Holy Spirit is the only true KEY to The Word of God. Nevertheless, the petition for the Holy Spirit does not exclude earnest and energetic study." (Fritz Rienecker, 1897-1965)*

Reflection

The apostle Paul was the most learned man of all the early apostles. He was educated in the law of Moses and Jewish traditions by one of the most respected scholars of his day, a man by the name of Gamaliel (Acts 5:34; 22:3). Saul of Tarsus knew what it was to be taught by man; he later learned what it meant to be taught by the Spirit of God.

No Christian should be guilty of denigrating biblical scholars. We should listen to and read after those who have given themselves to the study of the Sacred Writings. Unlearned is the person who thinks God's methods with men does not include his using skilled pastors and teachers in one's growth in Christ.

However, we must keep clearly before us this fact: While we study and listen to those who are students of the Word, without the Spirit of God opening our eyes to the truth of God, we are as blind as Saul of Tarsus was prior to his conversion and subsequent Spirit-enlightenment.

Verse

We give ourselves to study Your Word,
 for thus You have taught us to do.
But vain is the reading of Your truth,
 unless our eyes are opened by You.

God's Method

The Word

[11]*Whenever Moses held up his hand, Israel prevailed, and whenever he lowered his hand, Amalek prevailed. [12]But Moses' hands grew weary, so they took a stone and put it under him, and he sat on it, while Aaron and Hur held up his hands, one on one side, and the other on the other side. So his hands were steady until the going down of the sun. [13]And Joshua overwhelmed Amalek and his people with the sword.*
Exodus 17:11-13

Voice from the Church

"Had the pleasure of hearing that above a hundred people set apart a day of prayer in behalf of me and my dear brother Howell Harris, etc. While our friends thus continue to uphold their hands, our spiritual Amalek will never prevail against us." (George Whitefield, 1714-1770)*

Reflection

Everyone needs of our prayers, especially those who are waging war on the frontlines in the Kingdom of God. The man Moses knew this. Moses had directed his assistant Joshua to lead the battle against God's enemies, the Amalekites. It was not enough for Joshua to lead his men, using human strategy and weapons of war. Something more would be required for victory. What was that "something"? Moses ascended the hill to intercede, with Aaron and Hur. With upraised hands, Israel prevailed; with lowered hands, the enemy prevailed.

Have we learned this lesson? Or do we find ourselves doing the work of God without using the means he has placed at our disposal? Human efforts apart from prevailing prayer are worthless, no matter how spectacular our programs and performances appear. If we are to experience success as God counts success, we must persevere in prayer to God.

Verse

How often we have gone to war, O God,
  without Your wise guidance and strength.
Suffering defeat, we have wondered why,
  until the hands were raised at length.

Christian Models

The Word

> [7]*Remember your leaders, those who spoke to you the word of God.*
> *Consider the outcome of their way of life, and imitate their faith.*
> [8]*Jesus Christ is the same yesterday and today and forever.*

Hebrews 13:7-8

Voice from the Church

"No man is quite the same after contact with a saint. He may fly from him, and even, in the obduracy of his sinning, hug his sin the tighter, but always, uneasily, he remembers." (W. E. Sangster, 1900-1960)*

Reflection

If you were asked to select one or more Christians whose moral qualities and saintly character are strikingly Christlike, who would you name? While the Lord Jesus is the disciple's model *par excellence*, the Spirit wishes to so imprint the image of Christ upon us, that our walk with Christ is an example to our fellow believers.

The writer of the Hebrews Letter joined his exhortation with the reminder that "Jesus Christ is the same yesterday and today and forever." In other words, the same Christ who formed their leaders into exemplary Christians, is the same indwelling Christ who can make these first-century believers (and us) into people who are strong in faith, demonstrating godly behavior.

The Spirit of God has raised up, in every generation, a holy seed. He has sprinkled this seed across every denominational line and placed his devout followers on every continent. These are the people we are to imitate; they may not all be leaders, but they all resemble Jesus. Look for such people to emulate.

Verse

I knew a woman with a shining face,
  who lived her life with uncommon grace.
Though tried and tested to the very core,
  she triumphed joyfully whate'er she bore.
I consider her life and would imitate her faith.

Pure Intentions

The Word

"Beware of practicing your righteousness before
other people in order to be seen by them, for then you will
have no reward from your Father who is in heaven."
Matthew 6:1

Voice from the Church

"If your labors prove unsuccessful and you are much troubled by that, it is certain proof you did not expect to be rewarded simply for your [good] intentions, which you might have, if they had been pure and just." (Jeremy Taylor, 1613-1667)*

Reflection

In our walk with the Lord, it is more important as to *why* we perform acts of worship, ministry, and righteousness, as it is in doing the deed itself. Anything done—even in Jesus' name—which is motivated by vanity and pride, out of rivalry or for the praise of man, is repulsive in the eyes of God.

Jesus rebuked those, who in the performance of holy things were more concerned about what people thought than what God knew about them. Jesus did not upbraid the Pharisees for engaging in righteous acts; he excoriated them for performing such to gain people's attention and applause. Moral and religious service done for self-exaltation and adoration from others is an abomination to our holy God.

One of the most beautiful acts of service that a servant of Christ can perform is a deed done from a pure heart, when no one else is around, and no one else is looking except an all-seeing God.

As Christians, we should always be "playing" to an audience of One. Praise from God is what counts.

Verse

Why we do what we do
in the name of our Lord,
must be done with an eye
on Him, not on the crowd.

The Merciful

The Word
"Blessed are the merciful, for they shall receive mercy."
Matthew 5:7

Voice from the Church
"There is a morality that hardens, that makes one more severe with others the more one has learned to be severe with oneself. This is a tempting route of sacrifice-centered, spiritual-disciplines-focused, perfectionist, higher-life, and conscious raising ethics. But the first test of obedience to *Jesus'* ethic is not whether obedience makes one morally tougher but whether it also makes one mercifully softer." (Frederick D. Bruner, b. 1932)*

Reflection
There is a kind of religion that is true and yet false. This kind of religion is well-acquainted with the *letter* of the Law, but to such people the *spirit* of the Law is like a foreign language. *Letter Religion* is orthodox in its creed and well-versed in its belief system. But it is as cold and unattractive as the North Pole—and just as lifeless.

Our Lord's chief critics, when he ministered here on earth, were the religious elite: men steeped in the Hebrew Scriptures and cultic traditions. These were leaders who were stricter on others than they were on themselves. Why? Because their hearts were hard.

To show mercy to the weak and wayward, to the fainthearted and immature is not to be weak in one's self or untrue to the Word of God. Jesus was full of both grace and truth; we are to be filled with the same. Every repentant sinner is an object of God's mercy. Every repentant Christian, who has failed in his walk with the Lord, is likewise a recipient of a merciful God's grace.

Jesus said the merciful will be blessed. Do you want to be blessed?

Verse
I quickly picked up a stone,
  and was about to hurl;
Instead, I reached out and touched
  a sore, and he was healed.

Dealing with "Thorns"

The Word

So to keep me from becoming conceited because of the surpassing greatness of the revelations, a thorn was given me in the flesh, a messenger of Satan to harass me, to keep me from becoming conceited.
2 Corinthians 12:7

Voice from the Church

"To be a sacramental personality means that the elements of the natural life are presenced by God as they are broken providentially in His service. We have to be adjusted into God before we can be broken bread in His hands. Keep right with God and let Him do what He likes, and you will find that He is producing the kind of bread and wine that will benefit His other children." (Oswald Chambers, 1874-1917)*

Reflection

We are by nature stiff-necked and stouthearted. We are born with a mind that is twisted and contaminated by sin. While redeeming grace joins the repentant and believing sinner to God through the Lord Jesus Christ, there remains much in the disciple of Christ that requires transformation. God often uses suffering and affliction to bring us into fuller compliance with his will and likeness.

With Paul, God used "a thorn"—an infirmity of the flesh. Without it the apostle would have become a conceited, self-absorbed evangelist. The Lord mercifully used this ever-present weakness of the apostle "to keep me from becoming conceited."

While we often ask God to remove the thorn, as Paul first did, we fail to hear, like Paul, that God wants the thorn to remain to keep us low at the feet of Jesus. Embrace your thorn to the glory of God; God will use it to make you, not break you.

Verse

"Remove this thorn," was my supplication
  to God day after day.
His reply? "Let it stay;
  I will use this thorn for your perfection."

Differences

The Word

[22]"The glory that you have given me I have given to them, that
they may be one even as we are one, [23]I in them and you in me,
that they may become perfectly one, so that the world may know
that you sent me and loved them even as you loved me."
John 17:22-23

Voice from the Church

"Doctrinal differences between believers should never lead to personal
antagonism. Error must be opposed even when held by fellow members
of Christ, but if that opposition cannot coexist with a true love for all
saints and a longing for their spiritual prosperity then it does not glorify
God nor promote the edification of the Church." (George Whitefield, 1714-
1770)*

Reflection

One of the most difficult challenges we face in the Body of Christ is
how to disagree agreeably. Often our disagreements occur over second-
ary issues. Then there are occasions when disagreements surface regarding cardinal beliefs. Many of these disagreements could be resolved if
brothers and sisters in Christ were filled with the love and grace of
Christ. Prayerful, charitable deliberations have a way of bringing differing parties into harmony.

But where there is prideful obstinacy, no resolution to differences can
be reached. Many of our divisions occur because we are strong in ourselves instead of being strong in the Lord. Often, we are standing for our
own way instead of for biblical truth. Even in fighting for truth, we fail
because of the *way* we engage. As one once cautioned, "Be careful in
fighting a dragon, lest you become one."

Verse

He drew a circle that shut me out—
Heretic, rebel, a thing to flout.
But Love and I had the [grace] to win:
We drew a circle and took him in! (Edwin Markham, 1852-1940)**

True Humanity

The Word
And the Word became flesh and dwelt among us, and we have seen his glory, glory as of the only Son from the Father, full of grace and truth.
John 1:14

Voice from the Church
"True humanity is true godliness; true holiness is true manliness or true womanliness! Whatever is dehumanizing them, cannot be the fruit of the Spirit's ministry in us. Whatever makes you less human must be carnal, not spiritual." (Sinclair B. Ferguson, b. 1948)*

Reflection
Sin is an intruder; it is a foreign matter introduced in the Garden. The first man was created pure and holy; he was innocent and uncontaminated by any moral defect. There were no barriers to Adam's walk with God; he walked in perfect fellowship with his God—until the Fall.

The Lord Jesus Christ was the second Adam, who was "holy, innocent, unstained, separated from sinners" (Heb. 7:26). Jesus, though the Son of God, was also the Son of Man. He was God; he was man—he was the God-Man, always walking in holy fellowship with and submission to his Father.

Christians are called to walk in fellowship with God. Anything that impedes our walk will affect our fellowship. Anything that affects our fellowship is an intruder, creating darkness which the God of light wishes to dispel.

We are only a true person, as God means us to be, when through grace we rid ourselves of everything that makes us less than a man and woman of God. In other words, we are called to godliness—in the power of the Spirit.

Verse
Made to live in fellowship with my God,
By grace I refuse to be a mere clod.
When darkness seeks my way to overtake,
I flee to Him, lest communion I break.

Trust and Obey

The Word
[24] *"Everyone then who hears these words of mine and does them will be like a wise man who built his house on the rock. [25] And the rain fell, and the floods came, and the winds blew and beat on that house, but it did not fall, because it had been founded on the rock."*
Matthew 7:24-25

Voice from the Church
"From the human point of view there are countless possibilities of understanding and interpreting the Sermon on the Mount. Jesus knows only one possibility: simply go and obey." (Dietrich Bonhoeffer, 1906-1945)*

Reflection
As the Father's mouthpiece, the Word made flesh never once commanded his disciples to do one thing but what he expected them to do. Jesus knew well that whatever he commanded his followers to do, they could perform, as long as they looked to him in faith. Even a petulant, blustering Simon Peter could walk on water, if only he kept his gaze on the Lord Jesus.

What loving and wise parent does not expect a maturing child to obey him or her? And would a parent ever demand from a child what that child could never perform?

It is one of Satan's persistent lies in telling us (even from some pulpits) that we can't render consistent, obedient service to our Lord. True, such acts of loving and faithful obedience may not meet the standards of the scribes and the Pharisees. But that's not the standard by which we are measured. God knows we are naturally weak. But he also knows he has given us the Spirit to empower us to obey. Let us never think that God demands less from us than a faithful walk.

Verse
I said, "I can't; the hill is much too steep."
He said, "You can, if your eyes on Me keep."
I found I could, by in His Word trusting.
He said, "There's another hill—keep walking."

Falling into the Earth

The Word

> [24] *"Truly, truly, I say to you, unless a grain of wheat falls into the earth and dies, it remains alone; but if it dies, it bears much fruit. [25] Whoever loves his life loses it, and whoever hates his life in this world will keep it for eternal life."*
>
> John 12:24-25

Voice from the Church

"Oh, Eternal Love, my soul desires and chooses you. Come, Holy Spirit, inflame our hearts with your love. We love or we die. We die and we love. We die to all other loves in order to live to Jesus' love. Savior of our souls, may we sing forever, *Vive, Jésus!* Live, Jesus, whom I love! Reign forever. Amen." (Francis de Sales, 1567-1622)*

Reflection

Who wants to die? Who aspires to be *hidden*, as it were, where no one but God alone sees? And yet our Lord said that if there is no death, there can be no resurrection; where there is no burial, there can be no regeneration.

The words of our text were addressed to Greeks, men who were seeking for wisdom and possibly a hero to follow. They may have been only curiosity seekers, or they may have been sincere. We don't know. What we do know is this: Many times we approach God for one thing, then we discover he sees in us a need he wishes to meet that will satiate our deepest longings.

With God, death must precede life—abundant life; loss must precede gain. Before God could bless the world fully, God's Lamb must die. With us, there can be no fruitfulness and abundant blessing, until we die to our pet sins and twisted self.

Verse

I once was the object of my love,
  lifted high with my innate pride.
Then I was shown my sinful self
  and died, looking on the Crucified.

Singing Praises to God

The Word

Let the word of Christ dwell in you richly, teaching and admonishing
one another in all wisdom, singing psalms and hymns and
spiritual songs, with thankfulness in your hearts to God.
Colossians 3:16

Voice from the Church

"The Spirit not only inspires a new hymnody in every renewal within
the church, but makes the best of former hymnodies come to life with
new vigor." (Gordon Fee, b. 1934)*

Reflection

The psalms and hymns and spiritual songs have always played an important role in the congregations I served as well as in my personal walk
with God. How can a disciple of the Lord Jesus restrain himself from
lifting his heart to his Redeemer in songs of praise and thanksgiving?
Impossible. The Son of God himself was a singer: "In the midst of
the congregation I will sing your praise" (Heb. 2:12).

Just this morning, while reading in the Book of Hebrews, I was meditating on God's promised rest to his people. Two hymns came to mind:
"Near to the Heart of God" and "Sweetly Resting." I went to YouTube
and heard a beautiful choir sing each and sang along with them. God
gives his people a song in their heart from the moment of their new
birth. "I will sing to the Lord, because he has dealt bountifully with
me" (Ps. 13:6).

My Guatemalan Christian friend asks me occasionally, as I'm drinking my early morning coffee, "Pastor, have you sung yet this morning?"
He includes singing in his devotional time. It's no wonder he exudes the
joy of the Lord. Have you sung praises to God today?

Verse

Then sings my soul, My Saviour God, to Thee,
How great Thou art, How great Thou art.
Then sings my soul, My Saviour God, to Thee,
How great Thou art, How great Thou art! (Stuart K. Hine, 1899-1989)**

Bearing our Cross

The Word
And he said to all, "If anyone would come after me, let him
deny himself and take up his cross daily and follow me."
Luke 9:23

Voice from the Church
"To bear the cross is to display the royalty of heaven, while to deny the
cross is to defend our mean selves; to indulge in self-pity is to degrade
ourselves, while to play the man's part in the power of the Spirit is to
please Him who defended not Himself." (V. Raymond Edman, 1900-1967)*

Reflection
Early Christians never wore a cross of gold or silver around their necks.
To them, the cross was not a beautiful crafted piece of adornment to be
worn; the cross was a call to sacrificially and faithfully follow Jesus
Christ. The cross meant to those noble saints a death to self and, if need
be, a martyr's death.

To take up one's cross daily simply (and not always so simple) means
to identify ourselves with Jesus Christ in the face of the world's frown.
When Simon Peter denied having any relationship to the Lord Jesus in
the presence of his Lord's enemies, he failed to bear his cross. When
Paul and Silas sang praises to God at midnight in a Roman prison, they
were triumphantly bearing their cross, displaying their faithful identity
to Christ while incarcerated for preaching the gospel.

Jesus said, "For whoever is ashamed of me and of my words in this
adulterous and sinful generation, of him will the Son of Man also
be ashamed when he comes in the glory of his Father with the holy angels" (Mark 8:38). There are times when we must bear our cross quietly;
at other times, we are called of God to speak up courageously.

Verse
Must Jesus bear the cross alone,
And all the world go free?
No, there's a cross for everyone,
And there's a cross for me. (Thomas Shepherd, 1665-1739)**

Authenticity

The Word

⁴*For we know, brothers loved by God, that he has chosen you, ⁵because our gospel came to you not only in word, but also in power and in the Holy Spirit and with full conviction. You know what kind of men we proved to be among you for your sake.*

1 Thessalonians 1:4-5

Voice from the Church

"Sermons graced by prayer and spiritual hunger take on a tangible vitality. Hearers sense an authenticity and compelling truth they cannot neglect because the preacher speaks of truths personally experienced." (Gary M. Burge, b. 1952)*

Reflection

In George MacDonald's *The Curate's Awakening*, his primary fictitious character is a Scottish pastor, who in the book's beginning is an unconverted man. Rev. Thomas Wingfold's sermons consisted of preaching other men's sermons, which were boringly read to an equally bored congregation. Because the man himself was inauthentic, his sermons had no ring of authenticity about them. Fortunately for the pastor, he had a faithful layman who eventually led him into a genuine relationship with the Lord Jesus. Thereafter Wingfold delivered *messages*, not mere sermons. The messages rang true because the preacher had become a true person. The congregation readily discerned the difference.

A man cannot preach what he does not see. One cannot preach with conviction without experiencing truth for himself. Truth flowing through a true man is a powerful weapon in the hands of the Spirit of God. Pray that your pastor will be a true man filled with the Spirit of power.

Verse

A man came to town to be the pastor;
  he was plain and quite unpolished.
But when he stood and preached God's Word,
  all soon saw he knew the Master.

A Blessèd Reality

The Word

[1]*Therefore, since we have been justified by faith, we have peace with
God through our Lord Jesus Christ. [2]Through him we have
also obtained access by faith into this grace in which we
stand, and we rejoice in hope of the glory of God.*
Romans 5:1-2

Voice from the Church

"In the evening I went very unwillingly to a society in Aldersgate Street,
where one was reading Luther's preface to the *Epistle to the Romans.*
About a quarter before nine, while he was describing the change which
God works in the heart through faith in Christ, I felt my heart strangely
warmed. I felt I did trust in Christ, Christ alone for salvation: And an
assurance was given me, that he had taken away my sins, even mine,
and saved me from the law of sin and death." (John Wesley, 1703-1791))*

Reflection

A church member may very well go on in life, filling his or her positions and responsibilities faithfully and even zealously, yet all the while
never having experienced God's justifying and regenerating grace. This
is the sad history of many in the church.

However, our merciful Lord relentlessly pursues and awakens those
who will listen to his call. It comes as a shock to some clergy and lay
people, when they discover they had never been born again, though they
had been serving as a pastor, teacher, elder, or deacon. The Church of
England minister, John Wesley, fell into this category: he preached for
some years before he personally met Jesus Christ in saving grace.

How about you, dear reader? Is the Lord Jesus Christ *real* to you? If
not, would you seek him today?

Verse

I once knew the Jesus of the printed page;
I read the Gospels of the olden age.
But then there came a blessèd reality—
Christ became real to me personally.

What Change Grace Has Wrought!

The Word
> [1]*And you were dead in the trespasses and sins* [2]*in which you once walked, following the course of this world, following the prince of the power of the air, the spirit that is now at work in the sons of disobedience—* [3]*among whom we all once lived in the passions of our flesh, carrying out the desires of the body and the mind, and were by nature children of wrath, like the rest of mankind.*
>
> Ephesians 2:1-3

Voice from the Church
"'No man is justified by faith whose faith does not make him just' is a sound aphorism." (Purkiser, Taylor & Taylor)*

Reflection
Justification is an act whereby God counts the repentant, believing sinner as just or righteous (see Rom. 4:5). At the moment one is justified by faith, he is also adopted (see Rom. 8:15), regenerated (see 1 John 5:12), and sanctified (see e.g., 1 Cor. 6:11). "Sanctify" has a dual meaning: to be set apart for holy purposes and to make *actually* holy. When we experience God's merciful converting grace, we are set apart to Christ and from the world. By his Spirit, we are increasingly conformed to the image of Christ (2 Cor. 3:18). Also, God wishes to make each walking-in-the-light believer holy through and through (1 Thess. 5:23; 2 Cor. 7:1)—in heart and life (no, this doesn't mean we cannot sin).

Note three phrases in the above text: *"once walked," "once lived,"* and *"were by nature"*—each in the past tense. This is the work of the Spirit, operating in the genuine disciple of Christ, all made possible because of our Lord's atoning death and poured-out Spirit. For the Christian, there is a *before* and *after*—and *not yet*.

Verse
I'm not the person I used to be,
  thanks to Your mercy, O Christ.
I'm not the person I want to be,
  thus daily I keep our tryst.

God's Faithful Prophets

The Word
⁷But when he saw many of the Pharisees and Sadducees coming to his baptism, he said to them, "You brood of vipers! Who warned you to flee from the wrath to come? ⁸Bear fruit in keeping with repentance."
Matthew 3:7-8

Voice from the Church
"I was born to go to war and give battle to sects and devils. That is why my books are stormy and warlike. I must root out the stumps and bushes and hack away the thorns and brambles. I am the great lumberjack who must clear the land and level it." (Martin Luther, 1483-1546)*

Reflection
Some servants of the Lord are called to a hard and difficult ministry. When the prophet Isaiah heard from the Lord what his task would be, he answered: "How long, O Lord?" The Lord's response? "Until cities lie waste without inhabitant, and houses without people, and the land is a desolate waste, and the Lord removes people far away, and the forsaken places are many in the midst of the land" (Isa. 6:11-12). That's one difficult assignment! When Jeremiah was commissioned by the Lord, he was told that his ministry would be "to pluck up and to break down, to destroy and to overthrow, to build and to plant" (Jer. 1:10). Not a ministry to be coveted!

All of God's servants are not prophets, but each minister is called to speak prophetically: that is, they are to proclaim and apply God's Word to particular situations and issues, in the power of the Holy Spirit. We should thank God for those men and women, who across the ages have served as God's faithful mouthpieces.

Verse
And though this world, with devils filled, should threaten to undo us,
We will not fear, for God hath willed His truth to triumph through us:
The Prince of Darkness grim, we tremble not for him;
His rage we can endure, for lo, his doom is sure,
One little word shall fell him. (Martin Luther, 1483-1546)**

Removed "Scales"

The Word

[17]*So Ananias departed and entered the house. And laying his hands on him he said, "Brother Saul, the Lord Jesus who appeared to you on the road by which you came has sent me so that you may regain your sight and be filled with the Holy Spirit." [18]And immediately something like scales fell from his eyes, and he regained his sight.*

Acts 9:17-18

Voice from the Church

"Never shall I forget the gain to conscious faith and peace which came to my own soul not long after I had appropriated the crucified Lord as the sinner's Sacrifice.... It was a new development of insight into the love of God, a new discovery into divine resources." (H. C. G. Moule, 1841-1920)*

Reflection

Paul would never have become the evangelist and teacher he became without having been filled with the Holy Spirit. Though three days before he had had a divine revelation of the Lord Jesus Christ on the Damascus road, that experience alone was insufficient to make Paul an effective minister of the gospel. What Paul experienced in Damascus was not unlike what the apostles previously experienced, after they were told by their Lord to "Stay in the city until you are clothed with power from on high" (Luke 24:49).

Like the Ephesian elders in Acts 19, many of Christ's followers live as though they have never heard there is a Holy Spirit. Where the Holy Spirit is welcomed in his blessed fullness, there will be present light and power, victories and blessings, changed lives and charged testimonies. Have you had the "scales" removed from your eyes?

Verse

Thou canst fill me, gracious Spirit,
Though I cannot tell Thee how;
But I need Thee, greatly need Thee,
Come, O come and fill me now. (Elwood H. Stokes, 1815-1897)**

Spirit-Conviction

The Word
*[37] Now when they heard this they were cut to the heart, and said
to Peter and the rest of the apostles, "Brothers, what shall we do?"
[38] And Peter said to them, "Repent and be baptized every one of
you in the name of Jesus Christ for the forgiveness of your
sins, and you will receive the gift of the Holy Spirit."*
Acts 2:37-38

Voice from the Church
"Biblical, Spirit-filled preaching will always convict of sin and unrighteousness in the lives of hearers." (Harold J. Ockenga, 1905-1985)*

Reflection
Visiting with my Aunt Nellie (who is now with the Lord), in her living
room a good many years ago, we were discussing the things of God and
the work of the church. My aunt (my father's sister) had attended church
her whole life. She enjoyed good preaching and faithful pastors. And
she knew what it was to experience the presence and power of the Holy
Spirit during the services in the little village church where she attended.
During our conversation—while then in her mid-eighties—she said to
me, lamenting the condition of her local church, "Junior [I'm named
after my father], there is no conviction in our services!" I've heard the
same complaint, repeatedly.

Where the Holy Spirit is *manifestly* present, when sinners and careless
Christians are in attendance, there will follow as the night follows the
day, the convicting power of the Holy Spirit: "And when he comes, he
will convict the world concerning sin and righteousness and judgment." (John 16:8). Where there are praying, Spirit-filled people, there
will be found authentic conviction of sin.

Verse
*Thus might I hide my blushing face
While His dear cross appears,
Dissolve my heart in thankfulness,
And melt my eyes to tears.* (Isaac Watts, 1674-1748)**

The Spirit Gives Life

The Word

> *"It is the Spirit who gives life; the flesh profits nothing;*
> *the words that I have spoken to you are spirit and are life."*
> John 6:63 NASB

Voice from the Church

"The answer to experientialism is not creedalism or confessionalism but a theology of Word and Spirit in which truth does not remain external and historical but becomes by the action of the Spirit internal and existential." (Donald G. Bloesch 1928-2010)*

Reflection

The word for "flesh" in the above text is the Greek word *sarx*. When using the word "flesh" in this context, Jesus doesn't have in mind our physical bodies. He has reference to people exercising human abilities without the enabling power of God. The scribes and Pharisees were adept apologists; they could readily quote a biblical text in answer to any question. They were fundamentally orthodox in what they believed. And to be biblically orthodox is good and right. However, one can be straight as a poker and just as cold and dead. While heresy has slain its thousands, dead orthodoxy has slain its tens of thousands.

The life-giving Spirit, operating through the incarnate Christ, was transformative in all who believed. The same holds true today: Where the Word is proclaimed (and lived), and the Spirit is operating freely in its proclaimers, life appears—the very life of God.

Verse

It is the life-giving Spirit
and He alone who changes hearts.
Human effort remains futile,
failing to affect the inner parts.
Away with our fallen egos!
Away with dependence on self!
The letter alone will slay us;
the Spirit gives life of Himself.

Serving with Humility

The Word

[26] *For consider your calling, brethren, that there were not many wise according to the flesh, not many mighty, not many noble;* [27] *but God has chosen the foolish things of the world to shame the wise, and God has chosen the weak things of the world to shame the things which are strong,* [28] *and the base things of the world and the despised God has chosen, the things that are not, so that He may nullify the things that are,* [29] *so that no man may boast before God.*
1 Corinthians 1:26-29 NASB

Voice from the Church

"I pray God, with my whole heart, sooner to crush me utterly, with the most dreadful destruction, than to suffer me to take the least honor to myself of anything which He has been pleased to do by me for the good of others. I am only a poor nothing. God is all-powerful. He delights to operate and exercise His power by mere nothings." (Madame Guyon, 1648-1717)*

Reflection

It seems to be a rare person that God can trust fully to carry out his assignments ... with humility. And even when God does find a humble person, too often the messenger eventually becomes lifted up with pride. King Saul served God commendably, until he was overtaken by his own ego. King Hezekiah ruled well, until he failed to give God the glory (it must be difficult for a person in authority to remain humble). As long as we feel spiritually bankrupt ("Blessed are the poor in spirit"), God's grace is able to abound in and through us. Once we begin to glory in our *service* for God, God will withdraw his blessing from us—no matter how impressive our ministry may appear to undiscerning people.

Verse

He was the King of Israel; I was just a donkey.
I don't know why He chose me that day.
I had done nothing spectacular. But I carried Him
along while the crowd sang His praises.

Jesus Is Coming Again

The Word

[32]*"But concerning that day or that hour, no one knows, not even the angels in heaven, nor the Son, but only the Father.* [33]*Be on guard, keep awake. For you do not know when the time will come."*
Mark 13:32-33

Voice from the Church

"Christ is not only coming in power at the last day, but the power of His coming is to be consistently operating in the present day. As God has appointed the moon to lift the tide by its attraction, that it may flood and fill all the indentures of the coast, so has He ordained this great event of Christ's *Parousia* to draw up the faith and hope and love of the Church, when these have ebbed towards the world." (A. J. Gordon, 1836-1895)*

Reflection

Jesus knew the tendency among his own followers was that they would succumb to spiritual drowsiness. Thus, by means of parables and precepts, he repeatedly warned his disciples to "Be on guard, keep awake. For you do not know when the time will come."

It is emotionally impossible to keep oneself on "tiptoes" in view of Christ's return to earth. However, while we cannot always keep *emotionally* excited about Jesus' return to earth, we can order our lives *volitionally* with a view to his return.

Are you living your life in view of meeting your Lord some day? Are you holding this world's goods lightly or tightly? Are you prepared to give a good account, by God's grace? John Wesley was once asked what he would do if he knew the Lord Jesus would return the next day. His reply? "Just what I had planned on doing." That may sound a bit farfetched; but it was said by a person who lived a well-ordered life.

Verse

If our Lord should come tonight,
With the bright angelic host,
Would He find us in His vineyard,
Every servant at his post? (Harriet E. Jones,1823-1915)**

Reconciled

The Word

[18]*All this is from God, who through Christ reconciled us to himself and gave us the ministry of reconciliation; [19]that is, in Christ God was reconciling the world to himself, not counting their trespasses against them, and entrusting to us the message of reconciliation.*
2 Corinthians 5:18-19

Voice from the Church

"It is the consistent teaching of the Scripture that man could not overcome the cause of enmity. The barrier which the sin of man had erected the wit of man could not find means to remove. But in the death of Him whom God 'made sin' for man the cause of enmity was squarely faced and removed. Therefore a complete reconciliation results, so that man turns to God in repentance and trust, and God looks on man with favor and not in wrath." (Leon Morris, 1914-2006)*

Reflection

Sinful man can never in a million years enter a right relationship with God without God having first taken the initiative to reconcile man to himself. It was man in the Garden who deliberately chose to walk away from his Creator and God. Adam and Eve were under no compulsion to do so; nevertheless, they chose to forsake their benevolent Father for what they wrongly believed to be a more pleasurable existence.

But because God is merciful as well as righteous, fallen man and God were brought back together through the reconciling, atoning death of the Lord Jesus Christ. For those who turn from their sins and look to God's Lamb, the circle of reconciliation is completed. And yet not quite, for the reconciled become ambassadors of reconciliation. Let us pray to be faithful ambassadors.

Verse

My God is reconciled; His pardoning voice I hear;
He owns me for His child; I can no longer fear:
With confidence I now draw nigh,
And "Father, Abba, Father," cry. (Charles Wesley, 1707-1788)**

"In the Cross of Christ I Glory"

The Word

[18]*For the word of the cross is folly to those who are perishing,*
but to us who are being saved it is the power of God.
[19]*For it is written, "I will destroy the wisdom of the wise,*
and the discernment of the discerning I will thwart."
1 Corinthians 1:18-19

Voice from the Church

"Apart from the Spirit, the Cross stands inert, a vast machine at rest, and about it lie the stones of the building unmoved. Not till the rope has been attached can the work proceed of lifting the individual life through faith and love to the place prepared for it in the Church of God." (Henry B. Swete, 1835-1917)*

Reflection

Apart from Jesus Christ becoming our sacrifice for sin on that ignominious yet noble cross some two thousand years ago, it would be impossible for sinful man to enter a joyful relationship with the holy God. Apart from the Holy Spirit of God effectively applying Christ's work on the cross to individual, repentant sinners, the death of Christ would have been in vain—for the unrepentant.

Redemption is gloriously Trinitarian: God the Father loved the sinful world; God the Son freely gave himself as our substitutionary sacrifice for sin; God the Holy Spirit convicts the sinner of sin and administers redeeming grace to each believing person.

There is power in the very message of the cross of Christ. Every time the atoning death of Christ is proclaimed by one individual to another person—or to a multitude—the Holy Spirit attends such a proclamation with power. Let us glory in the cross of Christ!

Verse

In the cross of Christ I glory,
Towering o'er the wrecks of time;
All the light of sacred story
Gathers round its head sublime. (John Browning, 1792-1872)**

Daily Cleansing

The Word
*[8]Peter said to him, "You shall never wash my feet." Jesus answered
him, "If I do not wash you, you have no share with me."
[9]Simon Peter said to him, "Lord, not my feet only but also my
hands and my head!" [10]Jesus said to him, "The one who has bathed
does not need to wash, except for his feet, but is completely
clean. And you are clean, but not every one of you."*
John 13:8-10

Voice from the Church
"Nowhere does The Word of God promise a once-for-all cleansing. We
are to walk in the light if we are to know continuous cleansing. Let this
be clearly understood and then we shall not fall into the error of trying
to live today on the cleansing of yesterday. We must guard against any
deliberate choice of things unclean and ever cultivate the attitude of
entire surrender to the known will of God." (Duncan Campbell, 1898-1972)*

Reflection
Who among us can go through a week, a day, but what we accumulate
some of this world's soil on the surface of our "feet"? The minor inad-
vertences, the inattention given to moral duties, the infractions of the
royal commandment to love our neighbor as ourselves, the sins of omis-
sion—these require the cleansing blood of the Lord Jesus Christ.

When Jesus knelt before Simon Peter to wash his feet, Peter had already made up his mind: "You shall never wash my feet." On the surface, Peter's response sounded impressive: he was unworthy to have
God's Son to wash his feet! But Jesus didn't see it that way; he saw the
pride of the disciple's heart as well as the dirt on his feet.

Are you too proud to permit Jesus to wash your "feet" today?

Verse
*Though I have walked with you today
  in holy communion and love,
I notice some soil on my "feet,"
  which needs the cleansing of your blood.*

Keep to Your Calling

The Word

⁴As servants of God we commend ourselves in every way:
by great endurance, in afflictions, hardships, calamities, ...
⁵beatings, imprisonments, riots, labors, sleepless nights, hunger; ...
⁸through honor and dishonor, through slander and praise.
We are treated as impostors, and yet are true.

2 Corinthians 6:4-5, 8

Voice from the Church

"To fulfill our calling even when it isn't wanted forces us to be sure of what we're doing. It drives us to our knees in prayer, in attentive listening, in humility. Then we're released from the scramble for human approval and can do our work solely to please God." (Marva J. Dawn, b. 1948)*

Reflection

If the ministry you are faithfully engaged in isn't appreciated and affirmed as much as you think it should be, you're in good company— neither was Christ's nor the apostle Paul's.

Recently a longtime friend of mine authored a book and distributed it among many of his friends. Several months afterward he lamented to me, "I haven't heard one word of acknowledgement from any of them except one." My answer: "We live in a thankless culture, which has infected the church as well; don't be discouraged."

While expressions of gratitude are appreciated when given, the called servant of Christ neither seeks accolades nor should despair when he doesn't receive them. We are servants of Christ; we are called to follow him and do his bidding, even when our efforts are unappreciated, or rejected, or even opposed. We stand or fall before our own Master; we look to him only for commendation.

Verse

He was despised and rejected;
they refused the Man who could help;
They clung to themselves and their sins.
Walking away, He went to others.

"I saw the Lord"

The Word
[1]In the year that King Uzziah died I saw the Lord sitting upon a throne,
high and lifted up; and the train of his robe filled the temple....
[5]And I said: "Woe is me! For I am lost; for I am a man of unclean
lips, and I dwell in the midst of a people of unclean lips;
for my eyes have seen the King, the Lord of hosts!"
Isaiah 6:1, 5

Voice from the Church
"No man whose inward eyes have really seen that overwhelmingly holy Christ in Isaiah 6 ever talks again about his own sanctity." (J. Sidlow Baxter, 1903-1999)*

Reflection
An authentic encounter with the Three-in-One God will drive a person to his knees. By nature, we are rigid and stiff-necked, with proud hearts and haughty eyes. We easily condemn in others what we condone in ourselves. Only a vision of a holy God will disclose the filthiness of a corrupt heart. Once a person has caught a glimpse of God and the depravity of his own heart, he will never look with condescension toward another human being.

Self-righteous people are haughty; self-righteous people are judgmental; self-righteous people are self-centered. One of God's most difficult tasks is to get religious people to admit they are fallen, sinful, and desperately in need of deliverance—from sin and themselves.

A low view of God leaves us in our sin; an exalted view of a thrice-holy God brings cleansing and freedom, selflessness and fruitful service. Have you seen the Lord "high and lifted up"? One is never the same after such an encounter.

Verse
Take away our bent to sinning;
Alpha and Omega be;
End of faith, as its Beginning,
Set our hearts at liberty. (Charles Wesley,1707-1788)**

Christ's Slaves

The Word
> [16]Do you not know that if you present yourselves to anyone as obedient slaves, you are slaves of the one whom you obey, either of sin, which leads to death, or of obedience, which leads to righteousness? [17]But thanks be to God, that you who were once slaves of sin have become obedient from the heart to the standard of teaching to which you were committed, [18]and, having been set free from sin, have become slaves of righteousness.

Romans 6:16-18

Voice from the Church
"In twentieth-century Christianity we have replaced the expression 'total surrender' with the word 'commitment,' and 'slave' with 'servant.' But there is an important difference. A servant gives service to someone, but a slave belongs to someone. We commit ourselves to do something, but when we surrender ourselves to someone, we give ourselves." (Murray J. Harris, b. 1939)*

Reflection
At the stroke of God's justifying and regenerating grace, the new-born son of the Father is transferred from one kingdom and dominion to another. He no longer is under the rule and reign of Satan. He has gone from being a slave to sin and disobedience, to be a slave of the Lord Jesus Christ and righteousness.

Whereas slavery to sin and unrighteousness is tyrannical, debilitating and deadly, a voluntary submission to the Lord Jesus provides true freedom and joyful liberty. To surrender to Jesus Christ is righteousness, joy and peace.

To whom do you belong?

Verse
No longer am I my own;
To Christ the Lord I belong.
By His blood He paid the price;
Nothing is a sacrifice.

The Place of Prayer

The Word

[15]*But now even more the report about him went abroad, and great crowds gathered to hear him and to be healed of their infirmities.* [16]*But he would withdraw to desolate places and pray.*

Luke 5:16-17

Voice from the Church

"Enabled to spend nearly the whole day in prayer, praise, and confession. The day was fine, not too warm, and I wandered among the woods near old Rusco, quite alone, speaking with the Lord." (Andrew Bonar, 1810-1892)*

Reflection

Unless our prayer-life keeps pace with our service for Christ, we have no "bread" to offer the spiritually hungry. Too much of our Christian service is fruitless because of a misplaced focus. Impoverished hearts are incapable of communicating words of life to the dead and dying.

Some of us have warm hearts and empty heads. Others have full heads and empty hearts. The Lord Jesus Christ's ministry was always fresh because he was continually renewed by the Spirit of God. The Word of God dwelt in him richly, and the power of God flowed through him freely, because he knew the importance of spending time alone with his Father. This aloneness was necessary because he was the Son of Man, though also the Son of God.

How much more important it is for you and me to regularly "withdraw to desolate places and pray." Yours may not be a literal wilderness; it may be your bedroom, attic, basement, or study. But wherever your place of prayer is, when you arrive there—pray. Your Father hears, and you will leave prepared to serve again.

Verse

Oh, the pure delight of a single hour
That before Thy throne I spend,
When I kneel in prayer, and with Thee, my God
I commune as friend with friend! (Fanny Crosby, 1820-1915)**

The God of Beauty

The Word

As for the rich in this present age, charge them not to be haughty,
nor to set their hopes on the uncertainty of riches, but on
God, who richly provides us with everything to enjoy.

1 Timothy 6:17

Voice from the Church

"I recall a clergyman once telling me after a wonderful concert that for the first time in his life he realized that by enjoying the beauty of music he was obeying God, while before that experience obedience had always been associated with unpleasant tasks for him." (Diogenes Allen, 1932-2013)*

Reflection

Before I surrendered my life to the Lord Jesus Christ, I vividly recall how Satan repeatedly told me that if I became a Christian I would never really be happy. Satan certainly lived up to his character and reputation—what a liar!

Who in the history of the Christian Church ever underwent as many difficulties as the apostle Paul did? And who ever experienced as much joy?

Accumulating wealth, apart from God, leads to futility, emptiness, and despair. Why? Because riches provide no built-in guarantee. Since God is the giver of every good and perfect gift, his gifts satisfy man's deepest needs. Everything God provides, he does so for our enjoyment. Enjoyment!

Music is one of our Father's enjoyable gifts to us. How I enjoy congregational hymns, choral arrangements, instrumentals, listening to my wife Emily at the keyboard, and so-called secular arrangements by accomplished composers. God is the God of aesthetics, the God of beauty.

Verse

Across the pure wafting wind,
I heard a familiar sound—
It was a tune, sweetly played;
My heart leapt as it unwound.

The Word Applied

The Word

> *For whatever was written in former days was written for our instruction, that through endurance and through the encouragement of the Scriptures we might have hope.*

Romans 15:4

Voice from the Church

"Spiritual reading is made by action of the Spirit to contain meanings the author never thought of. God makes use of the words and actions of others to impart hidden truths. If He wills to enlighten us by such means, we should avail ourselves of this light. Everything which becomes an instrument of His divine action has a value far surpassing its natural and apparent worth." (Jean-Pierre de Caussade, 1675-1751)*

Reflection

The God-inspired writers of the Sacred Scriptures were moved by the Holy Spirit to pen their narratives, prophecies, poetry, and letters. By the meticulous administration of the Spirit, every word was written in order that the readers would be instructed, reminded, and edified. This is true of both Testaments.

God has given us his words for "a lamp to [our] feet and a light to [our] path" (Ps. 119:105). The apostle says that God gave us his words "that through endurance and through the encouragement of the Scriptures we might have hope."

The words that were penned by these holy men of old have been used by the Spirit to make application in the lives of God's people far beyond the original writers' understanding. It was the Spirit who first inspired the words, and it is the Spirit who applies the words for our profit—never in contradiction to the inspired Writings.

We continually marvel at our God's ways among men.

Verse

Unfold Your words to me, O God,
*   that I may clearly see the way.*
If I fail to see the right path,
*   surely my feet will go astray.*

Peace and Holiness

The Word
^{14}*Pursue peace with all people, and holiness, without which no one will
see the Lord: ^{15}looking carefully lest anyone fall short of the grace
of God; lest any root of bitterness springing up cause trouble, and by
this many become defiled; ^{16}lest there be any fornicator or profane
person like Esau, who for one morsel of food sold his birthright.*
Hebrews 12:14 NKJV

Voice from the Church
"If we love Christ, then we must be holy. If we wish to glorify Christ,
then we must be holy. If we wish to show gratitude to Christ, then we
must be holy. If we would not be found traitors at the last day to his
crown, honour and dignity, then we must be holy." (John Owen, 1616-1683)*

Reflection
Peace and holiness are a pair of graces beautifully joined by the Spirit;
the people of God are to be characterized by both. There is no such thing
as contentious and ugly holiness. Where true holiness is found, there
you will find true peace; where true peace is found, there you will find
true holiness.

Christians are called to a life of holy living and peace with all people.
Of course, lived-out truth invariably brings division between sinners and
saints ("I came not to bring peace but a sword"), and between believers
who sometimes are motivated by the "flesh."

We are to "pursue" a life of peace and holiness—so says the Spirit. To
"pursue" these graces of the Spirit does not imply we will not obtain
either. But lest we forget: Unless God gives peace and holiness, we cannot be at peace with others, nor walk a holy path. Grace is given *within*
so that we might walk with God and other *without*.

Verse
*I fear to fall short of your grace, O God,
   lest my heart causes others to stumble.
Help me to choose the path of peace and holiness,
   thereby seeing You and building up my brothers.*

"Consider"

The Word
¹*Therefore, holy brethren, partakers of a heavenly calling, consider
Jesus, the Apostle and High Priest of our confession; ²He was faithful
to Him who appointed Him, as Moses also was in all His house.*
Hebrews 3:1-2 NASB

Voice from the Church
"The word ... (*katanoein*) is suggestive. It does not mean simply to look
at or to notice a thing. Anyone can look at a thing or even notice it without really seeing it. The word ["consider"] means to fix the attention on
something in such a way that its inner meaning, the lesson that it is designed to teach, may be learned." (William Barclay, 1907-1978)*

Reflection
The word "consider" (Greek: *katanoein)* appears 14 times in the NT. Of
the seven occurrences in The Letter to the Hebrews, note these four exhortations the Spirit says we are to "consider."

• Christians are to "consider" the faithfulness of the Lord Jesus
Christ as an incentive to be faithful (3:1-2).
• Christians are to "consider how to stir up one another to love and
good works," in view of "the Day drawing near" (10:24-25).
• Suffering Christians are to "consider" how Jesus himself suffered
opposition, so they won't become "weary or fainthearted" in their
"struggle against sin" (12:3-4).
• Christians are to "consider" the "outcome" of the lives their godly
leaders lived, so that they might "imitate their faith" (13:7).

Verse
*Too often I have heard and read
  Your Word, O Lord, without giving
    full attention to what You said.
Is it any wonder the shield
  of faith slipped from my hand, leaving
    me defenseless and full of dread?*

Loving, Serving, Following

The Word
> [17]*He said to him the third time, "Simon, son of John, do you love
> me?" Peter was grieved because he said to him the third time,
> "Do you love me?" and he said to him, "Lord, you know everything;
> you know that I love you." Jesus said to him, "Feed my sheep...."*
> [19]*And after saying this he said to him, "Follow me."*
> John 21:17-19

Voice from the Church
"Thanks be to thee, O Lord Jesus Christ, for all the benefits which thou
hast given us; for all the pains and insults which thou has borne for us.
O most merciful Redeemer, Friend, and Brother, may we know thee
more clearly, love thee more dearly, follow thee more nearly; for thine
own sake." (Richard of Chichester, 1197-1253)*

Reflection
To know Christ is to love Christ; to love Christ is to follow Christ. It is
fundamentally impossible to know and love Christ without following
him in full obedience. If we are deficient in our obedience, it is because
our love for Christ is defective. "Whoever has my commandments and
keeps them, he it is who loves me. And he who loves me will be loved
by my Father, and I will love him and manifest myself to him" (John
14:21). The struggle many Christians have in their walk with God can
be reduced to a single issue: their heart fails to be renewed often with
the love of Christ.

What a chore and drudgery the Christian life becomes when our love
for God/Christ wanes. When our love for Christ is lukewarm, we begin
to chaff at his commands; it also affects all our relationships. The greater our love, the greater our motivation to serve.

Verse
May Thy rich grace impart
Strength to my fainting heart, my zeal inspire!
As Thou hast died for me, O may my love to Thee,
Pure warm, and changeless be, a living fire! (Ray Palmer,1808-1887)**

More Love

The Word

> [9]*And it is my prayer that your love may abound more and more, with knowledge and all discernment, *[10]*so that you may approve what is excellent, and so be pure and blameless for the day of Christ, *[11]*filled with the fruit of righteousness that comes through Jesus Christ, to the glory and praise of God.*
>
> Philippians 1:9-11

Voice from the Church

"There is no need to pressure with rules and regulations anyone who loves. Love is the most pressing teacher of them all. The loving heart already urges to conform to the will and intentions of the beloved. Love is a magistrate with quiet authority. It needs no police force or army. Whoever takes pleasure in God will greatly desire to please God. Love is the condensation of all theology." (Francis de Sales, 1567-1622)*

Reflection

The Word of God *informs* us as to how we can reciprocate the wondrous love of God that has been shed abroad in our hearts by the Holy Spirit. The Christian does not make choices and critical ethical decisions based on what he *feels*. Love requires boundaries; *agape* love must be instructed. The Word of God is our lamp and our light.

When one loves God much, the yoke of Jesus is light and not burdensome. The one filled with God's love will run to keep his commandments and do those things that are pleasing in his sight. For example, the Seventh Commandment is not burdensome to me, for my love for my love for God and my wife enables me to be faithful to her with joy. Our love for God never abrogates his laws but is an expression and fulfilment of them.

Verse

More love to Thee, O Christ, more love to Thee!
Hear Thou the prayer I make on bended knee.
This is my earnest plea: More love, O Christ, to Thee;
More love to Thee, more love to Thee! (Elizabeth P. Prentiss, 1818-1878)**

A Real Person

The Word

> [2]And the angel of the Lord appeared to him in a flame of fire out of the midst of a bush. He looked, and behold, the bush was burning, yet it was not consumed. [3]And Moses said, "I will turn aside to see this great sight, why the bush is not burned." [4]When the Lord saw that he turned aside to see, God called to him out of the bush, "Moses, Moses!" And he said, "Here I am."
> Exodus 3:2-4

Voice from the Church

"Theology books are always written in the third person. They present God as an object to be studied, and one rarely hears of anyone being converted while reading a theology book. The only way a person can ever be converted is if God is understood not in the third person but in the first person. He must become the subject and we must become the object. Unfortunately, most of Christianity is a massive effort to keep God in the third person. But there is no salvation until he is the first person and we deal with him face-to-face." (Dennis F. Kinlaw, 1992-2017)*

Reflection

The *manner* in which Yahweh appeared to Moses in the wilderness is not to be replicated. That is, who else has experienced a noncombustible shrub? God does not intend for phenomena to be repeated, precisely.

However, God does want to become to each one of us a Person—a Person with whom we walk in a right relationship with, a Person whose fellowship we come to enjoy. We never can become a *real* person until we come to know the personal God. This becomes possible through God's communication to us in Word and Spirit.

Is God your Father *real* to you today?

Verse

We stumble through life, groping for something,
  until we meet Reality and find we were nothing.
Stripped of our masks, with our eyes now seeing,
  we discover the Father and with joy are found weeping.

Jars of Clay

The Word
⁶*For God, who said, "Let light shine out of darkness," has shone
in our hearts to give the light of the knowledge of the glory of God in
the face of Jesus Christ.* ⁷*But we have this treasure in jars of clay,
to show that the surpassing power belongs to God and not to us.*
2 Corinthians 4:6-7

Voice from the Church
"Today I saw as I went home some old crocks and broken bricks and
pieces of all sorts of earthenware put by the side of the road because the
road is going to be widened, and I thought to myself, 'If the Lord would
only use me as an old broken crock to help to make a roadway for him
to ride through London, so that he might be glorified, I would be glad to
be thus honoured.'" (Charles H. Spurgeon, 1834-1892)*

Reflection
Fallen man, who was born with a propensity to glory in his achievements, requires a spiritual transformation and an ongoing reminder as to
who he is and to whom he belongs. The same God who spoke light into
existence is the same God who has enlightened believers, through the
Lord Jesus Christ. It is this indwelling glory and knowledge that is the
Christian's treasure—not our exploits and good deeds.

The more we accomplish in Jesus' name, the higher we climb on our
respective ecclesiastical ladders, the more we claw our way to the top—
the greater our susceptibility for taking credit for our labors and works
of righteousness.

We are merely "jars of clay"; if we fail to give God the glory, we have
miserably failed. It is well that we should ask God not to do more
through us than we can adequately handle with humility.

Verse
He thought he was serving powerfully;
he became pleased with his feats carelessly.
Then he went to his room and fell on his knees,
and was reminded the Spirit for him grieves.

Godly Courage

The Word

> By faith [Moses] left Egypt, not fearing the wrath of the king; for he endured, as seeing Him who is unseen.
> Hebrews 11:27 NASB

Voice from the Church

"He strengthened and confirmed his heart with spiritual courage and resolution to abide in his duty unto the end, without fear and despondency.... Moses had a distinct apprehension of God in His omnipresence, power, and faithfulness; this gave him a fixed trust in Him, that He would protect him and be faithful to him in the discharge of his promise." (John Owen, 1616-1683)*

Reflection

The prophets of old were told by God not to fear the face of man. That is, they were not to be intimidated in discharging their prophetic responsibilities when men disapproved of the messages they delivered from God. On the other hand, they were to fear God—meaning to walk before God with reverential awe, remembering he is holy, righteous, and just.

It is not every day that we are confronted with making a courageous moral choice. But when we are—in our family, on the job, in the classroom, in a committee meeting—our decision will clearly reveal the kind of person we are. Did we make our decision in the fear of God, or did we come down on the side of the fear of men?

We will not be prepared to identify with God and his words in the critical hour, if we have failed to fill our minds with the truth of God day by day. The "sword of the Spirit" must be always close at hand; the Invisible One must always be kept in view.

Whom do you fear?

Verse

Turn your eyes upon Jesus,
Look full in His wonderful face,
And the things of earth will grow strangely dim,
In the light of His glory and grace. (Helen H. Lemmel, 1864-1961)**

When Pain is a Blessing

The Word
[8] *"Oh that I might have my request, and that God would fulfill my hope,*
[9] *that it would please God to crush me, that he would let loose his hand
and cut me off!* [10] *This would be my comfort; I would even exult in pain
unsparing, for I have not denied the words of the Holy One."*

Job 6:8-10

Voice from the Church
"If pain were a curse—and nothing but a curse—well might we doubt
the justice on the throne, but if pain is a ladder to a better life, then light
falls on the sufferings of the innocent. It is not the anger of heaven that
is striking them. It may be the love of heaven that is blessing them.
There are always tears and blood on the steps that lead people heaven-
ward, to where the angels are." (George H. Morrison, 1826-1928)*

Reflection
While pain (emotional, physical) and suffering is the common lot of all
humanity, not everyone profits from it. But for the Christian, even the
slightest approach of some variety pain causes one to lift his or her heart
to the Father of mercies and the God of all kinds of comfort.

We are so forgetful, and we tend to be naturally forgetful of our loving God's manifold blessings toward his children. Therefore, when
some form of pain comes—suddenly, unexpectedly—the maturing believer lifts his heart almost involuntarily toward the throne grace, asking
what he may learn and how he may grow by this mysterious providence.

Will we be delivered from the pain? In time. However, while the pain
is with us, let us not deny the "words of the Holy One"; instead, let us
draw nearer to God and allow his grace to triumph in and through us,
using the pain as a stepping stone to make us more like Jesus.

Verse
I walked a mile with Sorrow;
And ne'er a word said she;
But, oh! The things I learned from her,
When Sorrow walked with me. (Robert Browning Hamilton, 1880-1950)**

Revival

The Word

[1]"He who has the seven Spirits of God and the seven stars, says this: 'I know your deeds, that you have a name that you are alive, but you are dead. [2]Wake up, and strengthen the things that remain, which were about to die; for I have not found your deeds completed in the sight of My God. [3]So remember what you have received and heard; and keep it, and repent,'"
Revelation 3:1-3a NASB

Voice from the Church

"Revival I define as a work of God by his Spirit through his Word bringing the spiritually dead to living faith in Christ and renewing the inner life of Christians who have grown slack and sleepy." (J. I. Packer, b. 1926)

Reflection

There can be no revival among believers without the recognition that we have drifted away from our spiritual moorings. There can be no revival among believers without coming to terms with our lukewarmness, lack of spiritual zeal, indifference toward lost people, disunity in the Body of Christ, absence of *koionia* (genuine Christian fellowship), moral compromises in our private lives, prayerlessness, and the absence of daily submission to the Lord Jesus Christ.

Our lack can only be resolved with a renewed awareness of the holiness of God. Such an awareness occurs when the Spirit of God searches hearts intensely through the Word of God. When God moves upon the hearts of honest, thirsty seekers, the sleepy are awakened, and the dead and dying are brought to new life.

Have you become sleepy in your walk with God?

Verse

O Holy Ghost, revival comes from Thee;
Send a revival, start the work in me;
Thy Word declares Thou wilt supply our need;
For blessings now, O Lord, I humbly plead. (J. Edwin Orr, 1912-1987)**

"My heart's desire"

The Word

> Brothers, my heart's desire and prayer to
> God for [Israel] is that they may be saved.
> Romans 10:1

Voice from the Church

"There is no reason in the world why you cannot become so steadfast in your personal prayer life that Christ will count on you to help build His church and advance His kingdom in many parts of the world. Beginning with your family, your church, and your community, you can play a significant part through normal daily prayer that will make a difference, even in distant lands." (Wesley Duewel, 1916-2016)*

Reflection

While we can bless people in a variety of ways, one of the richest blessings we can give to another person is to offer their names before the throne of grace. Do you have a prayer-burden for the unsaved—those in your family, neighborhood, church, workplace, in government, etc.?

What is your "heart's desire" for the sinner? The apostle Paul's "heart's desire" for his own people was "that they might be saved."

If one were to ask the typical church member what his or her "heart's desire" for their child would be, their answer would be revealing. Would they reply, "A good education at a famous university"? Or, would they say, "Upon graduation that they would find a notable position with a renowned company"?

What about man's spiritual standing before God? What about the lost of the world? Have we become so hardened because of the prevalence of sin, that we are no longer moved with the thought of people being lost forever. What is your "heart's desire" for people?

Verse

Rescue the perishing, care for the dying,
Snatch them in pity from sin and the grave;
Weep o'er the erring one, lift up the fallen,
Tell them of Jesus the mighty to save. (Fanny Crosby, 1820-1915)**

A More Excellent Name

The Word
³ᵇ*After making purification for sins, he sat down at the right hand of the*
Majesty on high, ⁴having become so much better than angels as
the name he has inherited is more excellent than theirs.
Hebrews 1:3b-4

Voice from the Church
"His name which is more excellent than [angels] may be inferred from
the context to be the title 'Son.' If He is said to have 'inherited' the
name Son, this does not mean that the name was not His before His ex-
altation. It was clearly His in the days of His humiliation (Heb. 5:8). It
was His, indeed, ages before His incarnation: this is the plain implica-
tion of the statement in Hebrews 1:2." (F. F. Bruce, 1910-1990)*

Reflection
Christ's human name was "Jesus," because he was mankind's savior
from sin (Matt. 1:21). However, Hebrews 1 says that Jesus was given a
"more excellent" name. The name that is "more excellent" is "Son."
Jesus is the eternal Son of the Father; he was "Son" before he was given
the name of "Jesus." The Son was "begotten" as "Jesus" in his incarnation: "You are my Son, today I have begotten you" (Heb. 1:5).

To demonstrate how much more the Son is superior to all created beings, he is contrasted to angels. The Son is worshiped by angels, that is
why he is superior to them: "Let all the angels of God worship
him" (Heb. 1:6). The Son is in fact Deity: "Your throne, O God, is forever and ever, the scepter of uprightness is the scepter of your kingdom" (Heb. 1:8). The Son was given an exalted position: "Sit at my
right hand until I make your enemies a footstool for your feet" (Heb.
1:13). "Son"—what a name!

Verse
"You are my dear Son, the Only Begotten;
Sit at my right hand, making intercession.
Your enemies I promise to make one day
a footstool for Your feet, for they turned away."

A Better Possession

The Word
[34]*For you had compassion on those in prison, and you joyfully accepted the plundering of your property, since you knew that you yourselves had a better possession and an abiding one.* [35]*Therefore do not throw away your confidence, which has a great reward.*
Hebrews 10:34-35

Voice from the Church
"John and Betty [Stam] were ready to 'baptize with blood a stony plot, till souls shall blossom from the spot.' It happened during the Long March of the Red Army to northwest China, an event famous for the army's bravery and heroism, as well as the suffering it inflicted on the civilian population. The Stams and their baby girl had just settled in their new assignment when a Red unit attacked their city and the Stams were captured. Early the next day (December 7, 1934) John and Betty Stam knelt side by side and were beheaded." (Kari Torjesen Malcolm, 1925-2014)*

Reflection
It has been reported there were more martyrs for Christ in the twentieth century than all the previous nineteen centuries combined. From the first martyr Stephen, to the present crucifixion of Christians in the country of Nigeria and elsewhere, God's favored people have willingly given their own blood in service to the Lamb of God, who laid down his life as an atoning sacrifice for them. We in the Western World know practically nothing of physically suffering for our faith in Christ. But our hearts should bleed for those who are suffering for the Lord Jesus. We care too much for our bodies and our possessions (just listen to the average prayer request). Those who are on the church's frontlines need our prayers.

Verse
Tortured and killed for Thy dear Name,
Lord, give them grace to count all but loss,
May they hold steadfast to the end,
Sharing the sufferings of the cross. (Susan H. Peterson, 1950-2004)**

A Better Resurrection

The Word

Women received back their dead by resurrection;
and others were tortured, not accepting their release,
so that they might obtain a better resurrection.
Hebrews 11:35 NASB

Voice from the Church

"A student at the University of Uruguay said to me: 'Professor McDowell, why can't you intellectually refute Christianity?'

"For a very simple reason," I answered. "I am not able to explain away an event in history—the resurrection of Jesus Christ." (Josh McDowell, b. 1939)*

Reflection

We have two recorded instances in the Old Testament of individuals being raised from the dead: The prophet Elijah was the human instrument in the raising of the widow of Zarephath's son (1 Kings 17:17-24); and Elisha raised the son of the Shunammite woman (2 Kings 4:18-37). There are three accounts of individuals raised through the ministry of Jesus: a twelve-year-old girl (Luke 8:41, 49-56); a young man (Luke 7:12-15); and Lazarus (John 11:1-44).

And, yet, the writer of Hebrews says there were those saints living under the Old Covenant who "were tortured, not accepting their release, so that they might obtain a better resurrection." "Not accepting their release"! Why? Their release would have provided them with a new life, as it were. But they didn't opt for that. They wanted a "better resurrection"—"better" because it would be everlasting; "better" because it would prove their faithfulness to their Lord; "better" because it would usher them into the presence of the King of kings and Lord of lords.

Verse

To accept their freedom
would have been the obvious choice.
But they looked far ahead,
by paying the ultimate price.

Christian Sacrifices

The Word

> [15]*Through him then let us continually offer up a sacrifice of praise to God, that is, the fruit of lips that acknowledge his name.* [16]*Do not neglect to do good and to share what you have, for such sacrifices are pleasing to God.*
> Hebrews 13:15-16

Voice from the Church

"I cannot help earnestly coveting the privilege of introducing the Gospel to a new land and people. When I heard the new language and saw a few portions of the people, I felt that if I could be permitted to reduce their language to writing, and perhaps translate the Scriptures into it, I might be able to say that I have not lived in vain." (David Livingstone, 1813-1873)*

Reflection

Under the Old Covenant, the life and worship of Israel were replete with sacrificial offerings. Although the Lord Jesus was the fulfilment of all that was represented by the former sacrifices, there yet remains sacrifices to be offered by each believer. Note some of these sacrifices.

• "I appeal to you therefore, brothers, by the mercies of God, to present your bodies as a living *sacrifice*, holy and acceptable to God, which is your spiritual worship (Rom. 12:1).

• "You yourselves like living stones are being built up as a spiritual house, to be a holy priesthood, to offer spiritual *sacrifices* acceptable to God through Jesus Christ" (1 Pet. 2:5).

• "Through him then let us continually offer up a sacrifice of praise to God, that is, the fruit of lips that acknowledge his name. [16]Do not neglect to do good and to share what you have, for such *sacrifices* are pleasing to God (Heb. 13:15-16).

Verse

No longer do we present the blood of beasts,
*   for these sacrifices were made obsolete.*
Because God's Lamb on our behalf was offered,
*   our bodies, thanks, and good deeds are now proffered.*

Equipped to Serve

The Word

[20]Now may the God of peace who brought again from the dead our Lord Jesus, the great shepherd of the sheep, by the blood of the eternal covenant, [21]equip you with everything good that you may do his will, working in us that which is pleasing in his sight, through Jesus Christ, to whom be glory forever and ever. Amen.
Hebrews 13:20-21

Voice from the Church

"No one else will ever receive the unique calling or special gifting that Bezalel and Oholiab were given to build a house for God. Yet their example serves as a reminder that God will equip us to do whatever he calls us to do. Neither Bezalel nor Oholiab had ever built a tabernacle before. Nevertheless, God called them to build it, and when he called them, he also equipped them.... When God calls us to do something, we are to trust that he will also give us whatever we need to fulfill that calling." (Philip G. Ryken, b. 1966)*

Reflection

Those whom God is pleased to call to either a special or a so-called common service, he will equip with the grace and gifts necessary to fulfil his calling. Whether you're a parent, teacher, pastor, missionary, doctor, businessman, laborer, etc.—if God has placed you where you are, he will enable you to serve him and your fellow man competently and efficiently, with joy and contentment.

While one may not always remain in their present employment, he or she should be at their best—whether they wait on tables or perform surgeries. God equips us as well as expecting us, by his grace, to improve our natural skills.

Verse

Give of your best to the Master;
Give Him first place in your heart.
Give Him first place in your service;
Consecrate every part. (Howard B. Grose, 1851-1939)**

Our Father in Heaven

The Word
14For this reason I bow my knees before the Father, 15from whom every family in heaven and on earth is named, ...
Ephesians 3:14-15

Voice from the Church
"In the implicit interaction between father and child more than bare obedience is essential. There must come the compelling joy of finding deep delight in His company. Over and over our Father fills our little lives with the overflowing abundance of His bounties. He enfolds us in His great strong arms of love. He pours into our souls a song of serenity." (W. Phillip Keller, 1920-1997)*

Reflection
The relationship that the Son of Man had (and has) with God was that of Son and Father. This eternal interrelatedness is more than the human mind can fully comprehend.

During his earthly life and ministry, the Lord Jesus routinely addressed and referred to the First Person of the Triune God as "Father." Jesus spoke of his "Father's house" (Luke 2:49; John 2:16). When he prayed, the Son directed his prayers to his Father. For example, in his High Priestly prayer (John 17), Jesus addressed God three times as "Father" (vv. 1, 5, 24), once as "Holy Father" (v. 11), and one time as "Righteous Father" (v. 25).

The Son of Man was always aware who he was in relationship to God. And the Father knew whom he had sent into the world. For at Jesus' baptism there was the speaking Voice: "This is my beloved Son, with whom I am well pleased" (Matt. 3:17). Lest we forget, Jesus taught the twice-born to pray, "Our Father in heaven ..." (Matt. 6:9).

Verse
I once only thought of God as God—
remote and distant, so uninvolved.
Then the Wind blew one warm summer night;
I awoke, looking up, cried, "My Father!"

"O, Heavenly Father ..."

The Word

For through him we both have access in one Spirit to the Father.
Ephesians 2:18

Voice from the Church

"As John Hyde came before the people ... he spoke three words in Urdu and three in English, repeating them three times" *'Ai Asmani Bak,* O, Heavenly Father.' What followed, who can describe? It was as if a great ocean came sweeping into that assembly. Hearts were bowed before the Divine Presence as the trees of the wood before a mighty tempest. It was the ocean of God's love being outpoured through one man's obedience. Hearts were broken before it." (Author Unknown)*

Reflection

None has ever discovered the depths of our Father's love and caring concern for each of his children. We believe that God is holy, just, and righteous. We also believe he is our Father in heaven, speaking to us through the revelation of his Son, the Lord Jesus Christ.

One day the disciple Philip requested of Jesus, "Lord, show us the Father." What was our Lord's reply? "Whoever has seen me has seen the Father" (John 12:8-9).

When reading the Gospel narratives through the eyes of the Spirit, our Father in heaven is revealed to us through the life and ministry of his beloved Son. When we see Jesus' care for the vulnerable and disenfranchised, we see the Father. When we see Jesus meeting the needs of the hurting, hungry, suffering, sorrowing, diseased, and bedridden, we see what our Father is like. When we see Jesus forgiving the sinner, upbraiding the self-righteous, and patiently teaching his followers, we see the true revelation of God the Father. "O, Heavenly Father ..."

Verse

Children of the heav'nly Father
Safely in His bosom gather;
Nestling bird nor star in Heaven
Such a refuge e'er was given. (Karolina W. Sandell-Berg, 1832-1903)**

The Father's Discipline

The Word

^{7}*It is for discipline that you have to endure. God is treating you as sons. For what son is there whom his father does not discipline?* ^{8}*If you are left without discipline, in which all have participated, then you are illegitimate children and not sons.*
Hebrews 12:7-8

Voice from the Church

"One day [Amy Carmichael] was telling the Good News to an old lady by interpretation. Just when she seemed ready to turn to Christ in faith, she noticed Amy's hands. It was very cold that day, and Amy was wearing fur gloves.... 'I went home, took off my English clothes, put on my Japanese kimono, and never again, I trust, risked so much for the sake of so little.'" (Elisabeth Elliot, 1926-2013)*

Reflection

We must never think of our heavenly Father's discipline as punishment. Quite the contrary. Though we may feel we've been to the "woodshed" on occasions, the Father always relates to his children in a manner that is full of love, albeit, full of truth. Our Father in heaven—through Word and Spirit—speaks to our needs, faults, failures, and sins, plainly and clearly. At times, we feel the severity of the "rod."

Wherever we have fallen short of his plan for us; whenever we need to adjust our conduct, lifestyle, and relationships—the Father is training our conscience to listen to his voice to please him more fully and bless others more consistently.

The purpose of the Father's discipline is "that we may share his holiness" (Heb. 12:10). When we resist his discipline, it shows we are disinterested in his conforming us to the image of his Son.

Verse

My heart flinched when the Word came strong that day;
*   for I had stumbled in my walk with God.*
But knowing He had corrected in love
*   made it easier to accept His rod.*

High and Lifted Up

The Word

> [12]*Young men and maidens together, old men and children!*
> [13]*Let them praise the name of the Lord, for his name alone*
> *is exalted; his majesty is above earth and heaven.*
>
> Psalm 148:12-13

Voice from the Church

"Before the Christian Church goes into eclipse anywhere there must first be a corrupting of her simple basic theology. She simply gets a wrong answer to the question, 'What is God like?' and goes on from there. Though she may continue to cling to a sound nominal creed, her practical working creed has become false. The masses of her adherents come to believe that God is different from what He actually is; and that is heresy of the most insidious and deadly kind." (A W. Tozer, 1897-1963)*

Reflection

True worship is never casual. When men and women of old were faced with God Almighty, they didn't sit nonchalantly with a cup of coffee in hand, legs crossed, waiting for the next joke to be told from the pulpit. No, worshiping from the heart, their minds were intent on God—high and lifted up.

The fundamental challenge our church generation faces today is, "What kind of God are we supposed to be worshiping?" How many typical congregants enter the church doors with thanksgiving and praise? How many of us would rather be entertained and experience a performance, than to behold the One who inhabits eternity whose name is holy? Until our view of God changes, our worship of God will remain mundane, nothing more than the natural man can offer to a figment of his manufactured imagination.

Verse

Praise to the Lord, the Almighty, the King of creation!
O my soul, praise Him, for He is thy health and salvation!
All ye who hear, now to His temple draw near;
Praise Him in glad adoration. (Joachim Neander, 1650-1680)**

Worshiping in Spirit

The Word

[23] "But the hour is coming, and is now here, when the true worshipers will worship the Father in spirit and truth, for the Father is seeking such people to worship him. [24] God is spirit, and those who worship him must worship in spirit and truth."

John 4:23-24

Voice from the Church

"'God is Spirit': it is not merely that he is a Spirit among other spirits; rather, God himself is pure spirit, and the worship in which he takes delight is accordingly spiritual worship—the sacrifice of a humble, contrite, grateful and adoring spirit.... Sincere heart-devotion, whenever and wherever found, is indispensable if men and women would present to God worship which he can accept." (F. F. Bruce, 1910-1990)*

Reflection

The natural man is overly impressed with religious trappings: symbols, ritualistic styles of worship, historical monuments and places, architectural structures—all of which shall eventually pass away.

Years ago, a group was touring one of London's famous cathedrals. Before the group exited the building, a member of the group took the guide aside and asked him, "Sir, can you tell me the last time someone was converted in this sanctuary?" The guide shook his head in response. In essence, the inquirer was asking if there was ever anything of reality which took place in that ornate structure.

There are many spiritual guides and helps in assisting one in their walk with God; however, if one never experiences the reality of God's forgiveness, cleansing, and empowering—every help can become a hindrance. When Spirit meets spirit—there is reality, there is worship.

Verse

The building and the place
will in time be effaced.
But my spirit will live on;
I will worship God alone.

Worshiping in Truth

The Word

[23] *"But the hour is coming, and is now here, when the true worshipers will worship the Father in spirit and truth, for the Father is seeking such people to worship him.* [24] *God is spirit, and those who worship him must worship in spirit and truth."*

John 4:23-24

Voice from the Church

"Only by serious searching of scripture and its consensual tradition of interpretation, with earnest daily application, will postmodern persons become active hearers of the Word." (Thomas C. Oden, 1931-2016)*

Reflection

God calls his people to be people of truth. Not truth as I see it, or truth as you see it, but objective truth as God sees it and has revealed to us through the Incarnate Word of God and the Written Word.

In many church traditions, so much of the so-called worship is superstitious: men through the ages have dictated forms and ceremonies that have prevented congregants from directing their worship to God alone, without human mediators.

So much worship is vain worship: certain prayers repeated over and over again, people walking in disobedience to God, and offering lip-service without heart obedience.

To worship God in "truth" is to exalt the name of his Son, the Lord Jesus Christ. (see John 12:13).

To worship God in "truth" is to offer one's body to God, consecrated to him alone (see Rom. 12:1-2).

To worship God in "truth" is to worship with a good conscience (see Matt. 5:23-25).

Verse

In vain do we enter God's house to worship,
singing praises and listening to His Word,
if we leave with hands dirty and hearts impure,
unchanged by the Spirit, resisting the Lord.

The Forgotten Among Us

The Word

> *And a man lame from birth was being carried, whom*
> *they laid daily at the gate of the temple that is called the*
> *Beautiful Gate to ask alms of those entering the temple.*
>
> Acts 3:2

Voice from the Church

"As a teenager, Bramwell Booth never forgot the first time his father led him into an East End [London] pub: gas-jets playing eerily on men's inflamed faces, drunken disheveled women openly suckling tiny children, the reek of gin and shag tobacco and acrid bodies. After a moment, seeing the appalled look on his son's face, William Booth said quietly: 'These are our people. These are the people I want you to live for and bring to Christ.'" (Richard Collier, 1924-1996)*

Reflection

How often the church has forgotten the down-and-out while catering to the well-to-do and people of position and influence in the community. Are the poor shunned or accepted in your local church? Are the world's disenfranchised sought out with an effort to win them to the Lord Jesus Christ? In his inaugural message, Jesus announced, "he has anointed me to proclaim good news to the poor" (Luke 4:18). On another occasion, our Lord remarked, "the poor have good news preached to them" (Matt. 11:5).

The church has mostly forgotten the poor and tattered, the downtrodden and destitute. If we are shipping thousands of dollars overseas while the alcoholic is sitting on our doorstep, we are not loving our neighbor as ourselves. Could it be that we need to start a mission to reach those who won't enter our beautiful buildings?

Verse

He held out his hand, day after day;
Most clung to their robes and turned away.
But one day there came two men close by:
Full of the Spirit, hearing his cry.

Doing Our Duty

The Word

> [7] *"Will any one of you who has a servant plowing or keeping sheep say to him when he has come in from the field, 'Come at once and recline at table'?* [8]*Will he not rather say to him, 'Prepare supper for me, and dress properly, and serve me while I eat and drink, and afterward you will eat and drink'?* [9]*Does he thank the servant because he did what was commanded?* [10]*So you also, when you have done all that you were commanded, say, 'We are unworthy servants; we have only done what was our duty.'"*

Luke 17:7-10

Voice from the Church

"My life as a worker is the way I say 'thank you' to God for His unspeakable salvation." (Oswald Chambers, 1874-1917)*

Reflection

Who among us deserves praise for his service in the Lord's vineyard? It is our merciful God who has called and gifted us. It is the Lord of the Vineyard who has sustained and preserved us in the work to which we have been appointed.

Let us never seek to be acknowledged for any good work we have performed for the King of kings. If we have truly been serving our Lord, with an eye single to his glory and praise alone, what praise can any man add to our Lord's commendation? The ancient worthies—such as Noah, Abel, and Enoch were commended by God for their obedient acts of faith. None of these sought the praise of men. He who seeks the praise of men will never receive the praise of God. To do our duty before God is our calling; we are his servants, not man's. In serving others, let us seek the praise of God alone.

Verse

I have simply done my duty, Father;
An unworthy servant I am.
To do what You have commanded, Father,
Is my offering to Your Lamb.

Walking

The Word

These are the generations of Noah. Noah was a righteous
man, blameless in his generation. Noah walked with God.
Genesis 6:9

Voice from the Church

"When a debate starts up in my mind about whether something is right
or wrong, I'll cut short the debate by deciding to treat it as wrong
whether or not it actually is, since I'll rarely suffer harm that way and I
may well suffer damage if I go with the self-justification." (Robertson
McQuilkin, 1927-2016)*

Reflection

Note a few NT references about how a Christian is to "walk" in this
present evil world.

• We were buried therefore with him by baptism into death, in order
that, just as Christ was raised from the dead by the glory of the Father,
we too might **walk** in newness of life (Rom. 6:4).

• "Let us **walk** properly as in the daytime, not in orgies and drunken-
ness, not in sexual immorality and sensuality, not in quarreling and jealousy" (Rom. 13:13).

• "For we **walk** by faith, not by sight" (2 Cor. 5:7).

• "But I say, **walk** by the Spirit, and you will not gratify the desires of
the flesh" (Gal. 5:16).

• "And **walk** in love, as Christ loved us and gave himself up for us, a
fragrant offering and sacrifice to God" (Eph. 5:2).

• "For at one time you were darkness, but now you are light in the
Lord. **Walk** as children of light" (Eph. 5:8).

Are you walking with God today?

Verse

How beautiful to walk in the steps of the Savior,
Stepping in the light, stepping in the light,
How beautiful to walk in the steps of the Savior,
Led in paths of light. (Eliza E. Hewitt, 1851-1920)**

"Train yourself for godliness"

The Word

> [7]Have nothing to do with irreverent, silly myths. Rather train yourself for godliness; [8]for while bodily training is of some value, godliness is of value in every way, as it holds promise for the present life and also for the life to come.
>
> 1 Timothy 4:7-8

Voice from the Church

"O my brother, cast not away the confidence of making progress in godliness; there is yet time, the hour is not yet passed. Why wilt thou defer thy good purpose from day to day? Arise and begin in this very instant, and say, 'Now is the time to be doing, now is the time to be striving, now is the time to amend thyself.'" (Thomas à Kempis, 1380-1471)*

Reflection

It is important that we care for our bodies; after all, we are told that our body is the temple of the Holy Spirit (1 Cor. 6:19). And many need to care for the body more than they are. Having said that, as it is with many habits, we tend to the extreme: we care more for the body than we do our soul and spirit.

The Holy Spirit reminds us that the most important training exercises we can engage in is the training that produces godly character and conduct. My goal six days a week is to take a brisk 20-25 minutes' walk. But if I exercise my body without daily training my inner life, what has it really profited me? Many of us are running on empty. Our souls have dried up. We're barely making it from day to day. What is the remedy? We must set aside daily time to get still before God. We must feed on his Word and commune with our Father in heaven. We must exercise regularly if we are to face each day successfully. Are you exercising?

Verse

His spirit grew faint in the battle,
His hands hung low and weak were his knees.
But then he found fresh bread and water;
Renewed, he rose, feeling a cool Breeze.

The World

The Word

> [15]*Do not love the world or the things in the world. If anyone loves the world, the love of the Father is not in him.* [16]*For all that is in the world—the desires of the flesh and the desires of the eyes and pride of life—is not from the Father but is from the world.* [17]*And the world is passing away along with its desires, but whoever does the will of God abides forever.*
>
> 1 John 2:15-17

Voice from the Church

"Ultimately, when we touch the things of the world, the question we must ask ourselves always is: 'How is this thing affecting my relationship with the Father.'" (Watchman Nee, 1903-1972)*

Reflection

Every secular system in this world is *of* the world: governments, economics, politics, the arts and sciences, entertainment industry, corporations, businesses, etc. If an enterprise is not governed by God's principles, it is *of* this world.

To be *of* this world is to embrace the world's desires (lusts). When our lives are directed by our natural and soulish appetites, when we satisfy our cravings by the inordinate desires of the flesh, when aspirations, plans and goals are concentrated on ourselves—we are identifying with the "world."

To boast of our accomplishments, possessions, positions is to be infected with the spirit of the world. To be *of* this world is the antithesis of being *of* God. The reason we are not to love the world is because it's temporary. To do the will of God is not to love the world, for in doing the will of God we abide with him forever.

Verse

Is it hard to serve God, timid soul? Has thou found
Gloomy forests, dark glens, mountaintops on thy way?
All the hard would be easy, all the tangles unwound,
Wouldst thou only desire, as well as obey. (Frederick W. Faber, 1814-1863)**

Kept from Evil

The Word
> [15] *"I do not ask that you take them out of the world, but that you keep them from the evil one. [16] They are not of the world, just as I am not of the world."*
> John 17:15-16

Voice from the Church
"Believers are ... neither to withdraw from the world nor to become indistinguishable from it, but rather, as ones consecrated by the truth and separated from evil, they are to witness to God's Son, aided by the Spirit." (Andreas J. Köstenberger, b. 1957)*

Reflection
When the Lord Jesus prayed that the Father would not take his disciples "out of the world," he was asking that his followers would not be removed from present society. No man can function properly in this life without employment, engaging in business, exchanging money, etc. Though some Christians attempt to isolate themselves from society to the extreme, this is not God's usual plan for his people.

There are certain practices and businesses which are inherently evil. The Christian is to refrain from participating in anything that is contrary to God's standard of righteousness: "Abstain from every form of evil" (1 Thess. 5:22). However, most of us are employed by and do business with companies that are not guided by biblical principles. And most of the people we work with are unbelievers. Are we to quit our job and isolate ourselves from unbelievers because they are *of* this world? Jesus said we should not; he prayed otherwise.

We live in a fallen wicked world. The Lord Jesus prayed that his disciples would be kept from the evil one. Are you willing to be kept?

Verse
Never a battle with wrong for the right,
Never a contest that He doth not fight;
Lifting above us His banner so white;
Moment by moment I'm kept in His sight. (Daniel W. Whittle, 1840-1901)**

The Light of the World

The Word
Again Jesus spoke to them, saying, "I am the light of the world. Whoever follows me will not walk in darkness, but will have the light of life."
John 8:12

Voice from the Church
"The light of divine holiness which shines upon us from God the Father, through the glorious face of our Lord Jesus (2 Cor. 4:6) and is shed within us by the communicating Holy Spirit (Rom. 5:5) is the joy and gladness of our infinite creator! That holiness is meant to infill our minds and hearts." (J. Sidlow Baxter, 1903-1999)*

Reflection
Before the Incarnate God invaded our human domain, the prophet foretold the glorious event by announcing, "The people who walked in darkness have seen a great light; those who dwelt in a land of deep darkness, on them has light shone" (Isa. 9:2). That "light" was the "Light of the world"—God's Son, the Lord Jesus Christ.

In John's Prologue (1:1-18) to his Gospel, he says of Jesus, "In him was life, and the life was the light of men" (1:4). The Lord Jesus emitted light (holiness and truth) to mankind because he himself was the source of life—eternal life. Where there is no life there is no light. The presence of light presupposes life.

Darkness (sin) is the antithesis of light. To follow Christ is to walk in the light. Not to follow Christ is to walk in darkness. How can we claim to be a follower of the Lord Jesus and walk in darkness? Jesus is light. To follow Jesus is to walk in righteousness and truth. If you have a question about any action or activity, hold it up to the Light. Does it pass the Light test?

Verse
My heart was dark;
The night was drear.
Then Jesus came close
And made all things clear.

Lights in the World

The Word

> [14]"You are the light of the world. A city set on a hill cannot
> be hidden.[15]Nor do people light a lamp and put it under a basket,
> but on a stand, and it gives light to all in the house. [16]In the same
> way, let your light shine before others, so that they may see your
> good works and give glory to your Father who is in heaven."
> Matthew 5:14-15

Voice from the Church

"They love one another. They never fail to help widows; they save orphans from those who would hurt them. If they have something, they give freely to the man who has nothing; if they see a stranger, they take him home, and are happy, as though he were a real brother. They don't consider themselves brothers in the usual sense, but brothers instead through the Spirit, in God." (Aristides of Athens, d. 134 AD, describing Christians to Emperor Hadrian)*

Reflection

What the sun is to our planet, the Lord Jesus is to all humanity; what the moon is to Earth, Christ's followers are to this world. The former is the source of holiness and truth, the latter are Christ's reflectors and witnesses to holiness and truth—in word and deed.

The darker the night, the brighter the lights. Our culture is increasingly becoming darker. As cream rises to the top, the quality of our lives will be seen for what they are against the backdrop of a wicked and perverse age.

Light is never forced; it simply shines. Each Christian is a light—in the home first, then in the shop, classroom, marketplace, etc. Where a Christian walks, light is present—to the glory of the Father.

Verse

He aspired to do something great;
Jesus said, "Stoop down; wash their feet."
He wanted to travel abroad;
Jesus said, "Go home to your friends."

Radiant Lights

The Word

> [14]*Do all things without grumbling or disputing,* [15]*that you may be blameless and innocent, children of God without blemish in the midst of a crooked and twisted generation, among whom you shine as lights in the world,* [16]*holding fast to the word of life.*
> Philippians 2:14-16a

Voice from the Church

"I met a man with a shining face—and I mean shining. It was a face having upon it the glow of heaven and the glory of God.... My first meeting with this man was in the month of May, 1906, and, little as I dreamed it then, that meeting was destined to prove the crossroad which was to lead to the settling of one of the greatest issues of my life. Certainly I needed to meet somebody, for spiritually I had a deep-rooted need." (Harry E. Jessop, 1884-?)*

Reflection

The world (and the church) is in need of radiant lights. Jesus said of John the Baptist that he was a "burning and shining lamp" (John 5:35). We can't shine unless we burn—burn with the very holy love of Jesus; burn with the very fiery power of the indwelling Holy Spirit.

A lamp doesn't emit light unless it is fueled by energy. The Holy Spirit is the Christian's indwelling energy. You say that you are a Christian. You say that you are a disciple of Jesus Christ. You say that you have been born again. Where then is the energy? Where is the light?

I thank God for the burning and shining lights I have come across during my spiritual pilgrimage. God wants to make you a radiant light in this world—a radiance that is not self-conscious; a radiance that is not aware of its own whiteness. It's the radiance of Christ, of holiness.

Verse

There flowed from her a radiancy,
Though beset with heartaches and trials.
Mostly she lived in obscurity,
But her influence crossed the miles.

The Word of God

The Word
> *All Scripture is breathed out by God and profitable for teaching,*
> *for reproof, for correction, and for training in righteousness.*
> 2 Timothy 3:16

Voice from the Church
"I have learned to ascribe the honor of infallibility only to those books that are accepted as canonical. I am profoundly convinced that none of these writers has erred. All other writers, however they may have distinguished themselves in holiness or in doctrine, I read in this way: I evaluate what they say, not on the basis that they themselves believe that a thing is true, but only insofar as they are able to convince me by the authority of the canonical books or by clear reason." (Martin Luther, 1483-1546)*

Reflection
The Lord Jesus heard the Word regularly read in the Temple and synagogue. The Apostles were men of the Word, and men as well through whom additional revelation was communicated by the Holy Spirit (the New Testament). In the words of Peter, "You should remember the predictions of the holy prophets and the commandment of the Lord and Savior through your apostles" (2 Pet. 3:2).

The written Word (the 66 books we call the "Bible") is God-breathed; it is "living and active, sharper than any two-edged sword, piercing to the division of soul and of spirit, of joints and of marrow, and discerning the thoughts and intentions of the heart" (Heb. 4:12). "Heaven and earth will pass away, but my words will not pass away" (Mark 13:31). What shall we do with God's truth? The answer: "Let the word of Christ dwell in you richly" (Col. 3:16).

Verse
I wanted a sure word from God;
Certainty I needed for this vessel of clay.
I heard a Voice: "Take up the Book."
I read; the Spirit turned my night into clear day.

Dependence

The Word

> *"I am the vine; you are the branches. Whoever abides in me and I in him, he it is that bears much fruit, for apart from me you can do nothing."*
> John 15:5

Voice from the Church

"I have sometimes heard Christian people talk as though God, having done what he's done in Jesus, now wants us to do our part by getting on with things under our own steam. But that is a tragic misunderstanding. It leads to arrogance, burnout, or both. Without God's Spirit, there is nothing we can do that will count for God's kingdom. Without God's Spirit, the church simply can't be the church." (N. T. Wright, b. 1948)*

Reflection

Apart from the grace of God, autonomous man endeavors to carve out a course for his life that is centered around himself; he has no interest in being accountable to anyone outside of his own ego.

Those who have accepted the call of Christ, to be his followers, have repudiated a self-driven life; the gospel has been embraced, sins have been forgiven, and the Holy Spirit has taken up residence within. But the regenerated man is still free—free to daily make choices that are either God-honoring or self-pleasing. He is free to assert his own will, disregarding the will of God.

The heart of man requires a fundamental heart-cleansing, Spirit-filling, and a mind renewal that empowers him to make righteous choices, to the glory of God. Without the strength of the Spirit, we remain helpless against the forces of evil. It is only by relying on the power of Christ that we can conquer in his name.

Verse

I said to myself, "I know I can do this."
Self-assured was I; my strength was strong.
He let me fail, until I was much broken;
Then I confessed to how I was wrong.

Controlling Love

The Word

^{14}For the love of Christ controls us, because we have concluded
this: that one has died for all, therefore all have died; ^{15}and he
died for all, that those who live might no longer live for
themselves but for him who for their sake died and was raised.
2 Corinthians 5:14-15

Voice from the Church

"In the heart of Africa, among the great lakes, I have come across black
men and women who remembered the only white man they ever saw
before—David Livingstone; and as you cross his footsteps in that dark
continent, men's faces light up as they speak of the kind Doctor who
passed there years ago. They could not understand him; but they felt the
Love that beat in his heart." (Henry Drummond, 1851-1897)*

Reflection

The call of God to serve others, in the name of Jesus, is a call from
above. This call is more than a human sympathy that one person may
feel for another's plight. To feed the hungry and clothe the naked and
treat the wounded and diseased, may be driven by self-gratification or a
desire to seek merit before God. But the love of God goes deeper than
human affection and passion. Once shed abroad in man's heart and controlled by God's indwelling Spirit, the love of God is motivated by the
Cross of Christ. God's love is selfless and pure, enduring and persistent,
clear-eyed and discerning. God's love is boundless and impartial in its
service; it does not consider the sacrifice and cost in going to the lost
and ministering to the Body of Christ.

In a self-driven age, God's people must refuse the world's mold, being transformed into the very image of the selfless Christ.

Verse

Rejecting its shame and seeming loss,
Our Lord joyfully went to the Cross.
With Christ's love controlling our own life,
Serving others is no sacrifice.

Real Knowledge and Discernment (1)

The Word
[9]*And this I pray, that your love may abound still more and more in real knowledge and all discernment,* [10]*so that you may approve the things that are excellent, in order to be sincere and blameless until the day of Christ;* [11]*having been filled with the fruit of righteousness which comes through Jesus Christ, to the glory and praise of God.*
Philippians 1:9-11 NASB

Voice from the Church
"Clearly, knowledge and discernment without love could easily become supercilious, overbearing, casuistical. But love without knowledge and discernment is soon a parody of itself. The Christian love for which Paul prays is regulated by knowledge of the gospel and comprehensive moral insight." (D. A. Carson, b. 1946)*

Reflection
Of the many prayers we hear prayed on behalf of others, it is rare to hear anyone pray for Christians like the apostle Paul. Attending the typical prayer service, one will hear repeated requests for the physical and material needs of our fellow believers. Of course, our Father in heaven cares about these matters, but should they dominate our prayers? What about the deeper needs? How often do we hear prayers like Paul prayed?

Believers are in need of "real knowledge" and discernment." To possess knowledge that is real is to understand the true gospel of the Lord Jesus Christ. To have "discernment" is to possess the ability to separate truth from error; it has a sensitive moral insight. For this to occur, the Spirit says the *agape* love of God must exceed the ordinary, to overflow, "abound still more and more." To possess real knowledge and discernment, we must be continually filled with the holy love of Jesus.

Verse
To have my eyes opened to Your truth,
To distinguish the real from the false,
I ask that my heart be filled, O God,
With Your great love displayed on the Cross.

Excellent Things (2)

The Word

[9] *And this I pray, that your love may abound still more and more in real knowledge and all discernment,* [10] *so that you may approve the things that are excellent, in order to be sincere and blameless until the day of Christ;* [11] *having been filled with the fruit of righteousness which comes through Jesus Christ, to the glory and praise of God.*
Philippians 1:9-11 NASB

Voice from the Church

"Love displays itself in knowledge and discernment. In proportion as it abounds it sharpens the moral perceptions for the discernment of what is best." (Marvin Vincent, 1834-1922)*

Reflection

The first of two purpose clauses appear in verse 10 of the above text: "so that." The reason Paul prays that the Philippians' "love may abound still more and more in real knowledge and discernment" is "so that you may approve things that are excellent."

These converts had grown up in a culture saturated with every kind of evil and perversion, not unlike our own generation. The recipients of this letter were mostly Gentile believers, who never had the privilege of hearing the Law and the Prophets in the local synagogue each week, as did the Jewish population.

Mind renewal is necessary for moral discernment. To "approve" means we are to examine, put to the test what our culture considers acceptable practice and behavior. After a careful examination, we are to embrace the kind of attitude and conduct that God considers morally "excellent." Christians are a counterculture minority. The mind of Christ and the mind of the world are antithetical to each other.

Verse

The Spirit is forming a people
  shaped by the truth of God.
These saints do not follow the masses—
  excellence they applaud.

Sincerity (3)

The Word
⁹And this I pray, that your love may abound still more and more in real knowledge and all discernment, ¹⁰so that you may approve the things that are excellent, in order to be sincere and blameless until the day of Christ; ¹¹having been filled with the fruit of righteousness which comes through Jesus Christ, to the glory and praise of God.
Philippians 1:9-11 NASB

Voice from the Church
"How have we managed to divorce holiness of life from imputed righteousness? How does one have the righteousness of Christ credited to his or her account and yet live without any regard for holiness? How can it be that nominalism is now called Christianity (which is holiness unto the Lord) and Christianity is regarded as fanaticism? Oh, for a divine visitation that brings the issue of holiness into focus in our lives so that we truly believe: 'Be holy; for I am holy.'" (Richard Owen Roberts, b. 1931)*

Reflection
The purpose of being able to "approve things that are excellent" is that God's people may be "sincere."

The word "sincere" suggests a transparent purity. In the time of Paul, should a crack occur in a piece of pottery, it was often repaired with wax. When a buyer, for example, was considering purchasing a vase, he would hold it up to the light of the sun, to see if it had been repaired with wax. If he saw wax, he would not make the purchase.

The Christian should be constantly lifting into the light of God's holiness moral issues with which he is confronted. If it passes the "light test," the believer can be said to be "without wax"; he is sincere.

Verse
To be "sincere" is to inspect
  our deeds in the light of God's light.
To be "sincere" is to walk in
  His light that we might see more light.
To be "sincere"—hate the darkness.

Blamelessness (4)

The Word

[9]*And this I pray, that your love may abound still more and more in real knowledge and all discernment, *[10]*so that you may approve the things that are excellent, in order to be sincere and blameless until the day of Christ; *[11]*having been filled with the fruit of righteousness which comes through Jesus Christ, to the glory and praise of God.*
Philippians 1:9-11 NASB

Voice from the Church

"C. H. Spurgeon once wrote as follows: 'There is a point of grace as much above the ordinary Christian as the ordinary Christian is above the world.' Of such he says: 'Their place is with the eagle in his eyrie, high aloft. They are rejoicing Christians, holy and devout men doing service for their Master all over the world, and everywhere conquerors through Him that loved them." (Thomas Cook, 1867-1947)*

Reflection

To be "blameless" is to live without guilt before God. When he was 99 years of age, Yahweh's command to Abram was: "I am God Almighty; Walk before Me, and be blameless" (Gen. 17:1). To be "blameless" is to walk before God with integrity of heart and life; it is to walk before God with a complete heart, a united heart, an undivided heart.

God was revealed to Abram as *El Shaddai*, the God who is sufficient, God Almighty—sufficient to enable Abram (under Old Covenant Law) to live before God blamelessly. If this was God's expectation under the Old Covenant, how much more is this his expectation under the New. Not that Abram never failed. But let's never lower God's standard of holiness to excuse our failures, our sins. By the power of the Spirit, God's grace can enable you today to live a blameless life.

Verse

They teach I must sin every day,
*   and sin in almost every way.*
They distort the plain Word of God;
*   they don't know the Spirit's power.*

In This Present Life (5)

The Word

[9]*And this I pray, that your love may abound still more and more in real knowledge and all discernment,* [10]*so that you may approve the things that are excellent, in order to be sincere and blameless until the day of Christ;* [11]*having been filled with the fruit of righteousness which comes through Jesus Christ, to the glory and praise of God.*
Philippians 1:9-11 NASB

Voice from the Church

"The text teaches us to pray that we will test out and approve for ourselves the highest and best and holiest things—all with a view to the day of Jesus Christ. Even now, Paul's prayer insists, Christians are to be as holy as pardoned sinners can be this side of eternity. And we are to pray toward that end." (D. A. Carson, b. 1946)*

Reflection

There is a perfection which will be realized by God's holy people when they are ushered finally into the presence of the glorified Lord Jesus Christ: "But you have come to ... the spirits of the righteous made perfect" (Heb. 12:22-23). There is an evangelical perfection (completeness) which God calls his people to in this life. In one sense we are not perfect: "Not that I have already obtained it or have already become perfect, but I press on so that I may lay hold of that for which also I was laid hold of by Christ Jesus" (Phil. 3:12). On another level, we are called to perfection: "For I am confident of this very thing, that He who began a good work in you will perfect it until the day of Christ Jesus" (Phil. 1:6). "Let us therefore, as many as are perfect, ..." (Phil. 3:15). This is not a form of *perfectionism*; it is to will one will—the will of God; it is to be wholly Christ's—until the day of Christ.

Verse

I make no excuses for my failure;
I chose to purse a selfish pleasure.
Lord, I want You as my only treasure—
Cleanse and make me wholly Thine.

To the Glory of God (6)

The Word
[9]*And this I pray, that your love may abound still more and more in real knowledge and all discernment,* [10]*so that you may approve the things that are excellent, in order to be sincere and blameless until the day of Christ;* [11]*having been filled with the fruit of righteousness which comes through Jesus Christ, to the glory and praise of God.*
Philippians 1:9-11 NASB

Voice from the Church
"There is no *static* level of supposed sinlessness through supposed erad-ication. Nay, they who walk with God most closely are most keenly aware of inhering liabilities to sin which still linger and would immedi-ately reassert themselves, apart from the continual infilling of the Holy Spirit." (J. Sidlow Baxter, 1903-1999)*

Reflection
The thirsty-hearted know well that every spiritual blessing they receive comes though the Lord Jesus Christ and is communicated to us by the blessed Holy Spirit. We have no righteousness of our own; it is all of grace. The greatest evangelist and teacher who ever walked this earth was the apostle Paul. Having founded many local churches and having preached the gospel to practically every known region in his day, yet Paul considered himself "the very least of all the saints" and "the least of the apostles" (Eph. 3:8; 1 Cor. 15:9). The higher he ascended in grace, the lower Paul became in his own eyes.

Those who have been "filled with the fruit of righteousness" are fully aware who is the *Source* of every good and perfect gift which comes from above. There is no room for self-righteousness; there is no room for boasting. All glory and praise are given to God alone.

Verse
I cannot keep this temple free
from each defilement of sin;
I welcome You to take control,
uniting my heart within.

Working Out What God Works In

The Word

Work out your own salvation with fear and trembling, [13]for it is God who works in you, both to will and to work for his good pleasure.
Philippians 2:12b-13

Voice from the Church

"There is ... a great difference between true holiness wrought in us by the Holy Spirit and a morally decent life produced by self-effort. Moreover the life of holiness wrought in us by the Holy Spirit needs to be kept pure and undefiled by the Spirit of God and the blood of Christ, whereas the morally decent life, produced by self-effort, endeavours to keep itself pure by 'good resolutions.'" (John Owen, 1616-1683)*

Reflection

Without the grace of God working within us, all our efforts in Christian service, as well as our endeavors to form Christlike character, are futile. But take courage, as a child of God, the Spirit of God is operating within you; he goes to the very tap root of your inner nature, prompting you to will his will. With an undivided heart to work with, God will use you as you serve others in Jesus' name.

The challenge you daily face is: Will you "work out" what God "works in you"? Is God prompting you to lay aside some impediment as you run this Christian race (see Heb. 12:1)? Are you in some way being selfish in your marriage, as an employee, in your ministry position (see Phil. 2:3-4)? Are you in any way defiling your spirit or your body (see 2 Cor. 7:1)? Are you manifesting the love of Jesus to those individuals he places in your pathway (see Matt. 22:39)? In the words of the holy apostle, "Work out your own salvation with fear and trembling, for it is God who works in you."

Verse

I trust in You, O living God,
to work Your grace freely within,
That I might keep in step with You,
working out what You work within.

Be Holy

The Word
> [14]As obedient children, do not be conformed to the
> passions of your former ignorance, [15]but as he who called
> you is holy, you also be holy in all your conduct, [16]since
> it is written, "You shall be holy, for I am holy."
> 1 Peter 1:14-16

Voice from the Church
"God must weary of our doctrinal involutions no less than our practical evasions. On any scheme known to theology—whether of terms or of concepts, whether Calvinist, Lutheran, or Arminian—we doddering, defaulting, defeated Christians would be driven to our knees, driven to the Cross, driven to Pentecost, if only we took with passionate seriousness this inviolable claim of the Father, 'You shall be holy, for I am holy.'" (Paul S. Rees, 1900-1991)*

Reflection
The doctrine and life of holy living is nonsectarian and transdenominational in nature, for it is a biblical call from God himself, who is essentially holy and has sent his *Holy* Spirit to make a *holy* people.

To be sure, many trappings and eccentricities have besmirched God's call to holy living. But only the cynical, dismissive, and uninformed would repudiate this high and holy calling.

The Holy Spirit alone, applying God's revealed Truth, is able to shape each follower of our Lord into a godly, Christlike person. No written codes of conduct devised by ecclesiastical bodies avail; imposed rules do not make for godly character. Nonetheless, the pulpit must teach, exhort, and warn lest the sheep go astray. But let us make sure we teach the plain Word of God and not our own notions.

Verse
I hear Your call, my Lord,
  to walk the holy way.
By your power alone
  I walk the narrow way.

Hating our Life

The Word

[25] *"Whoever loves his life loses it, and whoever hates his life in this world will keep it for eternal life. [26]If anyone serves me, he must follow me; and where I am, there will my servant be also. If anyone serves me, the Father will honor him."*

John 12:25-26

Voice from the Church

"Teach us, good Lord, to serve thee as thou deservest; to give and not to count the cost; to fight and not to heed the wounds; to toil and not to ask for rest; to labour and not to ask for any reward save knowing that we do thy will. Through Jesus Christ our Lord." (Ignatius Loyola, 1491-1556)*

Reflection

God both demands and deserves, from his people, unqualified loyalty to his Son, the Lord Jesus Christ. He who gave his all to and for us, must not receive anything less from us. We must forsake all to follow Christ; we must abandon ourselves and take up our cross to serve him. Anything less is to love ourselves; anything less is treason.

There is no place for halfhearted disciples among the Lord's followers. Divided hearts look back to Sodom. The person looking back is not fit for the kingdom of God.

The Son of God left all to become the Son of Man: "For you know the grace of our Lord Jesus Christ, that though he was rich, yet for your sake he became poor." (2 Cor. 8:9). What have you left behind to become a disciple of the Lord Jesus? You say that you left your sin behind. That's not good enough! Jesus didn't leave "sin" behind; he left the riches and glory of heaven. We must leave behind whatever the Holy Spirit puts his finger on.

Verse

Since my eyes were fixed on Jesus,
I've lost sight of all beside;
So enchained my spirit's vision,
Looking at the Crucified. (Mary D. James, 1810-1883)**

A Mature Faith

The Word
> ¹¹*And he gave the apostles, the prophets, the evangelists,*
> *the shepherds and teachers, ¹²to equip the saints for the work of*
> *ministry, for building up the body of Christ, ¹³until we all attain to the*
> *unity of the faith and of the knowledge of the Son of God, to mature*
> *manhood, to the measure of the stature of the fullness of Christ, ...*
> Ephesians 4:11-13

Voice from the Church
"Creeds do not ensure orthodoxy, for no individual church holds all the truth of the Church. The great body of truth is the property of the catholic church [i.e., the universal church], not any section, nor yet of any individual member thereof." (G. Campbell Morgan, 1863-1945)*

Reflection
The great creeds of the church were hammered out by its leaders when the truth, as it is found in Jesus, was under severe attack. The creeds are not to be despised, but, of course, no creed contains all the truth, nor did the formulators intend them to.

The Holy Spirit calls all true followers of Christ to "the unity of the faith and of the knowledge of the Son of God, to mature manhood, to the measure of the stature of the fullness of Christ." The Head of the church, the risen Christ, will not be content until this is achieved among his Body.

This is not a call to organizational unity—we will never see that in this world. But Christ does call each of his people to an *organic* unity of the Spirit, in truth and fellowship. Whenever we divide over anything that is not either plainly affirmed or forbidden by the Word of God, we are being childish instead of demonstrating maturity in Christ.

Verse
A sectarian spirit is prideful,
  separating true brothers and sisters.
The Holy Spirit unites truth and grace,
  making us one in Christ Jesus our Lord.

Really Caring

The Word

> ^{9}He went on from there and entered their synagogue. ^{10}And
> a man was there with a withered hand.... ^{13}Then he said to
> the man, "Stretch out your hand." And the man stretched
> it out, and it was restored, healthy like the other.

Matthew 12:9-10, 13

Voice from the Church

"I once heard a pastor say that if we had x-ray eyes and could see the real condition of the people in front of us when we preach and teach, we would break down and bawl." (Frederick D. Bruner, b. 1932)*

Reflection

The spiritual, emotional, physical, and material needs of some people may be obvious to us, while the needs of others are unknown—at least, to us. Daily we encounter suffering individuals, each of whom has a name and a need. Some needs are greater than others, but we all have needs.

There are those among us who are carrying heavy burdens. Often people only need a word of encouragement. Do we care? If we never really *see* people as individuals, we will never get to know them; we will never know how they are hurting.

I have often wondered how many times the man with the "withered hand" had come and gone from the house of worship, without any expectation of being made whole. Then there came that one special Sabbath, when someone took notice of his affliction and lifted his load. The "someone," of course, was Jesus of Nazareth. Jesus really *saw* the man that day and cared—cared enough to make a difference in one person's life. All around you are suffering people. How much do you care?

Verse

He could have seen me and turned away—
He didn't; He met my deepest need.
Now I must reach out to my brothers,
Showing Christ's love in word and in deed.

God Uses Suffering

The Word

> [15] But the Lord said to [Ananias], "Go, for he is a
> chosen instrument of mine to carry my name before the
> Gentiles and kings and the children of Israel. [16] For I will
> show him how much he must suffer for the sake of my name."
> Acts 9:15-16

Voice from the Church

"If God healed everyone immediately where would be the opportunity for character training? If God delivered everyone from conflict, oppression, and opposition at the first call, where would be the opportunity for the perseverance that creates character?... If Jesus' human experience in leadership could not be perfected without suffering, could our training for heavenly rulership be perfected without it?" (Paul E. Billheimer, 1897-1984)*

Reflection

We are spoiled disciples! Believers in the Western World can only imagine what the Suffering Church is experiencing in other parts of the world. All people suffer—to one degree or another. But not all people suffer because of their identification with Jesus. We should continually pray for those who are suffering for Jesus' sake.

But while we may not be suffering because of our loyalty to the Lord Jesus, we may be undergoing deprivations, afflictions, trials, emotional pain, an estranged relationship, or some other difficulty. How are you handling it? Are you still rejoicing in the Lord? Or have you become a complainer, or bitter, or have fallen into the slough of self-pity?

What our merciful Father cannot do for us in the *smooth* times, he is able to perfect us as we walk (crawl?) through the *rough* times.

Verse

It is the branch that bears the fruit,
That feels the knife
To prune it for a larger growth,
A fuller life. (Annie Johnson Flint, 1866-1932)**

A Mere Christian

The Word
And in Antioch the disciples were first called Christians.
Acts 11:26

Voice from the Church
"A worried airplane passenger asked a calm fellow traveler, 'Are you a Christian Scientist?' 'No,' was the reply, 'just a Christian.' One never needs to be a Christian plus. It is never Christ *and*, and it is never a Christian *and*. One is a Christian or anti-Christian. You do not have to add anything to a Christian, for everything that goes with it is included in that good word." (Vance Havner, 1901-1986)*

Reflection
The first Christians were called by that name, not so much out of admiration but out of derision. In time, however, the name *Christian* became a badge of honor, worn proudly by the followers of the Lord Jesus. To self-identify as a Christian could cost one his employment, his marriage, his life.

It is understandable why, over these past two thousand years, that some have added a qualifying term to the name "Christian." Since the name had come to mean almost nothing in some locations, denominations, and so forth, and because of the many divisions in the Body of Christ, a variety of qualifiers were created (such qualifiers are too numerous to attempt to mention).

It is probably too idealist to think that, in this world, we will ever rid ourselves of all the "qualifiers"; however, if each of us, by the power of the indwelling Spirit, would simply strive to live up to that worthy designation—"Christian"—it would be an expansive blessing to the church as well as to the world.

Verse
For me 'twas not the truth you taught,
To you so clear, to me so dim,
But when you came to me you brought
A sense of Him. (Beatrice Cleland, 1904-2005)**

"Behold, he is praying"

The Word

> [10]*Now there was a disciple at Damascus named Ananias.*
> *The Lord said to him in a vision, "Ananias." And he said,*
> *"Here I am, Lord."* [11]*And the Lord said to him, "Rise and go*
> *to the street called Straight, and at the house of Judas look*
> *for a man of Tarsus named Saul, for behold, he is praying."*
> Acts 9:10-11

Voice from the Church

"Prayer is not one among many manifestations of spiritual life; it is not even enough to say that it is the first and most important. It stands by itself, and is preeminent. It is *the* manifestation of our personal relation to God; it is the essential and immediate expression of our filial relation in Christ to the Father." (Adolph Saphir, 1831-1891)*

Reflection

Saul of Tarsus was a praying man long before he met the risen Christ on the Damascus Road; however, as with many in his own day and in ours, his prayers were little more than a ritual. His prayers were orthodox in nature, fervent in spirit, and often lengthy. But prayer is never *real* prayer until God becomes real to the pray-er. And God never becomes real to the pray-er until we have a real encounter with his Son, the Lord Jesus Christ. It is then that God becomes one's very own Father in heaven.

When God ceases to be *real* among those who name the name of Christ, prayer becomes a drudgery. When prayer is merely a spiritual exercise to be performed instead of a time of fellowship with our Father, then prayer has devolved into something to be gotten done with; then we can get on with what is real—our daily chores and duties.

When God becomes real to us, prayer becomes real.

Verse

I bowed on my knees,
But my heart was cold.
I stayed there until
The fire was restored.

Before a Watching World

The Word
[34] *"A new commandment I give to you, that you love one another: just as I have loved you, you also are to love one another.* [35] *By this all people will know that you are my disciples, if you have love for one another."*
John 13:34-35

Voice from the Church
"We may be true Christians, really born-again Christians, and yet fail in our love toward other Christians. As a matter of fact, to be completely realistic, it is stronger than this. There will be times (and let us say it with tears), there will be times when we will fail in our love toward each other as Christians." (Francis A. Schaeffer, 1912-1984)*

Reflection
Christ's commandment to his disciples, that they should love one another, was not a new commandment. What was new about the commandment was its standard of measurement: "just as I have loved you." And a high standard this is.

It is this standard that Christ has set for each of his followers to pursue—a standard of self-sacrificial love demonstrated among brothers and sisters in Christ, before a watching world.

The *label* Christ calls each of us to wear is not something manufactured from gold or silver—it is the label of *agape* love. The source of this love is God, and it is imparted to each repentant believer who receives the Lord Jesus Christ. But this love must be carefully maintained and fueled by an obedient walk before God, and before the family of God. When we fail in love we have failed God, for God is love. When we fail in love we have given the onlooking unbeliever another excuse why he or she does not wish to become a Christian.

Verse
He observed up close the pure love
they showed toward one another.
He then thought, as he walked away,
"I would like to be their brother."

When We Fail to Love

The Word

"Pray then like this: ... and forgive us our debts,
as we also have forgiven our debtors."
Matthew 6:9a, 12

Voice from the Church

"While on the complex of roads entering Bristol, I had been unwilling to take [my wife's] advice and as a consequence took a wrong turn; but I had justified myself. She said nothing, and I was inclined to drop the matter—with myself in the right, of course. But the Spirit whispered I was not to leave the matter there. 'I'm sorry,' I said. 'I was quite wrong over that question of the way.' 'Thank you, darling,' she said, and so we drove on ..." (Roy Hession, 1908-1992)*

Reflection

There are a variety of terms the Word of God uses when speaking of the matter of sin. One word is translated "debts," as in the above text.

In financial terms, a debt is something that is owed to another. When we say we are "in debt," we mean we owe, for example, a lending institution so much money. Morally and biblically speaking, we incur a debt before God when we fail to meet his standard of love. Since love is the fulfilling of the moral law of God (see, for example, Rom. 13:8), when we fail to meet his standard of love, we have incurred a debt before God and possibly with someone else. These "debts" are not the result of some deliberate violation against God or man (or should not be); they are inadvertent failures we experience toward one another in our daily walk. Our "debts" should be less frequent as we mature in Christ, but they will never be totally absent from us in this world—at least it appears so to me. Debts require forgiveness, God's forgiveness.

Verse

I saw she looked wounded,
from what I had spoken.
I said, "I'm sorry, dear."
She said, "All's forgiven."

"On a Hill Far Away"

The Word

> *For the word of the cross is folly to those who are perishing,*
> *but to us who are being saved it is the power of God.*
> 1 Corinthians 1:18

Voice from the Church

On a hill far away stood an old rugged cross,
The emblem of suff'ring and shame;
And I love that old cross where the Dearest and Best
For a world of lost sinners was slain. (George Bennard, 1873-1958)*

Reflection

As I write this, it is Holy Week, early in the morning and still dark. I've just returned from taking a short trip to view a cross on a hill far away. The cross was erected approximately 70 years ago and is maintained by a local electric utility. It stands 50 feet in height and is illuminated with over 100 bulbs. I parked my vehicle a mile or so away and gazed on the impressive site. I reflected, expressing my gratitude to our gracious and merciful God for the Cross, for God's Lamb, for Christ's voluntary offering of himself for the sins of the world, including mine.

Of course, the original Cross was quite different from the one I viewed this morning. It was much smaller, made of wood, bloody, and on it hung the God-Man—the crucified Christ who gave his life as a ransom for sinners.

There was nothing pretty about that first Cross on a hill far away: criminals were present, gamblers at its base, women were wailing, and fearful disciples stood at a distance. There were soldiers and mockers, deserters and deniers. What was beautiful is what took place on that middle Cross—the Just One dying for the unjust, to bring us to God!

Verse

In the cross of Christ I glory,
Tow'ring o'er the wrecks of time;
All the light of sacred story
Gathers round its head sublime. (John Bowring, 1792-1872)**

The Suffering Servant (1)

The Word

Who has believed what he has heard from us?
And to whom has the arm of the Lord been revealed?
Isaiah 53:1

Voice from the Church

"That this chapter speaks of none but Jesus must be evident to every unprejudiced reader who has ever heard the history of his sufferings and death. The Jews have endeavored to apply it to their sufferings in captivity; but, alas for their cause! they can make nothing out in this way. Allowing that it belongs to our blessed Lord, ... then who can read Isaiah 53 ... without being convinced that his death was a vicarious sacrifice for the sins of mankind?" (Adam Clarke, 1760-1832)*

Reflection

I feel ashamed each time I read about Isaiah's Suffering Servant; I feel such because I don't weep (It should cause us to weep, shouldn't it?). However, whether my tears flow or not, my heart breaks anew when I slowly and repeatedly read and meditate on these piercing words written some eight centuries before this Servant came to earth.

"Who has believed what he has heard from us?" The truth is, comparatively few, though in the millions: "He came to his own, and his own people did not receive him" (John 1:11). Until eyes are opened, men are blinded by this prophecy: "For to this day, when they read the old covenant, that same veil remains unlifted, because only through Christ is it taken away" (2 Cor. 3:14).

The "arm of the Lord"—the almighty strength of God—was manifested in and through the Suffering Servant, though his strength came through suffering and death, not by the might of man. Let us worship.

Verse

Dead in our deep sins and transgressions,
God's Servant was announced to all.
But who believes He's God answer,
To Adam's lamentable fall?

The Suffering Servant (2)

The Word

For he grew up before him like a young plant, and like a root
out of dry ground; he had no form or majesty that we should
look at him, and no beauty that we should desire him.
Isaiah 53:2

Voice from the Church

"The language of Messianic prophecy is often obscure. The divine intent in this obscurity is to remind the prophecy understandable only by true believers in God who are taught by the Holy Spirit.... Many of these passages cannot be interpreted except in the light of the entire content of the Word of God." (John F. Walvoord, 1910-2002)*

Reflection

In speaking of the Servant who was yet to be revealed, agricultural terms are used to describe his early years: "plant," "root," and "ground." The Word made flesh did not come to this world as a fully-grown man; his birth and human growth was like any other, though absent of sin. And his coming was "like a root out of dry ground." The life of God was manifested ("root") among a very arid and parched people ("dry ground"). How beautiful to see this Rose of Sharon bloom amidst a dry and thirsty wasteland! This should give hope to God's people in every generation!

When the Suffering Servant was finally revealed, there was nothing humanly and naturally attractive about him: "He had no stately form or majesty that might catch our attention, no special appearance that we should want to follow him" (Isa. 53:2 NET). Christ's true beauty came from his inherent holiness; his attraction was God's Spirit upon him.

Human charisma was not God's answer to man's dilemma.

Verse

His beauty and majesty
Lay not in His appearance;
His attraction was that He
Was God's Deliverance.

The Suffering Servant (3)

The Word

*He was despised and rejected by men, a man of sorrows
and acquainted with grief; and as one from whom men hide
their faces he was despised, and we esteemed him not.*
Isaiah 53:3

Voice from the Church

"He is not only not desired, but he is despised and rejected, abandoned and abhorred, a reproach of men, an object, one that men were shy of keeping company with and had not any esteem for, a worm and no man. He was despised as a mean man, rejected as a bad man.... Men, who should have had so much reason as to understand things better, so much tenderness as not to trample upon a man in misery—men whom he came to seek and save rejected him." (Matthew Henry, 1662-1714)*

Reflection

Words like "despised," "rejected," "sorrows," and "grief," are not words we normally associate with "the One who is high and lifted up, who inhabits eternity, whose name is Holy" (Isa. 57:15). And yet, these are the very terms the inspired prophet employs in describing the kind of reception the Suffering Servant would receive when he came into this world and would face by the multitudes thereafter.

Sin both hardens and blinds us to the holiness and goodness of a gracious and merciful God. It has always been this way. Nevertheless, God took the *chance*! Knowing how his very own Son would be treated, knowing that he was "holy, innocent, unstained, separated from sinners" (Heb. 7:26) would be the object of unfathomable cruelty—the Father sent him, and the Son freely came. The Son must suffer; the redemption of man was at stake.

Verse

"Man of Sorrows," what a name
For the Son of God who came
Ruined sinners to reclaim!
Hallelujah! What a Savior! (Philip P. Bliss, 1838-1876)**

The Suffering Servant (4)

The Word
⁴Surely he has borne our griefs and carried our sorrows; yet we esteemed him stricken, smitten by God, and afflicted. ⁵But he was pierced for our transgressions; he was crushed for our iniquities; upon him was the chastisement that brought us peace, and with his wounds we are healed.
Isaiah 53:4-5

Voice from the Church
"Martin Luther's beloved wife once said to her husband that she could not believe the story of Abraham and Isaac because God would never treat a son like that. 'But Katie,' Luther replied, 'he did treat his Son like that.'" (R. C. Sproul, 1939-2017)*

Reflection
The atoning, substitutionary death of the Suffering Servant, God's unique Son, was the wonder of angels and will forever be the worshipful enthrallment of believing, redeemed saints: "in Christ God was reconciling the world to himself" (2 Cor. 5:19).

That this Servant and Son has "borne," and "carried" all the "griefs" and "sorrows" that we have ever experienced and ever shall—on the Cross for us—is utterly incomprehensible to the human mind. But more than that—it was for our "transgressions" and "iniquities" that he was "pierced" and "crushed."

Our very human sympathy is stirred to its depths when we read the account of Abraham's willingness to offer his beloved son Isaac in sacrifice to God, at Yahweh's direction. But that Almighty God would offer his Son as an atoning sacrifice for the sins of the entire world is still unimaginable, until we discern his Father-heart toward us.

Verse
See from His head, His hands, His feet,
Sorrow and love flow mingled down!
Did e'er such love and sorrow meet,
Or thorns compose so rich a crown? (Isaac Watts, 1674-1683)**

The Suffering Servant (5)

The Word

All we like sheep have gone astray; we have turned—every one—to his own way; and the Lord has laid on him the iniquity of us all.
Isaiah 53:6

Voice from the Church

"This is the thrust of the whole chapter, not just that he would be despised and rejected, oppressed and afflicted, ... but in particular that he would be pierced for our transgressions, that the Lord would lay on him the iniquity of us all, ... that he would himself bear their iniquities." (John R. W. Stott, 1921-2011)*

Reflection

The most logical conclusion one could draw from the sheep going astray, and everyone turning to his own way, would be that these rebellious, stubborn "sheep" would be chastised by their Shepherd. But, no, it is the Shepherd himself—the Suffering Servant—that is to bear the iniquity of the sheep—fallen, sinful humanity.

This is the wonder of wonders of the Father's and Son's participation and joint self-giving and agony in the redemption story and atoning event. That man should be punished for willfully turning his back upon a benevolent God would only be justice; we would deserve such treatment from a holy and righteous God. But that this holy God should offer his Son, and that his most beloved Son should freely take upon himself that which is justly due to straying sheep (you and me), is beyond human comprehension: "the Lord has laid on him the iniquity of us all"! God's Lamb became the undeserving substitutionary sacrifice for we who deserve nothing but eternal death and hell. This is mercy; this is grace; this is love.

Verse

Was it for crimes that I had done
He groaned upon the tree?
Amazing pity! grace unknown!
And love beyond degree! (Isaac Watts, 1674-1748)**

The Suffering Servant (6)

The Word
He was oppressed, and he was afflicted, yet he opened not his mouth; like a lamb that is led to the slaughter, and like a sheep that before its shearers is silent, so he opened not his mouth.
Isaiah 53:7

Voice from the Church
"The men of the Bible had their school of suffering—one in silent waiting, another in prison, one in exile among mountains and caves, another in the desert. Someone has said, 'We are wounded in order that we may learn from the great Physician how to bind up wounds and give aid. God visits us with trials in order to teach us to carry the burdens of others. We ourselves must first go to school before we can be teachers of others.'" (George Steinberger, 1865-1904)*

Reflection
From the human perspective, one of the most remarkable occurrences of the Cross Event was the silent suffering of the Suffering Servant. Yes, we have the seven words Christ spoke, but in dying as well as in life the Son of Man never once cast aspersions, was ungrateful, never became harsh and censorious, and was never vengeful. The fact is, one of his closest apostles said of him, "When he was reviled, he did not revile in return; when he suffered, he did not threaten, but continued entrusting himself to him who judges justly" (1 Pet. 2:23).

Has not God's Lamb demonstrated for us, when faced with the most adverse difficulties and sufferings that a person has ever experienced, how we should respond when undergoing our minor (in comparison) sufferings? Peter said that the Lamb left us "an example, so that you might follow in his steps" (1 Pet. 2:21).

Verse
No mortal can with Him compare
Among the sons of men;
Fairer is He than all the fair
Who fill the heav'nly train. (Samuel Stennett, 1727-1795)**

The Suffering Servant (7)

The Word

[8]By oppression and judgment he was taken away; and as for his generation, who considered that he was cut off out of the land of the living, stricken for the transgression of my people? [9]And they made his grave with the wicked and with a rich man in his death, although he had done no violence, and there was no deceit in his mouth.
Isaiah 53:8-9

Voice from the Church

"The phrase 'by oppression and judgment' is two nouns presenting concomitant aspects of the same fact. The judgment was in fact employed as an instrument of oppression. It seemed as though the Servant must die without descendants, which was regarded as a great misfortune in that society." (Kenneth L. Barker & John Kohlenberger)*

Reflection

The Lord Jesus Christ was treated with the utmost cruelty and was unfairly judged and punished. This innocent, sinless, and holy Son of God was taken before both religious and civil rulers, who themselves were sinners and being judged by God for their wickedness.

Fifty days following his death, Peter announced to Christ's tormentors, "this Jesus, [who was] delivered up according to the definite plan and foreknowledge of God, you crucified and killed by the hands of lawless men" (Acts 2:23). "Lawless men" killed the Righteous One: "For Christ also suffered once for sins, the righteous for the unrighteous, that he might bring us to God." (1 Pet. 1:18). The Servant's death was a vicarious one: "stricken for the transgression of my people." This is the wonder of the Cross: "God shows his love for us in that while we were still sinners, Christ died for us" (Rom. 5:8).

Verse

He saw me plunged in deep distress
And flew to my relief;
For me He bore the shameful cross
And carried all my grief. (Samuel Stennett, 1727-1795)**

The Suffering Servant (8)

The Word
Yet it was the will of the Lord to crush him; he has put him to grief;
when his soul makes an offering for guilt, he shall see his offspring; he
shall prolong his days; the will of the Lord shall prosper in his hand.
Isaiah 53:10

Voice from the Church
"What good father could *wish* for his son to be crushed? It is only possible if there was some unquestionably greater good to be obtained. And what greater good could possibly justify the crushing of the Servant? The answer is given in the second half of the verse. It is when the 'life' of the Servant is offered as a sin offering that God's purpose in bringing him to this place is realized ('prosper')." (John N. Oswalt, b. 1940)*

Reflection
The heart of the Father must have been crushed as well as the heart of the Son, when the Servant trod the winepress alone.

The sufferings and death of Christ were the will of the Father. There was no other way to obtain redemption for fallen man: "it was the will of the Lord to crush him."

This is holy ground. It is one thing for sinful man to offer up a guilt offering for his own sins; he is guilty and deserving of punishment and death. It is quite another matter, infinitely greater, for the Father to offer up his sinless Son for the sins of the entire world. God's Lamb must be crushed; the Father's Lamb must die a most ignominious death.

It is only through this crushing that resurrection ("he shall prolong his days") shall come; it is only through crushing that glorious fruit shall spring forth ("the will of the Lord shall prosper in his hand"). Before life there must be death; before resurrection there must be crushing.

Verse
We may not know, we cannot tell,
What pains He had to bear;
But we believe it was for us
He hung and suffered there. (C. Frances Alexander, 1818-1895)**

The Suffering Servant (9)

The Word

> Out of the anguish of his soul he shall see and be satisfied; by
> his knowledge shall the righteous one, my servant, make many
> to be accounted righteous, and he shall bear their iniquities.
>
> Isaiah 53:11

Voice from the Church

"But suppose when he offers himself to us, we respond that we don't
need a sin offering. Suppose we have rejected the 'old-fashioned' idea
of sin and consider ourselves to be as worthy as the next person of the
blessings of God. What then? It would be as though, after all the labor
and struggle, the baby is stillborn. Then indeed it was for nothing. Then
indeed the Savior finds no satisfaction in the offering he made." (John N.
Oswalt, b. 1940)*

Reflection

I will never forget the night, when standing by the bedside of my wife
Emily, she gave birth to our second daughter (fathers were not allowed
in the delivery room when our first daughter was born). Following several hours of labor and anguish, there suddenly came great relief and joy
and satisfaction: a child was born; the agony had ended—for her (and
me). Christ's suffering of course was infinitely greater.

It is through the substitutionary, atoning death of the Suffering Servant that the ungodly may be justified ("accounted righteous"): "It was to
show his righteousness at the present time, so that he might be just and
the justifier of the one who has faith in Jesus" (Rom. 3:26). This is
grace, God's marvelous grace: "For by grace you have been
saved through faith. And this is not your own doing; it is the gift of
God, not a result of works, so that no one may boast" (Eph. 3:8-9).

Verse

There was no other good enough
To pay the price of sin;
He only could unlock the gate
Of heaven and let us in. (C. Frances Alexander, 1818-1895)**

The Suffering Servant (10)

The Word

*Therefore I will divide him a portion with the many, and he shall divide
the spoil with the strong, because he poured out his soul to death
and was numbered with the transgressors; yet he bore the sin
of many, and makes intercession for the transgressors.*
Isaiah 53:11

Voice from the Church

"That 'wondrous Cross' reaches out its reconciling arms to encircle all
worlds and beings and ages. It cost God more to hang nail-suspended on
Calvary than to create ten million stellar thoroughfares. The redemptive
meaning of that Cross ... was erected on the green mound outside old
Jerusalem, and will be shining through the universe when the biggest
alpha-star has burned itself to a cinder. It writes God's sublime 'V' sign
over the whole universe." (J. Sidlow Baxter, 1903-1999)*

Reflection

The conclusion of the Suffering Servant's Song ends in glorious triumph
and victory. The language employed is taken from the field of battle and
conquest. One recalls the records of war and conflict in Old Testament
battles. Following the clash of swords and shedding of blood, the spoils
were those of the victor.

The Servant conquered at Calvary; the empty tomb attested his victory. But wonder of wonders, for those who have died and risen with this
conquering Lamb—to these the spoils will be shared. For we are "heirs
of God and fellow heirs with Christ, provided we suffer with him in
order that we may also be glorified with him" (Rom. 8:17).

Let the Lamb of God forever be praised, by those who have been purchased by his own blood and have trusted in his name.

Verse

He was lifted up to die;
"It is finished" was his cry;
now in heaven exalted high:
Hallelujah, what a Savior! (Philip P. Bliss, 1838-1876)**

Breaking Up Fallow Ground

The Word

> Sow for yourselves righteousness; reap steadfast love;
> break up your fallow ground, for it is the time to seek the
> Lord, that he may come and rain righteousness upon you.

Hosea 10:12

Voice from the Church

"Conversion to God is not so easy and so smooth a thing as some would have us believe it is. Why is man's heart compared to fallow ground, God's Word to a plough, and his ministers to ploughmen, if the heart indeed has no need of breaking in order to receive of the seed of eternal life?" (John Bunyan, 1628-1688)*

Reflection

Soil that has lain dormant for an extended period tends to hardness and inflexibility. I found this to be so, when as a young man I worked for several summers on the farm of a brother-in-law. But what a change occurred with the soil in the spring, when the fallow ground was turned over with the shares of a plough. What had once been hard became pliable and receptive, for the anticipated sowing of seed.

Apart from grace, our hearts are hardened toward God, truth, and others. Through regenerating and renewing grace, hearts that had lain fallow become softened by the Spirit of God. Thus, the Lord spoke through the prophet, "And I will give them one heart, and a new spirit I will put within them. I will remove the heart of stone from their flesh and give them a heart of flesh." (Ezek. 11:19).

If our hearts are hard, we must take measures to break up the "fallow ground." Afterward, the "rains" of grace will fall. God is merciful; will we sincerely seek him today?

Verse

A hardness had gradually formed,
  freshness and softness disappeared.
He knelt to break the "ground" in prayer;
  clouds soon gathered and rain appeared.

Keeping Our Focus

The Word

²⁰If with Christ you died to the elemental spirits of the world, why, as if you were still alive in the world, do you submit to regulations— ²¹"Do not handle, Do not taste, Do not touch" ²²(referring to things that all perish as they are used)—according to human precepts and teachings?

Colossians 2:20-22

Voice from the Church

"We may point out the great difference that has come to exist between the Christianity of the early days and that of today: To us it has become a performance, a keeping of rules, while to the men of those days it was, plainly, an invasion of their lives by a new quality of life altogether." (J. B. Phillips, 1906-1982)*

Reflection

Whenever we take biblical principles and extrapolate from them a system of man-made rules and impose the same on our brothers and sisters in Christ, we have joined the cult of the Pharisees. Furthermore, if in our sincere interest in living a godly life, we formulate a code of conduct in that effort, those rules tend to become the end instead of the means toward Christian maturity. The apostle warned, "These have indeed an appearance of wisdom in promoting self-made religion and asceticism and severity to the body, but they are of no value in stopping the indulgence of the flesh" (Col. 2:23). We are prone to accept the "shadows" for the "substance": "These are a shadow of the things to come, but the substance belongs to Christ" (Col. 2:17). The Spirit writes truth on our hearts, and this truth has, of course, behavioral implications. But we must guard against making the ethics of the Christian faith foundational. Christ is our life—not man-made rules.

Verse

Satan is a crafty foe,
working to divert our gaze.
Let our minds be fixed on Christ,
the Word directing our ways.

Examining the Scriptures

The Word

> [10]The brothers immediately sent Paul and Silas away by night
> to Berea, and when they arrived they went into the Jewish
> synagogue. [11]Now these Jews were more noble than those in
> Thessalonica; they received the word with all eagerness,
> examining the Scriptures daily to see if these things were so.
>
> Acts 17:10-11

Voice from the Church

"For it is agreed by all that the Spirit of God, who is the Spirit of unity, cannot contradict himself. So if the interpretation or opinion of any theologian, Kirk [Church], or council, is contrary to the plain Word of God written in any other passage of the Scripture, it is most certain that this is not the true understanding and meaning of the Holy Ghost, although councils, realms, and nations have approved and received it. We dare not receive or admit any interpretation which is contrary to any principal point of our faith, or to any other plain text of Scripture, or to the rule of love." (The Scots Confession, 1560)*

Reflection

It is the prerogative of the Spirit of God to enlighten our naturally darkened minds to truth. And when this light is given, we can expect no more until we walk in the light. The sacred Word of God is our primary source of revelation. This Word must be read prayerfully and studied carefully. And we must guard against drawing definitive conclusions regarding "deep truth" when examining this Word in isolation from others. Great harm has come to the church because someone has received a "special revelation" from God about what a particular truth means. Teachers have a responsibility to preach and teach only the plain Word.

Verse

Let me hear Your voice alone, O Lord,
whenever I read Your sacred words.
And may my heart not be lifted high,
as another points me to Your truth.

Who is My Neighbor?

The Word
[36]"Which of these three, do you think, proved to be a neighbor to the man who fell among the robbers?" [37]He said, "The one who showed him mercy." And Jesus said to him, "You go, and do likewise."
Luke 10:36-37

Voice from the Church
"In the morning we cannot know yet who our neighbor will be that day. The condition of our hearts will determine who along our path turns out to be our neighbor, and our faith in God will largely determine whom we have strength enough to make our neighbor." (Dallas Willard, 1935-2013)*

Reflection
The question of, "Who is my neighbor?" is not a matter of geographical proximity; it is a matter of a providential encounter.

Whether or not we are neighborly depends on whether we have taken note of the person our sovereign Lord has placed in our path and responded to that person's need.

We can't be a neighbor to someone if we really don't *see* him. We can't be a neighbor to someone if we are preoccupied with ourselves. We can't be a neighbor to someone if we don't have the wherewithal to meet that person's need, or don't take the time to explore how a need can be met.

There are legitimate needy people, and then there are lazy people. I'm not under obligation to give assistance to an individual who has the mental and physical abilities to secure employment but won't. God has not called us to enable a person's laziness.

To be a neighbor is to demonstrate the love of God to a fellow creature in legitimate need. Words must give place to deeds.

Verse
He sat in rags; his feet were lame.
We were rushing to a big conference,
To learn how we might grow our church.
We hardly noticed; he was a nuisance.

The Word Made Effective

The Word

> [4]*For we know, brothers loved by God, that he has chosen you,* [5]*because our gospel came to you not only in word, but also in power and in the Holy Spirit and with full conviction.*
> 1 Thessalonians 1:4-5

Voice from the Church

"I'm a Welsh preacher, living in ... the South West of England. I pastor two neighbouring Evangelical Churches. Last year I listened to an Australian evangelical ... speak on the power of God's Word. He had many excellent things to say about the subject, concluding with Luther's comment on the Reformation: 'The Word of God did it.' In the Q & A session that followed his address, I asked him to comment on the relationship between Word and Spirit in preaching. The speaker didn't really know how to respond." (Guy Davies, n.d.)*

Reflection

The ministry of the Son of Man was effective not simply because he quoted Scripture when he preached, or because what he said was biblical truth, but because he himself was anointed with power from on High. The words of God spoken by a man of God is an awful weapon in the hand of God. The gospel proclamation of the apostle Paul, among pagan people, was effective because Paul was a God-called, Spirit-filled minister of righteousness. He spoke with the very power of the Holy Spirit; he was convinced that what he proclaimed and taught was the very truth of God. Someone once said after listening to a certain preacher, that the message was noted for its lameness, tameness, and sameness.

The Lord Jesus and the apostles were full of conviction, boldness, freshness, and power. Pray that your pastor will be filled with the same.

Verse

When he rose and preached God's sacred Word,
I knew before me a man of God stood.
His words were simple, but filled with power.
I left church thinking it was worth the hour.

The Choked Word

The Word

> [18] *"And others are the ones sown among thorns. They are those who hear the word, [19]but the cares of the world and the deceitfulness of riches and the desires for other things enter in and choke the word, and it proves unfruitful."*
> Mark 4:18-19

Voice from the Church

"At its deepest level, concupiscence creates the illusion that *having* constitutes *being*, that *consuming* can combat *anxiety*. It fosters the illusion that *getting* and *owning* will actually make us immortal." (Ted Peters, b. 1941)*

Reflection

The Lord Jesus likened the Word of God to seed sown in a field. For seed to grow properly, there must be soil preparation and cultivation. Seed sown in unprepared soil doesn't bode well for a fruitful harvest. But even one grain of seed sown in prepared soil, and subsequently cared for by the planter, will result in a splendid harvest, giving great satisfaction to the sower.

The reason some people never produce consistent fruit for God is because the Word of God has been strangled, choked. In his parable, Jesus said the "cares of the world and the deceitfulness of riches and the desires for other things enter in and choke the word."

Have you allowed anxiety and worry to choke faith and confidence in God? Is your heart set on what wealth can bring, instead of laying up treasures in heaven? What else is there that has invaded your heart, robbing you of fruitfulness? Is your trust in the Lord, or are you overcome by "other things"?

Verse

You say your trust is in your Father,
  then why the worry and fear?
Plant your feet solidly on the Word,
  then watch each care soon disappear.

Radical Surgery

The Word

¹²So then, brothers, we are debtors, not to the flesh, to live according to the flesh. ¹³For if you live according to the flesh you will die, but if by the Spirit you put to death the deeds of the body, you will live. ¹⁴For all who are led by the Spirit of God are sons of God.

Romans 8:12-14

Voice from the Church

"This active life of fellowship is at every moment characterized by mortification and vivification. As mortification, holiness is the laying aside of that which has been put to death at the cross of the Son of God; as vivification, holiness is the living out of that which has been made alive in the Son's resurrection." (John Webster, 1955-2016)*

Reflection

Often Romans 8:14 has been quoted by God's people in support of personal decision-making. In other words, the Spirit of God gives us personal guidance. Now, without question, the Holy Spirit does lead God's people into all truth necessary for their salvation and sanctification (see John 16:13, for example). However, in the above text, Paul addresses another matter; he is exhorting believers "to put to death ["mortify," KJV] the deeds of the body."

What does Paul mean by his exhortation? Simply this: Whatever we engage in with our body that is proscribed by the Word and Spirit of God, we must excise, cut it off ("put to death"). The disciple of Jesus Christ is to perform radical surgery on anything that cannot pass the light of God's scrutiny. Paul says of such believers who live this way: "For all who are led by the Spirit of God are sons of God." Are you putting to death everything that interferes with your walk with God?

Verse

I thought I surely could.
The Word and Spirit said, "You can't."
I walked to the edge;
I clearly knew the Dove was grieved.

Jesus is Lord

The Word

[8]*But what does it say? "The word is near you, in your mouth and in your heart" (that is, the word of faith that we proclaim);* [9]*because, if you confess with your mouth that Jesus is Lord and believe in your heart that God raised him from the dead, you will be saved.*
Romans 10:9-10

Voice from the Church

"The confession 'Jesus is Lord' ascribes to him a degree of honour which cannot be surpassed: in saying that, we say all. 'Jesus is Lord' remains the sufficient Christian confession. But it carries with it the corollary on which he himself insisted: that those who call him 'Lord' should do what he says" (Luke 6:46). (F. F. Bruce, 1910-1990)*

Reflection

For the Christian who acknowledged Jesus as Lord instead of Caesar in the first-century church, it could mean a certain death. When we confess, "Jesus is Lord," it spells death to self-rule.

When a believer confesses that Jesus is Lord, every rival to his lordship is dethroned. Such a true confession is radical, setting the course for one's life. It is a confession that is made once, and a confession that is affirmed repeatedly by the believer as he walks in obedience with God.

To confess, "Jesus is Lord" has implications for every area of the Christian's life. For when this confession is sincerely made from the heart, it means we have turned over the reins of our life to the Lord Jesus Christ; we no longer are in control.

To confess "Jesus is Lord" means we do the things that he says. To assert our will contrary to his will is to deny his lordship.

Verse

I confess, "Jesus is Lord,"
No longer am I my own.
He now reigns supreme alone,
every idol overthrown.

Devout Christians

The Word
> And they devoted themselves to the apostles' teaching and
> the fellowship, to the breaking of bread and the prayers.
> Acts 2:42

Voice from the Church
"One of the Devil's finest pieces of work is getting people to spend three nights a week in Bible studies.... We invest all this time in understanding the text, which has a separate life of its own, and we think we're more pious and spiritual when we do it. But the Bible is all there to be lived. It was given to us so we could live it. Most Christians know far more of the Bible than they're living. They should be studying it less, not more. You just need enough to pay attention to God." (Eugene H. Peterson, b. 1932)*

Reflection
I wonder if one were to take a poll, asking a broad variety of believers what they thought a Christian should be *devoted* to, what the results would look like. Would the answers resemble the devotion of the first-century Christians, as reflected in Acts 2:42?

The Apostles' teaching. This included both written and verbal communications (the Gospels, Letters, Prophecy).

Fellowship. The believers regularly gathered for mutual edification, building up one another, bearing each other's burdens.

Breaking of Bread. They regularly remembered the Lord's death and promised return, by eating the broken bread and drinking from the common cup.

Prayers. Their custom was to meet in homes for times of extended prayer. Are you a devout Christian?

Verse
Their faith was pure and simple,
   their risen Lord very real.
They often met together
   lest they lose their first love's zeal.

True Relatives of Jesus

The Word
> *32And a crowd was sitting around him, and they said to him, "Your mother and your brothers are outside, seeking you." 33And he answered them, "Who are my mother and my brothers?" 34And looking about at those who sat around him, he said, "Here are my mother and my brothers! 35For whoever does the will of God, he is my brother and sister and mother."*
> Mark 3:32-35

Voice from the Church
"Do as many kind gestures as you wish, do as many dazzling works as you please—but you will only be rewarded for doing the will of the sovereign Master." (François Fénelon, 1651-1715)*

Reflection
If you dare think you have a special relationship with God because you have been baptized, confirmed by the church, or a member of a certain denomination—read again the words of the Lord Jesus: "For whoever does the will of God, he is my brother and sister and mother."

You say that it is impossible to do the will of God? Are you sure you are not taking refuge in such a lie because you are clinging to some idol, some sin?

The natural, sinful heart can provide a thousand reasons for not doing the will of God: "No person is perfect"; "God doesn't expect me to obey everything Jesus taught—after all, I'm only human." If these are your excuses, then don't be so presumptuous as to call Jesus Lord.

Who are those who have a vital relationship with the Lord Jesus Christ? Those who are doing the will of God. If we have a problem with that, then let's talk to God about it.

Verse
I said, "The standard is too high."
Then I saw my will was too strong.
I relinquished control to Him;
His will then became my glad song.

The Use of Time

The Word

> [4] "We must work the works of him who sent me while it
> is day; night is coming, when no one can work. [5]As long
> as I am in the world, I am the light of the world."
> John 9:4-5

Voice from the Church

"I finished my sermon on the Wedding Garment; perhaps the last that I shall write. My eyes are now waxed dim; my natural force is abated. However, while I can, I would fain do a little for God before I drop into the dust." (John Wesley, 1703-1791, one year before he died at age 87)*

Reflection

Time is one of the most precious commodities given to man, and how often it is wasted on things that don't really matter. This is not to say that there is no place for recreation and relaxation. However, in an age when the god of entertainment is consuming the Body of Christ, who among us will rise and say to himself, "Enough is enough!"? What should be done in moderation has become our obsession.

Writing to the Ephesian believers, the apostle exhorted, "Look carefully then how you walk, not as unwise but as wise, making the best use of the time, because the days are evil. Therefore do not be foolish, but understand what the will of the Lord is" (Eph. 5:15-17).

Regrettably, many Christians are using their retirement years pursuing a lifestyle of pleasure. With so much work that needs to be done in the Kingdom of God, how can we foolishly fritter away our days consumed with lesser things? As long as we are in this world, we are to be light and salt. What work are you engaged in to the glory of God? Do you need to reevaluate how you are using your time?

Verse

Anna and Simeon were old in age,
  but neither thought of quitting the race.
Daily they were engaged in prayer and praise,
  and speaking of Messiah all their days.

Prayer is Dependence

The Word

⁶*Do not be anxious about anything, but in everything by prayer and supplication with thanksgiving let your requests be made known to God.* ⁷*And the peace of God, which surpasses all understanding, will guard your hearts and your minds in Christ Jesus.*

Philippians 4:6-7

Voice from the Church

"Prayer consists ... simply in telling God day by day in what ways we feel we are helpless." (Ole Hallesby, 1879-1961)*

Reflection

Prayer to the God and Father of our Lord Jesus Christ is essentially an act of helplessness. When we pray, if we do so honestly, we are confessing our need of and dependence on God.

We are finite creatures. This means that everything about us is limited, fragile, and dependent. We are dependent on God for the air we breathe, the food we eat, for the water we drink, and for the measure of health we enjoy—and much more. The Lord of all creation not only "upholds the universe by the word of his power" (Heb. 1:3), he likewise is the provider and sustainer of his people.

Anxiety is an intruder, a foreign object in the life of the trusting child of God. When you seriously think about it, how can you be worried about anything when you consider that you are cared for by the One who provides for the birds of the air, the beasts of the field, and, furthermore, is your own Father in heaven. Away with worry, fret, and anxiety! Don't allow them to tyrannize you.

Does a nursing baby have any worries? No, the child lives in total dependence upon his mother. We are needy; let us go to God in prayer.

Verse

Oh, what peace we often forfeit,
Oh, what needless pain we bear,
All because we do not carry
Everything to God in prayer. (Joseph M. Scriven, 1819-1886)**

Moving Mountains

The Word

^{23}*"Truly, I say to you, whoever says to this mountain, 'Be taken up and thrown into the sea,' and does not doubt in his heart, but believes that what he says will come to pass, it will be done for him. ^{24}Therefore I tell you, whatever you ask in prayer, believe that you have received it, and it will be yours."*

Mark 11:23-24

Voice from the Church

"Faith in the Lord Jesus endues prayer with a species of omnipotence; whatsoever a man asks of the Father in his name, he will do it. Prayer has been termed the gate of heaven, but without faith that gate cannot be opened. He who prays as he should, and believes as he ought, shall have the fullness of the blessings of the Gospel of peace." (Adam Clarke, 1760-1832)*

Reflection

One day the Lord Jesus cursed a fig tree, because of its lack of fruitfulness. In passing by the same tree the next morning, Peter marveled, "'Rabbi, look! The fig tree that you cursed has withered.' And Jesus answered them, 'Have faith in God'" (Mark 11:21-22).

"Mountains" represent difficult, humanly impossible obstacles. These mountains may be a sinful addiction, a compulsive disorder, or something like anger, that you have no mastery over. Mountains don't just go away—they must be removed. A mountain is something that cannot be removed through only concentrated human effort. A mountain cannot be removed by mere human reasoning or counseling. For their removal, mountains require the power of God released through radical faith ... and obedience. All things are possible with God, with your cooperation.

Verse

Faith, mighty faith, the promise sees,
And looks to that alone;
Laughs at impossibilities,
And cries, "It shall be done!" (Charles Wesley, 1707-1788)**

One Another

The Word

We are to grow up in every way into him who is the head, into Christ, ¹⁶from whom the whole body, joined and held together by every joint with which it is equipped, when each part is working properly, makes the body grow so that it builds itself up in love.
Ephesians 4:15-16

Voice from the Church

"Becoming a better Christian is not a matter of individual personal development. It is growing in the body with the other members of it. The "me and my God" mentality is contrary to the essence of the Christian life." (Simon Chan, b. 1951)*

Reflection

There are approximately 48 "one another" passages in the New Testament. These 48 occurrences can be reduced to 12 essential attitudes and actions Christians are to demonstrate toward each other. For example, they are to love one another, pray for each other, encourage one another, bear one another's burdens, and so on.

When we are born gain, we become a member of the Body of Christ. As members, we have a joint-connection to each other member. We are relatives. The term "brothers" is used approximately 230 times in the NT; it is a word which identifies close family relations.

Christians should not live in isolation from each other: "Whoever isolates himself seeks his own desire; he breaks out against all sound judgment" (Prov. 18:1). We are organically connected and mature better when we have close associations with at least a few other brothers and sisters in Christ. "But woe to him who is alone when he falls and has not another to lift him up!" (Eccles. 4:10). We need one another.

Verse

He struggled up the hill, all alone;
little was the progress he made.
A brother joined him in the steep climb;
this gift from God became his aid.

God's Settled Word

The Word

> *Forever, O Lord, Your word is settled in heaven.*
> Psalm 119.89 NASB

Voice from the Church
"If we ultimately appeal to human reason, or to logic, or to historical accuracy, or to scientific truth, as the authority by which Scripture is shown to be God's words, then we have assumed the things to which we appealed to be a higher authority than God's words and one that is more true or more reliable." (Wayne Grudem, b. 1948)*

Reflection
The Word of God is self-authenticating. That means we need no extrabiblical source to validate for us that which the Word of God says is true.

Frequently we hear preachers and teachers of the Word of God citing some archeological study, for example, that has *verified* as fact an ancient biblical site or person that is mentioned in the Bible. Well, that is very nice of them to take the time and expense to do so! However, we believe every Word of God to be true, and don't require outside investigators to confirm the matter for us. That is not to suggest that biblical archeology doesn't have its place, but its *place* is not to confirm what has previously been written by inspired men of God.

We may, with conviction and confidence, read God's Word, knowing that it is infallible and trustworthy. Furthermore, every word that has been written is "profitable for teaching, for reproof, for correction, and for training in righteousness" (2 Tim. 3:16). To quote Paul's words, addressing another matter: "Let God be true though everyone were a liar" (Rom. 3:4).

Verse
Soon all we see and touch and know
Will fade and fall away.
But praise the Lord! The truth remains,
The gracious Word of God. (Ken Bible, b. 1950)**

Methods and Means

The Word

And, behold, the Lord passed by, and a great and strong wind rent the mountains, and brake in pieces the rocks before the Lord; but the Lord was not in the wind: and after the wind an earthquake; but the Lord was not in the earthquake: [12]*And after the earthquake a fire; but the Lord was not in the fire: and after the fire a still small voice.*

1 Kings 19:11-12 KJV

Voice from the Church

"The road to the Promised Land of spiritual power always leads through desert places where 'the still small voice' has a chance to be heard." (Glenn R. Phillips, 1894-1970)*

Reflection

God is not in the business of duplicating his methods in revealing himself to his servants. He told one man to build an ark, another to construct a tabernacle for worship, another to command the people to encompass a city seven times, another to wash in a river seven times, another to fill her jars with oil; examples like these could be multiplied.

While God's *methods* among men are unique to the occasion and person, God's *means* of advancing his work on earth are substantially the same. He locates an individual (or a group of people), who seeks the heart of God. He reveals himself to this person through Word and Spirit and special providence. God speaks; the person listens.

God has a challenge on his hands: we want him to repeat the way he has spoken to us before. God is not obligated to do so. He may have used "fire" on one occasion, as he did with Elijah. But on another occasion God speaks quietly, in a low voice. Don't ask God to repeat his methods. Simply develop a listening ear.

Verse

I had been on a Mount;
the altar was ablaze.
Then came another day—
the Lord God changed His ways.

The Pruning

The Word
[1] *"I am the true vine, and my Father is the vinedresser.* [2]*Every branch in me that does not bear fruit he takes away, and every branch that does bear fruit he prunes, that it may bear more fruit."*
John 15:1-2

Voice from the Church
"The husbandman's hand (God the Father's) manages the pruning-knife of affliction, in order to [facilitate] his people's improvement in grace and holiness; he had rather see his vine bleed, than see it barren." (William Burkitt, 1650-1703)*

Reflection
Vine pruning is a radical and necessary procedure to ensure the healthy growth of the vine. Without pruning, the vinedresser cannot expect to see a healthy harvest of grapes.

It is natural for us to resist the Vinedresser's knife. We understandably recoil from the pain. But there can be no growth without the knife. We cannot be brought to spiritual maturity and health without holding very still, while all that is either unclean or is an impediment to fruitfulness is cut away from our heart and life.

Our heavenly Vinedresser uses a variety of instruments to expose our lack and need of him. These "instruments" may be affliction, trials, adversities, difficult people, personal infirmities, emotional trauma, sicknesses, failure—and so much more. The Vinedresser will use his knife to excise from our heart that which prevents us from producing the fruit of righteousness and good works, amid our trials. If we refuse the knife, we will eventually be severed from the Vine. What does the Vinedresser wish to prune in your heart?

Verse
It appeared to be a "little" thing,
  but I stumbled over it often.
I saw if I were to be healthy,
  I must submit to the Dresser's knife.

Looking to Jesus

The Word

"Look unto me, and be ye saved, all the ends of
the earth: for I am God, and there is none else. "
Isaiah 45:22 KJV

Voice from the Church

"Just fixing his eyes on me, as if he knew all my heart, he said, 'Young man, you look very miserable.' Well, I did, but I had not been accustomed to have remarks made from the pulpit on my personal appearance before. However, it was a good blow, struck right home. He continued, 'And you will always be miserable—miserable in life and miserable in death—if you don't obey my text; but if you obey now, this moment, you will be saved.' Then lifting up his hands, he shouted, as only a Primitive Methodist could do, 'Young man, look to Jesus Christ. Look! Look! Look! You have nothing to do but look and live!'" (Charles Spurgeon, 1834-1892)*

Reflection

Whenever the Spirit of God brings us to the place of repentance, he always reveals to us the defilement of our heart and the nature of our sins. This cannot be done without the Spirit shining his light within, causing us to take a long, close look at ourselves. This process may take moments or hours, even days.

However, after our sin and sins have been revealed to us, we cannot stop there, groveling in our past failures. The deep work of repentance moves from confession to faith. We must lift our inner eyes and look away to sin's remedy: "Behold, the Lamb of God, who takes away the sin of the world!" (John 1:29)—even my sin. If we don't look to Jesus, our life will be filled will remorse instead of faith.

Verse

Life is offered unto you, hallelujah!
Eternal life thy soul shall have,
If you'll only look to Him, hallelujah!
Look to Jesus who alone can save. (William A. Ogden, 1841-1897)**

The Cleansing Blood

The Word

⁸If we say we have no sin, we deceive ourselves, and the truth is not
in us. ⁹If we confess our sins, he is faithful and just to forgive
us our sins and to cleanse us from all unrighteousness.
1 John 1:8-9

Voice from the Church

"Anna [Waterman] was discouraged at the path her husband followed because it was causing him to miss work on some of his hangovers. So she asked a lady in her town in California to meet with her and help her pray for Charles to be saved. His wild life went on for three or more years and one night when ... he finally arrived at home, he told Anna he wanted to be saved. She immediately called her friend ... and they led him to the Lord. He begged the Lord for forgiveness and to clean up his life, which the Lord did." (Cyberhymnal.org)*

Reflection

This morning I received a text message from my oldest sibling, Sharon. She wrote, "I will be forever amazed at your life so drastically changed by our God." I am sorely in need of much more change! And, thanks be to God, he continues to change me (see 2 Cor. 3:18).

During my devotional time today, I recalled the gospel testimony song authored by Anna W. Waterman, "Yes, I Know." It had been years since I had heard this song sung. I discovered that it was written following her husband's wonderful conversion (all conversions are wonderful!). Charles and Anna eventually moved to the little town of Lodi, Indiana. Evidently their lives were such a beautiful witness to Christ's atoning blood, that the local church where they attended was named in their honor: Waterman Baptist Church. To God be the glory!

Verse

Come, ye sinners, lost and hopeless,
Jesus' blood can make you free;
For He saved the worst among you,
When He saved a wretch like me. (Anna W. Waterman, b. 1875-?)**

Being Diligent

The Word

> ¹³But according to his promise we are waiting for new
> heavens and a new earth in which righteousness dwells.
> ¹⁴Therefore, beloved, since you are waiting for these, be diligent
> to be found by him without spot or blemish, and at peace.
>
> 2 Peter 3:13-14

Voice from the Church

"Each day ... let us be eager and careful to keep this bright robe of ours without spot or wrinkle. Even in things that are considered to be trifles, let us keep close watch, so that we may also be able to escape serious sins. If we shall begin to scorn some sins as insignificant, little by little as we walk the way of life we will come to falls which are disastrous." (John Chrysostom, 349-407)*

Reflection

At the moment of God's justifying grace, the repentant sinner is also called to live a changed life, a holy life. Our gracious God accepts us as we are, but never leaves us to be what we were. Every known sin is left behind, with God continuing his wonderful transforming grace, until the moment we leave this world.

May we never resort to the thinking that our holy God will allow us to continue in willful disobedience to him. If we persist in willful sin, it is proof that we do not know God nor wish to be conformed to the likeness of his Son. "No one born of God makes a practice of sinning, for God's seed abides in him; and he cannot keep on sinning, because he has been born of God" (1 John 3:9). In the words of Chrysostom, "Let us be eager and careful to keep this bright robe of ours without spot or wrinkle." By the strength of God, you will be enabled.

Verse

Through the gates to the city in a robe of spotless white,
He will lead me where no tears will ever fall;
In the glad song of ages I shall mingle with delight;
But I long to meet my Savior first of all. (Fanny Crosby, 1820-1915)**

In Christ Jesus (1)

The Word

[30]But by His doing you are in Christ Jesus, who became to us wisdom from God, and righteousness and sanctification, and redemption, [31]so that, just as it is written, "Let him who boasts, boast in the Lord."
1 Corinthians 1:30-31 NASB

Voice from the Church

"Once they were involved in the old solidarity of sin and death, when they lived 'in Adam' and shared the fruits of his disobedience. Now that old solidarity has been replaced by the new solidarity of righteousness and life, by which men and women of faith are incorporated 'in Christ.'" (F. F. Bruce, 1810-1990)*

Reflection

The little phrase "in Christ Jesus" may be small as to the number of words; however, it is fraught with significance. This expression (and similar wording) occurs over 240 times in the New Testament.

To be "in Christ" means for the Christian that he is no longer "in Adam." To be "in Christ" means that at the moment of justifying, regenerating grace, the Christian has been granted a new identity, a new status, a new position. We are united with Christ, we belong to Christ, we are incorporated into Christ.

Paul says it is by God's "doing you are in Christ." Through God's gracious act, we have been placed in union with his Son. While faith is the operative response from the human side, it is God who takes the initiative, it is God who has made this transference (from in Adam to in Christ). We cannot give birth to ourselves; we cannot place ourselves into Christ. Our new identity is a gift from God.

Believer, you are "in Christ Jesus." What an identity!

Verse

In Christ I now am;
no more in Adam I live.
God said it is so;
my all to Him I now give.

Christ our Wisdom (2)

The Word

[30]But by His doing you are in Christ Jesus, who became to us wisdom from God, and righteousness and sanctification, and redemption, [31]so that, just as it is written, "Let him who boasts, boast in the Lord."
1 Corinthians 1:30-31 NASB

Voice from the Church

"The use of 'you' and 'us' indicates Paul's word concerns all Christians and that he is speaking of what Christ had done for all believers. We also see here that Paul has been using the term "wisdom" ... inasmuch as Christ, in whose work the divine wisdom reveals itself, is our wisdom from God so that we know God through Him." (F. W. Grosheide, 1881-1972)*

Reflection

Paul uses the word "wisdom" 18 times in 1 Corinthians, 16 of which are used in the first chapter. He writes of God's wisdom in contrast to man's. The people to whom Paul wrote lived in a culture where worldly wisdom was prized: "For indeed Jews ask for signs and Greeks search for wisdom" (1 Cor. 1:22).

Human philosophies are void of God's saving, sanctifying power, which is man's greatest and essential need. Christ is God's power and wisdom (see 1 Cor. 1:24).

The Lord Jesus Christ is the supreme wisdom of God, because he reveals God to us and shows us the way to God. Christ is God's wisdom, because it is through him that we are reconciled and rightly related to God. Worldly wisdom has no saving message. One never hears about the Cross in human philosophies; they never lead one to God: "the world through its wisdom did not come to know God" (1 Cor. 1:21).

Are you looking to God or to human wisdom for your answers?

Verse

Man's philosophies, devised by a darkened mind,
leave the soul impoverished for all humankind.
Only God's wisdom, revealed in the cross of Christ,
can save every sinner—a message most sublime.

Christ our Righteousness (3)

The Word
³⁰*But by His doing you are in Christ Jesus, who became to us wisdom from God, and righteousness and sanctification, and redemption,* ³¹*so that, just as it is written, "Let him who boasts, boast in the Lord."*
1 Corinthians 1:30-31 NASB

Voice from the Church
"The righteousness that comes from God is related to 'the righteousness of God' which in the gospel is revealed from 'faith for faith' (Rom. 1:17). God's righteousness makes possible a true righteousness in the believer." (Purkiser, Taylor, Taylor)*

Verse
In Christ, at the Cross, the righteous judgment of God was revealed against sin: "For the wrath of God is revealed from heaven against all ungodliness and unrighteousness of men, who by their unrighteousness suppress the truth" (Rom 1:18).

Not only was God's wrath against unrighteousness revealed at the Cross, but God's abundant mercy was also revealed: "It was to show his righteousness at the present time, so that he might be just and the justifier of the one who has faith in Jesus" (Rom. 3:26). It is through God's grace that redeemed sinners become the very righteousness of God: "For our sake he made him to be sin who knew no sin, so that in him we might become the righteousness of God" (2 Cor. 5:21).

By offering up his Son on our behalf, and by embracing through faith God's Gift for us, we are made right with God and such a resolute faith is declared by God as righteousness: "And to the one who does not work but believes in him who justifies the ungodly, his faith is counted as righteousness" (Rom 4:5). The righteous are to live righteously.

Reflection
By our effort we try to achieve righteousness;
But it was the Cross that exposed our foolishness.
It is now by grace through faith that we are made right—
This is God's way, stooping in Christ, curing our plight.

Christ our Sanctification (4)

The Word
^{30}*But by His doing you are in Christ Jesus, who became to us wisdom from God, and righteousness and sanctification, and redemption, ^{31}so that, just as it is written, "Let him who boasts, boast in the Lord."*
1 Corinthians 1:30-31 NASB

Voice from the Church
"It is only in the presence of Christ that life can be what it ought to be. Epicurus used to tell his disciples, 'Live as if Epicurus saw you.' There is no 'as if' about our relationship to Christ. The Christian walks with him and only in that company can a man keep his garments unspotted from the world." (William Barclay, 1907-1978)*

Reflection
The Son of God was absolutely holy before, during, and after his incarnation: "For it was indeed fitting that we should have such a high priest, holy, innocent, unstained, separated from sinners, and exalted above the heavens" (Heb. 7:26). Whatever holiness redeemed sinners receive is only *relative* holiness; only God is essentially and absolutely holy.

With the fall of man in the Garden, the image of God in man became defaced, distorted, and defiled. We are marred, fallen creatures. God's plan, through Christ, is that his justified and regenerated people be renewed in the image of Christ, who is "the image of the invisible God" (Col. 1:15). God the Holy Spirit has been given to God's people to conform them into the likeness of Christ: "For those whom he foreknew he also predestined to be conformed to the image of his Son" (Rom. 8:29). The Spirit is persistent in this work. As salvation is by grace through faith, so is sanctification. To whatever degree we may reflect the image of Christ, it is God's doing, with our cooperation.

Verse
When I behold God in His perfections
I'm aware how far short I truly fall.
But He has given me His Holy Spirit,
Making me more like Christ, my all in all.

Christ our Redemption (5)

The Word
*[30]But by His doing you are in Christ Jesus, who became to us wisdom
from God, and righteousness and sanctification, and redemption, [31]so
that, just as it is written, "Let him who boasts, boast in the Lord."*
1 Corinthians 1:30-31 NASB

Voice from the Church
"Redemption ... must be regarded as encompassing the whole of our
salvation; and the Apostle is clearly thinking in terms of our ultimate
glorification. We are not finally 'redeemed' until our bodies have been
redeemed. But our bodies are not yet redeemed. So we can say that we
are redeemed, and that we are yet to be redeemed. I am not fully redeemed until my body has been changed." (Martyn Lloyd-Jones, 1899-1981)*

Reflection
The saving act of God, in his Son, the Lord Jesus Christ is God's wonderful and mysterious redemption for lost sinners. Our salvation has
been purchased at the cost of the life of the Lord Jesus, and by his shed
blood we have been redeemed, forgiven: "In him we have redemption
through his blood, the forgiveness of our trespasses, according to the
riches of his grace" (Eph. 1:7). There is no other path to the forgiveness
of sins, except by the atoning sacrifice of Jesus Christ.

The redemption of the saints' bodies will be experientially realized
when "this mortal will have put on immortality" (1 Cor. 15:54). In the
meantime, "we ourselves, who have the firstfruits of the Spirit, groan
inwardly as we wait eagerly for adoption as sons, the redemption of our
bodies" (Rom. 8:23).

Christ Jesus has been made to us redemption, through his death, for
time and for eternity—from sin and from fallen corporality.

Verse
Redeemed, how I love to proclaim it!
Redeemed by the blood of the Lamb;
Redeemed through His infinite mercy,
His child and forever I am. (Fanny Crosby, 1820-1915)**

The Christian's Boast (6)

The Word
[30]*But by His doing you are in Christ Jesus, who became to us wisdom from God, and righteousness and sanctification, and redemption,* [31]*so that, just as it is written, "Let him who boasts, boast in the Lord."*
1 Corinthians 1:30-31 NASB

Voice from the Church
"True humility is closer to self-forgetfulness. The really humble person is unaware of his own importance—or lack of it—in the wider circles of life." (Martin Israel, 1927-2007)*

Reflection
Expressions of arrogance are almost pandemic in the Body of Christ. How we love to draw attention to ourselves. Too many of our so-called concert artists, special singers, musicians of all stripes, and, yes, preachers, promote themselves instead of exulting in the cross of Christ. It's a wonder that some religious performers are not struck down, as was Herod of old, for not giving glory to God.

In the above text, the beloved apostle reminds us that wisdom, righteousness, sanctification, and redemption are God's "doing." And because it is God's "doing," we are to "boast in the Lord."

Do you remember how grateful to God you were when you were first converted? Your heart was filled with thanksgiving to the Lord, and you went among your family and friends telling them about the great things the Lord had done for you. But in time, your relationship with Christ became stale, devolving into a perfunctory performance instead of maturing into an intimate friendship. Because of this, you no longer sincerely deflected praise given to you to Christ. Inwardly, you slowly began to die to Christ. We must repent of our prideful ways.

Verse
Forgive us, O Lord, for our prideful ways,
Accepting for ourselves man's empty praise.
May our lips and life point others to You,
For it is Your grace in all that we do.

The Test

The Word

[11]For no man can lay a foundation other than the one which is laid, which is Jesus Christ. [12]Now if any man builds on the foundation with gold, silver, precious stones, wood, hay, straw, [13]each man's work will become evident; for the day will show it because it is to be revealed with fire, and the fire itself will test the quality of each man's work.
1 Corinthians 3:11-13

Voice from the Church

"On that day we will not be asked to tell our stories or explain our theology; instead, all our actions will be shown to us, each thing that we did both privately and publicly: 'For God shall bring every secret work into judgment, with every secret thing, whether it be good, or whether it be evil'" (Eccl. 12:14). (Jonathan Edwards, 1703-1758)*

Reflection

Jesus Christ must be at the center and circumference of our life and ministry. Man-made schemes and human religious philosophies will never stand the test of the coming Day, no matter how impressive they may appear to the easily flattered eye.

The all-seeing God knows not only *what* we do, but *why* we do it. Are we masquerading as a Christian, or has the Spirit of God effectually wrought an ego-shattering, crucifying blow to our inborn pride and self-determined will?

Are we trying to impress people or please God? If we are trying to impress people with our performance, we are merely building a life of nothing but "wood, hay, straw"—each combustible, incapable of withstanding Judgment fire. We are called to build on Christ alone. Everything else will be consumed.

Verse

He assumed he had done well,
so most people had told him.
On applause he loved to dwell—
'til God finally broke him.

Praying for One Another

The Word
> [18]*[P]raying at all times in the Spirit, with all prayer and*
> *supplication. To that end, keep alert with all perseverance,*
> *making supplication for all the saints,* [19]*and also for me, ...*
> Ephesians 6:18-19a

Voice from the Church
"A Christian fellowship lives and exists by the intercession of its members for one another, or it collapses. I can no longer condemn or hate a brother for whom I pray, no matter how much trouble he causes me. His face, that hitherto may have been strange and intolerable to me, is transformed in intercession into the countenance of a brother for whom Christ died, the face of a forgiven sinner." (Dietrich Bonhoeffer, 1906-1945)*

Reflection
We can never overestimate the importance of supplicating the throne of grace for our brothers and sisters in Christ. God depends upon the intercession of the saints to further his work on earth. Does that sound strange to our ears? It is certainly not strange to God's, for he himself initiated this prayer-plan. Sovereign though he is, spiritual battles are not won, sinners are not saved, believers do not mature, circumstances do not change—apart from the prevailing prayers of God's people.

The apostle Paul constantly urged believers to pray for one another and for God's servants. The weapon of earnest, believing prayer is the one weapon Satan fears the most, and the one weapon that the church first relinquishes in her downward spiral.

John Wesley once wrote, "God does nothing but in answer to prayer." Lord, teach us to pray—for one another—earnestly, persistently, to the glory of Christ Jesus.

Verse
Restraining prayer, we cease to fight;
Prayer makes the Christian's armor bright;
And Satan trembles, when he sees
The weakest saint upon his knees. (William Cowper, 1731-1800)**

Christ in Me

...been crucified with Christ. It is no longer I who live, but ...st who lives in me. And the life I now live in the flesh I live by faith in the Son of God, who loved me and gave himself for me.
Galatians 2:20

Voice from the Church

"If there was a conception of Christ that I did not have, and that I need-ed, because it was the secret of some of these other lives I had seen or heard of, a conception better than any I had yet had, and beyond me, I asked God to give it to me. I had with me the sermon I had heard, 'To me to live is Christ,' and I rose from my knees and studied it. Then I prayed again. And God, in His longsuffering patience, forgiveness, and love, gave me what I asked for. He gave me a new Christ—wholly new in conception and consciousness of Christ that now became mine." (Charles G. Trumbull, 1872-1941)*

Reflection

To speak of the indwelling Christ is more than a theological statement and should be something more than Christian jargon or a religious cli-ché.

To say that "Christ lives in me" is impossible without experientially undergoing "I have been crucified with Christ." Yes, every true believer was in a real sense taken to the cross of Christ in his death. But some-thing more—the benefits of Christ's death must be appropriated by me, and I must undergo a deep death to my own ego for me to say with the apostle, "Christ lives in me."

Are you experiencing the vitality of the living Christ dwelling in you? Or are you merely testifying to some past experience?

Verse

With Christ I have been crucified,
  no longer does the "I" now live.
Christ in me completely resides;
  by Him I'm enabled to thrive.

Christt our Life

The Word
> *³For you have died, and your life is hidden*
> *with Christ in God. ⁴When Christ who is your life*
> *appears, then you also will appear with him in glory.*
> Colossians 3:3-5

Voice from the Church
"It is a very broken way of putting the deepest mystery in the Bible, but I can only ask that the Holy Spirit may make you know what it is to have Jesus as the center and origin of your life. The fountain and origin hitherto has been self, has it not? O cursed self, Barabbas, Barabbas, to the cross! The world says: 'Not Christ, but Barabbas, self.' The Christian says: 'Not Barabbas, but Christ.'" (F. B. Meyer, 1847-1929)*

Reflection
The life we have in Christ is his life, not our own. We must not think in terms of Christ's indwelling life as only the gift of eternal life. We have received eternal life at the moment we were born anew. However, God wants us to come to the place in our walk with him, that day by day we have a consciousness that Christ himself is our very life—the very oxygen we breathe, as it were, the very energy of our walk with him.

The Lord Jesus once said of his followers (his "sheep"), "I came that they may have life and have it abundantly" (John 10:10). The one who gives us life is our very life. Christ is the Person in whom we live, through whom we serve, and by whom we witness and pray and worship. Christ is our All in all. We are dependent on him for everything. We live our life in total reference to him. We constantly consult him by Word and Spirit. Without him we can do nothing. He is our life. Apart from Christ there is death; with him and by him there is abundant life.

Verse
You are my very life, O Christ;
* all deadness flees from Your presence.*
Why should I try to self-produce—
* not live in total dependence?*

Strength through Weakness

The Word
[32]*And what more shall I say? For the time would fail me to tell of Gideon and Barak and Samson and Jephthah, also of David and Samuel and the prophets:* [33]*who ... out of weakness were made strong, ...*
Hebrews 11:32-33 NKJV

Voice from the Church
Years ago, when I was an immature and inexperienced first-year seminary student, I found myself invited to conduct revival services in an Eastern port city.... When I arrived, I learned that I was scheduled to speak twenty-six times. I had only rough notes on a half-dozen talks that could in no way be called sermons. You can imagine my terror. For the next seven days, when I was not in the pulpit, I lived on my knees before my open Bible. There was only one evening service out of fourteen where there were no seekers after Christ. My weakness proved his strength.... That was when I began to learn that the greatest gift we have to offer to God is our weakness. (Dennis F. Kinlaw, 1992-2017)*

Reflection
How often, when facing humanly impossible situations, we petition God to make us strong. We cry out to God for strength, when God wants us to freely acknowledge our weakness. Gideon was weak; Barak, Samson, Jephthah, and David were weak men. They each were incapable of defeating the enemies of God. But they acknowledged their weaknesses. It was then God could use them as mighty instruments of his own making.

We should never presume that because we have equipped ourselves for God's chosen assignments, that such will ensure victory. No! Victories are given through weak servants who confess their weakness. Our weakness should drive us to our knees.

Verse
He was only a young lad,
But he knew the strength of God.
His trust was not in himself;
The giant fell to the sod.

Things Above (1)

The Word

> [1]*If then you have been raised with Christ, seek the things that are above, where Christ is, seated at the right hand of God.* [2]*Set your minds on things that are above, not on things that are on earth.* [3]*For you have died, and your life is hidden with Christ in God.*
> Colossians 3:1-3

Voice from the Church

"To seek heavenly things is to set our affections upon them, to love them and let our desires be towards them. Upon the wings of affection the heart soars upwards, and is carried forth towards spiritual and divine objects. We must acquaint ourselves with them, esteem them above all other things, and lay out ourselves in preparation for the enjoyment of them." (Matthew Henry, 1662-1714)*

Reflection

It is an impossibility to be a seeker after "things "above" without having died first to sin and rising to new life. Having died and risen in Christ, we are now united with him and indwelt by the Holy Spirit. It is an axiomatic truth, that we are not fit to live on this earth until we have experienced a little of heaven here below. Having died and risen, we have been given heavenly appetites and holy desires.

It is no wonder that so many professing Christians have no interest in *"things above"*—they have never experienced the reality of having died and risen. You will never have a passion for "the things that are above, where Christ is, seated at the right hand of God," unless you have first undergone a radical spiritual death to the old self, and been raised to a new life in Christ. Only then will you become a seeker after "things above."

Verse

He tried his best to live a Christian life,
  repeatedly making a vow and resolution.
Then one day he knelt at the Cross of Christ—
  there experiencing a radical solution.

Things Above (2)

The Word

¹If then you have been raised with Christ, seek the things that are above, where Christ is, seated at the right hand of God. ²Set your minds on things that are above, not on things that are on earth. ³For you have died, and your life is hidden with Christ in God.
Colossians 3:1-3

Voice from the Church

"No indwelling sin can be tolerated by an indwelling Christ; for he came into the world to save his people from their sins." (Adam Clarke, 1760-1832)*

Reflection

Without appropriating by grace though faith Christ's death and resurrection, any attempt to live a Christian life amounts to will-worship— trying harder, resolving to do better (moralistic). Yes, the will is always involved in walking with God, but having experienced a new birth, with the Holy Spirit indwelling his people, the believer goes forth in newness of life energized by power from on High.

Having undergone a spiritual death and resurrection, the disciple of the Lord Jesus will no longer tolerate willful sin. He has repudiated the old life, has been raised to new life in Christ, and consequently becomes a seeker of "things above." He is now a new creation in Christ Jesus., with all things becoming new.

The believer will be assaulted vigorously by his Adversary to lay aside the shield of faith. And if momentarily the shield is lowered, one must confess his sin, raise the shield again, receiving his Father's merciful forgiveness. As with the ancient saints of old, the follower of the Lord Jesus "desire[s] a better country, that is, a heavenly one" (Heb. 11:16)—pressing upward.

Verse

I'm pressing on the upward way,
New heights I'm gaining every day;
Still praying as I'm onward bound,
"Lord, plant my feet on higher ground." (Johnson Oatman, Jr., 1856-1922)**

Things Above (3)

The Word
> [1]*If then you have been raised with Christ, seek the things that are above, where Christ is, seated at the right hand of God.* [2]*Set your minds on things that are above, not on things that are on earth.* [3]*For you have died, and your life is hidden with Christ in God.*
> Colossians 3:1-3

Voice from the Church
"A pastor invited a young man to become a Christian and received the reply, 'Religion for my grandfather was an experience, for my father it was a tradition, and for me it is a nuisance.' Too often we have left out the experiential aspect of walking with Christ." (Myron S. Augsburger, b. 1929)*

Reflection
The Spirit, in the above text, exhorts believers to "seek the things that are above." We'll get to what that means later. For now, let's concentrate where these "things above" are located. We discover that they are not to be found in some secretive, mysterious place in the ethereal world. Neither do they reside within us. No, they "are above, where Christ is, seated at the right hand of God."

Whatever these "things" may be, they are found where Christ is. And where is the crucified, risen, ascended Christ?—"seated at the right hand of God." The Lord Jesus Christ is located now in the position of power and authority: "All authority in heaven and on earth has been given to me" (Matt. 28:18). This is more than a symbolic position; the Father delegated to his obedient, risen Son total rulership over Christ's church: "he put all things under his feet and gave him as head over all things to the church" (Eph. 1:22). What and where are you seeking?

Verse
Why are we so impoverished,
  surviving on fragments below?
With Christ there is more than enough;
  seek—to you His graces will flow.

Things Above (4)

The Word

> ¹*If then you have been raised with Christ, seek the things that are above, where Christ is, seated at the right hand of God.* ²*Set your minds on things that are above, not on things that are on earth.* ³*For you have died, and your life is hidden with Christ in God.*
> Colossians 3:1-3

Voice from the Church

"Now, ... the Way to the Celestial City lies just through this Town, where this lusty Fair is kept; and he that will go to the City, and yet not go through this Town, must needs go out of the World. The Prince of Princes himself, when here, went through this Town to his own Country ..." (John Bunyan, 1628-1688)*

Reflection

Now, what "things that are above" are we to seek and set our minds on? Let's keep with this one letter and simply note two things (there are so many more throughout Scripture).

Spiritual knowledge. This is only discovered at the right hand of God, on one's knees, with the open Word of God. And God will also use godly mature men and women to assist us in experiencing this kind of knowledge, as Apollos was taught by Priscilla and Aquila. God desires that we be "filled with the knowledge of his will" (1:9).

God's power. The servants of Christ require great strength in order to perform their respective tasks given to them by God. This strength comes from above, never from our own resources or those of others. We will faint long before the race is finished, unless we daily seek God for his gracious enabling power: "being strengthened with all power according to his glorious might" (1:11).

Verse

From Thee, the overflowing spring,
Our souls shall drink a fresh supply,
While such as trust their native strength
Shall melt away, and droop, and die. (Isaac Watts, 1674-1748)**

Things Above (5)

The Word

> [1] *If then you have been raised with Christ, seek the things that are above, where Christ is, seated at the right hand of God.* [2] *Set your minds on things that are above, not on things that are on earth.* [3] *For you have died, and your life is hidden with Christ in God.*

Colossians 3:1-3

Voice from the Church

"It is said that Ignatius of Loyola once had dug for the novices of his order a grave, having them buried except for their heads, asking, 'Are you dead?' To those who answered yes, he would reply, 'Rise then, and begin to serve, for I want only dead men to serve me." (Thomas C. Oden, 1931-2016)*

Reflection

The Spirit's exhortation that we are to always seek and to set our minds on *"things above"* is contrasted with "not on things that are on earth."

What are you seeking? What is your mind set on? Is it fame or fortune, status and success (as the world counts success), for the praise and adulation of your peers. What are you seeking? Is the world shaping your thinking and mindset, or are you being shaped and transformed by the Spirit of God? Does the way you are using your time, finances, and abilities reflect a Christian mind or a worldly mind?

Jesus lived and ministered in this world. But his thinking did not originate from the world but from his Father. The antidote to being conformed to the world's thinking is to seek and to set our minds on *"things above"*: God's holiness and righteousness, truth and grace, wisdom and knowledge—and so much more. These things are "where Christ is, seated at the right hand of God."

Verse

He caught a glimpse of the City,
Never turning back again.
For his eyes were fixed on the King,
The Savior who ransomed him.

Things Above (6)

The Word

¹If then you have been raised with Christ, seek the things that are above, where Christ is, seated at the right hand of God. ²Set your minds on things that are above, not on things that are on earth. ³For you have died, and your life is hidden with Christ in God.
Colossians 3:1-3

Voice from the Church

"There is nothing in the realm of the natural or the spiritual that is good, but we receive it from Him. All these gifts are purely of grace. We have done nothing to deserve them. They come from the bountiful hand of a generous God. Some think that what they receive comes from the hands of others, or from the efforts of their own hands. Many in the world cannot see the hand of the Lord in anything." (J. Nieboer, n.d.)*

Reflection

We conclude this section by noting a text in the *Epistle of James*. While located in a different context than the one we've been meditating on, what James says about things "from above" harmonizes with Colossians 3:1-3: "Every good gift and every perfect gift is from above, coming down from the Father of lights, with whom there is no variation or shadow due to change." (James 1:17).

The apostle has been addressing the subject of trials and temptations in the Christian's walk with God. He cautions his readers not to think that God is the source and cause of any form of "evil." Instead, all that that comes from "above" is a "gift" that is "good" and "perfect."

We should never settle for lesser things, the things that will eventually pass away. We live in this world, but our heart should be in heaven, where the Lord Jesus sits at the right hand of God.

Verse

Only through the Word and Spirit
Can we break the present world's mold—
Always seeking those things above,
Which God from us will not withhold.

The New Birth (1)

The Word

Jesus answered him, "Truly, truly, I say to you, unless
one is born again he cannot see the kingdom of God."
John 3:3

Voice from the Church

"Without realizing what I was doing, I had cut myself off from many of 'the boundless riches of Christ' (Eph. 3:8). I had amassed information about Christ without knowing him in the warmth and intimacy of a personal relationship." (Alister McGrath, b. 1953)*

Reflection

The apostle John employs the term "born," with reference to a spiritual birth, a total of 18 times (9 in his Gospel, 9 in 1 John). The language of a birth, in addition to our natural birth, proved to take the learned Nicodemus by surprise, when told by the Lord Jesus that he must be "born again": "Nicodemus said to him, 'How can these things be?' Jesus answered him, 'Are you the teacher of Israel and yet you do not understand these things?'" (John 3:9-10).

The truth of the necessity of a new birth, in order to experience God's rule and reign in one's life, has been a conundrum to many lost and religious people ever since Jesus walked on this earth. Those who are spiritually blind, as was Nicodemus, place their arrogant trust in trying to follow the letter of the Law, engaging in good works, attempting to treat people right, without realizing they need new life from above.

Just as a person cannot give birth to himself, we cannot generate God's life in ourselves. We believe and receive this new life by faith; it is God who gives us birth, newness of life. Have you been born again? Have you received God's Son, in whom is life?

Verse

Ye children of men, attend to the Word,
So solemnly uttered by Jesus the Lord;
And let not this message to you be in vain,
Ye must be born again. (William T. Sleeper, 1819-1904)**

The New Birth (2)

The Word

> *If you know that he is righteous, you may be sure that*
> *everyone who practices righteousness has been born of him.*
> 1 John 2:29

Voice from the Church

"One area of adjustment was made the very day after my conversion. Out of habit I went to the barber shop where a group used to play cards. But fortunately and providentially I picked up a pocket New Testament.... As the group gathered at the card table, I went to the barber's chair and began to read the New Testament. They called me to join them as usual in the card game. I replied: 'No, I've been converted.'" (E. Stanley Jones, 1884-1973)*

Reflection

No Christian should ever ridicule a fellow believer about how God dealt with that person in their new-found faith. While all conversions to Christ are similar as to its substance, how this new life in Christ is applied ethically with each one is very personal. The things that identified us as sinners—our fleshly habits and practices—will be exposed by the light of God's truth and holiness; the Holy Spirit calls the new believer to a righteous lifestyle. And some of these things we leave behind are not inherently sinful, but prove to be an impediment to spiritual growth (see Heb. 12:1).

The apostle John declares that every person who has been born of God "practices righteousness." What is this righteousness? We find it on the pages of God's Word, and he writes it on our heart. A person who says he is a Christian, and does not live a righteous life, lives a lie; he has been deceived. God's children walk a righteous walk.

Verse

Thine eye diffused a quickening ray—
I woke, the dungeon flamed with light;
My chains fell off, my heart was free,
I rose, went forth, and followed Thee. (Charles Wesley, 1707-1788)**

The New Birth (3)

The Word

> *No one born of God makes a practice of sinning,*
> *for God's seed abides in him; and he cannot keep*
> *on sinning, because he has been born of God.*
> 1 John 3:9

Voice from the Church

"At last, at long last, I had been converted in the realm of my will. No longer did I evade God's hands. He was free now to work out His good purposes in my affairs. To put it in rough language: My Master, at last, had flung His lariat of love around me. And now I bore His brand." (W. Phillip Keller, 1920-1997)*

Reflection

The phrase in the above text—"makes a practice of sinning"—literally should be rendered, "does no (or, "not") sin." The reason some versions (e.g., ESV) render the Greek phrase as they do is an attempt to clarify the phrase's meaning. In other words, a person who has been born of God does not "practice" sinning. The rendition is good and bad. It is good in the sense that it renders the present indicative active verb as something that is ongoing, "makes a practice of sinning." It is unfortunate in the sense that it leads one possibly to deduce: "The sin I'm committing is not a *practice*; I do it just once in awhile." Satan loves this rationalization! The "sin" John has in mind here is *willful* sin. He affirms that a person who has undergone a new birth experience will no longer choose to keep on sinning; the sinful habit has been broken. How can this be? Because God's "seed"—the very life and implanted Word of God—abides in the new convert. He cannot *willfully* sin because he does not *want* to. Note: this does not preclude a momentary failure (see 1 John 2:1-2).

Verse

O thou God of my salvation,
My Redeemer from all sin;
Moved by thy divine compassion,
Who hast died my heart to win. (Thomas Olivers, 1725-1799)**

The New Birth (4)

The Word
> *Beloved, let us love one another, for love is from God, and*
> *whoever loves has been born of God and knows God.*
> 1 John 4:7

Voice from the Church
"There are people who are unloving, unkind, always criticizing, whispering, backbiting, pleased when they hear something against another Christian. Oh, my heart grieves and bleeds for them as I think of them; they are pronouncing and proclaiming that they are not born of God." (Martyn Lloyd-Jones, 1899-1981)*

Reflection
One of the first evidences that a person has been truly born of God is a new love for other people. It was so with my own conversion. Before I ever stood up from the altar of prayer that Sunday evening in August, 1961, God had given me a love for my stepmother, whom, I'm sorry to say, I hated before I stepped out to surrender my heart to Christ that warm summer night.

How can we say we love God and speak the way we do about other people, including those in the family of God? One of the tests as to whether we are a true Christian is this love test, especially how we relate to fellow believers: "We know that we have passed out of death into life, because we love the brothers. Whoever does not love abides in death" (1 John 3:14). The love of which the apostle speaks does not originate in us: "for love is from God." This love is *divine* love, love from above; it is the love of God. Following our conversion to Christ, we see people differently, because we have been made—and are being made—into a different person. Are you different?

Verse
When the Lord Jesus entered in,
I was suddenly born again.
With this new life from above,
I discovered I could love.

The New Birth (5)

The Word
*Everyone who believes that Jesus is the Christ has been born of God,
and everyone who loves the Father loves whoever has been born of him.*
1 John 5:1

Voice from the Church
"Belief is the touchstone of spiritual life. Belief in itself is an intellectual judgment regarding the truth of a proposition; yet Christian Belief is essentially more than this. It is an act of the intellect which has moral and spiritual presuppositions, which is the response not of the reasoning faculty alone, but of the whole personality to the data presented." (Robert Law, 1860-1919)*

Reflection
Faith and love are intricately connected, in both the conversion experience and life of the Christian. Where you find the one, there is invariably the other.

To believe that the long-expected Jesus is the Messiah, the Father's uniquely anointed Son, is foundational to the Christian faith. True faith has an object; that object is also the cornerstone of Christianity—the Lord Jesus Christ. John was an eyewitness; we were not. Yet we believe: "Though you have not seen him, you love him. Though you do not now see him, you believe in him and rejoice with joy that is inexpressible and filled with glory" (1 Pet. 1:8). One cannot be born from above, without believing that Jesus is the Father's anointed Son.

Accompanying such faith will be the ability to love the Son's Father and the Father's children. Often in speaking of Jesus, we neglect our Father's role in Redemption. To love the Father is to love his children. Faith and love—they are bound together.

Verse
When Jesus is passing by,
each one who believes is saved.
To the Father and the Son—
may they forever be praised!

The New Birth (6)

The Word
For everyone who has been born of God overcomes the world.
And this is the victory that has overcome the world—our faith.
1 John 5:4

Voice from the Church
"If I could ascend some high mountain and look out over this wide land, you know very well what I would see. Robbers on the high roads, pirates on the seas, in the amphitheaters men murdered to please applauding crowds, selfishness and cruelty, misery and despair under all roofs. It is a bad world—an incredibly bad world. But in the midst of it, I have found a quiet and holy people who have learned a great secret. They are the despised and the persecuted, but they care not. They have overcome the world. These people are called Christians, and I am one of them." (Cyprian, Bishop of Carthage, 210-258)*

Reflection
Are you overcoming the world, or is the world overcoming you? A *worldly Christian* is an oxymoron; the very idea was antithetical to first-century Christianity.

Charles Colson once shared the account of what happened in the life of the CEO of a large drugstore chain when he came to faith in Christ. This wealthy businessman immediately took measures to have all pornography removed from the shelves in his stores. A friend of mine once told me that when his wife left him, he had to get rid of his television, for he could not trust himself to watch it alone.

The world—"the desires of the flesh and the desires of the eyes and pride of life" (1 John 2:16)—must be overcome by God's people. This overcoming is one of the marks of the twice-born.

Verse
Against the foe in vales below
Let all our strength be hurled;
Faith is the victory, we know,
That overcomes the world. (John H. Yates, 1837-1900)**

To Pray Well is to Live Well

The Word

> And he said to them, "Well did Isaiah prophesy of you
> hypocrites, as it is written, "'This people honors me
> with their lips, but their heart is far from me ...'"
> Mark 7:6

Voice from the Church

"Unless the common course of our lives be according to the common spirit of our prayers, our prayers are so far from being a real or sufficient devotion that they become an empty lip labor or, what is worse, a notorious hypocrisy." (William Law, 1686-1761)*

Reflection

To pray well is to live well; to live well is to pray well.

The essence of prayer is simply talking with our Father in heaven. It involves many facets—praise and thanksgiving, adoration and worship, supplication and intercession, confession and petition. But no matter what facet of prayer the Christian engages in, the serious believer will pray with utter sincerity and transparency before his holy and righteous Father.

Some Christians assume an *unnatural spiritual posture* when they pray. While it's true we are praying to the high and lofty One who inhabits eternity whose name is holy, our Father in heaven doesn't require artificial tones in order to hear and honor our requests. Neither should we be casual nor flippant in our audience with the King.

We are to be *real* before God. There can be no pretense in honest prayer. And the Spirit will convict us when there is a hairs-breadth discrepancy between our prayers and the way we are living. To pray well is to live well; to live well is to pray well.

Verse

Sun of my soul, Thou Savior dear,
It is not night if Thou be near.
Oh, may no earth-born cloud arise
To hide Thee from Thy servant's eyes. (John Keble, 1792-1866)**

Tradition and Traditionalism

The Word

So then, brothers, stand firm and hold to the traditions that you were taught by us, either by our spoken word or by our letter.
2 Thessalonians 2:15

Voice from the Church

"To put it boldly, where there is no appreciation for tradition, for the rich heritage of reflective theologizing with its general consensus on the basic Christian verities, Protestantism has spawned a mass of individual heresies, all vying for the center stage as the single truth of God." (Gordon F. Fee, b. 1934)*

Reflection

Traditions can be either good, bad, or indifferent. The apostle Paul writes about good tradition—those practices and precepts that all Christians are to observe in all places and at all times: "So then, brothers, stand firm and hold to the traditions that you were taught by us, either by our spoken word or by our letter."

There are bad traditions: Man-made teachings that are a stumbling block to spiritual growth and godly living. Some of these actually nullify the Word of God; Jesus spoke of such: "You have a fine way of rejecting the commandment of God in order to establish your tradition!" (Mark 7:9).

There are traditions which are morally and biblically indifferent. For example, the set time for worship services; the order of a worship service; the missions to receive financial support; the placement of sanctuary furniture; and so forth. One tradition must be kept at all costs; man-made commandments must be shunned like the plague; indifferent traditions may be changed with wisdom.

Verse

Let us hold firmly to the once-for-all delivered faith;
Let us reject man's teachings, that produce burdens and death;
Let us wisely make changes in matters indifferent,
Relying on God's faithful guides: Word, Wisdom, and Spirit.

Truth and Change

The Word

> *⁹Do not be led away by diverse and strange teachings, for it is*
> *good for the heart to be strengthened by grace, not by foods,*
> *which have not benefited those devoted to them. ¹⁰We have an*
> *altar from which those who serve the tent have no right to eat.*
> Hebrews 13:9-10

Voice from the Church

"To stay at the point to which some revered teacher of the past has brought us, out of a mistaken sense of loyalty to him; to continue to follow a certain pattern of religious activity or attitude just because it was good enough for our fathers and grandfathers—these and the like are temptations which make the message of *Hebrews* a necessary and salutary one for us to listen to." (F. F. Bruce, 1910-1990)*

Reflection

It can very well be an intellectually and spiritually traumatic experience, when a follower of the Lord Jesus comes to a different understanding on a particular interpretation of Scripture, than the one held by someone he has revered in the faith. When we do differ from those we have been close to and esteem highly, we must be certain that the long view, reaching back in Evangelical biblical history, is on our side.

The *Letter to the Hebrews* was written to a people whose Temple was still standing at the time. They were well-versed in the rites and ceremonies of the Jewish faith. Suddenly, all had changed with the coming of Messiah, in whom the *substance* of truth had transcended the *shadows*. This tended to shake the faith of new believers.

God's revelation of truth never changes, though its application will vary with the times. The sure Word of God is our safety.

Verse

The Word of God,
*   both lamp and light,*
Will lead me sure
*   through this dark night.*

One Faith

The Word

> [11]*For it has been reported to me by Chloe's people that there is quarreling among you, my brothers.* [12]*What I mean is that each one of you says, "I follow Paul," or "I follow Apollos," or "I follow Cephas," or "I follow Christ." [13]Is Christ divided? Was Paul crucified for you? Or were you baptized in the name of Paul?*
> 1 Corinthians 1:1-13

Voice from the Church

"I'll tell you what, I've come to the point, and at my age [77 at the time of interview] ... where I wouldn't sell my soul for any man's system of theology yet I love them all. It's Christ, and the Word of God. I will lay down my life for the Word of God, but systems, all of them, need patch-work and help, in bridging over points. Everyone of them; tell me one that doesn't. And yet, we do love them all, and there's no perfect system." (Armin Gesswein, 1907-2001)*

Reflection

Armin Gesswein, the author of the above quote, was raised in a nominal Christian home. He was converted through listening to a radio broadcast, when Paul Rader was the preacher and pastor of the Moody Church in Chicago. Gesswein later joined and pastored for the Christian & Missionary Alliance. Then, still later, he became an associate evangelist for the Billy Graham organization for many years.

Through the centuries, God has raised up many godly men to stimulate and lead reformation and renewal and revival in the church. Unfortunately, many of us have tended to identify more with men than we have with the God and gospel these men proclaimed. We thank God for these men; however, we preach Christ and him crucified.

Verse

While some theologies are better than others,
each tend to separate a host of true brothers.
The Word of God is the sole standard of our faith;
the Spirit unites, our opinions separate.

A Clean Heart

The Word
Create in me a clean heart, O God, and renew a right spirit within me.
Psalm 51:10

Voice from the Church
"It takes infinite power for God to create the universe out of nothing. But it takes even greater power to make saints out of sinners. For the nothingness out of which God created the universe did not resist him; but sinners do. David prays: 'Create in me a clean heart,' and uses the word *'bara'* for 'create.' It is something only God can do. The verb is never used with any other subject except God." (Peter Kreeft, b. 1937)*

Reflection
The greatest miracle God performs in any thirsty-hearted person is the miracle of a clean heart. Such a heart cannot be produced by the will and resolution of man. It does not come through the rite of infant or adult baptism. One does not receive a clean heart by receiving Holy Communion. A clean heart is bestowed by God to the truly repentant and fully consecrated seeker after God.

There is no human longing and desire for which God does not have an answer. What defiles a person? A defiled heart. To those who majored on external righteousness at the expense of internal purity, the Lord Jesus said, "For from within, out of the heart of man, come evil thoughts, sexual immorality, theft, murder, adultery, coveting, wickedness, deceit, sensuality, envy, slander, pride, foolishness" (Mark 7:21-22). Christ always went to the "heart" of the problem.

King David cried out for a clean heart, and he received one (see 2 Sam. 12). Have you received a clean heart from the Lord? If not, seek his face today.

Verse
O Lord, my heart is my biggest problem;
My will is much too weak to obey.
Create within me a clean heart, O God;
By Your power, I will watch and pray.

God's Faithful Heralds

The Word
> *"And everyone who has left houses or brothers or sisters or*
> *father or mother or children or lands, for my name's sake,*
> *will receive a hundredfold and will inherit eternal life."*
> Matthew 19:29

Voice from the Church

"I never raised the question of whether missionaries received a salary. The fact is that even after I arrived in India, I never asked what I was supposed to get. I didn't know till I was handed my first month's salary—150 rupees or $50. I felt 'if God guides, God provides.' And he has. I have never wanted for a thing I've needed" [served in ministry for over 65 years]. (E. Stanley Jones, 1884-1973)*

Reflection

The church of the Lord Jesus Christ owes an immeasurable debt to those men and women of God who, in every respect, left behind all to follow the call of God. Through the centuries, thousands of Christ's disciples have bid goodbye to fatherland, parents, friends and family, in order to proclaim the gospel at some great distance and cost.

Each of the apostles of the Lord Jesus traveled far and wide, proclaiming the unsearchable riches of Christ. From the first century until the present, the heralds of Jesus Christ have crossed mountains, rivers and seas; slept under open skies; traveled in all kinds of weather; been pilloried, persecuted and prosecuted. Some of these, of whom the world is not worthy, have given their very life's blood in holy martyrdom. Others have not suffered such hardship, but have nonetheless been true to their calling. We are debtors! God will not be unmindful of these noble servants on that Great Day.

Verse
You who have left home and traveled afar,
  to raise the banner of Christ the Lord,
Our God will not forget your work of love,
  rewarding you for preaching His Word.

The King's Reign

The Word

> *"The time is fulfilled, and the kingdom of God*
> *is at hand; repent and believe in the gospel."*
> Mark 1:15

Voice from the Church

"During the past sixteen years I can recollect only two occasions on which I have heard sermons specifically devoted to the theme of the Kingdom of God.... I find this silence rather surprising because it is universally agreed by New Testament scholars that the central theme of the teaching of Jesus was the Kingdom of God." (I. Howard Marshall, 1934-1015)*

Reflection

The rule and reign of God among men was prophesied by the ancient prophets, including John, the last of the Old Covenant mouthpieces for Yahweh.

Bible students saw long ago, that what was to the evangelist Mathew the "kingdom of heaven" was called my Mark the "kingdom of God." Both designations are essentially the same. The terms speak of God's reign that arrived in the person of the Word made flesh; this kingdom is meant to dwell in the hearts of all who are receptive to its King; and there is coming a day when "the God of heaven will set up a kingdom that shall never be destroyed, nor shall the kingdom be left to another people" (Dan. 2:44). The King's intention in coming to earth was to plant his reign in the hearts of all who repented and believed the gospel. And this same King taught his disciples to pray to the Father, that his full reign and rule would be ultimately and universally completed: "Your kingdom come, your will be done, on earth as it is in heaven" (Matt. 6:10). Have you personally received God's rule?

Verse

A kingdom of righteousness and love
  has marched in with my King from above,
Overthrowing every native foe,
  breaking down heavily entrenched woe.

Heaven

The Word

> *"He will wipe away every tear from their eyes, and death shall*
> *be no more, neither shall there be mourning, nor crying, nor*
> *pain anymore, for the former things have passed away."*
> Revelation 21:4

Voice from the Church

"Even though we know a whole lot less about life after death than people like to think we know, what is certain is that our new understanding of God will be richer than we even dreamed of in our finest tributes, our most blessed sermons, or our deepest meditations. The blind will see—that includes all of us. On earth, we all walk with white canes. (Abraham Kuyper, 1837-1920)*

Reflection

We don't know a whole lot about life after death for the redeemed. We don't know because God chose not to reveal more than he did in his Word. But we know enough.

We know Jesus is in heaven and the saved will be forever with him: "I go to prepare a place for you? And if I go and prepare a place for you, I will come again and will take you to myself, that where I am you may be also" (John 14:2-3).

We know the redeemed will have a body like Jesus: "We await a Savior, the Lord Jesus Christ, who will transform our lowly body to be like his glorious body" (Phil. 3:20).

We know there will be no uncleanness in heaven: "Blessed are those who wash their robes, so that they may have the right to the tree of life and that they may enter the city by the gates" (Rev. 22:14).

Heaven is a place of grace reserved for a prepared people.

Verse

God has placed within us the longing
    for a perfect Home.
That perfect Home is Heaven, where God's
    Son awaits his own.

Gratitude for God's Servants

The Word

> [3]*Greet Prisca and Aquila, my fellow workers in Christ*
> *Jesus,* [4]*who risked their necks for my life, to whom not*
> *only I give thanks but all the churches of the Gentiles*
> *give thanks as well.* [5]*Greet also the church in their house.*
>
> Romans 16:3-5

Voice from the Church

"In Romans 16:3-16 Paul gives his greetings to no fewer than twenty-six persons. But heading the list are Prisca and Aquila ... 'who once risked their necks for my life' (v. 4). The expression 'risk the neck' refers literally to the exposing of the neck to the executioner's sword, and metaphorically (as here) to the exposure to mortal danger." (Murray J. Harris, b. 1939)*

Reflection

Paul was a gracious servant of the Lord Jesus, always expressing his gratitude for and to those who had assisted him in ministry. To feel and express gratitude, toward those who have made a meaningful contribution to our life and ministry, is something that should be done by God's people. We must not carelessly forget those whom God has used to stimulate our faith along our spiritual journey.

Recently I was faced with a ministry decision. I felt I should decline an invitation, because of the grueling travel schedule it would necessarily entail. After I notified the contact person of my decision, my Father took me to his "woodshed." The next day, God used a statement from an author, whom I highly esteem, to chasten me. I reversed my decision and wrote a word of appreciation to the writer about how God had used him. Should you contact someone today?

Verse

Forgive us, O Lord, for carelessly
  forgetting Your kind servant,
Who helped us freely and faithfully,
  though we didn't deserve it.

Perfecting Holiness (1)

The Word

Therefore, having these promises, beloved, let us cleanse ourselves from all defilement of flesh and spirit, perfecting holiness in the fear of God.
2 Corinthians 7:1 NASB

Voice from the Church

"A holy man will follow after purity of heart. He will dread all filthiness and uncleanness of spirit, and seek to avoid all things that might draw him into it. He knows his heart is like tinder, and will diligently keep clear of the sparks of temptation." (J. C. Ryle, 1816-1900)*

Reflection

The moment the Holy Spirit enters a person's life, in the act of regenerating grace, the new follower of the Lord Jesus Christ is infused with a holy desire to live a life pleasing to his Father in heaven. Where this desire is not present in a professing Christian, we are not hesitant to say that the person is not born of the Spirit of God; for where the Holy Spirit is present, holy desires will follow as surely as night follows the day.

God calls his people to total separation, consecration, and sanctification. In the chapter prior to our above text, God calls the Corinthian believers to separation: "Therefore, come out from their midst and be separate," says the Lord. 'And do not touch what is unclean; And I will welcome you'" (2 Cor. 6:17). In 2 Corinthians 7:1, these believers are called to total consecration and sanctification. This consecration and spiritual surgery require decisive action: "let us cleanse ourselves from all defilement of flesh and spirit." This is something we must do, in the strength of God. The apostle says that this crucial action is "perfecting" what God has already begun; it is a matter of cooperating with God in his work of molding the believer into the image of the Son.

Verse

How can we claim Christ Jesus as Lord,
when we allow filth into body and mind?
The temple of God our body is;
we must cleanse it all to fulfill His design.

Perfecting Holiness (2)

The Word
Therefore, having these promises, beloved, let us cleanse ourselves from all defilement of flesh and spirit, perfecting holiness in the fear of God.
2 Corinthians 7:1 NASB

Voice from the Church
"[Christians] belong to God. Christ lives in them. When a heathen judge demanded of Ignatius of Antioch, why he spoke of himself as *theophorus* ('bearer of God'), the martyr replied that it was because he was 'one who has Christ in his breast.' In Christians, he declared, the promise was fulfilled, 'I will dwell in them, and walk in them, and they shall be my sons and daughters, says the Lord Almighty.'" (Iain H. Murray, b. 1931)*

Reflection
When we are born again by the Spirit of God, we become forgiven of all our sins and receive a cleansed conscience; there is no more guilt because there is no more condemnation: "There is therefore now no condemnation for those who are in Christ Jesus" (Rom. 8:1). However, to experience the new birth is not the end of the story; the Spirit calls us to a holy walk—inside and outside. God wants to perfect what he has begun; and he will perfect all that we allow him to.

Since it is the *Holy* Spirit who indwells the believer, he will not tolerate anything in our lives that is *un*holy: our language, appetites, associations, attitudes, and entertainments. The Holy Spirit will apply pressure to our conscience until we rid ourselves from all that is unholy, or until we harden our heart and grieve him. Do we live with a reverential awe ("fear") of God? If we mean to be a true disciple of the Lord Jesus, we must not allow anything to keep us from maintaining a pure heart before him.

Verse
God has given to us the freedom,
  to be a true disciple or not.
Our Lord cannot make the choice for us,
  but will help us to do what we ought.

Perfecting Holiness (3)

The Word
Therefore, having these promises, beloved, let us cleanse ourselves from all defilement of flesh and spirit, perfecting holiness in the fear of God.
2 Corinthians 7:1 NASB

Voice from the Church
"Remember, you are *without* power; the enemy is a *strong* power, but God has *all* power. Therefore come with your utter lack of power to Him Who as the Almighty has eternal abundance of power, and you will be able to conquer the enemy's strong power. God's omnipotence is able to make your impotence triumph over all the energy of the adversary." (Erich Sauer, 1998-1959)*

Reflection
Some reading these devotionals are afraid of the word "perfecting." Your instinctive reaction may be, "Nobody is perfect or can be perfect in this world." When God calls us to total obedience and consecration and calls us to cleanse ourselves from everything that defiles his temple (our body), he identifies this as "perfecting holiness." Now, who are you to say that you can't comply with God's call? Of course, one is never to call himself "perfect." And, furthermore, there will always be future calls to obedience and separation, but don't be guilty of telling God that he can't really mean what he says (that's precisely what the Serpent told Eve in the Garden).

If we are serious about our walk with God, we won't want anything to defile God's temple or to affect our Christian witness. If you're not serious about being a follower of the Lord Jesus, then you will simply slough off texts like 2 Corinthians 7:1. Christians are not only forgiven—they're called to be disciples of the holy Son of God.

Verse
Nothing between my soul and my Savior,
So that His blessed face may be seen;
Nothing preventing the least of His favor;
Keep the way clear! Let nothing between. (Charles A. Tindley, 1851-1933)**

Perfection and Sanctification

The Word

For by a single offering he has perfected for
all time those who are being sanctified.
Hebrews 10:14

Voice from the Church

"In the divine program for the Church, are Christians to be like Tanta-
lus, who was in water up to his neck, yet could never quench his burning
thirst, and who saw trees laden with fruit waving their branches directly
over his head, yet could never reach them to satisfy his gnawing hunger;
or like Sisyphus who had to roll a huge stone up a steep mountainside,
and found that whenever he partially succeeded, the stone always rolled
down again?" (Steven Barabas, 1904-1983)*

Reflection

The perfection the Hebrews' writer speaks of, in the above text, is that
which has been accomplished through the atoning sacrifice of Jesus
Christ for believers. At the Cross, all believers were *proleptically* perfected; that is, they were made complete in anticipation of the day when
they would become partakers of God's holiness. These believers, who
were perfected by the offering of Christ on their behalf, are presently
"being sanctified," as they live in continual surrender and obedience to
their Lord, who is their Sanctifier.

The clause "he has perfected" is in the perfect active indicative tense,
which suggests an action has been completed and the results of the action are continuing. The phrase "those who are being sanctified," suggests that those who have been perfected by Christ's offering experience
his continuing infusion of holiness. All this is of God and his grace,
working in those who walk with him. To God be the glory!

Verse

Christ died not only for our sins to atone;
  through his death also I have been perfected.
I'm now being made holy by His Spirit,
  as, by grace, I live a life that is yielded.

Joy in the Midst of Trial

The Word
*[25]About midnight Paul and Silas were praying and
singing hymns to God, and the prisoners were listening to
them, [26]and suddenly there was a great earthquake, so that
the foundations of the prison were shaken. And immediately all
the doors were opened, and everyone's bonds were unfastened.*
Acts 16:25-26

Voice from the Church
"The double-discomfort of the lictors' rods and the stocks was not cal-
culated to fill Paul and Silas with joy, but about midnight the other prisoners, as they listened, heard sounds coming from the inmost part of the
jail—sounds not of groaning and cursing, but of prayer and hymn-
singing. 'The legs feel nothing in the stocks when the heart is in heav-
en,' says Tertullian." (F. F. Bruce, 1910-1990)*

Reflection
One would *naturally* think, in following the call of God, all would go
smoothly, absent any difficulties or apparent reverses. Not so! Having
received a vision from God to take the gospel to Macedonia, Paul and
his companions proceeded accordingly. Arriving in Philippi, a woman
by the name of Lydia was converted, with her household. Later, on their
way to a prayer meeting, Paul and Silas were arrested, beaten, and im-
prisoned, for disturbing the peace (preaching the gospel).

These men were where they were, at God's direction. What was their
response? We find them late at night "praying and singing hymns to
God." What resulted? The jailor and his household were converted; the
men were released, and they went on their way. Could it be that if more
people witnessed Christian joy, more would be converted?

Verse
*I have found the joy no tongue can tell,
How its waves of glory roll!
It is like a great o'erflowing well,
Springing up within my soul.* (Barney E. Warren, 1867-1951)**

When Tempted

The Word

> ^{1}And Jesus, full of the Holy Spirit, returned from the Jordan
> and was led by the Spirit in the wilderness ^{2}for forty days, being
> tempted by the devil. And he ate nothing during those days.

Luke 4:1-2

Voice from the Church

"In the experience of all those who know anything of what it is to follow in the footsteps of the Lord in God-appointed service, the power of the Spirit is never realized save through some wilderness of personal conflict with the foe. From such experience entered upon in the fullness of the Spirit, men go out either broken and incapable of service, or with the tread and force of conscious power." (G. Campbell Morgan, 1863-1945)*

Reflection

Following the descent of the Spirit upon Jesus at the Jordan River, he underwent temptations more severe than any ever experienced by another human being. Remember, Jesus was not only the Son of God, he was also the Son of Man, and as the Son of Man he was tempted—for forty long days. If the Adversary could prevent God's Anointed One from fulfilling the Father's purpose in the redemption events (death and resurrection), there would be no hope for mankind; Satan would have achieved victory. But because Jesus overcame the Foe in the wilderness and later in the Garden; and because he triumphed through death and resurrected life, we too can overcome: "For because he himself has suffered when tempted, he is able to help those who are being tempted" (Heb. 2:18).

Jesus left the wilderness in the power of the Spirit. So can we—whatever our *wilderness* may be—God being our helper.

Verse

Whatever temptation I may face,
I must not despair; Christ suffered as well.
He now sits at the Father's right hand,
and now gives me His help—grace upon grace.

Affliction

The Word

[66] *Teach me good judgment and knowledge, for I believe in your commandments.* [67] *Before I was afflicted I went astray, but now I keep your word.* [68] *You are good and do good; teach me your statutes.*
Psalm 119:66-68

Voice from the Church

"There are those to whom a sense of religion has come in storm and tempest; there are those whom it has summoned amid scenes of revelry and idle vanity; there are those, too, who have heard its still small voice amid rural leisure and placid contentment. But perhaps the knowledge which causeth not to err, is most frequently impressed upon the mind during seasons of affliction; and tears are often the softened showers which cause the seed of heaven to spring and take root in the human heart." (Sir Walter Scott, 1771-1832)*

Reflection

Who among us has never experienced distresses so severely as to cause persistent suffering and anguish? During such turmoil, our very powers of endurance and self-control are challenged. The emotional pain and anguish are almost unbearable. The faint of heart often stumbles under the load. Even the strong in spirit may be confused and question.

What do we seek as a refuge during times of affliction? Where do we flea—narcotics? a spending spree? food binging? isolating ourselves? What did the psalmist do when afflicted? He prayed and vowed to obey God: "I have sworn an oath and confirmed it, to keep your righteous rules" (Ps. 119:106). After the affliction subsided he was able to say, "It is good for me that I was afflicted, that I might learn your statutes" (Ps. 119:71). Let God be your refuge in affliction.

Verse

Come, ye disconsolate, where'er ye languish,
Come to the mercy seat, fervently kneel.
Here bring your wounded hearts, here tell your anguish;
Earth has no sorrow that heaven cannot heal. (Thomas Moore, 1478-1535)**

Forgiveness

The Word

*[14]"For if you forgive others their trespasses, your heavenly
Father will also forgive you, [15]but if you do not forgive others
their trespasses, neither will your Father forgive your trespasses."*
Matthew 6:14-15

Voice from the Church

"It was while I was going down the stairs that suddenly the light broke
in on me, as if a veil had been torn away. I saw that I had always borne a
grudge against my mother for being a saintly woman, because her saintliness put me to shame.... When I got home today I threw my arms
around my mother's neck and asked her to forgive me for all this." (Paul
Tournier, 1898-1986)*

Reflection

Having experienced the gracious forgiveness of God, we must extend
the same to those who have wronged us. Often, however, because we
have wronged others, we must seek their forgiveness as well. This can
be a very humbling ordeal, but a necessary one.

During one's initial repentance, in coming to faith in Jesus Christ, the
Holy Spirit will reveal to the seeker people he has wronged. What shall
he do? The Spirit will make it clear. If he is to live in peace with God,
he must seek to be at peace with himself and others. This sometimes
requires an apology.

Furthermore, as we walk with God, a Spirit-shaped conscience will
inform us when we have caused an unnecessary offense toward another—a family member, a brother or sister in Christ, a coworker, etc.
What shall we do? Shall we override our conscience? Or shall we do the
right thing and make the necessary apology?

Verse

I saw her countenance suddenly fall,
  when a thoughtless word was spoken.
Afterward I went to my knees to pray.
  I could not. I returned—broken.

Receiving Glory

The Word

*"How can you believe, when you receive glory from one another
and do not seek the glory that comes from the only God?"*
John 5:44

Voice from the Church

"Charles Spurgeon in one place describes the clergyman who says,
'When I was preaching at such-and-such a place, fifteen persons came
into the vestry at the close of the service, and thanked me for the sermon
I had preached.' And Spurgeon, unable to restrain himself, lets fly furi-
ously at the complacent creature: 'You and your blessed sermon be
hanged! Take not to yourself the honour which belongeth to God only.'" (James Stewart, 1896-1990)*

Reflection

For the man or woman who has not submitted his or her ego to the cross
of Christ, there will always be the *natural* tendency to take credit that
should be passed on to God. The uncrucified "flesh" seeks to be praised,
adored, and acknowledged; it takes the glory instead of seeking "the
glory that comes from the only God."

When "glory" (praise) is given to you, how do you respond in your
heart? "Well, I deserved it; I worked hard to accomplish what I did." Or,
as we stroke our self-centered ego, "I'm glad someone realizes my importance." Or, on the other hand, "I thank you for your compliment, and
give glory to God."

Let us also heed the words of the wise man: "Let another praise you,
and not your own mouth; a stranger, and not your own lips" (Prov.
27:2). And when they do praise you, don't keep it—pass it on to the
One who is all-deserving.

Verse

He had stood so tall and straight;
*   the accolades were many.*
Then he took a mighty fall—
*   pride followed humility.*

Christ's Hands

The Word

> *"And whoever gives one of these little ones even a*
> *cup of cold water because he is a disciple, truly,*
> *I say to you, he will by no means lose his reward."*

Matthew 10:42

Voice from the Church

"During World War II, a church in Strasbourg, France, was destroyed....
When the rubble was cleared, a statue of Christ, standing erect, was
found. It was unbroken except for the two hands, which were missing.
In time the church was rebuilt. A sculptor, noticing the missing hands on
the statue of Christ, said, 'Let me carve a new statue of Christ, with
hands.' Church officials met to consider the sculptor's proposal. His
offer was rejected. A spokesman for the church said, 'Our broken statue
will serve to remind us that Christ touches the hearts of men, but He has
no hands to minister to the needy or feed the hungry or enrich the poor
except our hands.'" (George Sweeting & Donald Sweeting)*

Reflection

We are frequently guilty of asking God to do something, when God can
only perform some acts through our surrendered hands. While on earth,
the Lord Jesus used his hands to serve the hungry, the sick, and the distressed. Christ walked among men with great sensitivity; he could do so,
because he was not preoccupied with himself and his own needs.

If the grace of God is operating freely within us, our eyes will be alert
to those about us. If God's grace is impeded in our hearts, it will nega-
tively affect our service toward others. The Lord Jesus came to do his
Father's will. That will involved using his hands in serving others. We
are called to do the same.

Verse

When our eyes have been cleansed by God,
* we are able to see others clearly.*
When our eyes are turned inwardly,
* we're unable to serve others nobly.*

Whose Slave are We?

The Word

> *"No one can serve two masters, for either he will hate the one*
> *and love the other, or he will be devoted to the one and*
> *despise the other. You cannot serve God and money."*
> Matthew 6:24

Voice from the Church

"Bill Borden's father had left him a very large inheritance. But Bill did-n't cling to his riches, because he felt that everything he had was a trust from God. He gave away many millions of dollars, ... I was aghast. Since childhood I had thought being a millionaire was one of life's high-est goals. But here was Bill Borden, a college senior, giving away great wealth." (Scott Larsen, n.d.)*

Reflection

Not every disciple of the Lord Jesus is required by him to sell all his property and give the proceeds to the church and the poor, though some are. But each disciple of Christ is required to surrender himself and all he has to his Master, the Lord Jesus.

When one is a servant (a slave) of another, all he ever possessed has been turned over to his master. A slave owns nothing; he is owned by his master. The apostle acknowledged this when he wrote, "You are not your own, for you were bought with a price. So glorify God in your body" (1 Cor. 6:19-20). We are to glorify God with our body and every-thing we call our "own," which in fact is not our own, because we have surrendered ownership to our Master. We are simply God's stewards.

Who are you serving? What are you serving? Are you controlled by money, investments, property, things, or are you devoted to the Master, the Lord Jesus Christ?

Verse

It is not how much or how little we have,
but how much or how little "it" has us.
To surrender all we have to the Master—
is to be controlled by Him and not another.

"In the hands of Almighty God"

The Word
> [31] *What then shall we say to these things? If God is for us,*
> *who can be against us?* [32] *He who did not spare his own Son*
> *but gave him up for us all, how will he not also with him graciously*
> *give us all things?* [33] *Who shall bring any charge against God's elect?*
> *It is God who justifies.* [34] *Who is to condemn? Christ Jesus is the*
> *one who died—more than that, who was raised—who is at*
> *the right hand of God, who indeed is interceding for us.*
> Romans 8:31-34

Voice from the Church
"There was a day in Martin Luther's life when the road grew suddenly dark and threatening, and death seemed very near. 'The Pope's little finger,' thundered the Cardinal legate, 'is stronger than all Germany. Do you expect your princes to take up arms to defend you—a wretched worm like you? I tell you, No! And where will you be then? Tell me that!—where will you be then?' 'Then, as now,' cried Luther, in the hands of Almighty God!'" (James Stewart, 1896-1990)*

Reflection
Wherever God leads his children, we can be sure he is forever with them, for he does not forsake his own. This is a matter of faith—believing what God has spoken and is written. Because of this sure foundation, we need not check our "spiritual pulse" each time we are tried and tested. Our emotional clouds may hang low, as it were, and the assaults of the Enemy may come fast and furious; however, our status with God does not change with life's ebbs and flows, or with our own emotional fluctuations. Child of the Father, you must always believe that God is with you ... regardless. His Word never changes.

Verse
The storm may roar without me,
My heart may low be laid;
But God is round about me,
And can I be dismayed? (Anna L. Waring, 1823-1910)**

Knowing the Scriptures and Knowing God

The Word
> [39] *"You search the Scriptures because you think that in them you have eternal life; and it is they that bear witness about me, [40] yet you refuse to come to me that you may have life."*
> John 5:39-40

Voice from the Church
"True spirituality will be anchored in biblical revelation, but it will resist the temptation of biblicisim, which narrows the scope and purpose of revelation. We appeal not simply to the Bible as a book, but to the voice of the Holy Spirit as he speaks to us through the pages of the Bible and as he has guided the church through history." (Donald G. Bloesch, 1928-2010)*

Reflection
How is it that a person can be thoroughly knowledgeable as to the contents of the Bible and yet remain spiritually ignorant, without a true knowledge of God? How is it that a theology professor can lecture to students week after week, but experience no intimacy with God and is void of any real spiritual discernment and insight? How can a person quote at length memorized passages of Scriptures, nevertheless live a life of overt disobedience to God? The adversaries of the Lord Jesus were such people. They were schooled in the Hebrew Scriptures, taught the traditions of the fathers, were regular in their devotional exercises, yet the Baptist said of them, "among you stands one you do not know" (John 1:26). How could this be?

It could be because of the huge chasm that exists between knowing the Scriptures and knowing God. The Scriptures point to God and his Son, but absent the Spirit operating within, our eyes are blinded to the words we read. It is always—the Word and Spirit.

Verse
He stood week after week, quoting the Scriptures;
the people remained dead; words had no effect.
Then his heart was filled with the God of the Book;
the man was not the same; people left amazed.

The World's Most Powerful Force

The Word
[11]Now may our God and Father himself, and our Lord Jesus, direct our way to you, [12]and may the Lord make you increase and abound in love for one another and for all, as we do for you.
1 Thessalonians 3:11-12

Voice from the Church
"In the summer of 1988 Barbara and I visited a friend who spoke of his friendship with Dr. [Francis] Schaeffer and the man's touch. Once, my friend remembers, Schaeffer had in tow a successful architect who had 'dropped out' during the disillusionment of the sixties. He had not yet come to Christ, and he told my friend, 'I don't know if what Francis Schaeffer is telling me about Christianity is true or not. But I do know this: that man loves me.'" (R. Kent Hughes, b. 1942)*

Reflection
The most powerful force in the world is love—*agape* love. In his Ode to Divine Love, the apostle observed, "Love bears all things, believes all things, hopes all things, endures all things" (1 Cor. 13:7). What is the greatest fruit of the Spirit, and the grace which surpasses all other graces? Paul said it was divine love: "So now faith, hope, and love abide, these three; but the greatest of these is love" (1 Cor. 13:13).

One of the first evidences that a person has been truly born of God is the presence of *agape* love. Immediately following her conversion to Christ, Lydia invited Paul and his companions to be her guests—an expression of loving hospitality. Right after his own conversion, the jailer took the persecuted apostles "the same hour of the night and washed their wounds" (see Acts 16:11-34 for these two accounts).

The love of God, indwelling his people, is a mighty force for good.

Verse
O love of God, how strong and true!
Eternal, and yet ever new;
Uncomprehended and unbought,
Beyond all knowledge and all thought. (Horatius Bonar, 1808-1889) **

God's Unlikely Chosen

The Word

*25 "But in truth, I tell you, there were many widows in Israel
in the days of Elijah, when the heavens were shut up three
years and six months, and a great famine came over all
the land, 26 and Elijah was sent to none of them but only to
Zarephath, in the land of Sidon, to a woman who was a widow. "*

Luke 4:25-26

Voice from the Church

"We must remember throughout our lives that in God's sight there are
no little people and no little places. Only one thing is important: to be
consecrated persons in God's place for us, at each moment." (Francis A.
Schaeffer, 1912-1984)*

Reflection

The typical Jewish leader, during the days of Jesus' earthly ministry,
viewed himself and his people as superior to all others. These leaders
often treated Gentiles and society's disenfranchised with utter contempt.
Their provincial concept of religion built fences to keep "sinners" out,
instead of building bridges of grace to take sinners in.

Jesus was a popular person until his preaching became personal.
When he reminded his audience that one of Israel's foremost prophets
was directed by God to minister to a Gentile in the town of Zarephath,
his hearers were ready to throw Jesus over a cliff (see Luke 4:29).

But God often uses unlikely messengers to minister to unlikely people, as he did in the case of Elijah and a widow (see 1 Kings 17:8-24).
This foreign woman welcomed a messenger of God, and, in turn, was
both blessed materially and spiritually. Jesus did not fit the prescribed
mold of the leaders. Neither did a widow and a prophet.

Verse

Her need was extremely desperate,
* until the day the prophet stopped by.*
She welcomed and served him most gladly,
* and discovered God's gracious supply.*

Christianity's Foremost Hymnist

The Word

Oh sing to the Lord a new song, for he has done marvelous things!
His right hand and his holy arm have worked salvation for him.
Psalm 98:1

Voice from the Church

"The saying that a really good hymn is as rare an appearance as that of a comet is falsified by the work of Charles Wesley; for hymns, which are really good in every respect, flowed from his pen in quick succession, and death alone stopped the course of the perennial stream." (John Julian, b. 1932)*

Reflection

Intellectual and spiritual prejudice prevents the believer from enjoying what God has inspired. This is true when it comes to the songs Christians sing. For some, they have a prejudice against any song that has been authored in the last 50 years. For others, they have no appreciation for the time-tested hymns of the faith.

One of the most edifying things music leaders can offer their respective congregations is to acquaint them with classic hymns—hymns such as those written by the church's foremost hymnist, Charles Wesley (1707-1788). Wesley was the youngest son and eighteenth child of Samuel and Susanna Wesley. While historians differ as to the number of hymns he authored, some believe the number exceeds 6500. Wesley's lyrics are both excellent and biblical, though in more recent hymnals, some of words in his hymns have been altered (unfortunately), because the publishers disagreed with his theology. Wesley was no "milk and toast" author. He takes us to the height of God's excellency and extols the breadth of God's grace—to the uttermost salvation.

Verse

O for a thousand tongues to sing
My great Redeemer's praise,
The glories of my God and King,
The triumphs of His grace! (Charles Wesley, 1707-1788)**

"Make Me a Captive, Lord"

The Word

But now that you have been set free from sin and have become slaves of God, the fruit you get leads to sanctification and its end, eternal life.
Romans 6:22

Voice from the Church

"One of the blessings of discipleship to Jesus is that while it binds us to rigorous obedience it also sets us marvelously free. "Make me a captive, Lord, and then I shall be free." There are many gods in contemporary culture who only bind; they do not simultaneously bind and free. Jesus is the best of all gods, the liberator par excellence." (Frederick Dale Bruner, b. 1932)*

Reflection

Hymn writer and pastor George Matheson (1842-1906) was a remarkable person. Born with poor eyesight, he was intellectually gifted, earning a master's degree from the University of Edinburgh. Due to his poor vision and later blindness, he memorized his sermons and lengthy passages of Scripture. Some parishioners were not even aware he was blind.

One of Matheson's most popular hymns is "Make Me a Captive, Lord." The first line of the hymn reflects the biblical truth of the freedom the believer experiences though Jesus Christ, as well as the obedience we owe him. At the moment of our conversion to Christ, we are simultaneously set free from sin and made a bond slave of Jesus Christ. We are both free and a slave.

No Christian, indwelled by the Holy Spirit, wishes to use his freedom to commit sin. Never! He has surrendered his will to his Master. In the words of Matheson, "My will is not my own till Thou hast made it Thine."

Verse

Make me a captive, Lord, and then I shall be free.
Force me to render up my sword, and I shall conqueror be.
I sink in life's alarms when by myself I stand;
Imprison me within Thine arms, and strong shall be my hand.

Doing What He Says

The Word
"Why do you call Me, 'Lord, Lord,' and do not do what I say?"
Luke 6:46 NASB

Voice from the Church
"It is one thing for us to follow a grand custom and stand during the singing of the Hallelujah Chorus at the unforgettable climax of Part II of Handel's Messiah and so celebrate the ultimate victory of Christ. It is quite another thing for us to bow the knee before the crucified and exalted Lord of the universe and receive the metaphorical piercing of the ear as a sign and pledge of our joyful and willing slavery to him as long as we live." (Murray J. Harris, b. 1939)*

Reflection
No one can live in a saving relationship to the Lord Jesus Christ whose life is characterized by willful disobedience.

Through the years, when speaking with some people about their relationship with God, I've often heard them say something like, "Well, I pray; there's not a day goes by but what I pray."

As the Son of Man, the Lord Jesus was raised in a religious culture in which almost everyone prayed—in the Temple and synagogue, at home, and even in the marketplace, as did some prideful Pharisees. However, Jesus knew many of these prayers were worthless; they were worthless because the petitioner lived in disobedience to the Lord to whom he prayed: "Why do you call Me, 'Lord, Lord,' and do not do what I say?" Discipleship requires obedience to the Lord Jesus Christ. This is not slavish obedience. This is joyful, wholehearted submission to our Redeemer and Master. Let's not pretend to be a disciple of Jesus, if our life is not characterized by doing what he says.

Verse
By Thy blessed word obeying,
Lord, we prove our love sincere;
For we hear Thee gently saying,
"Love will do as well as hear." (Daniel S. Warner, 1842-1895)**

Prayer Should Be Uncomplicated

The Word
[7] *"And when you pray, do not heap up empty phrases as the Gentiles do, for they think that they will be heard for their many words.* [8] *Do not be like them, for your Father knows what you need before you ask him."*
Matthew 6:7-8

Voice from the Church
"As to prayer, you find much prayer a difficulty. And I understand you. Try, then, brief praying often, and whenever you pray, so it be with the deepest reverence of spirit, use the utmost freedom of words; the very homeliest, the very simplest; and I think you will find praying more and more a rest and less a task." (H. C. G. Moule, 1841-1920)*

Reflection
One of the challenges for those who teach or write about prayer is, that we should not give our audience the impression that to pray well is to pray at considerable length.

There were those in the time of Jesus (and ours as well), that prayed as though God would be required to hear and answer their petitions because they had prayed a lengthy prayer or had repeated some phrases repeatedly.

While it's true that there will be occasions when the child of God will spend some time at great length in his "closet" of prayer, this is not necessarily the rule for most Christians. To pray well is to pray unhurriedly, without distraction, and sincerely and honestly. To pray well is to listen well—to the Word and Spirit. The Spirit of God will teach the child of God how to spend his regular devotional times in Bible reading and prayer. Let us be willing to be taught by others but let us not be a slave to another's rule in this matter.

Verse
The time alone I spend with You, Father,
You do not judge by its length. But as I
Learn to know and love You more, I will
Often seek a place for us to meet.

God and Faith

The Word

And he said to the woman, "Your faith has saved you; go in peace."
Luke 7:50
And he went away, proclaiming throughout the
whole city how much Jesus had done for him.
Luke 8:39

Voice from the Church

"Faith is the imperial grace of Christ's system. A simple but very rare grace. Much of that which circulates as faith has but little if any elements of faith in it.... Faith is the divine energy implanted in the heart by God. By it we have the foundation, the sight, and the vital force of the unseen and eternal. An energy, it is that which masters everything for God; an eye that sees God in his nearness, majesty, and supremacy." (E. M. Bounds, 1835-1913)*

Reflection

Some years ago, I discovered a rather interesting phenomenon in the ministry of the Lord Jesus. When reading the Gospel accounts of several of the miracles Jesus performed, Jesus often remarked afterward that it was the person's faith which was the means of the miracle: for example, "Your faith has saved you." However, when individuals experienced a miraculous event, they often said, as in the above text, "how much Jesus had done for [them]."

Both are true and necessary, whenever God intervenes in the affairs and lives of men and women. It is God who is the primary source and cause of miracles, answers to prayer, and changed lives. And it is faith, on the part of the individual—or individuals—which cooperates with God Almighty in appropriating God's power.

Verse

I wondered if the thing could be done.
God said it could, if I would believe.
I trusted in the sure Word He gave;
I saw Him act; I give Him the praise.

Light and Darkness

The Word
[19]*"And this is the judgment: the light has come into the world, and people loved the darkness rather than the light because their works were evil. [20]For everyone who does wicked things hates the light and does not come to the light, lest his works should be exposed."*
John 3:19-20

Voice from the Church
"As Light, by its nature, cannot be self-contained, but is ever seeking to impart itself, pouring through every window and crevice, shining into every eye, bathing land and sea with its pure radiance; so God, from His very nature of Righteousness and Love, is necessitated to reveal Himself as being what He is. He is Light, and as such is always seeking to shine into the minds He has made in His own image." (Robert Law, 1860-1919)*

Reflection
Light and darkness in the Scriptures are metaphors for holiness and evil, righteousness and sin. Where one is present, of necessity the other must flee. Just as light and darkness cannot coexist in the same space, just so, righteousness and evil cannot coexist in the same person.

Man's greatest problem in receiving the Light of the gospel is not an intellectual hurdle. Man's fundamental problem is *moral*: he would rather cling to his sins than embrace the Light; he would prefer walking in moral darkness, than he would bowing before the God who "is light, and in him is no darkness at all" (1 John 1:5).

We are not passive bystanders in this matter. We are either actively pursuing the one or the other. Indifference is a choice; we cannot excuse ourselves. To love truth and righteousness is to receive the light and walk in it; to hate the Light is to love evil and our sins. We must decide.

Verse
Sitting in darkness, they saw a great Light.
They embraced the Truth, then fled their deep night.
What human wisdom failed to resolve in their mind,
They were forever changed when within the Light shined.

His Presence Makes the Difference

The Word

And the name of the city from that time on shall be, "The Lord Is There."
Ezekiel 48:35

As they were talking about these things,
Jesus himself stood among them.
Luke 24:36

Voice from the Church

"It is a great thing to be a listener. You want something for your soul, you want help. I don't want a great sermon. I want to feel the presence of God—that I am worshipping him, and considering something great and glorious. If I do get that I do not care how poor the sermon is." (Martyn Lloyd-Jones, 1899-1981)*

Reflection

I'm presently in my fifth decade of Christian ministry. Throughout this span I have witnessed many beautiful places of worship and listened to a host of delightful and edifying sermons. But what sticks in my mind to this day is neither great edifices of architectural wonder, nor the sermons which evidenced much study. What I still exult in are those houses of worship and messengers of the gospel which were saturated with the presence of the Holy One of Israel. One cannot easily forget a man or woman who walked on holy ground.

As creatures of God, we were made to have an appreciation for aesthetics—the beautiful things of life, such as attractive buildings. And we should admire a man who studies hard in sermon preparation. But what use is a beautifully designed building and a well-planned sermon, if the God of glory does not fill both? Unless the risen Christ shows up, all the rest is for naught.

Verse

As they walked along that one bleak day,
Their hearts were troubled, filled with dismay.
Then a Stranger suddenly came near;
Their hearts were warmed, for Jesus was there.

Anxiety (1)

The Word
> [6]*Humble yourselves, therefore, under the mighty hand of God so that at the proper time he may exalt you,* [7]*casting all your anxieties on him, because he cares for you.*
> 1 Peter 5:6-7

Voice from the Church
"The very act of casting our cares upon the Lord often changes them. In the village of Bethany, Martha was preparing dinner for Christ and his disciples. She was distracted with the concerns of a hostess, and resented the fact that her sister Mary was listening to Jesus instead of helping her. When she complained, Jesus gently rebukes her. In her anxiety about the many dishes of the dinner, she had forgotten the one serving that counted, the serving that Mary had chosen." (Edmund Clowney, 1917-2005)*

Reflection
We all have experienced mental sensations of anxiety from lesser to greater degrees. A mother may feel anxiety, as she waves goodbye to her child, leaving for the first day of school. Then, there is a husband, sitting by the bed of his dying wife, wondering what the future may hold for him, as he contemplates a future without her. Feelings of fear and apprehension may cover the breadth of one's life, including finances, job security, relationships, illness, death, and so much more.

What should we do when we begin to feel anxious about a matter? We have a sure Word from God: "Cast your anxiety once and for all upon the Lord!" How can we do this? Because the Word informs us, "He cares for you"! Placing your anxiety upon the Lord Jesus may not change the situation, but it will change *you*. Oh, the peace that Jesus gives amid every emotional pain.

Verse
All your anxiety, all your care,
Bring to the mercy seat, leave it there,
Never a burden He cannot bear,
Never a friend like Jesus! (Edward H. Joy, 1871-1949)**

Anxiety (2)

The Word
>⁶*Humble yourselves, therefore, under the mighty hand of*
>*God so that at the proper time he may exalt you, ⁷casting*
>*all your anxieties on him, because he cares for you.*
>1 Peter 5:6-7

Voice from the Church
"Where on the surface we may show a brave and even beautiful front to the world, down below may lie a whole host of fears and formidable fantasies. It is these unexpressed thoughts, impulses, and various imaginations which can wreak havoc with our health.... We may not even be aware that fears, anxieties, worry, and tension are nourished by the deep, innermost attitudes of the subconscious mind." (W. Phillip Keller, 1920-1997)*

Reflection
In the above text, there are two different Greek words used for "anxieties" and "cares." The word rendered "anxieties" simply means what we understand by the term: "a fear or dread about what may happen; a painful uneasiness of mind, usually over an impending ill." The cause of the anxiety may be real or imagined. On the other hand, the word rendered "cares"—"he *cares* for you"—means "to feel and experience genuine concern for a person or situation."

While the Christian may undergo anxiety about any number of things, he is not to carry these feelings. When such negative attitudes approach, he must learn to immediately "cast" them on his Mediator and Great High Priest, remembering that he "cares for you"—cares enough to carry your load. We need to learn to take our burden to the Lord and leave it there, as the Philadelphia pastor Charles A. Tindley exhorted us to do.

Verse
Leave it there, leave it there,
Take your burden to the Lord and leave it there;
If you trust and never doubt, He will surely bring you out.
Take your burden to the Lord and leave it there. (Charles A. Tindley, 1851-1933)**

Fishers of Men

The Word
> [16]*Passing alongside the Sea of Galilee, he saw Simon*
> *and Andrew the brother of Simon casting a net into*
> *the sea, for they were fishermen.* [17]*And Jesus said to them,*
> *"Follow me, and I will make you become fishers of men."*
> [18]*And immediately they left their nets and followed him.*
> Mark 1:16-18

Voice from the Church
"A friend of mine started keeping guinea pigs in his sixties. He was not an old fool, though some people suspected he was; he was a keen church school teacher. He had tried, and tried again, to win a boy in his class, but could make no close contact with him. Then he learned that the lad kept guinea pigs, and he took up the same hobby to tunnel a way to his heart." (W. E. Sangster, 1900-1960)*

Reflection
To engage in the task of introducing people to the Lord Jesus Christ, and persuading them to follow the Master, is not easy work. Since all people are born with a sinful propensity, with their back turned away from God, the witness for Christ must be filled with love and wisdom to be a successful fisher of men. While some are called to this ministry as a vocational service, most of us are little lights, pointing men and women to the Supreme Light of the world.

The new convert often falls into the trap of copying another person's methods, in seeking to win people to Christ. He will soon learn, however, that God will lead him to skillfully use his own gifts, and provide him with unique wisdom, in leading individuals to Christ. Each Christian is different, and each person we seek to win is different.

Verse
They were born and bred to be fishermen.
One eventful day, the Great Fisherman
  called, "Follow me, and I will make you be-
  come fishers of men." They followed; He did.

"All Things to All people"

The Word

[21] *To those outside the law I became as one outside the law (not being outside the law of God but under the law of Christ) that I might win those outside the law.* [22] *To the weak I became weak, that I might win the weak. I have become all things to all people, that by all means I might save some.*
1 Corinthians 9:21-22

Voice from the Church

"It is not enough ... to occasionally drop into another individual's world, preach to him, and go our way. Somehow, he needs to be brought into our world as well. If he isn't, the view he gets of us is so fragmented he could miss the total picture. He doesn't see the effects the grace of God has had in our day-to-day lives." (Jim Petersen, n.d.)*

Reflection

Not all Christians are called to be evangelists any more than all Christians are called to be vocational pastors. However, all Christians are called to be a light for Christ in this present evil world: "You are the light of the world" (Matt. 5:14).

Just as some men will study to develop skills to be effective fishermen, so those who are passionate about Christ will seek to study people, seeking the wisdom of God to be an effective witness to the glory of Christ.

We are neither called to compromise the gospel nor our witness in seeking to win people for Christ. However, the Spirit will reveal to us creative ways in developing relationships with those people he is drawing to Christ. In reaching people for Christ, we are called to be "wise as serpents and innocent as doves" (Matt. 10:16).

Verse

Rescue the perishing, duty demands it.
Strength for thy labor the Lord will provide;
Back to the narrow way patiently win them,
Tell the poor wanderer a Savior has died. (Fanny Crosby, 1820-1915)**

"Tell It to Jesus"

The Word
But the woman, knowing what had happened to her, came in fear and trembling and fell down before him and told him the whole truth.
Mark 5:33

Voice from the Church
"When we calmly reflect upon the fact that the progress of our Lord's Kingdom is dependent upon prayer, it is sad to think that we give so little time to the holy exercise." (E. M. Bounds, 1835-1913)*

Reflection
There is an old gospel song that one rarely hears anymore, which was written by Pastor Jeremiah Rankin (1828-1904); the title is "Tell It to Jesus." As a member of the human family, and a pastor as well, Rankin had learned that regardless of one's need, we can "Tell It to Jesus." That sounds rather quaint and simplistic, doesn't it? And yet, that is the essence of prayer: telling everything to our Father, through Christ our Mediator.

In his song, Rankin asks his singing audience eight questions: "Are you weary, are you heavyhearted?" "Are you grieving over joys departed?" "Do the tears flow down your cheeks unbidden?" "Have you sins that to men's eyes are hidden?" "Do you fear the gath'ring clouds of sorrow?" "Are you anxious what shall be tomorrow?" "Are you troubled at the thought of dying?" "For Christ's coming kingdom are you sighing?" He ends each verse with the refrain, "Tell it to Jesus alone." What a comfort to know that we can tell our God—everything, just as the woman in the above text of Scripture!

Dear child of God, what is it that you need to tell Jesus today? Be assured: he hears, and he cares. "Tell it to Jesus."

Verse
Tell it to Jesus, tell it to Jesus,
He is a friend that's well-known;
You've no other such a friend or brother,
Tell it to Jesus alone. (Jeremiah E. Rankin, 1828-1904)**

Christ is Everything

The Word

> ^{20}My confident hope is that I will in no way be ashamed
> but that with complete boldness, even now as always,
> Christ will be exalted in my body, whether I live or die.
> ^{21}For to me, living is Christ and dying is gain.
> Philippians 1:20-21 NET

Voice from the Church

"Andrew Bonar at the end of his sketch of Samuel Rutherford: 'Oh for his insatiable desires Christward! Oh for ten such men in Scotland to stand in the gap!—men who all day long find nothing but Christ to rest in, whose very sleep is pursuing after Christ in dreams.'" (John Stott, 1921-2011)*

Reflection

If you're like me, you are truly blessed to know, or to have known, at least a few Christians who demonstrate a passionate love for the Lord Jesus Christ. Such believers belong to "The Fellowship of Burning Hearts." Their personalities vary, as well as their backgrounds, but one thing sets them apart from all others: They live a sanctified life; they live to the glory of God; they continually abide in the Vine; while they live *in* the world they are not *of* the world; they are filled with a "joy inexpressible and full of glory"; they are more familiar with their Father in heaven than their closest earthly relative; they are neither self-righteousness nor condescending toward others; they are quick to confess their failures when they are wrong or have sinned; they show a genuine concern for others, and take confidential prayer requests seriously; they are transparently honest and without guile; they are totally human and singularly Christian in all they do; they haven't *arrived*, but are pressing forward and upward. To these saints—Christ is everything!

Verse

His name yields the sweetest perfume,
And sweeter than music His voice;
His presence disperses my gloom,
And makes all within me rejoice. (John Newton, 1725-1807)**

Knowing and Doing

The Word

[15] "*For I have given you an example, that you also should do just as I have done to you.* [16]*Truly, truly, I say to you, a servant is not greater than his master, nor is a messenger greater than the one who sent him.* [17]*If you know these things, blessed are you if you do them.*"

John 13:15-17

Voice from the Church

"Throughout Jesus' teaching these two words *know* and *do* occur constantly, and always in that order. We cannot do until we know, but we can know without doing. The house built on the rock is the house of the man who knows and does. The house built on the sand is the house of the man who knows but does not do." (Francis Schaeffer, 1912-1984)*

Reflection

During his earthly ministry, our Lord continually reminded the religious hierarchy, his disciples and the crowds, that being exposed to biblical truth is not the same as obeying God's words. The Lord Jesus taught his hearers, that those who are blessed by God are not those who *know* the truth of God, but those who *obey* the truth of God.

Many Bible studies and pulpit messages concentrate on the dissemination of biblical truth, without emphasizing the need to obey and apply the same. Information without practical obedience is both dangerous and worthless. We need orthopraxy as well as orthodoxy.

Years ago, when C. T. Studd (1860-1931) and F. B. Meyer (1847-1929) were travelling together, Meyer saw Studd on his knees, turning the pages of the Gospels. Meyer asked Studd, "What are you doing, Charlie?" Studd replied, "I'm reviewing Jesus' commands, and seeing if there are any I'm not obeying." We should repeatedly do the same.

Verse

They walked away, thinking how great
  was the truth they had just heard.
Then, one heard a Voice speaking,
  "Blessed are those who obey my word."

"Jesus, Priceless Treasure"

The Word
> [45] "Again, the kingdom of heaven is like a merchant
> in search of fine pearls, [46]who, on finding one pearl of
> great value, went and sold all that he had and bought it."
> Matthew 13:45-46

Voice from the Church
"A true Christian is a spiritual merchant, that seeks and finds this pearl of price; that does not take up with any thing short of an interest in Christ, and, as one that is resolved to be spiritually rich, trades high. He went and bought that pearl; did not only bid for it, but purchased it. What will it avail us to know Christ, if we do not know him as ours?" (Matthew Henry, 1662-1714)*

Reflection
It is amazing, indeed, the length to which men will go in search of treasure. From spending a few dollars, with the hope of winning a lottery, to investing millions of dollars in exploring for lost treasures in the sea, mankind will do almost anything to gain wealth.

What do you value most? Seriously, what is it you deem your greatest treasure—family? health? property? nature? friends? Johann Franck (1618-1677) considered all the above and came to the right conclusion. He wrote: "Jesus, priceless Treasure, / Fount of purest pleasure." Then he went on to personally testify, "Jesus is my Pleasure, / Jesus is my Choice. / Hence, all empty glory!" What a testimony!

To purchase the "Pearl of Great Price," one must "sell" everything he considers dear to experience the riches of God's inestimable Treasure, the Lord Jesus Christ. Having discovered this *Pearl*, you will then say with Andrew of old, "We have found the Messiah" (John 1:41).

Verse
Though the storms may gather, ...
Yea, whate'er I here must bear,
Thou art still my purest Pleasure,
Jesus, priceless Treasure! (Johann Franck, 1618-1677)**

Being Authentic

The Word

> *"Teacher, we know that you are true and teach*
> *the way of God truthfully, and you do not care about*
> *Anyone's opinion, for you are not swayed by appearances."*
> Matthew 22:16

Voice from the Church

"What I often pray with depth of earnest longing is this: O Lord, don't let me be veneer. Please make me solid oak. If I am cut, may I be the same all through. May I be solid brass, not a coating outside. Help me to be real in my love for You. May it be solid silver that is also being refined." (Edith Schaeffer, 1914-2013)*

Reflection

It has been over 35 years ago that I heard a renowned preacher lament, "I'm afraid we too often sell ourselves for more than we're worth." I've never forgotten those words. What was he saying? Simply this: That fallen man is susceptible to presently himself to others what he knows he is not. We want others to think the best of us, even if what they're seeing is not a true representation of who we are.

Such was the basic plague of Phariseeism in Jesus' day. These men were so consumed by their external righteousness, while neglecting internal holiness: "Now you Pharisees cleanse the outside of the cup and of the dish, but inside you are full of greed and wickedness" (Luke 11:39).

The more prideful we are, the more concerned we become with appearances. This is not to suggest that appearance is unimportant; however, what we appear to others should reflect our true selves. To be *sincere*, is to live transparently before God and authentically with others.

Verse

The fire will reveal whether we
* were made of gold or dust.*
If we lived for appearances,
* there's nothing left but crust.*

A Timely Warning

The Word

"Remember Lot's wife."
Luke 17:32

Voice from the Church
"She [Lot's wife] ... became a monument of Divine displeasure, and of her own folly and sin. It is a proof that we have loved with a *criminal* affection that which we leave with grief and anxiety, though commanded by the Lord to abandon it." (Adam Clarke, 1760-1832)*

Reflection
When we fail to seriously reflect upon our Lord's admonitions and warnings, we do so to our own soul's peril. When the Lord Jesus admonished his hearers to "Remember Lot's wife," he wasn't addressing *outsiders*, he was speaking to *insiders*—his own disciples. That's you and me.

Jesus was teaching his followers about impending Judgment and used Sodom and Lot's wife as illustrations of the certainly of future Judgment, the need to make necessary preparations to escape God's wrath, and that we should be on our guard against turning back (looking back).

This terse warning—"Remember Lot's wife"—is one of the shortest texts in Scripture, yet one of the most pungent. If God tells his people to remember something, we do well to often refresh our memories about what it is we are to remember.

Lot and his daughters escaped Sodom—so did his wife. However, upon barely making their escape, the wife and mother looked back, which all were told not to do: "Escape for your life. Do not look back or stop anywhere in the valley" (Gen. 19:17). Lot's wife looked back and immediately became a pillar of salt. Where are you looking?

Verse
It seemed to be such a minor thing—
    looking back from where she came.
But she was informed not to do so;
    Jesus warned the very same.

The Right *Look*

The Word

*¹Therefore, since we are surrounded by so great a cloud of witnesses,
let us also lay aside every weight, and sin which clings so closely,
and let us run with endurance the race that is set before us,
²looking to Jesus, the founder and perfecter of our faith, who for
the joy that was set before him endured the cross, despising
the shame, and is seated at the right hand of the throne of God.*
Hebrews 12:1-2

Voice from the Church

"There is life in a look, and power too; the life and power of a divine transformation, in which, as we behold, we are changed into the same image from glory to glory." (Andrew Murray, 1828-1917)*

Reflection

In Lot's wife, we have an example and a warning from Jesus not to look back to the world from which we were delivered. In the Letter to the Hebrews, we are exhorted by the Spirit to fix our eyes on our Lord and Leader: "looking to Jesus, the founder and perfecter of our faith."

Christians should not assume they are *safe,* because at one point in time they left the world of Sodom. All the Bible's exhortations for believers to persevere, and to stay spiritually awake, are meaningless unless it is possible for us to defect from the faith. To have at one time embraced the Word of God with joy is no guarantee that we will escape the Judgment of God (see the Parable of the Seed and Sower).

The grace of God *in* us must cooperate with the grace of God *for* us. God saves no one finally who obstinately refuses to cooperate with his grace ongoingly. We are to maintain a steadfast gaze on our Lord and Savior, empowered by his indwelling Spirit.

Verse

*He thought he would run the far race,
  with weights and sin loading him down.
But in laying them all aside,
  he looked Up; his feet did abound.*

The Presence of Power

The Word

> *One day He was teaching; and there were some Pharisees*
> *and teachers of the law sitting there, who had come from every*
> *village of Galilee and Judea and from Jerusalem; and the*
> *power of the Lord was present for Him to perform healing.*
> Luke 5:17 NASB

Voice from the Church

"I think it is fair to note that if there is one thing that differentiates the early church from its twentieth-century counterpart it is the level of awareness and experience of the presence and power of the Holy Spirit." (Gordon D. Fee, b. 1934)*

Reflection

There are two words in the Greek language (in which the NT was originally written) which we often confuse: "authority" and "power." The first word means (as in the case of Jesus) the delegated right to govern and rule; the latter word means the ability and energy to perform. In Matthew 28:18, Jesus announced to his apostles, "All authority in heaven and on earth has been given to me." In the above text, Luke notes, "the power of the Lord was present for Him to perform healing."

It must be observed, that while Jesus was given authority by his Father to perform many signs and miracles during his earthly ministry, the *power* to perform such was often withheld and restricted, because of a lack of obedience and faith on the part of his hearers. An example of this is noted by Matthew, "And he did not do many mighty works there, because of their unbelief" (Matt. 13:58).

It takes the active presence of God among us, or him to accomplish his will and purposes.

Verse

The Lord Himself walked among them,
* to heal inside and throughout.*
But some refused His truth and words,
* thus unchanged because of doubt.*

Bitterness

The Word

[14]Strive for peace with everyone, and for the holiness without which no one will see the Lord.[15]See to it that no one fails to obtain the grace of God; that no "root of bitterness" springs up and causes trouble, and by it many become defiled.
Hebrews 12:134-15

Voice from the Church

"When personal relations go wrong, in nine cases out of ten immediate action will mend them; but if that immediate action is not taken, they will continue to deteriorate, and the bitterness will spread in an ever-widening circle." (William Barclay, 1907-1978)*

Reflection

I've met a few bitter people across the years, some of which were Christians. I realize it sounds a bit odd, doesn't it, that a follower of the Lord Jesus would become embittered? However, many of us have witnessed this sad occurrence, if not experienced it ourselves.

In the Body of Christ, if a person allows himself, there are plenty of *natural* reasons for a person to become infected with a bitter spirit. We have all been sinned against—more than once—by our brothers and sisters in Christ. But how do we handle the offenses when they come?

Bitterness begins, like a physical wound, with a wounded spirit, then that wound is allowed to fester; it becomes rawer by the day. We become obsessed with what was said and done to us.

Esau became a bitter person; he had been wronged by his brother and his mother and was disappointed in his father. For twenty years, Esau and Jacob were estranged, until God met Jacob and Jacob met God in a fresh experience of grace. Christian, guard against bitterness!

Verse

She was deeply wounded in her spirit;
The hurt was real and most severe.
But she went to her knees to God in prayer—
Balm was given; God met her there.

The Spirit Makes the Difference

The Word

And with great power the apostles were giving their testimony to the resurrection of the Lord Jesus, and great grace was upon them all.

Acts 4:33

Voice from the Church

"Our generation is rapidly losing its grip upon the supernatural; and as a consequence the pulpit is rapidly dropping to the level of the platform. And this decline is due, we believe, more than anything else, to an ignoring of the Holy Spirit as the supreme inspirer of preaching." (A. J. Gordon, 1936-1895)*

Reflection

I wish every pulpit which preaches "grace, grace, grace" would be equally filled with the power of the Holy Spirit. Of the early church, the writer Luke personally witnessed, "and great grace was upon them all." Where there is "great grace" there will be "great power" upon the God's ministering servants, as there was with the apostles.

Lamentably, much of the contemporary church possesses everything but the power of the Spirit. We have nicely designed church buildings, many professionally trained musicians, seminary educated pastors, and busily engaged lay people, but how often do we leave a church service believing that the Lord Jesus has appeared—in edifying, convicting, encouraging, converting power?

It has been asked by concerned Christians, "If the Holy Spirit were removed from our church, would anyone notice the difference in the church's ongoing operations?"

The first-century church would have noticed, for there would have been no church without the Spirit. What about ours?

Verse

When he stood to preach the Truth of God,
A power rested on him from above.
The people experienced great grace,
For there was the presence of the Dove.

The Weeping Christ

The Word
> [41]And when he drew near and saw the city, he wept over it, [42]saying, "Would that you, even you, had known on this day the things that make for peace! But now they are hidden from your eyes."
> Luke 19:42-43

Voice from the Church
"At Nimes, Étienne de Grellet was once speaking to a group of eighty concerning 'the great love of God to us through our blessed Redeemer,' when officers and gendarmes entered to arrest him. With the others, they were constrained by his words 'to bend the knee with tears and prayers to the Lord God and to the Lamb,' and returned to the prefect saying that they had never heard one speak in such a fashion before." (S. D. Gordon, 1859-1936)*

Reflection
Tears are shed for a variety of reasons: grief and sorrow, anger and frustration, joy and happiness, agony and defeat. For the Son of Man, tears were shed over the loss of a friend (Lazarus); as he underwent extreme agony (in the Garden); and when he looked upon his sacred and favored homeland, that would be destroyed within forty years: they will "tear you down to the ground, you and your children within you. And they will not leave one stone upon another in you" (Luke 19:44).

An evangelist once told me that years earlier he had asked the Lord to give him tears. He then said, "Be careful what you ask for." I never heard him preach but what at some point during the message he wept.

Jesus wept over the city of David because "you did not know the time of your visitation" (Luke 19:44). Have you ever shed tears because people were rejecting the gospel of peace? Jesus did.

Verse
He came all the way from Heaven—
God's Son, proclaiming good news.
His own city turned Him away.
He wept; they held to their views.

God's Greatest Miracles

The Word
The believers in Macedonia and in Achaia ... report concerning
us the kind of reception we had among you, and how you
turned to God from idols to serve the living and true God.
1 Thessalonians 1:7b, 9

Voice from the Church
"The Church is called to live above her own ability. She is called to live on a plane so high that no human being can live like that in his own ability and power. The humblest Christian is called to live a miracle, a life that is a moral and spiritual life with such intensity and such purity that no human can do it—only Jesus Christ can do it. He wants the Spirit of Christ to come to His people. This afflatus, this invasion from above affects us mentally, morally, and spiritually." (A. W. Tozer, 1897-1963)*

Reflection
Excepting the Incarnation and Resurrection of Jesus Christ, the great miracle the Almighty God performs among his creation is the miracle of a changed life. This miracle of grace is greater than the creation of all God's physical creative acts, because it transforms fallen, moral beings, who were originally made in the image of God, into forgiven, sanctified children of our Father in heaven.

These transformed trophies of God's grace will in a future Day be placed on display for the entire universe to behold: "For it was fitting that he, for whom and by whom all things exist, in bringing many sons to glory" (Heb. 2:10); "Let us rejoice and exult and give him the glory, for the marriage of the Lamb has come, and his Bride has made herself ready" (Rev. 19:7).

Are you one of God's miracles? Have you made yourself ready?

Verse
Some were seeking for signs and wonders;
Some sought food, lasting but a day.
But when Jesus transformed great sinners,
Joy came that never went away.

When Salvation Comes Home

The Word
> [9]And Jesus said to him, "Today salvation has come
> to this house, since he also is a son of Abraham.
> [10]For the Son of Man came to seek and to save the lost."
> Luke 19:9-10

Voice from the Church
"In his seventeenth year, my father passed through a crisis of religious experience, and from that day he openly and decidedly followed the Lord Jesus. Every morning and evening, even to the last day of his life, a portion of Scripture was read, his voice was heard softly joining in the psalm, and his lips breathed the morning and evening prayer, falling in sweet benediction on the heads of all his children, many of them far way over all the earth, but all meeting him there at the throne of grace." (John G. Paton, 1824-1907)*

Reflection
No human being can estimate the future value to this world, of the person who has passed from the darkness of sin into the ineffable light of our merciful Father's pure holiness. When salvation comes to a home, whether it occurs in Jericho (as in the case of Zacchaeus), or in Scotland (as in the case of John G. Paton), or in the reader's home—that person's influence will affect every future generation for good, as each succeeding generation embraces the Lord Jesus.

Twenty-one centuries later, we are still reading about the change that came to a man and his household, because a God-thirsty son of Abraham sought to see Jesus of Nazareth, who had first sought to see him. Has Jesus been welcomed into your home. Has salvation come to your house? Jesus always makes a difference when he enters a heart and a home.

Verse
Living here with my Lord in a holy union,
Day by day, all the way holding sweet communion;
O what change grace hath wrought in my lowly station!
Since my soul has received full and free salvation. (Haldor Lillenas, 1885-1959)**

"Outsiders"

The Word

^{5}Walk in wisdom toward outsiders, making the best use of the time.
^{6}Let your speech always be gracious, seasoned with salt, so
that you may know how you ought to answer each person.
Colossians 4:5-6

Voice from the Church

"[The Colossians'] regular intercourse with unbelievers is to be governed by *wisdom*. This is no mirror human wisdom that comes from above. Indeed, as Paul has already stated, Christ is the source of this wisdom, and so, as the believer is in Christ, he is in touch with the wisdom which can guide his steps." (Herbert M. Carson, b. 1956)*

Reflection

The *English Standard Version* translators rendered the Greek word (*exó*) as "outsiders" in the above text. They use the same translation in four additional occurrences (1 Cor. 5:12, 14:23; 1 Thess. 4:12; 1 Tim. 3:7).

In our text, Paul expresses his concern as to how Christians should behave in the presence of nonbelievers ("outsiders"). We should listen to the Spirit's concern about this matter.

The Christian must have a significant relationship with "outsiders," if he is to be a "light." We cannot win people to Christ without interacting with them. On the other hand, in our contact with "outsiders," we must use "wisdom," lest their influence on us taints our influence for Christ toward them, thereby diminishing our witness.

In eating with sinners, we can be sure the Lord Jesus never laughed at their vulgar jokes, nor complained about people, events, and the providence of God. The Son of Man was both wise and winsome toward "outsiders." Those walking in the Spirit will do likewise.

Verse

We cannot be an effective witness for Christ,
    without showing God's sincere love toward people.
But be careful in the presence of "outsiders,"
    lest you grieve the Spirit, stooping to their level.

Unity of the Spirit

The Word

[1]I therefore, a prisoner for the Lord, urge you to walk in a manner worthy of the calling to which you have been called, [2]with all humility and gentleness, with patience, bearing with one another in love, [3]eager to maintain the unity of the Spirit in the bond of peace.
Ephesians 4:1-3

Voice from the Church

"I believe that in the present divided state of Christendom, those who are at the heart of each division are all closer to one another than those who are at the fringes." (C. S. Lewis, 1898-1963)*

Reflection

Church tensions and conflicts are as old as the church itself. From Acts 6—when the Hellenistic widows complained about failing to be cared for—to the present day, relating to one another in truth and love is the ongoing challenge of every Christian.

Some conflicts are serious, with rippling consequences. For example, in its early days, the church was about to be torn apart over the question of whether Gentiles were obligated to observe ceremonial Jewish ordinances (see Acts 15). For the most part, that issue was resolved to everyone's satisfaction.

Truth, humility, gentleness, and patience are the necessary ingredients in maintaining "the unity of the Spirit in the bond of peace." When any one of these graces is absent in the heart and life of a local church, dissension and estrangements are bound to occur.

There can only be true unity where there is the presence of biblical truth. We must cling to the truth of the gospel, but let's not trample underfoot our brothers and sisters in Christ while doing so.

Verse

Blest be the tie that binds
Our hearts in Christian love;
The fellowship of kindred minds
Is like to that above. (John Fawcett, 1739-1817)**

Forgiven

The Word

*And behold, some people brought to him a paralytic, lying
on a bed. And when Jesus saw their faith, he said to the
paralytic, "Take heart, my son; your sins are forgiven."*
Matthew 9:2

Voice from the Church

"Jesus Christ in his providence has placed me among you, that if I only
pass you on the street, you may have proof before your eyes of his gracious declaration, 'All manner of sin and blasphemy shall be forgiven to
men for the Son of man's sake.'" (John Newton, 1725-1807)*

Reflection

The sweetest words ever heard by a sinner during our Lord's earthly
ministry were these: "Your sins are forgiven." And it remains the same
today.

Guilt-laden, heavily burdened by the load he carries, when a man receives our merciful God's pardoning grace, it is cause for rejoicing. We
are told that even the angels of heaven rejoice when the lost has been
found.

It has been my privilege through the years to observe a wide variety
of people who have experienced God's forgiveness. I think of an alcoholic, an exotic dancer, a soldier, a company secretary, a country singer,
children and teenagers, a wealthy man in his eighties, a young carpenter,
and on and on I could go.

When a person is assured of God's forgiveness, when he or she realizes their sinful past has been wiped clean, words cannot describe what
one feels. How can we adequately describe a death to life event, a lost
and found experience? Forgiveness! Amazing grace!

Verse

Guilty I stand before Thy face;
On me I feel Thy wrath abide.
'Tis just the sentence should take place;
'Tis just—but O Thy Son hath died! (Charles Wesley, 1707-1788)**

Looking Outward

The Word

> [19]*I hope in the Lord Jesus to send Timothy to you soon, so that I too may be cheered by news of you.* [20]*For I have no one like him, who will be genuinely concerned for your welfare.* [21]*For they all seek their own interests, not those of Jesus Christ.*
> Philippians 2:19-21

Voice from the Church

"If there is any one message all our psychopagan prophets insist on, it is that we must love ourselves. But if there is any one message that Jesus and all his saints insist on, it is that we must deny ourselves. In Christ's psychology, the absolute oxymoron is 'St. Self.'" (Peter Kreeft, 1937)*

Reflection

Ever since the Great Fall, man has been born with a heart and mind turned inward. The history of the human family is a record of tragedy after tragedy because of this innate bent—a preoccupation with our wants and supposed needs. From the self-centered driver on the highway, to the political despot ruling the lives of millions, sinful self-interests have wreaked havoc on our planet.

It is only through our merciful God's regenerating and sanctifying grace, operating freely in the lives of receptive people, that man can be adequately programmed by the Spirit to look lovingly outward instead of selfishly inward.

Christians who have not allowed the Spirit of Christ to fully cleanse and conquer their self-centered disposition, and who fail to keep closely attached to the Vine, can cause repeated damage in their relationships. Their natural default mode to selfishness will often rise to the surface in testing times. To follow Christ is to forsake ourselves.

Verse

He came into our world to do His Father's will,
Leaving the glories of Heaven behind.
We will never fulfill our Father's plan for us,
By serving ourselves instead of mankind.

Our Supreme Example

The Word

*[7]For one will scarcely die for a righteous person—though perhaps
for a good person one would dare even to die— [8]but God shows
his love for us in that while we were still sinners, Christ died for us.*
Romans 5:7-8

Voice from the Church

"Sent as a young man of 19 to visit the capital cities of Europe, in order
to complete his education, [Count Nikolaus von Zinzendorf] found himself one day in the art gallery of Düsseldorf. He stood before Domenico
Feti's *Ecce Homo*, in which Christ is portrayed as wearing the crown of
thorns, and under it which the inscription reads: 'All this I did for thee;
what doest thou for me?' Zinzendorf was deeply convicted and challenged." (John R. W. Stott, 1921-2011)*

Reflection

Christ's self-offering on the Cross, some two thousand years ago, was
the most selfless act of love this world has witnessed. His death was not
a selfless death because he was a man; it was a most selfless death because he was the incarnate Son of God.

Many are the heroes who have given up their lives while thinking
more of others than they did about themselves. But Christ's act of self-
sacrifice was more than a heroic human act, it was an atoning sacrifice
for the ungodly by God's unique Son who gave up all his glorious innate prerogatives, making the Great Descent to this fallen world, clothing himself with the limitations of human flesh.

Even in those awful dying moments, the Lord Jesus was thinking of
others. He gave the future care of his mother into the hands of an apostle; he selflessly ministered to a condemned thief; and he prayed for the
forgiveness of those who were humanly responsible for his death. Such
is God's love!

Verse

Love so amazing, so divine,
Demands my soul, my life, my all. (Isaac Watts, 1674-1748)**

Serving Others

The Word

> *Now, brothers and sisters, you know about the*
> *household of Stephanus, that as the first converts of*
> *Achaia, they devoted themselves to ministry for the saints*
> 1 Corinthians 16:15 NET

Voice from the Church

"True Christians consider themselves as not satisfying some creditor, but as discharging a debt of gratitude. Accordingly theirs is not the stinted return of a strained obedience, but the large and liberal measure of voluntary service." (William Wilberforce, 1759-1833)*

Reflection

As followers of him who came into this world to serve others and not himself, we are likewise called to serve God by serving others. This call to serve others is not humanistic altruism. No, it is the very love of Christ indwelling and compelling the believer to selflessly consider the other person, by serving that person in the name of Jesus.

When the 120 were filled with the Spirit on the Day of Pentecost, they immediately left the prayer room for the streets of Jerusalem, proclaiming to all ethnicities "the mighty works of God" (Acts 2:11). Not all of us are called or gifted to be street preachers. However, all of God's people have been called to serve the body of Christ and others with their unique Spirit-giftedness.

Once the Holy Spirit enters to take control of our life, he is at work to decentralize our self-centered egos, purifying our heart, until we can see God more clearly and thereby see the needs of our brothers and sisters with greater clarity. If we are wrapped up in ourselves, we will always be blind to those around us.

Verse

To walk with Christ here below
* is to serve others without*
*   thinking, "What's in it for me?"*
*   This is to be a Christian.*

A Reason to Sing

The Word

"Behold, God is my salvation; I will trust,
and will not be afraid; for the Lord God is my
strength and my song, and he has become my salvation. "
Isaiah 12:2

Voice from the Church

"Many good Christians have God for their strength who have him not for their song; they walk in darkness: but light is sown for them. And those that have God for their strength ought to make him their song, that is, to give him the glory of it (see Ps. 68:35) and to take to themselves the comfort of it, for he will become their salvation." (Matthew Henry, 1662-1714)*

Reflection

The prophet was told of a Day, after God's people had returned from their transgressions and backslidings, that they would turn their eyes upon Yahweh once again. In that Day, the people of God will be fearless and unafraid, because the Lord alone would be their strength, song, and salvation.

Since the earnest of the Spirit has been given to God's people, and the kingdom of Christ is now within his people, it is our joy and privilege to walk through this world fearlessly, with a song of praise on our lips, experiencing strength and salvation through our Lord Jesus Christ.

My dear godly mother didn't have the benefits of listening to gospel music with the technology we now have. However, her days were filled with songs as she sang "psalms and hymns and spiritual songs, singing and making melody to the Lord with [her] heart" (Eph. 5:19). Let your children and grandchildren hear you praise the Lord in song.

Verse

When I failed to sense the nearness of God
in prayer, I began to sing a hymn of praise.
If we could learn this lesson as did David
long ago, joy would attend all of our days.

Armed with God's Strength

The Word

> [10]*Finally, be strong in the Lord and in the strength of his might.* [11]*Put on the whole armor of God, that you may be able to stand against the schemes of the devil.*
> Ephesians 6:11-12

Voice from the Church

"Oh, that God's children would understand that their own strength is one of their worst enemies! Could the workers in God's kingdom but see that their own power is the greatest hindrance to their bearing fruit for God!" (George Steinberger.1865-1904)*

Reflection

Will we ever learn one of the most important lessons God desires to inscribe indelibly on our hearts, that it is "Not by might, nor by power, but by my Spirit, says the Lord of hosts" (Zech. 4:6)?

How often we fail in the work of God and in our relationships, because we are strong in ourselves rather than strong in the strength of God. Like Samson of old, we go out to do battle with the enemy, not realizing that we have no strength and become a captive to the enemy.

We will never live in the strength of God without being continually aware of our own natural weaknesses and vulnerabilities. We are too presumptuous; we begin our days without waiting upon the Lord for renewed strength. And then we wonder why we fail. "They who wait for the Lord shall renew their strength; they shall mount up with wings like eagles; they shall run and not be weary; they shall walk and not faint" (Isa. 40:31).

Let us stay armed with the strength of God. Let us learn the secret of daily being renewed with the very strength of God.

Verse

Put on the Gospel armor,
And, watching unto prayer,
Where duty calls, or danger,
Be never wanting there. (George Duffield, 1818-1888)**

Word and Prayer

The Word

> [17]*Take the helmet of salvation, and the sword of*
> *the Spirit, which is the word of God,* [18]*praying at all*
> *times in the Spirit, with all prayer and supplication.*
> Ephesians 6:17-18

Voice from the Church

"As my devotional life developed, I learned that prayer brings power, but character grows through reading and obeying the Word of God—the Scriptures." (Kenneth N. Taylor, 1917-2005)*

Reflection

As I write this, there are two memories which come to mind. The first is of a trip I took with one of my mentors to a Bible conference where he was the speaker. Then well into his eighties, early in the morning this Bible scholar and preacher sat with an open Bible, and periodically looked up toward the ceiling (though I knew he was looking beyond the ceiling) in prayer. Then he would look down at the Word and read a little more. Then the routine would repeat itself.

I also think of an evangelist, who stayed in our home while conducting revival services in our local church. Walking down the hallway of our house one morning, his bedroom door being slightly open, I saw him on his knees, with an open Bible before him. He was reading the Word and praying.

The two go together—meditating upon the Word of God and praying to the God of the Word. When we learn the secret of combining these two exercises—unhurriedly—then we will have learned one of the most important lessons in our Christian walk. Nothing can defeat the child of God who arms himself with the Word and prayer.

Verse

It is not by the might of human wisdom,
Nor by the strength of our determined will,
But by the Word and power of the Spirit,
That we can take and conquer every hill.

False Prophets

The Word

"Beware of false prophets."
Matthew 7:15

Voice from the Church

"The false teachers [see Letter of Jude] were claiming to be so Spirit-filled that there was no room for law in their Christian lives. They claimed that grace was so abundant that their sin (if it must be called) provided greater occasion for it (cf. verse 4). They claimed that the salvation of the soul is what matters, and that what a man does with his body is immaterial, for it is bound to perish. Those who fussed about sexual purity seemed to them astonishingly naïve." (Michael Green, b. 1930)*

Reflection

False prophets/preachers have always been with us. What are some of the marks of false prophets?

• False prophets preach "another Gospel"—Christ plus their innovative interpretation of the Word of God.

• False prophets depart from the historical evangelical understanding of the faith—the once-for-all delivered faith.

• False prophets are full of themselves instead of being filled with the Spirit.

• False prophets attract a following to themselves, instead of making disciples of Christ; humility doesn't grace their ministry.

• False prophets inevitably refer to their "anointing," instead of pointing people to the Lamb of God.

• False prophets speak often of money; they are greedy and covetous.

• False prophets seek to build monuments to themselves, instead of ministering to the glory of God. Beware of false prophets!

Verse

The message we heard sounded almost right,
* except it didn't lead us to the Cross.*
Many were struck by a slick performance;
* Word and Spirit were absent—to our loss.*

Power to Live

The Word

> "This generation is an evil generation. It seeks for a sign,
> but no sign will be given to it except the sign of Jonah."
> Luke 11:29

Voice from the Church

"We want visible results, dramatic wonders, mighty works; and it is not always for these the Spirit of Power is given. Power may be as necessary for silence as for speech, and as mighty in obscurity as in high places. He comes to make us effective in all the Will of God. In the one Spirit there are diversities both of function and manifestation." (Samuel Chadwick, 1860-1932)*

Reflection

Those outside of Christ, as well as the spiritually immature, are invariably mesmerized by the sensational and spectacular displays of religious fervor and drama. The multitudes of Jesus' day lusted after signs and wonders: the greater the miracle, the greater the excitement. But what happened when there was no multiplication of bread and fish? How many loyal followers were at the Cross? Spirit-phenomena have periodically attended the proclamation of the Word throughout church history, especially in times of authentic revivals. However, signs and wonders are not to be sought, though the church should expect healings and answers to all kinds of prayers the righteous request.

The power of the Spirit, operating freely among God's people, will help us to overcome temptation; equip us to exercise our gifts; enable us to be faithful in all duties; empower us to rejoice always, pray without ceasing, and give thanks to our Father in every circumstance; and fill us with the very love of Christ for all people. Seek for these "signs."

Verse

When it is God who does the unusual,
*   don't be incredulous and deny.*
Our usual need is for His power today—
*   simply to walk and on Him rely.*

Our Reward

The Word

> [23] Whatever you do, work heartily, as for the Lord and not for
> men, [24] knowing that from the Lord you will receive the
> inheritance as your reward. You are serving the Lord Christ.
> Colossians 3:23-24

Voice from the Church

"I have met two classes of Christians: the proud who imagine they are humble and the humble who are afraid they are proud. There should be another class: the self-forgetful who leave the whole thing in the hands of Christ and refuse to waste any time trying to make themselves good. They will reach the goal far ahead of the rest." (A. W. Tozer, 1897-1963)*

Reflection

The disciple of the Lord Jesus fixes his gaze on his Master for his approval. To have his Lord's approval is greater than any other's, for it is his Master's commendation he ultimately seeks and not man's.

To serve others with excellence and humility is to serve our Lord. There will be occasions when the believer will not meet another's expectation, but this should never be because of an ethical or moral fault. The most noble Christians are the best employees and employers. It is these who engage in their work conscientiously and faithfully, because in the privacy of their mind they are laboring to please their Lord.

Often a Christian's witness is negated because of laziness, complaining, gossiping, and an overall lack of an excellent work ethic. Our verbal witness for Christ will have the greatest impact when others can readily see that we are a noble person on the job. Regardless how may earn an income, we must keep in mind that we are fundamentally serving our Lord. This is the greatest incentive to quality work.

Verse

He gladly performed His Father's will,
Without a thought of its outcome.
He could freely do the work of God,
Because with Him his mind was one.

The Lord our Guide

The Word
> And the Lord will guide you continually and satisfy your desire in
> scorched places and make your bones strong; and you shall be like a
> watered garden, like a spring of water, whose waters do not fail.
> Isaiah 58:11

Voice from the Church
"Clarification often comes through humble means, like writing and receiving letters, through conversations with friends, deliberately letting
the act of Lord's Day worship establish the boundaries and size of your
life. Somewhere in the midst of this prayerfulness you will make your
decision (without any guarantee that it is absolutely right). And then
God gives grace to live out what is decided." (Eugene Peterson, b. 1932)*

Reflection
Moral clarity is given to us through the written Word of God, informing
our mind and enabling us through the Spirit's strength to implement
God's imperatives for daily living. Making other critical choices (not
necessarily moral choices) is another matter: such as decisions involving
business, career, major purchases, ministry and family matters, and a
host of other important decisions.

For the person who values the Word of God and who seeks to walk
daily in fellowship with the Lord, God will often give his wisdom to us
through others. That has been my own experience. It is wise to seek
counsel from those who have knowledge and wisdom in the need you
require at a given time. Sometimes this guidance will come to us without another person's realizing he or she was God's instrument in supply-
ing the answer to our prayers. If we are on "praying ground" and are
patient, the Lord will graciously provide us with his guidance.

Verse
All the way my Savior leads me;
What have I to ask beside?
Can I doubt His tender mercy,
Who through life has been my Guide? (Fanny Crosby, 1820-1915)**

Fruit of the Spirit

The Word

[22]*But the fruit of the Spirit is love, joy, peace,
patience, kindness, goodness, faithfulness,* [23]*gentleness,
self-control; against such things there is no law.*
Galatians 5:22-23

Voice from the Church

"Concerning the "fruit of the Spirit" one should notice at once that the word "fruit" is singular; in other words, all virtue in the believer's life has but one source, namely, the Spirit. All other benefits, charismatic and moral alike, flow from the Spirit who is the primary all-inclusive gift. It is the fullness of the Spirit that evidences an abundance of fruit as manifested by the virtues." (Carl F. H. Henry, 1913-2003)*

Reflection

The Spirit of God is only allowed to produce an abundance of his fruit in and through us as we abide in the Vine, the Lord Jesus Christ (see John 15), are being continually filled with the Spirit (see Eph. 5:16) and are daily walking in the Spirit (see Gal. 5:16f).

Some of the most beautiful natural scenes we come across are those fields which are filled with acres of fruit trees, vineyards, or grain. These are all appealing to the eyes as well as enjoyable to the taste.

Fruit trees, grapevines, and corn, wheat, etc., are intended to produce a specific kind of fruit. What good is a grapevine that doesn't produce grapes—and quality grapes at that?

God intends his people to be channels through which the Holy Spirit can bear his fruit. This fruit cannot be self-produced; it can only appear as we cooperate with the Spirit as he works his will in us and as we live out his will through us.

Verse

*Being fully surrendered to the Vine,
the branch luscious fruit will bear.
But should it decide to go its own way,
It will wither and decay.*

To Whom Do You Belong?

The Word

Through [Christ] we have received grace and apostleship to bring about the obedience of faith for the sake of his name among all the nations, [6]including you who are called to belong to Jesus Christ.

Romans 1:5b-6

Voice from the Church

"And then I prayed my first real prayer. 'God, I don't know how to find You, but I'm going to try! I'm not much the way I am now, but somehow I want to give myself to You.' I didn't know how to say more, so I repeated over and over the words: *Take me.*" (Charles W. Colson, 1931-2012)*

Reflection

Many of us were asked the following questions in our traditional wedding ceremony: "Will you have this man/woman to be your husband/wife; to live together in the covenant of marriage? Will you love him/her, comfort him/her, honor and keep him/her, in sickness and in health; and, forsaking all others, be faithful to him/her as long as you both shall live?" Of course, the purpose of the questions was to elicit an unequivocal affirmative public response from both parties. The vow is supposed to discourage adultery and divorce, encouraging a lifelong commitment to each other.

Through the years, my wife Emily has written me little notes whenever I travelled. She has occasionally written, "Remember, you belong to me." It's not that she ever had cause to worry; she was simply expressing her love and our commitment to each other.

So it is in our relationship with the Lord Jesus: we "belong to Jesus Christ." We need this reminder ... often. Are you living out your identity with the Lord Jesus? To whom do you belong?

Verse

Once I belonged to another,
A slave to sin was I.
Now I belong to Christ Jesus—
None other shall now vie.

The Gift of Special Identity

The Word
> *Behold what kind of love the Father has given to us,*
> *that we should be called children of God—and we are!*
> 1 John 3:1a RIT

Voice from the Church
"And seeing of thy tender love to mankind, thou hast given thy dear and only Son to be unto us both a sacrifice for sin, and also an example of godly life, give us grace that we may always most thankfully receive this his inestimable benefit, and also daily endeavour ourselves to follow the blessed steps of his most holy life; who liveth and reigneth with thee and the Holy Ghost, ever one God, world without end. Amen." (William Burkitt, 1650-1703)*

Reflection
All people enter this world with God's imprint stamped on their moral personhood. But it is only those who have experienced God's regenerating grace who are truly children of God, and who qualify to look up and call this God "Father."

It is through our Father's demonstration of love through the Cross of his Son, the Lord Jesus Christ, that he confers upon redeemed sinners a special identity—"children of God." We have been given this new identity because of his love for us: "In this is love, not that we have loved God but that he loved us and sent his Son to be the propitiation for our sins" (1 John 4:10).

"Behold what kind of love the Father has given to us ..." This love is a special quality of love; it is the Father's benevolent gift bestowed upon repentant sinners; the gift he has bestowed is the gift of a new identity— "children of God"!

Verse
Of all the gifts we have received,
To be called a "child of God" is
A wonder our Father conceived—
Given to those who have believed.

Crossed Hands

The Word

> [13] And Joseph took them both, Ephraim in his right hand
> toward Israel's left hand, and Manasseh in his left hand
> toward Israel's right hand, and brought them near him.
> [14] And Israel stretched out his right hand and laid it on the head
> of Ephraim, who was the younger, and his left hand on the head
> of Manasseh, crossing his hands (for Manasseh was the firstborn).
>
> Genesis 48:13-14

Voice from the Church

"Sudden reversals come to us all—to wean us from confidence in men
and things; to stay us from building our nest on any earth-grown tree; to
force us to root ourselves in God alone." (F. B. Meyer, 1847-1929)*

Reflection

Disappointments are the result of unfulfilled expectations. In the above
Genesis 48 narrative, both Joseph (the father) and Manasseh (the
firstborn) experienced a painful disappointment and confusion. This was
because the firstborn son was to receive the greater blessing; instead, it
was conferred upon Ephraim.

How often God's children wrestle with our Father's providential will.
Since the human family is under the curse, because of our first parents'
sin, pain and suffering will be our lot. Furthermore, God will often take
his children by unexpected route, as he did with Israel on their journey
toward Canaan. His ways are higher than our ways.

Sometimes God will lead us to pray that a circumstance should be
changed; other times, he will lead us to bear and embrace a bitter disappointment, enabling us to eventually rejoice in his wisdom. However
God leads us, his mercy and peace will go with us.

Verse

Though sorrows befall us and Satan oppose,
God leads His dear children along;
Through grace we can conquer, defeat all our foes,
God leads His dear children along. (George A. Young, 1855-1935)**

"In Pains and Pleasures"

The Word

⁹"On the left hand when he is working, I do not behold him; he turns to the right hand, but I do not see him. ¹⁰But he knows the way that I take; when he has tried me, I shall come out as gold. ¹¹My foot has held fast to his steps; I have kept his way and have not turned aside."
Job 23:9-11

Voice from the Church

"Let all our employment be to know God; the more one knows Him, the more one desires to know Him. And as knowledge is commonly the measure of love, the deeper and more extensive our knowledge shall be, the greater will be our love; and if our love of God were great, we should love Him equally in pains and pleasures." (Brother Lawrence, 1614-1691)*

Reflection

When a disciple of the Lord Jesus Christ cannot see, yet believes, it is the highest expression of faith and knowledge of God. To love God, without seeking explanations why frowning providences have befallen us, is a mirror into the heart and life of a mature believer.

What more could the patriarch Job have undergone than he did? With the loss of material wealth, death of his children, opposition from his wife, and the severe attack on his body, this human monument of righteousness and humility maintained both his integrity and Yahweh's approval.

Job knew God; God knew Job. Those who have an intimate walk with their Father in heaven, though their faith be battered and bruised, will remain standing in the by God's grace, because of the faithful God who has made them strong in their weak places. Are you like Job, with your foot holding fast to God's steps while wading through tough times?

Verse

I kept to the path when the sun was bright,
But then came a storm in the black of night.
I was tossed to and fro, with little light.
When I thought I would fall, He held me tight.

Ultimate Devotion

The Word

> *"If anyone comes to me and does not hate his own father*
> *and mother and wife and children and brothers and sisters,*
> *yes, and even his own life, he cannot be my disciple."*
> Luke 14:26

Voice from the Church

"In words which can still bring tears to the eyes, St. Augustine describes the desolation into which the death of his friend Nebridius plunged him (*Confessions* IV, 10). Then he draws a moral. This is what comes, he says, of giving one's heart to anything but God. All human beings pass away. Do not let your happiness depend on something you may lose. If love is to be a blessing, not a misery, it must be for the only Beloved who will never pass away." (C. S. Lewis, 1898-1963)*

Reflection

We cannot truly follow Christ while glancing back over our shoulder, hankering after lesser loves. To possess a divided heart is to be loyal to neither object of one's affection and attention. According to the apostle James, the with a double mind needs to purify his heart (see James 4:8).

To have an affectionate attachment for another person is both natural and normal (within a Christian ethic). Jesus loved Lazarus; the apostle Paul often wept over those he cared deeply for. Without fond feelings toward people we truly care about, we are nothing but sterile, cold automata. The challenge for the Christian is to always see to it that his affection for another human being does not interfere with his devotion for the Lord Jesus Christ. Loving God/Christ with our all will allow us to love others properly, without them becoming an idol. To love God with our "all" enables us to love others as we should.

Verse

With what my God in Christ
  has done for me,
My single heart is His—
  ever shall be.

One in Christ Jesus

The Word

> There is neither Jew nor Greek, there is neither slave nor free,
> there is no male and female, for you are all one in Christ Jesus.
>
> Galatians 3:28

Voice from the Church

"What is called for in these days, as in any other time, is a church that is a genuine covenantal community defined by the gospel rather than a service provider defined by laws of the market, political ideologies, ethnic distinctives, or other alternatives to the catholic community that the Father is creating by his Spirit in his Son. For this, we need nothing less than a new creation where the only demographic that matters is in Christ." (Michael Horton, b. 1964)*

Reflection

All those who are "in Christ Jesus" constitute the church catholic (universal) and the church local. In our unregenerate state, we were "in Adam"; in our regenerate state, we are "in Christ Jesus.

Regardless of our previous state and our former sins, every person who has passed from death to life, from being lost to being found, from being blind to seeing—these and these alone comprise the church of the Lord Jesus Christ. We may be baptized with water, without being justified by faith; we may be a member of a local church without having experienced new life in Christ. Sacred rites cannot give a sinner spiritual birth.

Furthermore, as disciples of the Lord Jesus Christ, our identity in the church is not found in our secular credentials or positions. Whether high or low, poor or wealthy, educated or illiterate, or whatever our racial and cultural makeup—"in Christ Jesus" we are one. There is one church and one church alone. Those "in Christ Jesus" are the church.

Verse

Elect from every nation, yet one o'er all the earth;
Her charter of salvation: one Lord, one faith, one birth.
One holy name she blesses, partakes one holy food,
And to one hope she presses, with every grace endued. (S. J. Stone, 1839-1900)**

True Fellowship

The Word
> [36]And when he had said these things, he knelt down and
> prayed with them all. [37]And there was much weeping on the part
> of all; they embraced Paul and kissed him, [38]being sorrowful most of
> all because of the word he had spoken, that they would not see
> his face again. And they accompanied him to the ship.
> Acts 20:36-38

Voice from the Church
"Though we all have to enter upon discipleship alone, we do not remain alone.... If we take him at his word ... our reward is the fellowship of the Church. Here is a visible brotherhood to compensate a hundredfold for all we have lost." (Dietrich Bonhoeffer, 1906-1945)*

Reflection
We come to the Lord Jesus Christ alone; however, we don't remain alone.

The apostle Paul is a noble example of one who saw the importance of Christian community and Spirit-fellowship. Whenever he traveled, Paul companioned with at least one other person, for example, Timothy. And whatever city he entered, Paul first searched for Jewish believers or disciples of Christ or both. Paul believed in the organic unity of the body of Christ and emphasized its oneness in Christ.

Often one hears reports of certain local churches being so *friendly*. While it is well that people be "friendly," friendliness should not to be confused with true fellowship in the Spirit. If all we can talk about with other Christians are our common interests in family, sports, the weather, and politics—such *friendliness* is not what the historic church believed constituted true fellowship. True fellowship is a gift of the Spirit.

Verse
Join hands, then, members of the faith,
Whatever your race may be!
Who serves my Father as His child
Is surely kin to me. (William A. Dunkerley, 1852-1941)**

Caesar and God

The Word

> *"Therefore render to Caesar the things that are*
> *Caesar's, and to God the things that are God's."*
> Matthew 22:21

Voice from the Church

"Jesus did not join the political revolutionaries of His own day, and He remains sovereign over all politics today." (Timothy George, b. 1950)*

Reflection

Followers of Christ can fall into one of two *ditches* when it comes to one's relationship and involvement in the affairs of this world's political institutions. For some, they have become so immersed in and entangled by their political engagements, that their salt has lost it savor. For others, they have withdrawn themselves from any involvement in politics and may be suspicious of those Christians who believe such are called to serve in the political system of their country.

For the earnest Christian, wherever God's will truly leads, he is called to be both a witness for Christ ("light") and an influential preservative for truth, righteousness, and justice ("salt").

Anytime our duty intersects the world system, the Christian must be on his guard, for every institution of this world is permeated with secular views that are contrary to the kingdom of God. We must take care when rendering "to Caesar the things that are Caesar's" that we don't forget to render "to God the things that are God's." Being kept clean by the blood of Christ and his Spirit on the inside, we will live without contamination on the outside. Otherwise our life and words are powerless.

Yes, let us pay proper due to the state, but let us also make sure we honor God in all things.

Verse

Only as my eye remains clear
And my love for God warm
Can I serve in this fallen world
And not do myself harm.

Inside and Outside

The Word

> [12] Therefore, my beloved, as you have always obeyed, so now,
> not only as in my presence but much more in my absence, work
> out your own salvation with fear and trembling, [13] for it is God
> who works in you, both to will and to work for his good pleasure.
> Philippians 2:12-13

Voice from the Church

"Jesus has more to do in us than through us. Our inner changes of heart become much more important than the things we may achieve in front of other people." (James Houston, b. 1922)*

Reflection

During his earthly ministry, the Son of Man never once attempted to make a good impression on either his disciples or the crowd. His sole aim in his life and ministry was to please and glorify his Father, with whom he was intimately and organically connected.

We either seek to please men or God—we cannot do both simultaneously. If we fail to allow God to work deeply in the hidden parts of our life, our unsanctified self will dominate our public life. For true disciples of Christ, God is always at work "in" them ... instructing and correcting, admonishing and disciplining, guiding and controlling—in Word and Spirit.

What God works "in," we are to work "out." We are often in a rush to make a good impression on others; God is not impressed with such unsanctified motives. Let us cooperate with God's inner workings in our life, then we can be certain that "his good pleasure" will be done in and through us—to his glory alone. Otherwise, we will depend on self-effort, which is to walk in the flesh instead of walking in the Spirit.

Verse

Once it was my working, His it hence shall be;
Once I tried to use Him, now He uses me.
Once the power I wanted, now the Mighty One;
Once for self I labored, now for Him alone. (A. B. Simpson, 1843-1919)**

True Greatness

The Word

To me, though I am the very least of all the saints, this grace was given, to preach to the Gentiles the unsearchable riches of Christ, ...
Ephesians 3:8

Voice from the Church

"I went with Mr. [George] Whitefield to Blackheath, where were, I believe, twelve or fourteen thousand people. He a little surprised me, by desiring me to preach in his stead; which I did (though nature recoiled) on my favourite subject, 'Jesus Christ, who of God is made unto us wisdom, righteousness, sanctification, and redemption.' I was greatly moved with compassion for the rich that were there, to whom I made a particular application. Some of them seemed to attend, while others drove away their coaches from such an uncouth a preacher." (John Wesley, 1703-1791).*

Reflection

George Whitefield (1714-1770) and John Wesley (1703-1791) were two of our Lord's foremost evangelists in the 18th century. These men were used as the Spirit's flaming instruments of grace, to preach to more people than any other two servants of Christ prior to their time.

Whitefield and Wesley had known each other since their Oxford school days, and had developed a fond relationship, in Christ. The one was a Calvinistic Methodist (Whitefield), the other, an Arminian Methodist (Wesley). Notwithstanding their understanding of the finer points of Christian doctrine, note the honor and humility expressed in the above quote. Whitefield honored Wesley by inviting him to preach in his place; Wesley was humbled by such an invitation. This is true greatness, even while differing over some lesser doctrinal points.

Verse

A grace-filled heart embraces
All of God's true servants, while
A narrow heart excludes those
With differing convictions.

Holiness and Love

The Word
As servants of God we commend ourselves in every way: by ... puri-
ty, knowledge, patience, kindness, the Holy Spirit, genuine love; ...
2 Corinthians 6:4

Voice from the Church
"Not his holiness without his love: that is only harshness. Not his love
without his holiness: that is only compromise. Anything that an individual Christian or Christian group does that fails to show the simultaneous
balance of the holiness of God and the love of God presents to a watching world not a demonstration of the God who exists but a caricature of
the God who exists." (Francis A. Schaeffer, 1912-1984)*

Reflection
When "God's love has been poured into our hearts through the Holy
Spirit" (Rom. 5:5), his holiness and purity are also diffused throughout
the wellspring of our being. Thereafter it is the Spirit's mission to bring
into conformity the totality of our being and behavior "to mature manhood, to the stature of the fullness of Christ" (Eph. 4:13). *Agape* love
and the holiness of God, indwelling the disciple of Christ, by the very
presence of the Holy Spirit are experiential realities. Where the Spirit is
present—there is the love of God; where the Spirit is present—there is
the holiness of God.

The breakdown with Christians comes whenever we fail to live-out
what the Spirit works-in. I once heard someone pray, "Lord help me in
my actions, interactions, and reactions." I have often prayed that prayer
since first hearing it. Discipleship is neither automatic nor static; it is a
walk—a walk in the Spirit, in holiness, and in love. As we allow the
Spirit to refresh his graces in us, let us keep step with the Spirit.

Verse
Oh, that Your holy love would flow freely
and always from the wellspring of my heart,
That Christ and Christ alone may be honored,
as I walk in this world, doing my part.

Striving

The Word

> *Only let your manner of life be worthy of the gospel of Christ,*
> *so that whether I come and see you or am absent, I may hear*
> *of you that you are standing firm in one spirit, with one*
> *mind striving side by side for the faith of the gospel,*
> Philippians 1:27

Voice from the Church

"I find that often, after having plainly, fully and calmly stated my views to one who is opposing the truth as I see it, I am strongly tempted to strive for the last word; but I also find that God blesses me most when I there commit the matter into His hands, and by so doing I most often win my adversary." (Samuel L. Brengle, 1860-1936)*

Reflection

In the body of Christ, we are either "striving side by side" or striving against one another. We are either living in harmony with our brothers and sister in Christ or experiencing friction and disharmony with the same.

There can be no authentic unity in the church of Christ apart from walking in the Word and Spirit. Every other supposed *unity* is a falsehood—a lie against the truth. Unity without truth is uniformity without Christ, who is truth. Truth apart from unity leaves a raw scar among those in the church and causes those on the outside to scoff and mock. To contend for the truth as it is in Jesus is one thing; to be contentious while contending for the truth sours the truth of the gospel and discredits our witness. What to speak, when to speak, and how to speak are learned as we live under the Spirit's control. Let us strive together for the gospel, without striving with one another.

Verse

They walked with God in Peace and Love,
But failed with one another;
While sternly for the Faith they strove,
Brother fell out with brother. (James Montgomery, 1771-1854)**

The Sin that Clouds Our Thinking

The Word
For by the grace given to me I say to everyone among you not to think of himself more highly than he ought to think, but to think with sober judgment, each according to the measure of faith that God has assigned.
Romans 12:3

Voice from the Church
"Pride ... is a passion always to be in control so that all our desires get satisfied and in all relationships we dominate. So pride makes impossible a truly respectful attitude to other people, ... and it makes impossible a truly reverent attitude to God, which sees his glory as all that matters and ourselves as here to praise and please him in all that we do, starting with our treatment of others." (J. I. Packer & Carolynn Nystrom)*

Reflection
Every sinful "self" hyphenated word (for example: self-absorption, self-promotion, self-gratification, self-driven) speaks of an attitude of the heart that makes it impossible to act with integrity toward God and others. The very taproot of the unsanctified self is pride, which is the essence of sin. We can act pridefully in subtle and not so subtle ways: in conversation, making ourselves appear better than we really are; reacting in a touchy manner when shown a fault or mistake; accepting praise from others while failing to give glory to God; promoting our own accomplishments, when we actually asked for God's help in those endeavors; relating with condescension toward those we perceive to be beneath us. Any failure to walk in the Spirit provides an opening to act in the flesh—to act pridefully, which clouds both our vertical and horizonal relationships. Let's endeavor, by the power of the indwelling Spirit, to live without "earth-born" clouds.

Verse
All that is dross in my nature, O Lord,
Purify with your fiery Spirit.
May I honor you with each breath I take,
Knowing your grace is without limit.

Love and Obedience

The Word

[23] *Jesus answered him, "If anyone loves me, he will keep my word, and my Father will love him, and we will come to him and make our home with him.* [24] *Whoever does not love me does not keep my words. And the word that you hear is not mine but the Father's who sent me."*
John 14:23-24

Voice from the Church

"True love for God is expressed not in sentimental language or mystical experience, but in moral obedience." (Rienecker & Rogers)*

Reflection

For too many of us, the word "love," when used in reference toward God, conjures up thoughts of sentimentality and affection. While feelings of affection toward God—expressed by gratitude for blessings received—are an acceptable and worthy response for of all his children, mere sentiment is another matter.

Sentimentalism fails to give proper recognition to God and ends with the worshiper feeling good without translating his good feelings into doing good—in word and deed. When we are content to feel merely good—in our private devotions, attending public worship and Christian concerts—our religious experience results in a kind of mysticism that fails to honor God with obedience.

It is right that we have good feelings toward God—as we sing the psalms, hymns, and spiritual songs; however, *agape* love must not be reduced to feelings; *agape* love is action: "If anyone loves me, he will keep my word." Religious feelings without subsequent acts of obedience is not love. Remember, Jesus was not content to feel; his feelings moved him to action. We are called to follow his example.

Verse

I love Thee, I love Thee, I love Thee, my Lord;
I love Thee, my Savior, I love Thee, my God:
I love Thee, I love Thee, and that Thou dost know;
But how much I love Thee my actions will show. (Author Unknown)**

Stay Ready (1)

The Word
> [35] *"Stay dressed for action and keep your lamps burning,*
> [36] *and be like men who are waiting for their master to*
> *come home from the wedding feast, so that they may*
> *open the door to him at once when he comes and knocks."*
> Luke 12:35-36

Voice from the Church
"Nowhere are we told to watch for the coming of Christ. We are exhort-ed, rather, in view of the uncertainty of the time of the end, to watch. 'Watching' does not mean 'looking for' the event; it means spiritual and moral 'wakefulness.' We do not know when the end will come. There-fore, whenever it happens, we must be spiritually awake and must not sleep." (George Eldon Ladd, 1911-1982)*

Reflection
During his earthly ministry, the Lord Jesus sought to prepare his disci-ples for his glorious return to earth. On this subject, his words were di-rected toward his contemporary followers as well as toward those in future generations. It is clear from his exhortations, that Jesus was con-cerned that some of his disciples would eventually become spiritually listless and enervated by internal and external matters.

The immoral climate of our own generation pervades every sector of society and is impacting a large segment of Christ's church. A sleepy church is not a watchful, prepared, and praying church. Are we slouch-ing toward Gomorrah? Our "lamps" are either burning brightly or grow-ing dim. Are you staying wide awake and longing for our Lord's return? Or has your first love grown lukewarm. The Spirit cries, "Wake up, stay dressed for action and keep your lamps burning."

Verse
When Jesus comes to reward His servants,
Whether it be noon or night,
Faithful to Him will He find us watching,
With our lamps all trimmed and bright? (Fanny Crosby, 1820-1915)**

Stay Ready (2)

The Word

> [35] "Stay dressed for action and keep your lamps burning,
> [36] and be like men who are waiting for their master to
> come home from the wedding feast, so that they may
> open the door to him at once when he comes and knocks."
>
> Luke 12:35-36

Voice from the Church

"The long flowing robes of the east were a hindrance to work; and when a man prepared to work he gathered up his robes under his girdle to leave himself free for activity. The eastern lamp was like a cotton wick floating in a sauce-boat of oil. Always the wick had to be kept trimmed and the lamp replenished or the light would go out." (William Barclay, 1907-1978)*

Reflection

To prepare for work is as important as the work for which one prepares. For the surgeon to go into surgery or for the farmer to go out into his fields without having prepared his equipment, without having made adequate preparation for the task at hand, would be considered the height of foolishness. How much more necessary it is for the disciple of the Lord Jesus Christ to be prepared for his imminent return.

While God provides us with the grace to stay watchful, he cannot dress us for action nor keep our lamps burning. It is our responsibility to take the necessary steps and employ the essential Christian disciplines, in order that we may guard ourselves against sin, feed our souls on the Living Bread, and engage in good works—all in the power of the Spirit's wisdom, discernment and strength. We have been forewarned by the Master himself. Stay dressed with your lamp brightly burning—today and each day!

Verse

O watch, and fight, and pray;
The battle ne'er give o'er;
Renew it boldly every day,
And help divine implore. (George Heath, 1745-1822)**

Whose Strength?

The Word

> Samuel said, "When you were little in your own
> eyes, were you not head of the tribes of Israel? And
> did not the Lord anoint you king over Israel?"
>
> 1 Samuel 15:17 NKJV

Voice from the Church

"Oh, that God's children would understand that their own strength is one of their worst enemies! Could the workers in God's kingdom but see that their own power is the greatest hindrance to their bearing fruit for God!" (George Steinberger, 1865-1904)*

Reflection

What we think about ourselves and what God thinks about us may be at the opposite ends of the proverbial poles. No person can know himself apart from God's penetrating and illuminating Spirit. Self-deception blinds us to the reality of who we are and self-deception is one of the byproducts of sin.

Because disobedience distorts reality, we are prone to think we are more capable than we are, in the work of our Lord. Thus, we believe we are moving forward, making progress and achieving successes in the name of Jesus, when, from God's vantage point, we are a failure. Such was the case with King Saul, when he overtly disobeyed the voice of the Lord.

We are left unprotected and exposed to the Enemy's arrows, when we enter the Lord's battles in our own strength. Past victories do not ensure future victories, if we fail to keep low at the feet of Jesus.

To be forewarned is to be forearmed. The Scriptures faithfully warn us against the danger of self-dependence. Our strength is in God alone.

Verse

The sidelines are strewn with
undisciplined, careless men,
Who chose the convenient path,
failing to conquer within.

Doctrine and Life

The Word

Take heed to yourself and to the doctrine. Continue in them, for in doing this you will save both yourself and those who hear you.
1 Timothy 4:16

Voice from the Church

"Orthodoxy in matters of belief is not a substitute for holiness of life, either for the individual or for the church, because orthodoxy in biblical terms includes the moral outcome of that right belief." (David F. Wells, b. 1939)*

Reflection

One of the results of the Fall is that we humans are prone to extremes, even Christians. This is evident in many of our pulpits and pews. If one should question whether this assertion is true to the facts, all we must do is to take a casual look at social media.

There are those who aver that doctrine is unnecessary, and to listen to them it is soon clear that for them it isn't. They float from pillar to post in their self-made belief system. Others fail to make a vital connection between biblical teaching and their own behavior. Christianity to them is more cerebral than a dynamic relationship with the living God.

Then, there is the biblical balance: doctrine and life. Where the Spirit is present, in his informative and transformative power, there you will discover a holy symmetry and symphony of authentic Christianity. And how beautiful this is wherever it is seen.

The Christian is to seek to have an informed mind and a transformed life. The one should always result in the other. Our safety lies in being people of the Word who walking according to the Spirit. One without the other is like a boat with only one oar. Let us fill our minds with the Word, allowing the Spirit to energize us unto good works.

Verse

So let our lips and lives express
The holy Gospel we profess;
So let our walks and virtues shine,
To prove the doctrine all divine. (Isaac Watts, 1674-1748)**

Our Home, His Home

The Word

> For we know that if the tent that is our earthly home
> is destroyed, we have a building from God, a house
> not made with hands, eternal in the heavens.
>
> 2 Corinthians 5:1

Voice from the Church

"Just as I should seek in a desert for clean water, or toil at the North Pole to make a comfortable fire, so I shall search the land of void and vision until I find something fresh like water, and comforting like fire; until I find some place in eternity, where I am literally at home. And there is only one such place to be found." (G. K. Chesterton, 1874-1936)*

Reflection

To find our home in God and to be finally at home with God are both the Christian's present experience and future hope and promised reality.

Not to be at "home" is to be a wanderer, not unlike those the psalmist spoke of: "Some wandered in desert wastes, finding no way to a city to dwell in; hungry and thirsty, their soul fainted within them" (Ps. 107:4-5).

As wonderful as it is to find our home in God, and to have the assured hope of a future home with him, how blessed are those in whom God has made a home for himself: "If anyone loves me, he will keep my word, and my Father will love him, and we will come to him and make our home with him" (John 14:23). Have you found your "home"? Has God made his "home" in you?

The church is filled with restless people, people who have neither found their rest in God nor have allowed God to be at rest in them. Let us allow God to make his home in our heart.

Verse

For me to be at home with God,
Oh, what joy and peace and rest!
For God to be at home in me,
Makes me surely twice as blessed!

The Eye Gate

The Word

[34] *"Your eye is the lamp of your body. When your eye is healthy, your whole body is full of light, but when it is bad, your body is full of darkness.* [35] *Therefore be careful lest the light in you be darkness."*

Luke 11:34-35

Voice from the Church

"When Michelangelo was starting to paint unclad people, his teacher said to him, "Why are you doing this?" He said, "I want to see man as God sees man," and the teacher said to him, "But you're not God." I think that's a very strong junction to remind us that the eye gate and the ear gate ultimately affect the imagination." (Ravi Zacharias, b. 1946)*

Reflection

For those of us who have experienced God's infusion of life and light, through our Lord Jesus Christ, how we manage our eyes is a critical factor in our growth (or lack of growth) in spiritual knowledge and grace.

Our first parents took a great Fall, because they failed to guard their eyes. Achan brought shame on himself and his family and caused Israel's defeat at the battle of Ai—all because he left his eyes unprotected.

We either have healthy or unhealthy eyes, which reflects a healthy or unhealthy heart. How great has been the fall of many followers of Christ, because of either a momentary or habitual failure to guard their eyes. Eye-protection is a must if one is to keep a pure heart.

The shores of time are strewn with those who failed to take seriously our Lord's admonition recorded in Luke 11. Even the Old Testament patriarch Job saw the necessity of guarding his eyes: "I have made a covenant with my eyes; how then could I gaze at a virgin?" (Job 31:1).

Verse

For one to be full of light,
The eyes must be entirely whole.
It takes more than just one touch;
It takes discipline of the soul.

Fixed Vision

The Word

I have set the Lord always before me; Because
He is at my right hand I shall not be moved.
Psalm 16:8 NKJV

Voice from the Church

"It is our wisdom and duty to set the Lord always before us, and to see him continually at our right hand, wherever we are, to eye him as our chief good and highest end, our owner, ruler, and judge, our gracious benefactor, our sure guide and strict observer; and, while we do thus, we shall not be moved either from our duty or from our comfort." (Matthew Henry, 1662-1714)*

Reflection

Conversion and transformation by the Spirit requires our fixed attention on our Lord in all things. While it is psychologically impossible to be always *consciously* looking to the Lord Jesus, yet, for the thirsty-hearted saint there will be a subterranean undercurrent flowing steadily from the throne of God calling one onward and upward.

Our walk with God is just that, a walk. While there will be times when one may be diverted from his steadfastness, through trials and temptations, immediate confession and cleansing must occur if we are to refocus our gaze fixed on the Man at God's right hand.

God's greatest saints have learned to cultivate discipleship habits, which assist them in walking the "narrow road" toward the City of God. David is worthy of our emulation: "I have set the Lord always before me." Through grace this must be a settled fact for Christ-followers. With so much else clamoring for our time and attention, let us make certain where our inner and outer eyes are fixed.

Verse

Be Thou my Vision, O Lord of my heart;
Be all else but naught to me, save that Thou art;
Be Thou my best thought in the day and the night,
Both waking and sleeping, Thy presence my light. (Dallan Forgaill, 530-598)*

Earthen Vessels

The Word

*But we have this treasure in earthen vessels, so that the surpassing
greatness of the power will be of God and not from ourselves.*
2 Corinthians 4:7 NASB

Voice from the Church

"We are all frail, but do thou esteem none more frail than thyself." (Thomas à Kempis, 1380-1471)*

Reflection

That God would use men and women in the work of his kingdom, who
appear to be strong in mind, temperament, and natural ability seems
reasonable to us. But that God would take man—with all his innate infirmities—and use him to advance his purposes on earth must be a wonder to angels in heaven.

The most fragile vessel in the body of Christ can be used for God's
greatest good, if that vessel always keeps in mind that God is using it—
not because it is strong, but because it is totally weak apart from Almighty God.

Any good that flows from and through the disciples of the Lord Jesus
to others is all because these men and women recognize where the
source of their strength originates and is maintained—"the surpassing
greatness of the power will be of God and not from ourselves."

The Christian must never forget from whom his strength is derived.
God's strength will continue to make us strong, if we continue to recognize that we are nothing but earthen vessels.

It is well for us to often remember that we are mere channels, through
whom the power of God flows. The power belongs to God, not in the
channel.

Verse

Stand up! stand up for Jesus!
Stand in His strength alone;
The arm of flesh will fail you;
Ye dare not trust your own. (George Duffield, 1794-1868)**

The Trinitarian Faith is a Powerful Faith

The Word

> The grace of the Lord Jesus Christ and the love of God
> and the fellowship of the Holy Spirit be with you all.
> 2 Corinthians 13:14

Voice from the Church

"Without trinitarian contact with Christ in his Word, the Father in prayer, and each other's Spirit-given gifts in the apostolic fellowship of the church, we will be powerless in mission. We need Christ, we need prayer, we need gifts, and we need each other. When we have all four, we are a missionary church." (Frederick D. Bruner, b. 1932)*

Reflection

The Christian faith is a trinitarian faith: God in Three Persons: Father, Son, and Holy Spirit. Where the Spirit is at work in the world and the church, Christ is also present as well as the Father. One member of the Trinity should never be exalted at the exclusion of the other Two. The Christian faith is not a Jesus *only* faith. The Father sent the Son, the Son exalts the Father, and the Spirit glorifies the Son. The Christian is to honor each member of the Triune God. We address our prayers to the Father (as Christ did and taught); we pray in Jesus' name; and we are indwelt by and live in the power of the Spirit.

When the believer properly understands his relationship to each member of the Trinity and their relationship to one another, and enjoys the benefits of the Cross, Resurrection and Pentecost, he will be a blessing to God and to the church and the world. There is power in biblical, spiritual knowledge; there is power in the gospel; there is power in the preached Cross; there is power through the poured-out Spirit. Glory be to our God, the Three in One.

Verse

Holy, Holy, Holy! Lord God Almighty!
Early in the morning our song shall rise to Thee.
Holy, Holy, Holy! Merciful and mighty!
God in three persons, blessed Trinity! (Reginald Heber, 1783-1826)**

An Unpleasant Truth

The Word

> [5] *Therefore the wicked will not stand in the judgment,*
> *nor sinners in the congregation of the righteous;*
> [6] *for the Lord knows the way of the righteous,*
> *but the way of the wicked will perish.*
> Psalm 1:5-6

Voice from the Church

"Keep in full view of your mind that all who die unpardoned and unrenewed are utterly unfit for the presence of God and must be lost forever. They are not capable of enjoying heaven; they could not be happy there. They must go to their own place; and that place is hell. Oh, it is a great thing in these days of unbelief to believe the whole Bible!" (J. C. Ryle, 1816-1900)*

Reflection

While the gospel of the Lord Jesus Christ is for all, neither have all received it nor will all believe it. This truth is irrefutable, to all who carefully ponder the Word of God. It was because that God is a God of love, that he sent his one and only Son into the world for the salvation of humankind. However, some believe, and some do not. The believing ones are eternally saved; the unbelieving ones perish forever. That some men and women will be lost forever is an unpleasant truth to our sensitive ears. But unpleasant or not, this is the Word of the Lord and his Word remains forever. There was a time when our pulpits reminded the pews, more often than is done in many pulpits these days, that Hell is just as real as Heaven. However, those days are past and rarely is the subject broached. In this "feel good" age, the last thing we want to do is to make people *uncomfortable*. The Lord Jesus thought differently.

Verse

For those who have trusted Christ alone,
To them there is no condemnation.
But if we fail to accept God's Gift,
To perish is our destination.

Law and Love

The Word

[8]*Owe no one anything, except to love each other, for the one who loves another has fulfilled the law.* [9]*For the commandments, "You shall not commit adultery, You shall not murder, You shall not steal, You shall not covet," and any other commandment, are summed up in this word: "You shall love your neighbor as yourself."*

Romans 13:8-9

Voice from the Church

"Remember, the Pharisees called the Son of God a Sabbath-breaker. They kept the law of the Sabbath, they broke the law of love. Which was the worst to break? Which was the higher law to keep? Take care lest, in the zeal which seems to you to be for Christ, you be found indulging their spirit and not His." (F. W. Robertson, 1816-1853)*

Reflection

It is possible to keep the letter of the Law of God while at the same time breaking the Law of Love. The Law of Love does not break the Law of God, it fulfills it, completes it. Many of the Pharisees were well-versed in the Law of God (as well as their man-made laws); however, because their hearts were not permeated with the Law of Love, they broke the Law of God because they broke the Law of Love. They kept the husk of the Law and broke its kernel.

God's Law and God's Love are not antithetical to each other. His Law interprets his Love, and His Love is the expression of his Law. The Word and Spirit teach us how to walk in God's Law and how to express his Love. We fulfill God's moral Law when we righty love him and our neighbor. The two great commandments are for us today and every day. "Father, help me to love as you love."

Verse

The Law of God has been given,
To guide us all our days.
The Spirit of Love indwells us,
To walk in all His ways.

Practice What You Preach

The Word

*¹⁹If you are sure that you yourself are a guide to the blind, a light
to those who are in darkness, ²⁰an instructor of the foolish, a teacher
of children, having in the law the embodiment of knowledge and
truth— ²¹you then who teach others, do you not teach yourself?
While you preach against stealing, do you steal? ²²You who say
that one must not commit adultery, do you commit adultery?*
Romans 2:19-22

Voice from the Church

"Be a walking, talking, living example of what you preach, in every
silent moment of your life, known and unknown; bear the scrutiny of
God, until you prove that you are indeed an example of what He can do,
and then "make disciples of all nations." (Oswald Chambers, 1874-1917)*

Reflection

Those who are called to teach and instruct others are called by God to
live the truth they teach before sharing said truth. There is nothing
worse in the church than for a teacher of biblical truth to contradict the
truth he teaches by the life he lives. Does the man who teaches others to
exercise self-control have control over his own appetites? Does the
teacher who instructs his class that the body is the temple of the Holy
Spirit defile his own body? Does the minister who calls others to live a
life of holiness, live out the same calling in his own life?

Teachers of God's Word are held by God to a higher standard: "Not
many of you should become teachers, my brothers, for you know that
we who teach will be judged with greater strictness" (James 3:1). This
should cause each teacher/preacher to walk in the fear of God. Pray for
your church leaders that they will be people of integrity.

Verse

*I love the truth I hear you teach;
I love more the life that you live.
For when I see the way you walk,
I can believe the truth you taught.*

Sent by God

The Word
There was a man sent from God, whose name was John.
John 1:6

Voice from the Church
"Should the record of my poor and broken life lead any one to conse-crate himself to mission work at home or abroad that he may win souls for Jesus, or should it even deepen the missionary spirit in those who already know and serve the Redeemer of us all—for this also, and for all through which He has led me by His loving hand and gracious guidance, I shall, unto the endless ages of eternity, bless and adore my beloved Master and Saviour and Lord, to whom be glory for ever and ever." (John G. Paton, 1824-1907)*

Reflection
The above words, by John G. Paton (1824-1907), were written by a man who had served his Lord for many years as a pioneer missionary to the New Hebrides Islands in the South Pacific (now Vanuatu). By the time of his death, his Aniwa New Testament was printed, and missionaries had been established on twenty-five of the thirty islands.

This son of Scottish soil was raised in a home where prayer was of-fered daily by his father for the eleven children. His father had hoped to be a minister; however, God had other plans for him. His father vowed that if God would give him sons, that he would consecrate each of them to God's service. God gave him three, each eventually serving the Lord in Christ's vineyard. The torch of the gospel blazed brightly in the life and ministry of John G. Paton until his dying day; he was a God-sent man. Where does God wish to send you? Are you listening? We will never be sent until our ears are tuned to the voice of the Good Shepherd.

Verse
Bear the news to every land,
Climb the steeps and cross the waves;
Onward!—'tis our Lord's command;
Jesus saves! Jesus saves! (Priscilla J. Owens, 1829-1907)**

Lamp and Light

The Word

> *Your word is a lamp to my feet and a light to my path.*
> Psalm 119:105

Voice from the Church

"Almighty God and merciful Father, who hast appointed thy Word to be a light to our feet, and a lamp to our paths, and caused all Holy Scripture to be written for our learning; grant us the assistance of thy Holy Spirit, that we may in such ways read, mark, learn, and inwardly digest them, that by patience and comfort of thy Holy Word, we may embrace, and ever hold fast the blessed hope of everlasting life, which thou hast given us in our Saviour Jesus Christ." (William Burkitt, 1650-1703)*

Reflection

Unless we lowly creatures, whom God wishes to transform into the image of Christ, are enlightened by the revealed Word of God, we will be stumbling and bumbling along a dark journey, knowing neither where we are or where we should go.

But life need not be a dark tunnel on an uncertain path. God has graciously given us his written Word and Spirit, to reveal to us who we are and the life that we should be living. Those who are walking in darkness, love the dark. Those who are walking in the light of God, love the light. God is light, and his Word enlightens us by his Spirit. We are without excuse. God has spoken to us through his written revelation. Let us embrace it, obey it, and live it, in the power of the Spirit.

Have you listened to the Word of God today? Is the path you're walking an illuminated one? We have no excuse: The Word of God has been revealed and the Spirit is present. Let us embrace the Word and listen to the Spirit's voice.

Verse

Thy Word is a lamp to my feet,
A light to my path alway,
To guide and to save me from sin,
And show me the heav'nly way. (Ernest O. Sellers, 1869-1952)**

Persistence in Prayer

The Word

⁸ "I tell you, though he will not get up and give him anything because he is his friend, yet because of his impudence he will rise and give him whatever he needs. ⁹And I tell you, ask, and it will be given to you; seek, and you will find; knock, and it will be opened to you. ¹⁰For everyone who asks receives, and the one who seeks finds, and to the one who knocks it will be opened."
Luke 11:8-10

Voice from the Church

"It is the holy ... shamelessness of faith, which bridges over the infinite distance of the creature from the Creator, appeals with importunity to the heart of God, and ceases not till its point is gained. This would indeed be neither permissible nor possible, had not God, by virtue of the mysterious interlacing of necessity and freedom in His nature and operations, granted a power to the prayer of faith, to which He consents to yield." (C. F. Keil & F. Delitzsch)*

Reflection

Persistence and importunity in prayer were taught by the Lord, exemplified by the saints under the Old Covenant, and reinforced in the teachings of the holy apostles. We do not continue to supplicate the Lord, regarding a need, because our Father failed to hear our first request. Nor do we continue to supplicate the throne of grace because God is reluctant to hear the cries of his children. There are times when the Lord may tell us to pray no longer about a matter, as he once informed Paul concerning his "thorn in the flesh." God is under no obligation to answer our request when first offered. We are to persist in prayer until our petition is either answered or God tells us to stop.

Verse

O Thou by whom we come to God,
   the Life, the Truth, the Way,
The path of prayer thyself hast trod:
   Lord, teach us how to pray! (James Montgomery, 1854-1771)**

How to Live

The Word

> Let them give glory to the LORD, and
> declare his praise in the coastlands.
> Isaiah 42:12

Voice from the Church

"Jaraslov Pelikan's (1923-2006) *Bach Among the Theologians* concludes with a chapter titled "Johann Sebastian Bach—between Secular and Sacred." Pelikan points out that Bach began his compositions by writing *Jesu Juva* (Jesus, help) and closed them by writing *Soli Deo Gloria* (to God alone be the glory). These are also good grace notes for one of the most diligent and faithful of the "Lord's remembrancers," as Cotton Mather called church historians." (Timothy George, b. 1950)*

Reflection

Whether every human creature of God recognizes it or not, they are totally dependent upon the Creator and Redeemer for their very existence and wellbeing. And because we are dependent, we should seek God's help in matters both great and small and seek to give God alone the glory in all and for all things.

Since the entrance of sin and rebellion in the Garden, it is man's innate inclination to live independently and take the credit for all his accomplishments. Mature believers know better.

The very essence of prayer is an expression of our helplessness and dependence upon God— "Lord, help me," cried the Canaanite woman to Jesus (Luke 15:25).

There is no greater joy than to ask for God's help, and to live a life to the glory of God alone. Never be ashamed or hesitant to ask your Father for his help; he enjoys giving it to his children.

Verse

To You be the glory, O God—
Not unto us, not unto us.
For You are God and we are not;
We are but dust, we are but dust.

Sin and Holiness

The Word

> [12]*Not that I have already obtained it or have already*
> *become perfect, ...* [15]*Let us therefore, as many*
> *as are perfect, have this attitude; and if*
> *in anything you have a different attitude,*
> *God will reveal that also to you.*
> Philippians 3:12, 15 NASB

Voice from the Church

"In regard to the doctrine of *sinless perfection* as a heresy, we regard contentment with *sinful imperfection* as a greater heresy. And we gravely fear that many Christians make the apostle's words, "If we say we have no sin we deceive ourselves," the unconscious justification for a low standard of Christian living." (A. J. Gordon, 1836-1895)*

Reflection

Some years ago, I was in the company of a few men, who represented different doctrinal traditions. The question of "sin" entered the discussion, which became a bit lively. One person was quick to assert that all Christians sin. Another was just as quick to claim that he never sins. For the person who said, "All Christians sin," he should ponder what is meant by 1 John 3:8: "Whoever makes a practice of sinning is of the devil, ..." For the person who claimed, "I never sin," he should ask himself if ever needs the Advocate: "And if anyone sins, we have an Advocate with the Father, Jesus Christ the righteous" (1 John 2:1). To say, "All Christians sin," is a low view of God's call to holiness. To claim, "I never sin," is an exalted view of one's self.

God's greatest saints are the quickest to acknowledge their shortcomings. All Christians still fall short of God's glory (perfections).

Verse

Search me, O God, and know my heart today,
Try me, O Savior, know my thoughts, I pray;
See if there be some wicked way in me;
Cleanse me from every sin, and set me free. (J. Edwin Orr, 1912-1987**

Holy Examples

The Word

> Brothers, join in imitating me, and keep your eyes on
> those who walk according to the example you have in us.
> Philippians 3:17

Voice from the Church

"I am persuaded that I shall obtain the highest amount of present happiness, I shall do most for God's glory and the good of man, and I shall have the fullest reward in eternity, by maintaining a conscience always washed in Christ's blood, by being filled with the Holy Spirit at all times, and by attaining the most entire likeness to Christ in mind, will, and heart, that it is possible for a redeemed sinner to attain to in this world." (Robert Murray M'Cheyne, 1813-1843)*

Reflection

Years ago, I read about a businessman who kept on a wall in his office a picture of a godly pastor who had gone to be with the Lord. The man said he placed the picture there as a reminder to conduct his business with integrity. When he was tempted to violate his conscience, he would go into his office and look on the face of the departed saint. To reflect on the life of a man whom he knew had had a close walk with God, served as God's reminder to him to be true to God in all his business transactions.

Biblical examples are helpful incentives to godliness. It is also helpful to have known personally those who took their walk with God seriously. And to read about devout men and women, whose lives were filled with the fragrance of Christ, is a further stimulant for us, that we might run a faithful race to the very end.

Are you living the kind of life that you would want others to imitate?

Verse

Why should we prize the world's celebrities,
Who mostly live for the present,
When God has placed a few saints in our path,
Whose lives are clearly transcendent?

Whatever it Takes

The Word
Before I was afflicted I went astray, but now I keep your word.
Psalm 119:67

Voice from the Church
"Dearest Redeemer, make me humble, prepare me for Thy future mercies; and whenever Thou seest me in danger of being exalted above measure, graciously send me a thorn in the flesh, so that Thy blessings may not prove my ruin." (George Whitefield, 1714-1770)*

Reflection
Some of God's nearest and dearest servants have been some of his greatest sufferers. Some have suffered physically, as did Moses (speech impediment) and Jacob (afflicted thigh); others have suffered emotionally and psychologically, as did the hymn writer, William Cowper; and many others have suffered because of their Christian identity, bearing their cross to the glory of God.

There is something about suffering that drives us to our knees (or should). We either ask God for deliverance, or we supplicate the throne for grace to bear the cross patiently and joyfully.

Whatever may be your personal affliction (and if you don't experience one presently, you will eventually), allow God to use it for your good and his glory. Do you complain and chaff under this unfriendly providence? Is your affliction a burden or a blessing? God wants to sanctify every affliction, using it to mature us and bless others.

David was one of the most afflicted believers on record. He was besieged by his enemies and often beset with physical infirmities. Yet, he composed songs of praise to God, through all his sufferings.

Will you allow your Father to use your affliction to his glory?

Verse
Some through the waters, some through the flood,
Some through the fire, but all through the blood;
Some through great sorrow, but God gives a song,
In the night season and all the day long. (G. A. Young, 1903-?)**

Seeking God's Face

The Word

Then the king said to me, "What are you
requesting?" So I prayed to the God of heaven.
Nehemiah 2:4

Voice from the Church

"Most revolutions do not begin with people seeking God on their knees. But that is the kind that the world needs today—an army of people on their knees. An army of believers not seeking their own agenda for their lives, but an army seeking God's agenda for a lost world." (David & Kim Butts)*

Reflection

When Israel had sinned, Moses fell on his knees and interceded on their behalf with Yahweh (Num. 21). When God needed a prophet, he moved the heart of a barren woman to supplicate the throne of grace (1 Sam. 1). When the fallen walls of Jerusalem needed rebuilding, God touched the heart of Nehemiah to pray for wisdom and guidance (Neh. 2). Before the New Testament church was born, the hearts of 120 believers gathered for a prolonged concert of prayer (Acts 1).

One of the Spirit's primary methods and means in advancing the kingdom of Christ on earth is prayer—intercessory prayer. We have resorted to every other manufactured method to "grow" the church, but we have failed to keep first things first. Our efforts are sure to fail unless we first go to our knees, seeking the face of God for his power and plan. Too often we give lip service to this matter of prayer, then go our own way doing our own thing.

When our hearts are right with God, we make him our first and constant recourse. Are you seeking God's face today?

Verse

Before we go forth on a mission,
Before making bold proclamation—
God's plan is to seek Him for wisdom;
This comes by making supplication.

Inward or Outward?

The Word
> *¹⁵I do not ask that you take them out of the world, but*
> *that you keep them from the evil one ... ¹⁸As you sent me*
> *into the world, so I have sent them into the world.*

John 17:15, 18

Voice from the Church
"We have met Christian believers who were so obsessed by some particular *doctrine* of sanctification that instead of being drawn closer to Christ and made more like Him in practical, unselfish helpfulness toward others, they have been surreptitiously lured away from Him into a kind of cliquish, self-deluded spiritual *superiority*." (J. Sidlow Baxter, 1903-1999)*

Reflection
Our Father in Heaven has given birth to a people in order that he might not only prepare them for Heaven but make them vitally useful to others while they remain in this world. That being the case, there is no room for Christian cloisters, enclaves of spirituality where a select few have isolated themselves from needy people.

Before God could bring reformation and renewal to the 16th century church in Europe, he had to first force the monk Martin Luther out of the monastery. Before Christ could begin to build his church and advance God's kingdom on earth, he had to ignite, purify, and fill the hearts of timid disciples, who thereafter flooded streets and highways and byways with the glorious gospel of Jesus Christ.

Every person that has ever been reached with the gospel was reached because someone was sent and went. Are you living for yourself? Christ only sends the prepared. Has he prepared you? To whom is Christ sending you today? Go forth in the power of his Spirit.

Verse
Make me, O Lord, one of Your channels of blessing,
A life poured out in service to You.
I seek no gain or rewards down here;
I'm content to keep Your smile in view.

More than Pardon

The Word

> ⁴*For we know, brothers loved by God, that he has chosen you,*
> ⁵*because our gospel came to you not only in word, but also*
> *in power and in the Holy Spirit and with full conviction.*
> 1 Thessalonians 1:4-5

Voice from the Church

"A theology that has learned to speak in such a monotone about grace—always as pardon but not also as power—gives no guidance or direction to the serious Christian. The Christian life, engaged only in constant return to that pardoning word, goes nowhere." (Gilbert Meilaender, b. 1946)*

Reflection

For the Spirit-born child of God, the day of his conversion was so momentous that it is a day never to be forgotten. No more would a disciple of Jesus Christ forget the time that he passed from darkness to light, than the children of Israel would forget their passing through the Red Sea. God's pardoning grace should always be cherished. And it is cherished by those who have heard it.

However, the Christian is to have more than a testimony to a conversion event, he is also one who is indwelt by the Holy Spirit—the Spirit of power. The Holy Spirit was given to both make us holy and make us a blessing to others.

What evidence is there in your life of the Spirit's presence and power. Are you experiencing the indwelling power to live a pure life? Are you allowing God to help you to be sensitive to witnessing opportunities? Do you see any evidence of the Spirit's fruit maturing in you? Are you looking for opportunities to share your resources with those in need? Pardon, yes! Power, yes!

Verse

His pardoning voice I heard;
My acceptance was assured.
Now I look to Him for pow'r,
To walk the straight and narrow.

The Difference

The Word

Thus the Lord used to speak to Moses face to face, as a man speaks to his friend. When Moses turned again into the camp, his assistant Joshua the son of Nun, a young man, would not depart from the tent.
Exodus 33:11

Voice from the Church

"All ministers may be, and ought to be, so filled with the Holy Spirit that all who hear them shall be impressed with the conviction that 'God is in them of a truth.'" (Charles Finney, 1792-1875)*

Reflection

As important as it is for God's servants to receive all the formal education they possibly can, what qualifies them for service is not a diploma. As great as the distance is between reading about the Rocky Mountains and seeing them in person, the distance is vastly greater between being Word-taught and Spirit-taught.

While traveling with the Lord Jesus, the disciples heard each word he spoke. Nevertheless, until the day of Pentecost, the disciples lacked the power to minister effectively. Until they were filled and anointed with power, the ambassadors of Christ were incapable of fulfilling God's high calling.

After listening to an apostle following the day of Pentecost, God's people knew they had heard a God-called and God-filled man. God's people deserve no less today. Moses was on intimate terms with Yahweh, so was his assistant Joshua, who basked in God's presence.

For us to be effective ambassadors for Christ, God's presence and power must be a reality in our day-to-day walk. What about you? Are you one of God's filled vessels?

Verse

As soon as he stepped behind the pulpit,
I discerned an aura he brought with him.
He had come from God's very own presence,
And he brought that palpable sense with him.

The Indwelling Presence

The Word

To them God chose to make known how great
among the Gentiles are the riches of the glory of
this mystery, which is Christ in you, the hope of glory.
Colossians 1:27

Voice from the Church

"It was many years ago that I made my response to Christ, kneeling at my bedside in a school dormitory. I have not regretted it. For I have experienced what Lord Reith (the first director general of the BBC) once called 'the mystery and the magic of the indwelling Christ.'" (Ole Hallesby, 1879-1961)

Reflection

Before I became a Christian, my first love was the game of baseball. Every chance I got, I played it, read about it, and attended games. I still enjoy the game—especially watching my grandsons play.

While I played the game in high school and the little leagues, I was only an average player. But as kids will do, I often thought of myself as a great player while swinging the bat. However, I was only "great" in my own imagination. But I often thought, if a Micky Mantle or a Duke Snider could have miraculously slipped inside me—what a different player I could have been! These were two of my favorite heroes—men of power and speed.

For the Christian, the Lord Jesus Christ has come "inside," in the person of the Holy Spirit. Think of it—Christ in you! Now when facing challenges, it is not my power, but his power working in and through me. Are you allowing him to work, or is there a hindrance? His presence and power can make you what you ought to be. Are you willing?

Verse

In my own strength I am powerless,
Failing and stumbling with every step.
But a life of defeat I need not live,
For the living Christ is alive in me.

Acknowledging our Failures

The Word
David said to Nathan, "I have sinned against the Lord." And Nathan said to David, "The Lord also has put away your sin; you shall not die."
2 Samuel 12:13

Voice from the Church
"Like the mother who shares her defenses against infections with her baby, mature Christians can help younger Christians develop spiritual antibodies. Too often more mature believers are shy to confess their problems and weaknesses. This gives the impression that the older Christians live on a different plane of holiness and have never struggled. We forget that when we expose our weaknesses we are able to share how God has helped us handle them." (Paul Brand, 1914-2003)*

Reflection
We must observe the fine line between sharing our personal failures and projecting to others an air of perfectionism. Following two days of speakers celebrating his life and ministry, it was time for Dr. J. I. Packer to speak. He introduced his talk with these words: "Don't expect me to perform an evangelical striptease." Though his language was rather crude, what he was saying to a large crowd that had gathered in honor of his eightieth birthday, was, "I'm not prepared to share my private personal weaknesses in this setting." And rightly so.

There is a place for confession; however, personal failures should never be shared publicly. I've known some to do so with lasting damage. We all have feet of clay; however, extreme care must be taken if and when we expose our *dirty* feet to another person. God will lead you to a mature Christian when confession to man is necessary, as David did to Nathan. God will give us wisdom, if we ask.

Verse
There for me the Savior stands,
Shows His wounds and spreads His hands.
God is love! I know, I feel;
Jesus weeps and loves me still. (Charles Wesley, 1707-1788)**

Living Selflessly

The Word

*²Let each of us please his neighbor for his good, to build him up.
³For Christ did not please himself, but as it is written, "The
reproaches of those who reproached you fell on me."*
Romans 15:2-3

Voice from the Church

"Sin is fundamentally an orientation toward self. We won't let God be God of our lives. We run our lives our way, without him. Self is at the center of the picture. Repentance is reorienting ourselves toward God. It's putting God at the center. What matters most is no longer our pleasure or success or even our problems, but God's glory (2 Cor. 12:7-9)." (Tim Chester, n.d.)*

Reflection

From the moment we enter this world, we are naturally inclined to please ourselves. Though we teach children to share, such sharing goes contrary to their instincts and will. We are members of a fallen race; we are naturally selfish.

While training and proper culture may make some of us appear less preoccupied with our own interests than the interests of others, nevertheless, we were all born with a sinful, self-centered disposition. Only the redemptive grace of the Lord Jesus Christ, and the purifying ministry of the Holy Spirit, can radically transform a self-serving person into a self-denying, other-oriented disciple of Christ.

Jesus is our perfect example of a selfless life. We can only approximate the perfect selfless life of Christ here below; however, the Spirit of Christ in us will keep prodding us toward a life that is more and more characteristically selfless.

Verse

*More like the Master I would live and grow;
More of His love to others I would show;
More self-denial, like His in Galilee,
More like the Master I long to ever be.* (Charles H. Gabriel, 1856-1932)**

Grieving the Holy Spirit

The Word

> *And do not grieve the Holy Spirit of God, by whom*
> *you were sealed for the day of redemption.*
> Ephesians 4:30

Voice from the Church

"There is no word in the New Testament that more clearly and beautifully reveals the tenderness of the heart of God. The word "grieve" means literally 'to cause sorrow to.' To 'grieve the Spirit' therefore means to cause Him to have sorrow, to make Him sad." (P. Kluepfel, 1866-1944)*

Reflection

The Holy Spirit is God's agent on earth, administering the work of the Triune God among men. How we relate to the Spirit is very important. We are informed that the Spirit can be resisted (Acts 7:51), quenched (1 Thess. 5:19), insulted (Heb. 10:29 NASB), and grieved (Eph. 4:30).

Only a Christian is capable of grieving the Holy Spirit. That is so because the Christian is one who has a love-relationship with God. It is those we love who can grieve us, wound us, for it is those we deeply care about.

How do you think the Lord Jesus felt when he looked upon the thrice-denying Simon Peter? He didn't say anything to the unfaithful disciple. All he did was look at Peter; but it was a look of grief—enough for Peter to weep bitterly (Luke 22:62).

When we sin—in our actions, interactions, and reactions—we cause God to grieve. Genesis 6:6 records that when our Creator looked upon the wickedness of Noah's age, "it grieved him to his heart." Careful Christians want to live so as not to cause the Spirit to grieve. Let us purpose to bring joy to God and not grief.

Verse

O grieve not the Spirit wherewith ye are sealed,
Ye Christians, but rather obey;
And hearken with joy when He speaks through His Word,
And faithfully walk in His way. (P. Kluepfel, 1866-1944)*

Be Encouraged as You Read

The Word

> For whatever was written in former days was written for
> our instruction, that through endurance and through
> the encouragement of the Scriptures we might have hope.
> Romans 15:4

Voice from the Church

Re-living the Psalms with Christ changes our emotions, to focus upon worship of God. Walking through the Gospels with Christ, changes our behaviour, to virtue and service. Living in the Epistles, leads to relationships with Christ and his Church, that educate our enjoyment, and thus give joy to others. Hoping in the book of Revelation, leads to humility and peace, as one entrusts one's future to God. (James M. Houston, b. 1922)*

Reflection

When read in the proper frame of mind, one can never read the Scriptures without receiving some measure of profit. For the Christian, the Bible is never read alone; the Spirit is always present. We should always try to remember this.

The written Word of God is a book of instruction—from Genesis to Revelation. As disciples of the Lord Jesus Christ, we will never graduate from his school; we will always be learners. However, remember the education we receive from reading is meant for our instruction, that should lead to transformation. Unless truth is assimilated by Christ's followers, we become a people with full heads and cold hearts—we are neither changed nor do we become agents for change unless God's truth is translated into life and action. We receive encouragement from the Word and hope is kept alive, when we act upon the principles and precepts in the Word of God. Be encouraged!

Verse

Your words, O Lord, are sweet to my taste,
Giving me life as I walk in your ways.
Write them deeply upon heart and mind,
That You may be glorified all my days.

Refined Gold

The Word

I counsel you to buy from me gold
refined by fire, so that you may be rich.
Revelation 3:18

Voice from the Church

"You feel sorry for us in India because of our poverty in material things.
We who know the Lord in India feel sorry for you in America because
of your spiritual poverty. We pray that God may give you gold tried in
the fire which He had promised to those who know the power of His
resurrection." (Bakht Singh, 1903-2000)*

Reflection

Those of us in the Western World are often guilty of viewing those in
Third World countries with an attitude of condescension and pity. Living in comparative wealth and with many gospel privileges, we feel sorry for those who may not know where their next meal and article of
clothing will come from.

We forget that many of those living in material deprivation may be
wealthier than we are, for they have experienced the riches of God's
grace while living in poverty, while we may be living in spiritual poverty surrounded with the wealth of the world. In reality, who is richer?

Fred Paxford, C. S. Lewis' gardener and handyman, remarked after
the death of Lewis, "Jack [Lewis' nickname] had no idea of money. His
mind was always set on higher things."** Lewis could have easily died
a wealthy man. He didn't; he gave away practically all of his wealth.

We live in an acquisitive age, a consumer society, resulting in the
cares of the world and the deceitfulness of riches choking the Word.
What are you living for, this world or the next?

Verse

Riches I heed not, nor man's empty praise,
Thou mine Inheritance, now and always:
Thou and Thou only, first in my heart,
High King of heaven, my Treasure Thou art. (Mary E. Byrne, 1880-1931)***

Always Stretching for More

The Word

> [7]*But whatever gain I had, I counted as loss for the sake of Christ.* [8]*Indeed, I count everything as loss because of the surpassing worth of knowing Christ Jesus my Lord.*
> Philippians 3:7-8

Voice from the Church

"You will ask me, 'Are you satisfied? Have you got all you want?' God forbid. With the deepest feeling of my soul I can say that I am satisfied with Jesus now; but there is also the consciousness of how much fuller the revelation can be of the exceeding abundance of His grace. Let us never hesitate to say, 'This is only the beginning.'" (Andrew Murray, 1828-1917)*

Reflection

The above two quotations were written by men who, at the time of the respective ministries had served their Lord for many years. One was an apostle, the other was a pastor and evangelist. Both of their statements reflect holy aspirations for even a greater knowledge of Christ and growth in grace. Neither man was content with the measure of his spiritual growth; there was more inner and outer territory to conquer in the name of Jesus.

Spiritual complacency, inner discouragements, and mental ennui are a drag on the body and soul. We must never give in to the infirmities of the flesh and spirit. We must never allow the culture of the world and the spiritual listlessness of others to affect our pursuit of God. The spirit must be constantly fed and serving others our daily ministry—until the Lord calls us home. Content with Jesus? Yes! Satisfied with our growth and service? Never! The spirit must be continually fed if we are to be healthy and have *bread* enough to give others.

Verse

I want to scale the utmost height
And catch a gleam of glory bright;
But still I'll pray till heav'n I've found,
"Lord, lead me on to higher ground." (Johnson Oatman, Jr., 1856-1922)**

A Holy Priesthood

The Word
⁴*As you come to him, a living stone rejected by men but in the sight
of God chosen and precious, ⁵you yourselves like living stones are
being built up as a spiritual house, to be a holy priesthood, to
offer spiritual sacrifices acceptable to God through Jesus Christ.*
1 Peter 2:4-5

Voice from the Church
"The cleansing which we receive through the blood of Christ enables us
to assume the role of a priest before God, and our ministry in this capacity finds its highest expression in prayer for others. Hence the whole
purpose of redemption while we live on this earth culminates in intercession." (Robert E. Coleman, b. 1928)*

Reflection
Not all of us are called to be a church leader of one kind or another. But
each of is called by God to serve him as a priest.

Under the Old Covenant, a prophet spoke to the people the words
given to him by God. Under the same Covenant, a priest spoke to God
on behalf of the people. Priests were intercessors, mediators. Priests
brought God and people together, by means of their sacrifices and prayers.

While few are called to be prophets, all are called by God under the
New Covenant to serve him as a priest. We are "a holy priesthood." This
is a high and noble calling—to bring before the Great Hight Priest daily
the needs of others. Are you faithfully fulfilling your calling as a priest?
God is depending on you to intercede for those you care deeply about.
God wants to make you into a faithful and effective priest. Are you willing to become a caring intercessor?

Verse
*Not just for their bread and material needs,
Not for skies always blue and a life of ease,
But for a walk with Christ that is real and close
Is a prayer that God approves and honors most.*

Pride's Pitfall

The Word

[17]*The seventy-two returned with joy, saying, "Lord, even the demons are subject to us in your name!"* [18]*And he said to them, "I saw Satan fall like lightning from heaven."*

Luke 10:17-19

Voice from the Church

"I have heard with great joy of the way in which God is using you as the instrument of His power in different places in Wales.... I am praying that ... He will keep you humble. It is so easy for us to become exalted when God uses us as the instruments of His power." (Excerpt from a letter to Evan Roberts (1878-1951) from R. A. Torrey, 1856-1928)*

Reflection

The curse of a prideful heart is the number one cause of church leaders and all others falling from the pinnacle of power with God and men. This diabolical and insidious monster has slain more servants of the Lord than all other sins combined. Pride was what caused an angel to fall from Heaven and a third of Heaven's host with him. It was pride that took the throne of Israel from King Saul. King Hezekiah displeased the Lord because his heart was lifted up with pride.

There were three sins that evangelist Billy Graham continually prayed the Lord would save him from: the love of money, sexual immorality, and a proud heart. Each of God's people would do well to pray that prayer often, including church leaders. When the seventy-two returned from a successful mission, they were glowing with self-confidence. Jesus immediately sensed a problem. He knew the same sin that befell Lucifer could cause the downfall of these men. And it can be your downfall as well. Guard against pride!

Verse

My soul, be on thy guard;
Ten thousand foes arise;
The hosts of sin are pressing hard
To draw thee from the skies. (George Heath, 1745-1822)**

God's Answer to Conflict

The Word

Clothe yourselves, all of you, with humility toward one another, for "God opposes the proud but gives grace to the humble."
1 Peter 5:5

Voice from the Church

"In the autumn of 1906, having felt depressed for some time by the cold and fruitless condition of my out-stations, I was preparing to set out on a tour to see what could be done to revive them. There was a matter, however, between the Lord and myself, that had to be straightened out before he could use me ... Suffice to say that there was a difference between a brother missionary and myself." (Jonathan Goforth, 1859-1936)*

Reflection

One of the ongoing challenges every disciple of the Lord Jesus faces is the challenge of serving in unity with his brothers and sisters in Christ. It often comes as a shocking surprise to a new convert, that Christians don't always get along too well with each other. That's a fact, and a sad one at that.

Taking the New Testament alone, there are plenty of references to believers in conflict and exhortations to unity. The most apparent conflict in the NT was the dissension between Paul and Barnabas (see Acts 15:37f). Then there's the friction that arose between Euodia and Syntyche (see Phil. 4:2-3). Conflicts will come; we must learn how to handle them. God's antidote to conflict is *agape* love—a love which demonstrates a higher regard for a fellow member in Christ than for oneself. Self-sacrificing love is God's answer to dissension. We would do well to be so filled with and practice *agape* love, that conflict and dissension would never enter our respective churches.

Verse

O the deep, deep love of Jesus,
Love of ev'ry love the best;
'Tis an ocean vast of blessing,
'Tis a haven sweet of rest. (S. Trevor Francis, 1834-1925)**

Overcoming Jealousy

The Word
> ^{5}What then is Apollos? What is Paul? Servants through whom
> you believed, as the Lord assigned to each. ^{6}I planted, Apollos
> watered, but God gave the growth. ^{7}So neither he who plants nor
> he who waters is anything, but only God who gives the growth.
> 1 Corinthians 3:5-7

Voice from the Church
"I was speaking in Chicago at a conference of students. And one night I was miserable. The problem had nothing to do with anyone else, it was in me. There were two speakers, and I became jealous of my brother. He had preached better than I had ... Although I said nothing, my friend sensed that all was not well. He was a wonderful man of God. He turned to me and said, 'What's wrong, brother?' ... At last I said, 'I'm sorry, my brother, I was jealous of you because you preached better than I did.'" (Festo Kivengere, 1919-1998)*

Reflection
We tend to forget that God has sovereignly distributed his gifts to each member in the body of Christ as he wills. A jealous disposition may arise when we see how well God is using another person's gift. This attitude rarely occurs when the person being used is outside our own circle. It is more likely to occur when one of our peers or someone we perceive to be beneath us is being wonderfully used of God. Such was the case with King Saul toward young David. When following David's successful victory on the field of battle, Saul heard the women extoling David: "Saul has struck down his thousands, and David his ten thousands." Then we read, "And Saul was very angry, and this saying displeased him" (1 Sam. 18:7-8). Beware of jealousy!

Verse
He saw God mightily use another;
He silently thanked God for his brother.
Thus, he conquered with love and prayer,
Satan losing his chance to enter there.

God's Compassion

The Word
> *For we do not have a high priest who is unable to*
> *sympathize with our weaknesses, but one who in every*
> *respect has been tempted as we are, yet without sin.*
> Hebrews 4:15

Voice from the Church
"He will carry us in his arms till we are able to walk. He will carry us in his arms when we are weary from walking. But he will not carry us if we will not walk." (George MacDonald, 1824-1905)*

Reflection
Our finite minds are incapable of fathoming the infinite compassion and concern our Father in Heaven and our Great High Priest demonstrate toward us. David's prayer for God's people is expressed in these words, "Oh, save your people and bless your heritage! Be their shepherd and *carry them forever*" (Psalm 28:9, italics added). And our merciful God will do just that—"carry" his people like the good and loving Shepherd that he is. Why is this? "For he knows our frame; he remembers that we are dust" (Ps. 103:14).

However, remember this: while God sympathizes with our weaknesses, he does not sympathize with rebellion and deliberate sin. Make no excuses for purposely violating God's known laws and will. Doing so will take you straight to your Father's "woodshed."

Yes, God's is compassionate, but don't deliberately try his patience. "Today, if you hear his voice, do not harden your hearts as in the rebellion" (Heb. 3:15).

To be a Christian is to be tempted. However, when tempted, we are assured we have the sympathy of our interceding High Priest.

Verse
Was there ever kinder shepherd
Half so gentle, half so sweet,
As the Savior who would have us
Come and gather at His feet? (Frederick W. Faber, 1814-1863)**

Just When We Think He's Finished with Us

The Word

> [3]*So I went down to the potter's house, and there he was*
> *working at his wheel.* [4]*And the vessel he was making of*
> *clay was spoiled in the potter's hand, and he reworked*
> *it into another vessel, as it seemed good to the potter to do.*
> Jeremiah 18:3-4

Voice from the Church

"After spending seventeen years in a barren wilderness, baffled and frustrated in Christian work and witness, I suddenly came to realise that God had made provision for clean hands and a pure heart. And on my face in my own study at five o'clock in the morning I came to know the recovering power of the blood of Christ." (Duncan Campbell, 1898-1972)*

Reflection

The mercy and compassion of God never cease to amaze me. They never cease to amaze not only because of what I have seen him doing in the lives of others, but mostly because of what I've seen of his persistent patience toward me.

I was privileged to hear Duncan Campbell preach over fifty years ago. He was mightily used of God in the 1940s and 50s in the Hebrides Revival. However, after being God's spokesman to those people for many years, he fell because of pride. God used a sermon by a faithful, younger preacher and his young daughter to point Campbell back to the path of humility. He confessed the pride of his heart, and our merciful Lord began to use him mightily once more.

Oh, the mercy and compassion of God! Remember the prophet Jonah? He too strayed from God's calling and appointed mission, but God was merciful and recommissioned him. And God has been merciful to you.

Verse

It is God: His love looks mighty,
But is mightier than it seems;
'Tis our Father: and His fondness
Goes far out beyond our dreams. (Frederick W. Faber, 1814-1863)**

Idols

The Word

> [2]*The more they were called, the more they went away; they kept sacrificing to the Baals and burning offerings to idols.* [3]*Yet it was I who taught Ephraim to walk; I took them up by their arms, but they did not know that I healed them.*

Hosea 11:2-3

Voice from the Church

"God will resolutely turn His face from the prayers of all who cherish idols in their hearts. In the very postures commonly adopted in prayer, the bowing of the head or the bending of the knee, the sovereignty of God is acknowledged. To submit to this proper relationship between the Sovereign and the suppliant is the foundation of all prayer. Idolatry, however, denies this very thing." (Arthur Wallis, 1922-1988)*

Reflection

An idol is a symbol that one has created first in his imagination. A material object, activity, or philosophy is simply the sinful product of the imagination.

Whatever governs our lifestyle and controls our minds is either God or a god. We in the Western World may not bow down to obvious pagan idols; however, there are so many popular activities, objects, and activities that we have become slaves to that we hardly realize it. I think of a man by the name of Albert, who attended services where I pastored for some years; he was converted later, in his 80s. Attending stock car races was one of Albert's idols, often keeping him from attending church. Following his conversion, he told me, "Ralph, I haven't been to one since."

Idols are all around us. Are you paying homage to any? Are you sure?

Verse

Lord Jesus, I long to be perfectly whole;
I want Thee forever to live in my soul;
Break down every idol, cast out every foe—
Now wash me, and I shall be whiter than snow. (James L. Nicholson, 1828-1896)**

"Maintain the spiritual glow"

The Word

> ⁴*I sought the Lord, and he answered me and delivered*
> *me from all my fears. ⁵Those who look to him are*
> *radiant, and their faces shall never be ashamed.*
> Psalm 34:4-5

Voice from the Church

"Dr. James Moffat—who, it is alleged, translated the New Testament not into English but into Scots!—took considerable liberties with the original in his treatment of the text. 'In spirit zealous' [Rom. 12:11] is all the Greek really requires. But Moffat amplifies that. He gives us the striking and memorable paraphrase" 'Maintain the spiritual glow.'" (Ian Macpherson, n.d.)

Reflection

I've known a good many of our Lord's radiant saints across the years, some of whom are now deceased, but some I know are still very much alive. Thinking of those departed saints, others were common laborers, some were stay-at-home mothers, others were professional people, and others were in their teens. Regardless of their ages and responsibilities and education, one thing set each of these apart from all other Christians—each one demonstrated a supreme love and devotion to their God and his Son, Lord Jesus Christ. In sharing Jesus and God's saving grace, their faces would light up—they were radiant! Of these saints I've known, each had his or her own peculiar human weaknesses and foibles. The fact is, some of them had glaring faults. No matter! They glowed. They were contagious Christians. Just being in their presence, one was challenged to live a holy life, to walk carefully and joyfully before God. Do you know a few radiant saints? May their number be multiplied!

Verse

Rejoice in God's saints, today and all days!
A world without saints forgets how to praise.
Their faith in acquiring the habit of prayer,
Their depth of adoring, Lord, help us to share. (Fred Pratt Green, 1903-2000)**

"Present Yourselves to God"

The Word
[12]Let not sin therefore reign in your mortal body, to make you obey its passions. [13]Do not present your members to sin as instruments for unrighteousness, but present yourselves to God as those who have been brought from death to life, and your members to God as instruments for righteousness. [14]For sin will have no dominion over you, since you are not under law but under grace.
Romans 6:12-14

Voice from the Church
"The French have a most suggestive proverb: 'He is not escaped who drags his chain!' Gibbon tells of one of the Roman emperors who was brought from prison to the palace, and who sat for some hours on the throne with his fetters on his limbs. Thousands of those whom God has brought out of prison are in much the same condition. They are in the palace, but they carry about them the vestiges of the prison-life." (J. Gregory Mantle, 1853-1925)*

Reflection
Total surrender and devotion to God is the call of God to every born-again follower of the Lord Jesus Christ. God will accept nothing less from his children than service with a whole heart. Few of Israel's and Judah's kings served God with a whole heart. Though some served God with total devotion for a period, many eventually developed a divided heart, like King Hezekiah. God will not be fully satisfied with our worship and service until every faculty of the body and soul has been presented to him in full surrender and consecration. As long as we have pockets of reservation and resistance in our heart and behavior, God will not be able to bless and use us as he desires.

Verse
All to Jesus I surrender,
All to Him I freely give;
I will ever love and trust Him,
In His presence daily live. (Judson W. Van DeVenter, 1855-1939)**

An Audience of One

The Word

For am I now seeking the approval of man, or of God?
Or am I trying to please man? If I were still trying to
please man, I would not be a servant of Christ.
Galatians 1:10

Voice from the Church

"Hugh Latimer, who was martyred in Oxford for his faith, was frequently invited to preach before the king of England. 'One Sunday,' he writes, 'as I was in my study preparing myself by prayer and meditation before the service I heard a voice saying to me, "Latimer, Latimer, be careful what you preach today, because you are going to preach before the king of England."' 'After a little I heard another voice saying to me, "Latimer, Latimer, be careful what you preach today, because you are going to preach before the King of Kings."'" (John M. Drescher, 1929-2014)*

Reflection

Sooner or later the Christian will have to decide if he is going to be a man-pleaser or a God-pleaser. To be a man-pleaser is to fear man rather than to walk in the fear of God. To be a God-pleaser is to walk through life beholden to the Lord God omnipotent—to play, as it were, to an audience of One.

As exhorted in the pages throughout the New Testament, believers are to seek to please fellow believers for their good and edification. However, we must never seek the approval of man to advance a selfish agenda or for insincere purposes. It is well to be liked; it is better to be liked for the right reasons. To live with a single eye to the glory of God is to live a well-ordered life, a life that God honors. Are you living such a life, a God-pleasing life, by the strength of the Spirit?

Verse

Shall I, for fear of feeble man,
The Spirit's course in me restrain?
Or, undismayed, in deed and word
Be a true witness for my Lord? (Johann J. Winkler, 1670-1722)**

Walking in God's Wisdom

The Word

> ^{9}*And so, ... we have not ceased to pray for you, asking*
> *that you may be filled with the knowledge of his will in all*
> *spiritual wisdom and understanding, ^{10}so as to walk in a*
> *manner worthy of the Lord, fully pleasing to him: bearing fruit*
> *in every good work and increasing in the knowledge of God.*
> Colossians 1:8-10

Voice from the Church

"Throughout our earthly lives, it is always at the point of need—that moment of crisis when we cast about for some solution or answer or even some escape—that the opportunity is offered to us to choose. We will accept either the solutions, answers, and escapes that the world offers (and there are always plenty of those), or the radical alternatives shown to the mind attuned to Christ's." (Elisabeth Elliot, 1926-2015)*

Reflection

We will never face a crisis (and they are sure to come) or habitually make wise and righteous choices, unless we fill our minds with God's words, allowing the Spirit to guide our thinking. Poor choices are a mere reflection of a heart and mind left uncontrolled by the Word and Spirit.

David speaks of the righteous and blameless person, of the wise and understanding person, as one that "The law of his God is in his heart; his steps do not slip" (Ps. 37:31).

The Christian cannot live without looking back and having some regrets, regrets that came because of poor choices. However, as we grow in Christ, we should have fewer regrets. God has promised: "If any of you lacks wisdom, let him ask God, who gives generously to all without reproach, and it will be given him" (James 1:5).

Verse

That heavenly wisdom from above
Abundantly impart;
And let it guard, and guide, and warm,
And penetrate my heart. (Christopher Smart, 1722-1771)**

The Spirit Reminds Us

The Word

> [25] "These things I have spoken to you while I am still with you. [26] But the Helper, the Holy Spirit, whom the Father will send in my name, he will teach you all things and bring to your remembrance all that I have said to you.
> John 14:25-26

Voice from the Church

"If we try to apply the teaching of our Lord apart from the imparted nature of our Lord to our souls, we will make a muddle. It is not that we take the Sermon on the Mount as precepts and try to live up to them, but that when the Spirit of God brings some word of God back to our remembrance in certain circumstances—will we obey it?" (Oswald Chambers, 1874-1917)*

Reflection

I used to often pray, after reading the Scriptures, "Lord, if I could only remember everything I have just read, how much better it would be for me in my walk with you." Then one day the Lord brought to my remembrance the above words of the Lord Jesus. God will remind us of the words we have meditated on—just when we need his word for a particular time and situation. Jesus told his disciples this would be the case for them: "And when they bring you to trial and deliver you over, do not be anxious beforehand what you are to say, but say whatever is given you in that hour, for it is not you who speak, but the Holy Spirit" (Mark 13:11). It is well to memorize Scripture; however, we can never memorize enough Scripture to cover every future contingency. But the Holy Spirit, who indwells us, will bring to our minds the very word we need when we need it. You can depend on it!

Verse

I cannot trust my own memory,
To act according to God's truth.
But I do trust the Holy Spirit,
To keep my faulty mind renewed.

Gloom

The Word

⁴But he himself went a day's journey into the wilderness and came and sat down under a broom tree. And he asked that he might die, saying, "It is enough; now, O Lord, take away my life, for I am no better than my fathers." ⁵And he lay down and slept under a broom tree.

1 Kings 19:4-5

Voice from the Church

"For more than a whole week I have been tossed to and fro in death and in hell, so that I am still drained of all strength in my body and am trembling in all my limbs. I have lost Christ completely and have been shaken by the floods and storms of despair and blasphemy. However, as moved by the prayers of the saints, God has begun to have mercy on me and to snatch my soul from deepest hell." (Martin Luther, 1483-1546)*

Reflection

Many a saint has been cast down into the throes of discouragement and despondency and depression, if not despair. Some Christians will retort with platitudes, saying such emotions and feelings should not beset any of God's children.

I well remember the response an esteemed brother in the Lord gave to the idea that *real* Christians never experience severe emotional down times. He would quote the one line in Edward Mote's beautiful hymn: "When darkness seems to hide His face,"** and then add, "There are times in the life of the Christian when darkness not only "seems" to hide God's face, but in fact does." An apt observation! In such times, it's not that we are hidden from God, but that God is hidden from us. Every mature believer can testify to such experiences. No, God never forsakes his own, though at times it may feel like it.

Verse

His oath, His covenant, His blood,
Support me in the whelming flood.
When all around my soul gives way,
He then is all my hope and stay. (Edward Mote, 1797-1874)***

God is Faithful

The Word

> *I will also praise you with the harp for your faithfulness, O my*
> *God; I will sing praises to you with the lyre, O Holy One of Israel.*
> Psalm 71:22

Voice from the Church

"I do not intend to be one of those who bemoan little results, while 'resting in the faithfulness of God.' My cue is to take hold of the faithfulness of God and USE THE MEANS necessary to secure big results." (James O. Fraser, 1886-1938)*

Reflection

To be "faithful' is to be true to one's word and promises, to be reliable, trusted, and to be believed. The Bible is replete with references to God's faithfulness. For the Christian, the thought of an *unfaithful* God is unimaginable (or should be). The God of Abraham, Isaac, and Jacob, the God and Father of the Lord Jesus Christ is and always will be faithful. The God spoken of in the written Word is revealed to be and found to be a faithful God. The patriarchs and saints of old trusted in and depended upon God's word.

It is in the very nature of God to be faithful. He can be none other. The Word informs us that God is faithful and that his faithfulness is great (Ps. 31:5; Lam. 3:23); that he has never failed to keep one of his promises (Josh. 21:45); that he faithfully keeps covenant with his children (Deut. 7:9); that he is faithful to help us when facing temptation (1 Cor. 10:13); that he is faithful to forgive us when we have confessed our sin (1 John 1:9); that he will establish us and protect us against Satan (2 Thess. 3:3); and so much more. Yes, God is faithful, and because he is faithful we can trust his recorded and revealed words to be true.

Verse

Great is Thy faithfulness, O God my Father,
There is no shadow of turning with Thee;
Thou changest not, Thy compassions, they fail not
As Thou hast been Thou forever wilt be. (Thomas O. Chisholm, 1866-1960)**

"My Aim in Life"

The Word
¹⁰ *You ... have followed my teaching, my conduct, my aim in life, my faith, my patience, my love, my steadfastness,* ¹¹ *my persecutions and sufferings that happened to me at Antioch, at Iconium, and at Lystra— which persecutions I endured; yet from them all the Lord rescued me.*
2 Timothy 3:10-11

Voice from the Church
"There have been men before now who got so interested in proving the existence of God that they came to care nothing for God Himself ... as if the good Lord had nothing to do but *exist*! There have been some who were so occupied in spreading Christianity that they never gave a thought to Christ." (C. S. Lewis, 1898-1963)*

Reflection
How often, during the two millennia of the church's existence, have Christians taken doctrinal bypaths and swerved from preaching and teaching the centrality of Christ and the Cross. This sad fact occurred in the first century and has been with us ever since.

The apostles kept to the centralities. Paul reminded the church, "For I resolved to know nothing while I was with you except Jesus Christ and him crucified" (1 Cor. 2:2). Paul exhorted his son in the gospel to "preach the Word" (2 Tim. 4:2); he said there were those who had "swerved from the truth" (2 Tim. 2:18).

Paul's "aim in life" was to glorify God by faithfully proclaiming the gospel, exalting the Lord Jesus Christ, lifting high the cross, and to live a life pleasing to God. What is your aim?

If we will keep to the Word, walk in the Spirit, emphasizing the centrality of Christ and the gospel, we can never go wrong.

Verse
Many futile bypaths have lured
more than one of Your children, Lord.
I would proclaim and lift high Christ—
this my aim, in deed and in word.

God's Ways with Man

The Word

[8]For my thoughts are not your thoughts, neither are your ways my ways, declares the Lord. [9]For as the heavens are higher than the earth, so are my ways higher than your ways and my thoughts than your thoughts.

Isaiah 55:8-9

Voice from the Church

"Every now and then, I would catch a glimpse of a cross—not necessarily a crucifix; maybe two pieces of wood accidentally nailed together, on a telegraph pole, for instance—and suddenly my heart would stand still. In an instinctive, intuitive way I understood that something more important, more tumultuous, more passionate, was at issue than our good causes, however admirable they might be." (Malcolm Muggeridge, 1903-1990)*

Reflection

The thoughts and ways of the Lord God are beyond all human comprehension: "a God comprehended is no God at all," a mentor of mine would often say. This axiom certainly holds up when pondering the providential ways of God in the conversion of men and women.

For example, think of the conversion of Zacchaeus. Jesus is passing through the town of Jericho. Zacchaeus just *happened* to be on that road and climbed a tree to get a better glimpse of Jesus; and before the day ended Jesus was in the tax collector's home, and Zacchaeus was a changed man!

For me, I was invited to attend church to hear the pastor's farewell sermon. I didn't respond to the closing invitation, but the pastor walked down the aisle, invited me to give my life to Jesus, and I left church that evening a converted teen. At the time, I had no plans to become a Christian; however, Omniscience thought otherwise. What's your story?

Verse

God unchanging, God so dear,
God afar, and yet so near,
In thy majesty so fair,
Thou art present ev'rywhere. (Daniel O. Teasley, 1876-1942)**

Loving Ourselves at the Expense of Others

The Word

> *Behold, this was the guilt of your sister Sodom: she*
> *and her daughters had pride, excess of food, and*
> *prosperous ease, but did not aid the poor and needy.*
> Ezekiel 16:49

Voice from the Church

"To consume the best for yourself and give the crumbs to God is blasphemy. A heart that truly worships is a heart that gives its best to God in time and substance.... I have to wonder whether someday we may wake up to discover that all our incestuous spending on ourselves and our frantic construction of excessively luxurious places of worship—even as we ignore, for the most part, the hurting and the deprived world—filled God's heart with pain." (Ravi Zacharias, b. 1946)*

Reflection

When we think of the sins of Sodom, our minds instinctively identify Sodom with sexual immorality. And it's true to the facts: homosexuality and sexual deviance of every kind populated that region. But the sins of Sodom were more than those of a sexual nature. Ezekiel informs us that Sodom's sins consisted of pride, gluttony and hoarding, self-gratification, and an utter disregard toward the poor and needy.

How many of us Christians cry out against the sins of sexual immorality while we are blatantly guilty of the other prominent sins of Sodom? Social media is plagued with photos of Christians living sumptuously. We see few photos of Christians helping the needy. It's a snapshot of Evangelical narcissism. While denouncing obvious sins, we have fallen prey to Sodom's other sins. When will we repent? When will we turn from our wicked ways?

Verse

Search out our hearts and make us true,
Wishful to give to all their due;
From love of pleasure, lust of gold,
From sins which make the heart grow cold. (William B. Carpenter, 1841-1918)**

Divine Love

The Word

[20]*If anyone says, "I love God," and hates his brother, he is a liar;
for he who does not love his brother whom he has seen cannot love
God whom he has not seen.* [21]*And this commandment we have
from him: whoever loves God must also love his brother.*

1 John 3:20-21

Voice from the Church

"You cannot be receiving the life of Christ without becoming like Him.
You cannot walk with God without keeping His commandments. You
cannot know God without immediately, automatically loving Him. Love
always manifests itself by doing what the object of its love desires." (Martyn Lloyd-Jones, 1999-1981)*

Reflection

The first-century church was characterized by an upward and outward
look and love: they loved God and others with a sincere and pure *agape*
love. This love characterized these holy people wherever they were and
went. Their love was warm, but not soft; it was deep, and not superfi-
cial; it was pure, and not pharisaical. And this quality of divine love has
always characterized the true people of God; Jesus said it would be so:
"By this all people will know that you are my disciples, if you have love
for one another" (John 13:35).

When the church fails, it always fails first in its lack of true biblical
love—God's love. And when we fail in love, we become guilty of hate,
which is the absence of love—either passively or overtly.

When the fresh winds of renewal and revival blow across the church,
it always brings with it God's outpoured love. The people of God must
return to what has been lost among them—*agape* love.

Verse

Love divine, all loves excelling,
   joy of heav'n, to earth come down,
Fix in us Thy humble dwelling;
   all Thy faithful mercies crown. (Charles Wesley,1707-1788)**

Changed Lives

The Word

[18]*Also many of those who were now believers came, confessing and divulging their practices.* [19]*And a number of those who had practiced magic arts brought their books together and burned them in the sight of all. And they counted the value of them and found it came to fifty thousand pieces of silver.*
Acts 19:18-19

Voice from the Church

"So radical was the difference in my life that a few months after I became a follower of Jesus, our five-year-old daughter Alison went up to my wife and said, 'Mommy, I want God to do for me what he's done for Daddy.'" (Lee Strobel, b. 1952)*

Reflection

The proof as to whether a person has truly repented of their sins and believed on Christ as Lord and Savior, is whether they thereafter are living a changed life. Where there is no noticeable change in attitudes and actions following a confession of faith, we have every right to be suspicious of one's profession of faith.

There will always be ongoing change in one's life following the conversion event: "we all, ... are being transformed into the same image from one degree of glory to another' (2 Cor. 3:18). With that being said, however, true adult conversions are conspicuous with radical and observable change. There cannot be ongoing change without the change that comes with repentance. Repentance implies change and turning—a turning from our sins. In the Hebrew Scriptures, we often read the exhortation given to sinning people, to turn from their sins. Have you changed? Have you turned from your sins?

Verse

Living here with my Lord in a holy union,
Day by day, all the way, holding sweet communion;
Oh, what change grace hath wrought in my lowly station
Since my soul has received full and free salvation! (Haldor Lillinas, 1885-1959)**

Whose Kingdom Are We Building?

The Word
[29] *I know that after my departure fierce wolves will come in among you, not sparing the flock;* [30] *and from among your own selves will arise men speaking twisted things, to draw away the disciples after them.* [31] *Therefore be alert, remembering that for three years I did not cease night or day to admonish every one with tears.*
Acts 20:29-31

Voice from the Church
"It is important for Christians to be on their guard against building their own little empires…. Whatever excuses those outside may give to justify their grabs for power these do not apply to Christians. They of all people should bear in mind that they are accountable to God and that they are doing the work of God, not pursuing personal ambition." (Leon Morris, 1914-2006)*

Reflection
It is insidious and often imperceptible; it is frequently applauded and paraded before the undiscerning—this drive that some have in building their own kingdom. It happened to King Saul after the Spirit of the Lord left him: "Saul came to Carmel, and behold, he set up a monument for himself" (1 Sam. 15:12). It happened to Saul's son Absalom: "Now Absalom in his lifetime had taken and set up for himself a pillar which is in the King's Valley" (2 Sam. 18:18). These men erected their own monuments; they never wanted to be forgotten. We do remember them, but not in the way they thought we would.

True servants of the Son of Man are not engaged in building their own kingdoms and memorials. God servants know who is keeping the books. That's enough for them.

Verse
Arm me with jealous care
as in Thy sight to live,
And now Thy servant, Lord, prepare
a strict account to give! (Charles Wesley, 1707-1788)**

Believing, Not Achieving

The Word

⁸For by grace you have been saved through faith.
And this is not your own doing; it is the gift of God,
⁹not a result of works, so that no one may boast.
Ephesians 2:8-9

Voice from the Church

"In an era of performance-oriented religion, the rediscovery of grace presents a profoundly subtle challenge. Teaching a religionist grace is like teaching a workaholic how to relax. In a fast-paced culture of self-congratulatory striving, the Good News of grace is like a fresh breeze of relief." (Thomas C. Oden, 1931-2016)*

Reflection

The apostle Paul's emphasis on salvation by grace through faith was received, by those schooled in the Law of Moses, as utterly contrary to the Law and purposes of God. God's plan of salvation had been—even under the Old Covenant—misconstrued and reconstructed into a system whereby many of the Law's teachers taught that salvation was something to be *achieved*—not *received*.

Such teaching and practice are still a problem throughout Christendom. For those who have been enculturated to believe that nothing can be received without first earning it, salvation as a gift from God is a total conundrum, mindboggling, and reason-defying. Such a plan for man's redemption and eternal salvation is a huge stumbling block to many. Such was the case in Paul's day; such is the case today. Prior to his conversion, Paul made every effort to gain God's acceptance—then it was revealed to him that salvation was by grace through faith. You can neither earn or achieve salvation. It can only be received; it is a gift.

Verse

Oh, the love that drew salvation's plan!
Oh, the grace that brought it down to man!
Oh, the mighty gulf that God did span
　At Calvary! (William R. Newell, 1868-1956)**

This Present World

The Word

> *For Demas, having loved this present world,*
> *has deserted me and gone to Thessalonica.*
> 2 Timothy 4:10 NASB

Voice from the Church

"The love of the world, and the love of God, are like the scales of a balance, as the one falleth, the other doth rise: when our natural inclinations prosper, and the creature is exalted in our soul, religion is faint, and doth languish; but when earthly objects wilt away, and lose their beauty, and the soul begins to cool and flag in its prosecution of them, then the seeds of grace take root, and the divine life begins to flourish and prevail." (Henry Scougal, 1650-1678)*

Reflection

To abandon our Christian calling and to desert our post of duty, for anything less than the call of God on our life, is to embrace this present world instead of embracing the will of God.

Years ago, I was privileged to sit on a ministerial committee. It was our responsibility to review candidates for ordination, and other ancillary matters pertaining to the status of the denomination's ministers. A middle-aged minister came before the committee in one of its sessions prepared to surrender his credentials. The man was discouraged and planned to leave the ministry for a secular position. The committee was wise and compassionate in their counsel and encouraged the brother to hold fast to his calling. Which he did.

Often what lies behind discouragement is a deficiency of love for the Lord Jesus. When that occurs, the love for lesser things creeps in—the love of this present world.

Verse

What was in the city of Thessalonica,
  that caused Demas to desert the apostle Paul?
It was not so much as what was in the city,
  as what had entered his heart that induced his fall.

Grieving Over Misspoken Words

The Word
^{24}*And the Lord's servant must not be quarrelsome but kind to every-one, able to teach, patiently enduring evil,* ^{25}*correcting his opponents with gentleness. God may perhaps grant them repentance leading to a knowledge of the truth,* ^{26}*and they may come to their senses and escape from the snare of the devil, after being captured by him to do his will.*
2 Timothy 2:24-26

Voice from the Church
"Sorry for a hasty word, spoken to Lucas a week ago—rather, to his wife on the matter of salt. I guess he didn't understand that we did not bring supplies for them to buy. He says his spirit is changed and that he cannot feel the same again with me in the work. I sat an hour or more with him humbling myself ridiculously before other Indians to try to gain him. God knows if I gained; I strove to be meek. May the Spirit restore us to fellowship again." (Jim Elliot, 1927-1056)*

Reflection
Years ago, waiting for the service to begin, two evangelists were talking to each other; the question of tongue-control came up. H. Robb French leaned over to S. I Emery and asked, "Dr. Emery, could you tell me when a person should speak and when he shouldn't. With a broad smile, Dr. Emery shook his head and answered, "No, I can't." Years later, the same two men were at a different venue. Dr. Emery asked Brother French, "Have you gotten a good answer to the question you asked me a few years back, about when one should speak and when he shouldn't?" Brother French shook his head and answered, "No, I haven't."

Wisdom is needed, when to speak, what to say, and how to say it. When we fail in this matter, let us have grace to confess it.

Verse
Oh, be careful, little tongue, what you say,
Oh, be careful, little tongue, what you say.
There's a Father up above looking down in tender love,
Oh, be careful, little tongue, what you say. (Author Unknown)**

A Powerful Witness

The Word

[56]And he said, "Behold, I see the heavens opened, and the Son of Man standing at the right hand of God." [57]But they cried out with a loud voice and stopped their ears and rushed together at him. [58]Then they cast him out of the city and stoned him. And the witnesses laid down their garments at the feet of a young man named Saul. [59]And as they were stoning Stephen, he called out, "Lord Jesus, receive my spirit."
Acts 7:56-59

Voice from the Church

"Scarcely ever did I dine with him but his ardour in returning thanks, sometimes in an appropriate hymn, sometimes in prayer, has inflamed the souls of all present. In all the twenty-four years that I knew him, I never remember him to have spoken unkindly of anyone but once; and then I was struck with the humiliation he expressed for it in prayer next day." (Charles Simeon 1759-1836, writing of Henry Venn, 1796-1873)*

Reflection

Holy men and women are awful weapons in the hands of a holy God. Unbelievers may reject what Christians believe and teach, regarding the gospel of Christ; nevertheless, they cannot sincerely refute how graciously godly Christians behave under pressure and facing opposition.

One of the greatest arguments and witnesses for the reality of the crucified and risen Christ is a holy life. It is more than a coincidence that Saul, a radical persecutor of Christians, was soon converted after witnessing holy Stephen's reaction as he faced death at the hands of his tormentors. Surely, more sinners would be won for Christ, if they saw more of Christ in Christ's followers. A verbal witness backed by a Christlike life is an awful weapon in the hands of God.

Verse

Not merely in the words you say,
Not only in the deeds confessed,
But in the most unconscious way,
Is Christ expressed. (Beatrice Clelland, 1904-2005)**

Joy in the Midst of Trials

The Word

[32]*But recall the former days when, after you were enlightened, you endured a hard struggle with sufferings,* [33]*sometimes being publicly exposed to reproach and affliction, and sometimes being partners with those so treated.* [34]*For you had compassion on those in prison, and you joyfully accepted the plundering of your property, since you knew that you yourselves had a better possession and an abiding one.* [35]*Therefore do not throw away your confidence, which has a great reward.*

Hebrews 10:32-35

Voice from the Church

"Many Christians have sad faces because they refuse to go the second mile. Because of refusing, their hearts can no longer sing. Were they to go the second mile, they would feel so relieved that they could sing aloud for joy." (Watchman Nee, 1903-1972)*

Reflection

There is no earthly explanation for why certain believers face some of the most difficult trials imaginable and, yet, through it all, maintain a joyful composure.

No, there is no *earthly* explanation; however, there is a *heavenly* one: joy is given from above. Joy finds its source in the one "who for the joy that was set before him endured the cross, despising the shame" (Heb. 12:2).

Church history is replete with testimonies of Christians, who despite their difficult circumstances, possessed and demonstrated an observable joy, which is a fruit of the indwelling Holy Spirit.

Joy can be neither manufactured nor counterfeited. It comes from the Father above. Are you a joy-filled Christian? If not, why?

Verse

I have found the joy no tongue can tell,
How its waves of glory roll;
It is like a great o'erflowing well,
Springing up within my soul. (Barney E. Warren, 1867-1951)**

Fruit through Abiding

The Word

> [4]*Abide in me, and I in you. As the branch cannot bear fruit by itself, unless it abides in the vine, neither can you, unless you abide in me ...*[11]*These things I have spoken to you, that my joy may be in you, and that your joy may be full.*
> John 15:4, 11

Voice from the Church

"Do not confound *work* and *fruit*. There may be a good deal of work for Christ that is not the fruit of the heavenly Vine. Do not seek for work only. Oh! Study this question of fruit-bearing. It means the very life and the very power and the very spirit and the very love within the heart of the Son of God—it means the heavenly Vine Himself coming into your heart and mine." (Andrew Murray, 1828-1917)*

Reflection

We humans are meant to work, to be employed in labor that is both meaningful and fulfilling. This is true for all people, including Christians. There is no place in the kingdom of God for lazy and indifferent laborers.

It is well to remember, however, that while we are called to be productive and effective laborers in our Lord's vineyard, true fruit only results from a vital, faithful connection to the Vine. Jesus said, "As the branch cannot bear fruit by itself, unless it abides in the vine, neither can you, unless you abide in me" (John 15:4). In the words of Paul, "I planted, Apollos watered, but God gave the growth" (1 Cor. 3:6).

Yes, we are called to be diligent laborers, but remember, it is God who produces the fruit, the growth, as we joyfully abide in Christ, who is our very life.

Verse

Abide in Christ—this highest blessing gain;
Each day sweet fellowship with Him maintain.
Abiding, He and we are joined as one;
In constant fellowship, all barriers gone. (Author Unknown)**

God's Words are Reliable

The Word

> *The sum of Your word is truth, And every one*
> *of Your righteous ordinances is everlasting.*
> Psalm 119:160 NASB

Voice from the Church

"Critics of the Bible usually pour scorn on the idea that God has a plan of salvation for the world. We must not allow these rationalistic ideas to daunt us from following our Lord or his Word. We know full well that not one jot or tittle will pass away until everything is fulfilled. Time and again the New Testament exclaims, 'This happened that the Scriptures might be fulfilled.' Yes, what the Bible says is far more certain than many unbelievers would care to admit." (Kurt Koch, 1913-1987)*

Reflection

If the written Word of God is unreliable, if any part or doctrine it affirms is untrue, if what the prophets and the Lord Jesus and the apostles spoke and recorded is inaccurate—then Christians have no sure word to believe and proclaim.

Unbelief regarding the words of God first entered the human race in Eden's Garden. The Lord God had furnished Eden with a wide variety of beautiful trees, all to be enjoyed by the first couple and their offspring. However, there was one tree Adam and Eve were forbidden to eat: "but of the tree of the knowledge of good and evil you shall not eat" (Gen. 2:17).

The Serpent thought otherwise: "Did God actually say, 'You shall not eat of any tree in the garden'?" (Gen. 3:1). The woman took the bait, and through her the man. The world has never been the same. It is a fearful and eternally destructive matter, to disbelieve the words of God.

Verse

How firm a foundation you saints of the Lord,
  is laid for your faith in his excellent Word!
What more can he say than to you he has said,
  to you who for refuge to Jesus have fled? (George Keith, 1638-1716)**

One Fellowship

The Word

[15]*And when [Jehu] departed from there, he met Jehonadab the son of Rechab coming to meet him. And he greeted him and said to him, "Is your heart true to my heart as mine is to yours?" And Jehonadab answered, "It is." Jehu said, "If it is, give me your hand." So he gave him his hand. And Jehu took him up with him into the chariot.* [16]*And he said, "Come with me, and see my zeal for the Lord." So he had him ride in his chariot.*

2 Kings 10:15-16

Voice from the Church

"I thank God that he has given me a ministry of the Word that leaps over denominational walls and man-made barriers, and that I belong to a wide and loving fellowship of people who seek to honor Jesus Christ and bring sinners to faith in Him. I guess it's the broadness of my ministry that has upset the people who have a more narrow outlook on the Christian life than I do." (Warren Wiersbe, b. 1929)*

Reflection

The message and mission of the church of the Lord Jesus Christ have been sorely damaged through the centuries because of religious bigotry. Our opinions and prejudices have created unnecessary divisions and animosities in the body of Christ. My wife and I were visiting a church some time ago. In the foyer, a young man saw me carrying what he thought to be a Bible (it was an iPad). He asked, "Is that the King James Version?" I politely ignored the question. He asked again, "Is that the King James Version?" I replied, holding my iPad out to him, "All the versions are in here." His question was no doubt sincere, but uninformed. Let us unite around the truth, as it is found in Jesus!

Verse

You servants of God, your Master proclaim,
And publish abroad his wonderful name;
The name all-victorious of Jesus extol;
His kingdom is glorious and rules over all. (Charles Wesley, 1707-1788)**

One Body

The Word

[20]*"I do not ask for these only, but also for those who will
believe in me through their word,* [21]*that they may all be one,
just as you, Father, are in me, and I in you, that they also may
be in us, so that the world may believe that you have sent me."*
John 17:20-21

Voice from the Church

"My hearers are made up of all sorts ... My endeavor is to persuade
them to love one another ... Whether water baptism should be adminis-
tered by a spoonful or tubful, or in a river, or in Jordan, are to me points
of no great importance ... If a man loves Jesus, I will love him, whatever [denomination] he may be called by ... His differing from me will not
always prove him to be wrong, except I am infallible myself." (John Newton, 1725-1807)*

Reflection

If the prayer that Christ prayed, as recorded in John 17, means anything,
it means the Lord Jesus desired then and desires now, that there should
be an observable unity among his disciples. If this were true, observers
would readily acknowledge Christ was sent into the world by the Father.
Jesus prayed for this. Do we believe this is still his concern?

I have seen my share of divisions in the body of Christ—many of
them occurring over nonsensical issues led by flesh-driven people. Too
often self-willed leaders, with shrill voices domineering the church's
deliberations, precipitate friction and unnecessary separation among the
brethren. The *goats* wound untold numbers of *lambs*, with the entire
body suffering. Such actions are not the way of the Word and Spirit.
God has a better plan. Let us do his work in his way.

Verse

Christ prayed for Body oneness;
We ought to pray the same.
Then to seek by word and deed,
To glorify His name.

One Faith

The Word

[4]*There is one body and one Spirit—just as you were called to the one
hope that belongs to your call—* [5]*one Lord, one faith, one baptism,*
[6]*one God and Father of all, who is over all and through all and in all.*
Ephesians 4:4-6

Voice from the Church

"If the word *revelation* emphasizes God's initiative in making himself
known and *inspiration* denotes the process he employed, then *authority*
indicates the result. Because Scripture is the revelation of God by the
inspiration of the Spirit, it has authority over us." (John Stott, 1921-2011)*

Reflection

The inspired writer has noted there is one body, one Spirit, one hope,
one Lord, one baptism, one God and Father and one faith. Not many
faiths, but one faith.

There are three main branches in Christianity: Protestant, Orthodox,
and Roman Catholic. Within these three, there are hundreds of denominations, mostly within Protestantism. And, yet, the apostle said there is
only "one faith"—meaning core doctrinal beliefs that all true Christians
commonly confess.

Within these branches of Christianity, there are many differing convictions and preferences, and even heresies which have caused divisions
among the disciples of Christ. As the apostle wrote elsewhere, "The
Lord knows those who are his" (2 Tim. 2:19).

There is only "one faith." While there are many peripheral issues
which identify a variety of streams within Christianity, we should never
allow these to prevent us from experiencing the common fellowship we
have in Christ Jesus the Lord.

Verse

When we began to discuss
  minor issues that divide,
Our fellowship grew quite cool,
  'till the Lord drew near our side.

Sacred Places

The Word
> [14]*And Jacob set up a pillar in the place where he had spoken with him, a pillar of stone. He poured out a drink offering on it and poured oil on it.* [15]*So Jacob called the name of the place where God had spoken with him Bethel.*
Genesis 35:14-15

Voice from the Church
"When the Memorial Church moved farther out the Frederick Road to a new site, they cut the altar rail where I knelt and was converted and made it into a prayer desk with an inscription on it: 'At this spot Stanley Jones knelt and gave himself to Christ'... Tradition says that Zacchaeus used to go water the sycamore tree in which he first met the Lord. I understand that; I go periodically to that spot and water it with my tears of gratitude." (E. Stanley Jones, 1884-1973)*

Reflection
Whenever the Lord God reveals himself to his children in pardoning and saving grace, those places remain special and indelibly written on our memory. It was so with Abraham, Isaac, and Jacob, and it is so with you and me.

The sacred place for me is a small wood-framed church, on Ohio Street, in Columbus, Indiana. On a Sunday evening, in August 1961, I knelt at the mahogany stained altar, with my pastor kneeling in front of me and my brother beside me (no one stood in our church, when repenting of their sins!). My life was forever changed; Christ came in!

Places, in themselves, have no special power, but the God who reveals himself to us in special ways at specific places make those places sacred. Do you have a sacred place, where Christ first became real to you?

Verse
Happy the church, thou sacred place,
The seat of thy Creator's grace;
Thine holy courts are his abode,
Thou earthly palace of our God! (Isaac Watts, 1674-1748)**

A Second Touch

The Word

^{23}And he took the blind man by the hand and led him out of the village, and when he had spit on his eyes and laid his hands on him, he asked him, "Do you see anything?" ^{24}And he looked up and said, "I see people, but they look like trees, walking." ^{25}Then Jesus laid his hands on his eyes again; and he opened his eyes, his sight was restored, and he saw everything clearly.

Mark 8:23-25

Voice from the Church

"I began to realize why so many of the saints, whom modern-day Christians might regard enviously as the most godly of persons, were driven time after time to seek a deeper experience. Moody, who had evangelized two continents, struggled in his later years, yearning for a 'second' experience to overcome his inadequacies. Bonhoeffer, in prison, a giant before men, comforter and pastor to the other inmates, wrote of the wrenching of his soul in the unforgettable poem, 'Who Am I?'" (Charles Colson, 1931-2012)*

Reflection

While the experience of being justified and regenerated by faith should never be minimized by Christians, many of the disciples of the Lord Jesus have discovered, following the new-birth event, a deeper need. And many of these thirsty-hearted souls have gone on to testify to the Spirit's deeper work in them.

Such an experience has been identified by a variety of terms: entire sanctification, second work of grace, filling of the Spirit, baptism with the Spirit, etc. The terms we use are unimportant. What is important is the *substance* of what occurs in such an experience—purity and power.

Verse

It is more than Your forgiveness,
that I need, O Lord. I plead
For a deeper, inner cleansing—
power to obey Your Word.

Power to Live Victoriously

The Word

[17]So Ananias departed and entered the house. And laying his hands on him he said, "Brother Saul, the Lord Jesus who appeared to you on the road by which you came has sent me so that you may regain your sight and be filled with the Holy Spirit." [18]And immediately something like scales fell from his eyes, and he regained his sight.
Acts 9:17-18

Voice from the Church

"As a result of that experience, the Holy Spirit has always been real to me. I do not remember having had any specific teaching on the subject at that time, and I certainly was not seeking any sort of experience of the Spirit; nevertheless, from that night to this present day, the Person, work and reign of the Holy Spirit has been very precious and relevant." (Former chaplain to the US Senate, Richard C. Halverson, 1916-1995)*

Reflection

Every person who has been born of the Spirit is indwelt by the same Spirit: "Anyone who does not have the Spirit of Christ does not belong to him" (Rom. 8:9). However, not everyone who has been born of the Spirit has been filled with the Spirit—in the New Testament sense of the term.

There are several attending dynamics accompanying the filling of the Spirit. While God's regenerating work of grace provides the forgiveness of sins, this post-conversion experience will empower us to have consistent power over sinning, as we abide in Christ and walk in the Spirit. A multitude of believers have testified to the effects of such an experience. Their witness will be rejected by the suspicious. Be that as it may; those who have experienced this filling know better.

Verse

I ask not for wings to rise to Heaven,
I seek not for visions or dreams,
I need power to walk with You, O Christ—
Power to obey and to please.

The Pure in Heart

The Word

> [8]*And God, who knows the heart, bore witness to them, by giving them the Holy Spirit just as he did to us, [9]and he made no distinction between us and them, having cleansed their hearts by faith.*
>
> Acts 15:8-9

Voice from the Church

"The Holy Spirit came to cleanse. Live coals from off the altar fell upon that Upper Room company in a blessed ministry of purifying. The Holy Spirit of Love, interpenetrating their spirits, purified, sweetened, and transformed the springs of their being. The source was purified, the innermost nature cleansed." (Joe Brice, 1873-?)*

Reflection

God's saving and sanctifying ministries flow from Calvary and the Upper Room. Our hearts are "sprinkled clean" by the blood of Christ (Heb. 10:22); our hearts are "cleansed" by the purifying work of the Holy Spirit (Acts 15:9). From the one, the guilt of sin is cleansed; from the other, the source of sinning is purified.

All one must do to substantiate this truth—and there are many Scriptures attesting to this—is to make a careful study of the life of Simon Peter—before and after Pentecost. How we enjoy pointing to Peter's failures, to justify our own. But remember, it was Peter's vacillation and equivocation and self-justification and denials, that occurred before Pentecost. Yes, we have a record of Peter's failing after the Pentecost experience; however, no one can study his life without seeing the dramatic affect Pentecost had in his life. We are not to seek experiences; we are to seek God. Neither are we to wander aimlessly in the wilderness, when Canaan lies before us. Have you allowed the Spirit to purify your heart?

Verse

*Must we wait for Heaven, to receive a pure heart
  and enjoy day-by-day victory over sin?
Has not the blood of Christ and gift of the Spirit
  provided for you a much deeper work within?*

When We Miss the Mark

The Word

[1]*My little children, I am writing these things to you so that you may not sin. But if anyone does sin, we have an Advocate with the Father, Jesus Christ the righteous. [2]He is the propitiation for our sins, and not for ours only but also for the sins of the whole world.*

1 John 2:1-2

Voice from the Church

"I am grateful for Scripture's emphasis upon my life pattern rather than my acts, because there may be moments when I look the other way or when I slip from being in an intimate partnership with God. Occasionally, something shows up in my life that really does not fit the pattern of Christlike living. Then He checks me and brings me back to himself." (Dennis Kinlaw, 1922-2017)*

Reflection

The follower of Christ is favored with having both an "Advocate with the Father, Jesus Christ the righteous," and the indwelling Advocate of the Holy Spirit, "I will ask the Father, and he will give you another Advocate ... he dwells with you and will be in you" (John 14:16-17).

The Advocate within (Holy Spirit) teaches and guides us, guards and empowers us, convicts and encourages us. The Advocate above (Jesus Christ) pleads our case with the Father when we have failed, when we have sinned.

The Christian need not despair when he has failed in his walk with God: "we have an Advocate with the Father." The word "with" here means "face to face with." Our Savior and risen Lord is also our Advocate. Satan will destroy our faith and confidence when we have sinned, unless we flee to our Advocate on high, trusting in his intercessions.

Verse

Five bleeding wounds He bears;
  received on Calvary;
They pour effectual prayers;
  they strongly plead for me. (Charles Wesley, 1707-1788)**

"What about this man?"

The Word

²⁰*Peter turned and saw the disciple whom Jesus loved following them, the one who also had leaned back against him during the supper and had said, "Lord, who is it that is going to betray you?"* ²¹*When Peter saw him, he said to Jesus, "Lord, what about this man?"* ²²*Jesus said to him, "If it is my will that he remain until I come, what is that to you? You follow me!"*

John 21:20-22

Voice from the Church

"To him who obeys, and thus opens the door of his heart to receive the eternal gift, God gives the Spirit of His Son, the Spirit of Himself, to be in him, and lead him to the understanding of all truth.... The true disciple shall thus always know what he ought to do, though not necessarily what another ought to do." (George MacDonald, 1824-1905)*

Reflection

To teach and share the Word of God is both a privilege and responsibility, for those who called to do so. However, it is the Holy Spirit, the Spirit of Truth, who makes personal application of the truth in the hearts and lives of those who hear. We must trust the Spirit to do his work; we must not try to do the Spirit's work ourselves.

There will always be those among us who have developed stiff necks and hard hearts. If they won't listen to God, they won't listen to us. But sometimes we speak when God has not spoken to us. We can meddle in another's walk, when it is none of our business. There may be an occasion when we can speak to another for his edification; however, quite often we need to leave the brother or sister alone, trusting God to do his personal work without our help.

Verse

How God chooses to lead others
  is not for me to question;
For He is the sovereign Lord
  and leads by His own discretion.

"Blessed Quietness"

The Word
[23] *And a windstorm came down on the lake, and they were filling with water and were in danger.* [24] *And they went and woke him, saying, "Master, Master, we are perishing!" And he awoke and rebuked the wind and the raging waves, and they ceased, and there was a calm.*
Luke 8:23-24

Voice from the Church
"When Jesus rises, the storm stops. The calm comes from the power of His presence. As a strong quiet man steps in majestically among a crowd of noisy brawlers, his very appearance makes them ashamed and hushes their noise; so Jesus steps in among the elements, and they are still in a moment." (Lettie Cowman, 1870-1960)*

Reflection
The disciple of Christ is not immune from life's storms. But blessed is that disciple who has the peace of Christ on the inside while walking through the storms on the outside.

Inner peace cannot be manufactured; neither can it be conjured up. If we enjoy the peace that Christ gives, and no one can take away, this peace will be with us always—whether life's externals are stormy or calm.

Anyone can remain poised when all is going well—saint and sinner alike. But how do we react when the proverbial roof falls in?

The peace of Christ is not Stoicism; it's not merely keeping a "stiff upper lip" as we face trials and tribulations. No, Christ wants his peace to abide in us. Christ is the Master of the wind and the waves; he is the sovereign Lord. Why should we worry and fret? Receive God's peace today: "May the God of peace be with you all. Amen" (Rom. 15:33).

Verse
Blessed quietness, holy quietness,
Blest assurance in my soul!
On the stormy sea, He speaks peace to me,
And the billows cease to roll. (Manie P. Ferguson, 1850-1932)**

"Blessed Assurance"

The Word

> [15]For you did not receive the spirit of slavery to fall back into
> fear, but you have received the Spirit of adoption as sons, by
> whom we cry, "Abba! Father!" [16]The Spirit himself bears
> witness with our spirit that we are children of God.
>
> Romans 8:15-16

Voice from the Church

"During the forty years I have been in the ministry, I have met with at least forty thousand who have had a clear and full evidence that God, for Christ's sake, had forgiven their sins, the Spirit himself bearing witness with their spirit that they were the sons and daughters of God." (Adam Clarke, 1760-1832)*

Reflection

It is the privilege for each of God's justified and forgiven children, to receive assurance of their salvation. It is one thing to read the Scriptures and rationally deduce because we have confessed our sins that our sins are forgiven (1 John 1:9). It is another thing for the Holy Spirit to impress directly upon the repentant believing sinner's consciousness that God himself has heard his confession. The Spirit gives to the new-born child a new language: "Father! My Father!"

In 1982 I attended a Billy Graham Crusade in the city of Boston. Following an evening service, I returned to my hotel via the subway. As we travelled under the city, someone began singing, "Blessed assurance, Jesus is Mine." One by one, each Christian began to join in.

I'll never forget the night I left the church's altar. Before I rose to my feet, I knew I was a forgiven young man. No one had to tell me or try to convince me. I had received a blessed assurance from the Spirit himself!

Verse

Blessed assurance, Jesus is mine;
Oh, what a foretaste of glory divine!
Heir of salvation, purchase of God,
Born of His Spirit, washed in His blood. (Fanny Crosby, 1820-1915)**

Providential Influences

The Word
⁴⁰One of the two who heard John speak and followed Jesus was Andrew, Simon Peter's brother. ⁴¹He first found his own brother Simon and said to him, "We have found the Messiah" (which means Christ). ⁴²He brought him to Jesus. Jesus looked at him and said, "You are Simon the son of John. You shall be called Cephas" (which means Peter).
John 1:40-42

Voice from the Church
"Fortunately for both myself and others, ... there was one person who by her quiet, strong love saved me from utter ruin. She was a tiny, hunched-backed, plain woman who taught Scripture and English in the school.... No matter how far I wandered, God, by His gracious Spirit, used the sweet influence of this gallant little lady to move upon the heartstrings of a rough, tough young man." (W. Phillip Keller, 1920-1997)*

Reflection
I never cease marveling at the mysterious ways in which God uses the influence of other people in an individual's conversion and growth in grace and the advancement of Christ's kingdom on earth.

Where would Joshua have been without the influence of Moses? Would we have heard of Elisha without the influence of his mentor Elijah? Timothy became a pastor, because an apostle and evangelist by the name of Paul passed through the city of Lystra. Simon Peter was led to Christ by his brother Andrew.

We all have an influence with other people. Usually that influence goes out mostly unnoticed, as it should. By simply living an upright Christian life, the lives of others will be touched. Only eternity will tell how God has used you, if you will only be faithful to him.

Verse
When Andrew brought his brother
*   to Christ that day so long ago,*
He had no way of knowing
*   the results of that one kind act.*

Sacrifice and Worship

The Word

[28]*The whole assembly worshiped, and the singers sang, and the trumpeters sounded. All this continued until the burnt offering was finished.* [29]*When the offering was finished, the king and all who were present with him bowed themselves and worshiped.*
2 Chronicles 29:28-29

Voice from the Church

"True worship takes us low before it ever takes us high. Worship starts at the cross every time. It begins with what I see of myself there and continues on through to my grace and forgiveness. I worship as a forgiven sinner before I worship as a saint. And when I do worship as a saint, it's as an astonished one, knowing the truth about myself." (John Fischer, b. 1947)*

Reflection

Sacrifice and worship were inseparable under the Old Covenant. Where and when there were sacrifices offered for sin, the response was one of holy worship on the part of the individual and congregation. Worship often preceded, accompanied, and followed sacrificial offerings.

The Lamb of God was our sacrificial offering for sin. In every remembrance of his voluntary offering, we respond with heartfelt gratitude, "Amazing love! How can be, / that Thou, my God, shouldst die for me?"

The follower of God's Lamb never graduates from kneeling at the foot of the Cross. It is at the Cross where my redemption was purchased. It was at the Cross where my sins were borne. And it was at the Cross where I am forgiven. And what will my response be? A life lived as a sacrifice of thanksgiving to the glory of God in Christ my Lord.

Verse

Now I've given to Jesus everything,
Now I gladly own Him as my King,
Now my raptured soul can only sing
  of Calvary. (William R. Newell, 1868-1956)**

Until He's Finished with Us

The Word

⁶Then the people of Judah came to Joshua at Gilgal. And Caleb the son of Jephunneh the Kenizzite said to him, ... ¹⁰"Now, behold, I am this day eighty-five years old. ¹¹I am still as strong today as I was in the day that Moses sent me; my strength now is as my strength was then, for war and for going and coming. ¹²So now give me this hill country of which the Lord spoke on that day."
Joshua 14:6, 10-12

Voice from the Church

"I don't know whether I am to go on the shelf or not. If I do, I make Africa the shelf ... There is a Ruler above, and His providence guides all things. He is our Friend and has plenty of work for all His people to do. Don't fear of being left idle, if willing to work for Him." (David Livingstone, 1813-1873)*

Reflection

I remember hearing a preacher commenting about the gospel song "Let Me Burn Out for Thee." He said, as I recall, "I don't want to burn out for the Lord. Too many are suffering from burnout. I want to burn on." I think I understand what the preacher was trying to say, though I also agree with the sentiments that Bessie Hatcher was trying to communicate through the song.

Until the Lord himself is finished with us, we should never settle for a life of ease and self-satisfaction. I see too many of God's elderly people leaning back on their oars, at ease in Zion. As long as God gives you breath, there is work to be done. I love that old gospel song, "We'll Work Till Jesus Comes." Ask God to help you keep the flame alive in your soul, so that you can serve him by serving others, until the end.

Verse

We'll work till Jesus comes,
We'll work till Jesus comes,
We'll work till Jesus comes,
And we'll be gathered home. (Elizabeth K. Mills, 1805-1829)**

Our Common Lot

The Word

[36]*Others suffered mocking and flogging, and even chains and imprisonment.* [37]*They were stoned, they were sawn in two, they were killed with the sword. They went about in skins of sheep and goats, destitute, afflicted, mistreated*—[38]*of whom the world was not worthy—wandering about in deserts and mountains, and in dens and caves of the earth.*
Hebrews 11:36-38

Voice from the Church

"Someone once asked John Wesley's mother, 'Which one of your eleven children do you love the most?' Her answer was as wise as the question foolish: 'I love the one who's sick until he's well, and the one who's away until he comes home.' That, I believe, is God's attitude toward our suffering planet. He feels the pain of those suffering. Do we?" (Dr. Paul Brand and Philip Yancy)

Reflection

Suffering is the common lot of all humanity. Whether saint or sinner, cancer, strokes, heart attacks, emotional and physical pain—we all share some form of suffering. And for Christians, many suffer because of their identity with Christ and the cross.

The Spirit has reminded us to "weep with those who weep" (Rom. 12:15). The Lord Jesus wept over the loss of a true friend, the apostle Paul wept day and night over pastor and churches, that they would endure and mature. People suffer; we should suffer with them.

While drinking coffee one morning, an acquaintance who had lost a friend a few days before, asked, "Ralph it's alright to cry isn't it?" My response: "I once heard a father say to his son, 'Men don't cry.' But the Son of Man wept, and he was the perfect Man." Yes, it's alright to cry.

Verse

For me it was in the garden,
He prayed: "Not my will, but Thine."
He had no tears for His own griefs,
But sweat drops of blood for mine. (Charles H. Gabriel, 1856-1932)**

"By my Spirit"

The Word
Then he said to me, "This is the word of the Lord to Zerubbabel: Not by might, nor by power, but by my Spirit, says the Lord of hosts."
Zechariah 4:6

Voice from the Church
"God frowns on neither intelligence nor education, nor on people continuously pushing themselves to go beyond the supposed limits of their abilities. What he is concerned about is that spiritual work never be done solely in a natural way, only with natural endowments. Rather he wishes by the power of the Holy Spirit present and available, as in the life of Jesus, to make it possible for the followers of Jesus to exceed the real limits of their humanness and thus speak to the hearts of people with a life-creating, life-transforming power." (Gerald F. Hawthorne, 1925-2010)*

Reflection
For the church of the Lord Jesus to make progress and grow as he intended (and intends) it to, it requires more than what we can bring to the table. To do work for God without the Spirit of God is to fail, no matter how glamorous our so-called achievements appear to the natural man. Much of what takes place in our churches is nothing but that which is "full of sound and fury, signifying nothing." If the wisdom writer were to survey our multiplicity of ecclesiastical activities today, he might well respond, "Vanity of vanities, says the Preacher" (Eccles. 1:2). Without the fiery Holy Spirit pervading our hearts and ministries, all we do is nothing but a "noisy gong or a clanging cymbal" (1 Cor. 13:1).

Let us utilize all the means available, sanctifying them with the Word of God and prayer, making sure that we ourselves are filled with power from on high.

Verse
He had studied long and hard carefully,
  applying himself through it all prayerfully.
Then he went down on his knees pleadingly,
  that the Spirit would fill him powerfully.

Others

The Word

> [26]*When Jesus saw his mother and the disciple whom he loved standing nearby, he said to his mother, "Woman, behold, your son!" [27]Then he said to the disciple, "Behold, your mother!" And from that hour the disciple took her to his own home.*
>
> John 19:26-27

Voice from the Church

"After twelve days the authorities got to know of my family connections. While this was, of course, a great relief for me personally, from an objective point of view it was most embarrassing to see how everything changed from that moment. I was put into a more spacious cell which was cleaned for me daily by one of the men. When the food came round I was offered larger rations. I always refused, since they would have been at the expense of other prisoners." (Dietrich Bonhoeffer, 1906-1945)*

Reflection

One Christian grace which characterizes those who are mature in Christ and identifies those who have often journeyed the road of considerable suffering, is that grace which instinctively thinks of the needs of others.

The Lord Jesus Christ exhibited perfect selflessness as the Son of Man. Wherever he went he was thinking how he could serve individuals, including his mother during his last hour. Whether it was feeding the hungry, or giving the water of life to a sinful, thirsty woman, Jesus genuinely cared for people. He had no hidden agendas; he had no ulterior motives; he never used people to meet his own self-centered needs, for he was not self-centered. Jesus was focused on his Father and his Father's mission for himself, which was a mission to *others*. It is God's sanctifying grace that takes our focus off ourselves.

Verse

Lord help me live from day to day
In such a self-forgetful way
That even when I kneel to pray
My prayer shall be for—Others. (Charles D. Meigs, 1792-1869)**

Separation

The Word

*17 "Therefore go out from their midst, and be separate from them,
says the Lord, and touch no unclean thing; then I will
welcome you, ¹⁸and I will be a father to you, and you shall
be sons and daughters to me, says the Lord Almighty."*
2 Corinthians 6:17-18

Voice from the Church

"In many things we *must* be separate. But be careful that it is the right
kind of separation. If the world is offended by the separation that the
Bible requires, we cannot help that, but let us make sure we do not of-
fend by a separation that is foolish and unscriptural." (J. C. Ryle, 1816-1900)*

Reflection

I knew intuitively, before I rose from the altar of prayer the night of my
conversion, that I was to separate myself from some things and some
people. The Holy Spirit immediately spoke to me about the unclean
"things" I was to rid myself. And the Spirit also informed my conscience that I could no longer maintain *intimate* friendship with those
who were walking in darkness. "Do not be unequally yoked with unbelievers. For what partnership has righteousness with lawlessness? Or
what fellowship has light with darkness?" (2 Cor. 6:14).

However, there are separations that can be harmful. We should not
sever contacts with all unbelievers, otherwise we will have no witness to
them. And we should never separate ourselves from other Christians
with whom we don't see eye-to-eye with on things that are essentially
indifferent—a lesson I was slow in learning. Let us separate ourselves
from every sin and whatever impedes our walk with Christ, but let's
take care that our separations don't push us to Phariseeism.

Verse

*He was eager to please
  God in all that he did.
But the light that was giv'n
  he took home and it hid.*

Friendship

The Word

> [1]*As soon as he had finished speaking to Saul, the soul of Jonathan was knit to the soul of David, and Jonathan loved him as his own soul. [2]And Saul took him that day and would not let him return to his father's house. [3]Then Jonathan made a covenant with David, because he loved him as his own soul.*
>
> 1 Samuel 18:1-3

Voice from the Church

"C. S. Lewis was a strong, genial, stimulating, loving presence in my life from Oxford days through Davy's [Vanauken's wife] death and the immensity of grief that followed. He was, above all, a friend." (Sheldon Vanauken, 1914-1996)*

Reflection

There are a variety of facets that goes into making a true friendship. The degree of friendship that David and Jonathan experienced is (unfortunately) rare. There are relationships that have developed over time, between two persons, that may be called a genuine friendship. We never have many real friends. For friendships to develop requires an investment of time, and we only have so much time.

Each of us should have at least one or two faithful friends. And we should also make sure that we are friends with the Lord Jesus. Jesus was a friend—to sinners (a friend speaks truth to those he loves), and Jesus is a friend to obedient followers: "You are my friends if you do what I command you" (John 15:14).

Are you blessed to have a few Christian friends? Are you a friend of the Lord Jesus? If you are married, I hope your spouse is your best friend. And I hope you are an intimate friend with the Living Lord.

Verse

Friendship with Jesus!
Fellowship divine!
Oh, what blessed, sweet communion!
Jesus is a Friend of mine. (Joseph C. Ludgate, 1864-1947)**

The Peril of Success

The Word
[18] *"And when [a king] sits on the throne of his kingdom, he shall write for himself in a book a copy of this law, approved by the Levitical priests. [19] And it shall be with him, and he shall read in it all the days of his life, that he may learn to fear the Lord his God by keeping all the words of this law and these statutes, and doing them, [20] that his heart may not be lifted up above his brothers."*
Deuteronomy 17:18-20

Voice from the Church
"Isn't it interesting that when God uses our lives and we truly begin to soar as an eagle, it is easy to gravitate to one of two erroneous extremes. Either we embrace a false humility, failing to recognize and exercise our gifts as fully as we could; or we fall into the clutches of pride and arrogance so totally that God no longer uses us in mighty ways." (Charles R. Swindoll, b. 1934)*

Reflection
God only selects the humble to lead. Men may select those who are otherwise, but the person God chooses is humble, or one in whom he can develop true humility.

Every leader continuously faces the challenge of leading with humility or with pride. Each of us must resolve how we will respond to the accolades and the spotlight, if we are given a prominent place.

I heard Evangelist H. Robb French share how he handled praise and criticism following a sermon. When someone remarked how much they enjoyed the message, Robb said to himself, "Now, don't get puffed up!" When someone criticized his sermon, he would say to himself, "Now, don't get puffed down!" Now that's sanctified wisdom!

Verse
Forbid it, Lord, that I should boast,
Save in the death of Christ my God!
All the vain things that charm me most,
I sacrifice them to His blood. (Isaac Watts, 1674-1748)**

The Jealousy of God

The Word
[13] *"You shall tear down their altars and break their pillars and cut down their Asherim* [14] *(for you shall worship no other god, for the Lord, whose name is Jealous, is a jealous God),* [15] *lest you make a covenant with the inhabitants of the land, and when they whore after their gods and sacrifice to their gods and you are invited, you eat of his sacrifice."*
Exodus 34:13-15

Voice from the Church
"The sharpness of the description 'jealous' when applied to God suggests that there are two kinds of jealousy. In fallen man, jealousy can be selfish and irrational; in God, jealousy is pure love. The same divine fire which consumes idolatry, since it also yearns to show compassion, guarantees to keep Israel in his love." (Raymond C. Ortlund, Jr., b. 1950)*

Reflection
The Lord our God will never be content until we have fully capitulated to him and him alone. As both our Creator and Redeemer, God has made us for himself and purchased us with the very blood of his Son. By his Spirit, he is continually wooing his offspring to a point of complete abandonment to him, and a total surrender to the sovereignty of his Son, the Lord Jesus Christ.

We are naturally stiff-necked and hardhearted. It is only as we become penitentially broken before the high and lofty One who inhabits eternity, that God can begin to create within us a love and loyalty for him, previously unknown by us. God wants our all; and we will be restless until he has our all.

Are there any pockets of resistance remaining in you? Are there idols left unconquered? God is a jealous God. What are you waiting for?

Verse
All to Jesus I surrender,
All to Him I freely give;
I will ever love and trust Him,
In His presence daily live. (Judson W. Van de Venter, 1855-1939)**

The Marriage of the Lamb

The Word

⁶Then I heard what seemed to be the voice of a great multitude, like the roar of many waters and like the sound of mighty peals of thunder, crying out, "Hallelujah! For the Lord our God the Almighty reigns. ⁷Let us rejoice and exult and give him the glory, for the marriage of the Lamb has come, and his Bride has made herself ready."
Revelation 16:6-7

Voice from the Church

"The hope of the Christian is 'the Marriage of the Lamb' when faith shall be translated into sight, when our love for Christ shall be brought to its consummation in that happy day. However, it is not primarily the day itself which exercises the purifying hope so much as it is the Person with whom we shall be united." (George E. Ladd, 1911-1982)*

Reflection

At the consummation of all things, the Lord our God has prepared the grandest of all celebrations for the Lamb and the Lamb's Bride.

The Spirit, across the ages, has been seeking a Bride for the Lamb, similar to how Isaac's servant sought a bride for his master. Faithfully and persistently, the Spirit of God has been brooding over the face of the earth, convicting of sin and inviting all who will to come: "The Spirit and the Bride say, 'Come.' And let the one who hears say, 'Come.' And let the one who is thirsty come; let the one who desires take the water of life without price" (Rev. 22:17).

To each one who responds in faith to God's overtures of grace, to each of these is given the gracious privilege of entering an eternal marriage to the Lamb of God. And each respondent is invited and will be present at the Marriage Feast. Are you prepared for that day?

Verse

At the Lamb's high feast we sing,
Praise to our victorious King,
Who hath washed us in the tide
Flowing from his piercèd side. (Robert Campbell, 1814-1868)**

Milk or Meat?

The Word

You need milk, not solid food, [13]for everyone who lives on milk is unskilled in the word of righteousness, since he is a child. [14]But solid food is for the mature, for those who have their powers of discernment trained by constant practice to distinguish good from evil.
Hebrews 5:12b-14

Voice from the Church

"Simply put, the psychologizing of faith is destroying the Christian mind. It is destroying Christian habits of thought because it is destroying the capacity to think about life in a Christian fashion. It is as if the top-soil were being washed away, leaving the land barren and incapable of being cultivated. It can no longer sustain the bountiful harvest of being able to discern between good and evil." (David F. Wells, b. 1939)*

Reflection

Milk and meat, infants and adults—these are the contrasts the apostle sets before the believers in the above text. Evidently, there were believers indulging themselves in questionable conduct, conduct contrary to "the word of righteousness." These were mere infants as it were, immature Christians.

There has always been a great need in the body of Christ for those who are "skilled in the word of righteousness." those who soak their minds with the Word of God and those who have mature discernment.

We live in a morally murky age. The only way to live in this world, as God intends us to live, is to have our mind informed by the Word of God and our spirit continually filled with the Spirit of God. Otherwise, we will be misguided by whatever is culturally acceptable and currently fashionable. Are you drinking milk or eating meat?

Verse

Bowing in full surrender
Low at His blessèd feet,
Bidding Him take, break me and make,
Till I am molded, complete. (Oswald J. Smith, 1889-1986)**

One Righteous Man

The Word

> *⁸But Noah found favor in the eyes of the Lord. ⁹These*
> *are the generations of Noah. Noah was a righteous man,*
> *blameless in his generation. Noah walked with God.*
> Genesis 6:8-9

Voice from the Church

"Every day you and I are making decisions that help construct one kind of world or another. Are we co-opted by the faddish worldviews of our age, or are we helping to create a new world of peace, love, and forgiveness? How now shall we live? By embracing God's truth, understanding the physical and moral order he has created, lovingly contending for that truth with our neighbors, then having the courage to live it out in every walk of life. Boldly and, yes, joyously." (Charles Colson and Nancy Pearcey)*

Reflection

The Christian's moral compass is the written Word of God. The man Noah had no Bible; he was informed by and walked according to a theophanic revelation of God—God directly and verbally communicating to him. Noah listened, learned, obeyed, and pleased God. He was exceptional—no one else like him in his age.

And what an age it was, in Noah's time: "The Lord saw that the wickedness of man was great in the earth, and that every intention of the thoughts of his heart was only evil continually" (Gen. 6:5).

"Noah walked with God." Every day, every moment of every day—this man Noah walked with God, communed with God, obeyed God. No one else was walking with God. No one else was obeying God. What about you? Are you walking with God today?

Verse

My life, my love, I give to Thee,
Thou Lamb of God who died for me;
Oh, may I ever faithful be,
My Savior and my God! (Ralph E. Hudson, 1843-1901)**

Thinking

The Word

> Brothers, do not be children in your thinking.
> Be infants in evil, but in your thinking be mature.
> 1 Corinthians 14:20

Voice from the Church

"To think secularly is to think within a frame of reference bounded by the limits of our life on earth; it is to keep one's calculation rooted in this-worldly criteria. To think Christianly is to accept all things with the mind as related, directly or indirectly, to man's eternal destiny as the redeemed and chosen people of God." (Harry Blamires, 1916-2017)*

Reflection

Paul said of the wicked who refused to submit to God, that they were "futile in their thinking" (Rom. 1:21). God prophesied through Jeremiah of a day when he would "put my law within them, and I will write it on their hearts" (31:33). A Christian's thinking begins to change at the moment of his conversion—from thinking that once was futile and foolish, to thinking that is righteous and wise. This occurs because God has given such the gift of repentance. the gift of a changed mind.

From the time of new birth, the Holy Spirit indwells us, and through his presence he begins to increasingly conform our thinking to the very thinking of Christ Jesus. This doesn't happen overnight. But it does occur, as we day-by-day walk in the light of God. The Bible is full of exhortations how a disciple of Christ should think. We cannot expect to think correctly—toward God and others, about ourselves and this world, about this life and the next—unless our minds are under the control of the Spirit. We are called by the Spirit to "be renewed in the spirit of your minds" (Eph. 4:23). How is your thinking?

Verse

I want my mind controlled by You;
  all my heart daily renew,
That nothing subtle dim my view
  of You, my Lord and Savior.

Judgment for Christians

The Word
> [17]*For it is time for judgment to begin at the household of God;
> and if it begins with us, what will be the outcome for those who do
> not obey the gospel of God?* [18]*And "If the righteous is scarcely
> saved, what will become of the ungodly and the sinner?"*
> 1 Peter 4:17-18

Voice from the Church
"What Luther called 'Babylonian Captivity' is a falling for the spirit, style and system of the age, which is also a worldliness and an unfaithfulness that both saps the strength of the Church and brings it under the judgment of God. Have we done that? Ironically, we in the Western Christian Church have been undermined by the very modern world that the Christian faith was so instrumental in helping to create." (Os Guinness, b. 1941)*

Reflection
There are two texts in the books of Acts that frequently grip my soul. The one is found in Peter's Pentecost sermon, where he exhorts his audience, "Save yourselves from this crooked generation" (2:40). The other is a summary statement located in 9:31 and reads that the church was "walking in the fear of the Lord."

Since we will eventually stand before our Judge—not a judgment of salvation, but a judgment of works—how are we presently living our life? Peter said that judgment is to begin with us, "the household of God." The Spirit pleads with us to "save ourselves" from the sinful ways of our wicked culture—this present world.

The early church walked in "the fear of the Lord." Are we? Listen to the voice of the Spirit today.

Verse
*Are we prepared to give a good account
 before the Judge on that Great Day?
Having been washed in the blood of God's Lamb,
 let us be true lest we betray.*

Sincere Love

The Word

> [16]By this we know love, that he laid down his life for us, and we
> ought to lay down our lives for the brothers. [17]But if anyone
> has the world's goods and sees his brother in need, yet closes
> his heart against him, how does God's love abide in him? [18]Little
> children, let us not love in word or talk but in deed and in truth.

1 John 3:16-18

Voice from the Church

"The Christian form of love is not an abstract caring for humanity in general, or the sort that is often found in people who have little love for anyone in particular, nor is it a love for the common aspects of all humanity found in each person. It is a strong, overflowing love of each particular human being, warts and all." (Paul C. Vitz, b. 1935)*

Reflection

The love that God has poured into our hearts, by his Holy Spirit (Rom. 5:5), is not something natural. God's love, *agape* love, comes from above and is supernatural. It is the love that caused the Father to send his Son into a fallen world. It is the love that moved the Son to offer himself as a substitutionary sacrifice for sin and sinful people.

This love that comes from God and is given to receptive hearts, causes us to love as God loves—to love the sinner, the broken and hurting, the fallen and failing, the unloving and unfriendly, those who are enemies of the cross and despisers of Christians. This love creates big hearts, wide arms and deep pockets. This love gives and gives and keeps on giving—to the just and unjust. This love is not weak but strong; it is not passive but active; it will forgive when offended and will speak up when necessary. It is best seen in Christ and seasoned disciples.

Verse

O love of God, how rich and pure!
How measureless and strong!
It shall forevermore endure
The saints' and angels' song. (Frederick M. Lehman, 1868-1953)**

Justified by Faith

The Word

[11]Now it is evident that no one is justified before God by the law, for "The righteous shall live by faith." [12]But the law is not of faith, rather "The one who does them shall live by them." [13]Christ redeemed us from the curse of the law by becoming a curse for us—for it is written, "Cursed is everyone who is hanged on a tree."
Galatians 3:11-13

Voice from the Church

"Luther followed where his soul-struggles led him. In finding answers, he followed the Scriptures where they led him. He began his lectures on Romans with the following words: 'In the presence of God it is not by doing just works that one becomes just, but, having been made just, one does good deeds.'" (James M. Kittelson, 1941-2003)*

Reflection

We are either justified on God's terms or we seek to be justified on our own terms. We cannot have it both ways. To be justified on God terms, we must renounce our self-justification, our self-righteous ways.

Paul wrote of the unbelieving Jews of his day: "For, being ignorant of the righteousness of God, and seeking to establish their own, they did not submit to God's righteousness" (Rom. 10:3). The problem these people faced is the same faced by many religious people today: Trying to do right without first being declared right (justified) by God.

God's solution to self-justification and self-righteousness was given by the apostle in the verse following the one quoted above: "For Christ is the end of the law for righteousness to everyone who believes" (Rom. 10:4). Christ himself fulfilled all righteousness, that repentant sinners might be declared righteousness. It is by grace through faith. (Eph. 2:8).

Verse

Believing, we rejoice
To see the curse remove;
We bless the Lamb with cheerful voice,
And sing His bleeding love. (Isaac Watts, 1674-1748)**

The Blessing of Brokenness

The Word

[16]*For you will not delight in sacrifice, or I would give it; you will not be pleased with a burnt offering.* [17]*The sacrifices of God are a broken spirit; a broken and contrite heart, O God, you will not despise.*

Psalm 51:16-17

Voice from the Church

"If a man be proud of his strength or manhood, a broken leg will bruise him; and if a man be proud of his goodness, a broken heart will bruise him; because, ... a broken heart comes by the discovery and charge of sin and by the power of God upon the conscience." (John Bunyan, 1628-1688)*

Reflection

Before God can mightily use a man or woman he must first bruise and break him of his self-will, pride, and sin. God does not break one's will, but he does break our willfulness.

Before the patriarch Jacob became a blessing to his family and nation, God had to take him down to the brook Jabbok. There all alone, this deceiver and conniver wrestled not only with an angel, but he wrestled with his arrogance and self-sufficiency. Jacob was no match against the heavenly powers. He was smitten, bruised, and broken. Jacob lost; God won. Jacob thereafter walked with a limp; however, he became a powerful force in the hands of God.

A self-directed, willful life resists the Potter's hands. We can never be shaped into the vessel of our gracious God's choosing unless we accept the pressure he applies to our stubbornness. Total renunciation to self brings God's favor. We have a choice: Will we reject the right to rule our life, or will we bow to the lordship of Jesus Christ.

Verse

What sacrifices shall I bring, O God?
What offerings will you accept?
"Bring a broken spirit and contrite heart—
These offerings have great effect."

Beauty and Shame

The Word

> [20]*And she said, "The Philistines are upon you, Samson!"*
> *And he awoke from his sleep and said, "I will go out as at*
> *other times and shake myself free." But he did not know that*
> *the Lord had left him.* [21]*And the Philistines seized him and gouged*
> *out his eyes and brought him down to Gaza and bound him*
> *with bronze shackles. And he ground at the mill in the prison.*
> Judges 16:20-21

Voice from the Church

"If holiness and saintliness are one and the same thing, then it may be said that Thomas Cook lived the life of a saint and did honour to the life of holiness. If one may be permitted to say so, I have never known any man whose living so corresponded with his teaching as did that of my brother." (Vallance Cook, 1892-1936)*

Reflection

For our sovereign Lord to bestow great gifts on those whom he wills is marvelous to behold. For without the distribution of spiritual gifts throughout the body of Christ, the church could not function effectively; it would not exist as the church was designed to.

Spiritual gifts are necessary. But great grace is necessary in those who have received great gifts—the grace of holiness, the grace of Christlikeness. The man Samson was given powerful gifts—the gift to lead, the gift to conquer others. But Samson's grace was not commensurate with his gifts. His humility, patience, and self-control did not keep pace with his observable strengths. He failed to conquer himself.

God's holiness is a beautiful thing to behold in men; its opposite brings shame and pain.

Verse

All that I was, my sin, my guilt,
My death, was all mine own;
All that I am I owe to Thee,
My gracious God, alone. (Horatius Bonar, 1808-1889)**

Shining Lights

The Word

> [1]*Arise, shine, for your light has come, and the glory of the Lord has risen upon you.* [2]*For behold, darkness shall cover the earth, and thick darkness the peoples; but the Lord will arise upon you, and his glory will be seen upon you.*
> Isaiah 60:1-2

Voice from the Church

"God has called us to shine, just as much as Daniel was sent into Babylon to shine. Let no one say that he cannot shine because he does not have as much influence as some others may have. What God wants you to do is to use your influence you have." (D. L. Moody, 1837-1899)*

Reflection

Christians are called to be reflectors of the true Light. Just as John the Baptist was not that Light, neither are we. However, we are called to be little lights: "You are the light of the world" (Matt. 5:14).

Years ago, while attending a church camp in central Michigan, the campers were awakened early each morning with the ringing of a bell. After the bell was rung, a minister would quote the above verse: "Arise, shine, for your light has come, and the glory of the Lord has risen upon you." Wouldn't that be an excellent text to quote upon rising each morning?

God's light of truth and holiness have beautifully shone through his incarnate Son, the Lord Jesus Christ. And for believers, the God who said, "'Let light shine out of darkness,' has shone in our hearts to give the light of the knowledge of the glory of God in the face of Jesus Christ" (2 Cor. 4:6).

God has called us to shine in this world—in words and deeds.

Verse

She never sought the limelight,
And was content not to be known.
But the God who sees all things
Saw the loving deeds she had sown.

Consecrated Bodies

The Word

> I appeal to you therefore, brothers, by the mercies of
> God, to present your bodies as a living sacrifice, holy
> and acceptable to God, which is your spiritual worship.
> Romans 12:1-2

Voice from the Church

"If you were asked, 'Where does Christian holiness express itself?' how would you answer? Paul's answer? The body. His over-arching exhortation is, 'present your bodies as a living sacrifice.'" (Sinclair Ferguson, b. 1948)*

Reflection

There were those in Paul's day who thought the human body was inherently evil. This misguided thinking brought about two opposite views and practices. There were those who responded with extreme asceticism: punishing the body, depriving it of life's essentials. On the other hand, there were those who went to the other extreme: indulging their bodies in all sorts of debauchery and wickedness. For some, "If the body is evil, then let's try driving the demons out; for others, "If the body is evil, then let's treat life like a party, knowing no restraints."

The Christian view of the body is entirely different from the prevailing philosophies and practices of the first century and the twenty-first century. Because man was made in God's image, and because he has been redeemed by the blood of God's Son, he is to glorify God in his body (1 Cor. 6:20).

At some point—either at the conversion event or sometime later—to each of Christ's disciples will be revealed that their body, including every member, is to be dedicated wholly to the Lord. Have you made such a total consecration?

Verse

Let my hands perform His bidding,
Let my feet run in His ways;
Let my eyes see Jesus only,
Let my lips speak forth His praise. (Mary D. James, 1810-1883)**

Conscience and Love

The Word

[3]*Let not the one who eats despise the one who abstains, and let not the one who abstains pass judgment on the one who eats, for God has welcomed him.* [4]*Who are you to pass judgment on the servant of another? It is before his own master that he stands or falls. And he will be upheld, for the Lord is able to make him stand.*
Romans 14:3-4

Voice from the Church

"In fundamentals ... faith is primary, and we may not appeal to love as an excuse to deny essential faith. In non-fundamentals, however, love is primary, and we may not appeal to zeal for the faith as an excuse for failures in love. Faith instructs our own conscience; love respects the consciences of others. Faith gives liberty; love limits its exercise." (John R. W. Stott, 1921-2011)*

Reflection

When love and truth excel in the Body of Christ, there will be little quibbling about matters which are at the *circumference* of the Christian faith. However, where there is lack of knowledge in truth and faith, and an immaturity in spiritual growth and conduct, there will be no end to strife, judgmentalism, and confusion.

The first-century church quarreled over incidentals: dietary issues, Sabbath regulations, whether to eat meat which had first been offered to idols, and so forth. The succeeding generations of Christians have not done much better than the first, though the issues have differed.

Where the Scriptures are clear on what is essential to the faith, the church should speak with one voice. Where the Scriptures are silent on particular issues the church must not sit in judgment on another person's conscience.

Verse

In essentials—unity;
In non-essentials—liberty;
In all things—charity. (Rupert Meldenius, 1582-1651)**

Sent to Save

The Word

> [9]And Jesus said to him, "Today salvation has come
> to this house, since he also is a son of Abraham. [10]For
> the Son of Man came to seek and to save the lost."
> Luke 19:9-10

Voice from the Church

"As a teenager Bramwell Booth never forgot the first time his father led him into an East End pub: gas jets playing eerily on men's inflamed faces, drunken disheveled women openly suckling tiny children, the reek of gin and shag tobacco and acrid bodies. After a moment, seeing the appalled look on his son's face, William Booth said quietly, 'These are our people. These are the people I want you to live for and bring to Christ.'" (Richard Collier, 1924-1996)*

Reflection

Our mission is no different than that of the Son of Man's. The Lord Jesus was the "Sent One"—sent by the Father to lost people, to the lost individual. And each of us is sent as well—not from Heaven to earth, but to those in our respective spheres of influence. There will be those whom God calls to minister on foreign soil, and there will be those ordained to shepherd congregations. For most of us, however, our "sentness" will not be an official appointment by the church, but simply being a Christian neighbor and friend to all that God's providence directs us to.

Jesus "came to seek and to save the lost." Have we forgotten those without Christ are lost—lost from the Shepherd's fold, lost in sin, and will be lost eternally until and unless they are found? God wants to use you to seek someone who is lost. Who might that be?

Verse

Out in the desert hear their cry,
Out on the mountain, wild and high;
Hark! 'tis the Master, speaks to thee,
"Go, find My sheep where'er they be." (William A. Ogden, 1841-1897)**

Suffering and Comforting

The Word

³Blessed be the God and Father of our Lord Jesus Christ, the Father of mercies and God of all comfort, ⁴who comforts us in all our affliction, so that we may be able to comfort those who are in any affliction, with the comfort with which we ourselves are comforted by God.

2 Corinthians 1:3-4

Voice from the Church

"[John] Newton showed love in abundance to [William] Cowper during the worst years of his depression. Indeed, it seems probable that Cowper would have succeeded in committing suicide in the depths of his torments had it not been for Newton's constant attendance at his bedside, calming the affected poet from the effects of his nightmares, delusions, and hallucinations." (Jonathan Aitken, b. 1942)*

Reflection

As a young pastor, I remember reading the advice the Scottish New Testament scholar William Barclay gave to ministers: "Every sermon ought to provide a measure of comfort to the suffering."

There will always be those in our circles of influence who are suffering. We are called to care, to comfort, just as we have been given comfort by God and others.

Years ago, I was sitting in a local restaurant early one morning. A female stranger entered, walked to my table and asked if she could speak to me. I answered, "Of course." She sat down and commenced to share a sad tale (and didn't ask for money), taking several minutes. I listened, then she stood and asked, "Can I give you a hug?" "Certainly," I responded. And this lady, who happened to be black, left as suddenly as she came. She needed comfort, a listening ear. I never saw her again.

Verse

In this world of toil and sorrow
Many hearts are full of care,
Let us live to serve our Master,
And each other's burdens bear. (William J. Henry, 1867-1955)**

Saving and Losing

The Word

> [24] Then Jesus told his disciples, "If anyone would come
> after me, let him deny himself and take up his cross and
> follow me. [25] For whoever would save his life will lose
> it, but whoever loses his life for my sake will find it."
> Matthew 16:24-25

Voice from the Church

"We are to die to all claims of the self-indulgent life. Ambition, love of ease and comfort, wealth, employment, marriage, family, self-will must all be offered to Jesus. We must ask him to nail to the cross all that is unworthy of him, so that his life can be seen in our mortal bodies. For the disciple, as for the Lord, the crown is unattainable without the cross." (Michael Green, b. 1930)*

Reflection

Before I had surrendered my life to the Lord Jesus Christ, I remember being tormented with the thought: *If I were to become a Christian, look at all the things I would have to give up!*

It is one of Satan's tricks of his trade: "If you become a Christian, your life will be miserable, for you will never have the *fun* you're having now, nor will you have any friends."

Well, the truth is: I wasn't having fun; I was one miserable lost boy, suffering under the guilt of sin. And my friends were in the same *boat* I was in. I was trying to save my life and didn't realize I was losing it.

I did "give up" quite a bit when I came to Christ: a guilty conscience, a bitter heart, devious ways, foul mouth, filthy thoughts, all my sins, and a whole lot more. But in losing my life for Christ's sake, I found so much more—real Life, Abundant Life. How about you?

Verse

A life is wasted when saved for self;
*   it can be saved by losing itself.*
To lose is to gain; to save is to lose;
*   by losing we win when Christ we dare choose.*

How Do We React to Trials?

The Word

> [9]*But he said to me, "My grace is sufficient for you, for
> my power is made perfect in weakness." Therefore I will
> boast all the more gladly of my weaknesses, so that the power
> of Christ may rest upon me.* [10]*For the sake of Christ, then, I
> am content with weaknesses, insults, hardships, persecutions,
> and calamities. For when I am weak, then I am strong.*
> 2 Corinthians 12:9-10

Voice from the Church

"God knows best; and the true Christian reaction to suffering and sorrow is not the attitude of self-pity or fatalism or resentment. It is the spirit which takes life's difficulties as a God-given opportunity, and regards its troubles as a sacred trust, and wears the thorns as a crown." (James Stewart,1896-1990)*

Reflection

Our sufferings will either produce in us a bitter heart or fertile soil in which the grace of God can abound. We all suffer—to greater or lesser degrees. The question is: how will I react in my sufferings? Will I complain about the providence of God? Will I become embittered? Or will I receive the comforting and abounding grace of God?

Through the years, I have had opportunity to obverse how a wide variety of believers have handled their hurts, offenses, trials, heartaches, and adversities. We react to these dark clouds naturally or supernaturally, in the flesh or in the Spirit.

God's good, godly saints have learned to trust God in the darkest days and the toughest times. Because they were well-grounded before the storm came, they came through it better instead of bitter.

Verse

If placed beneath the northern pole,
Though winter reigns with rigour there;
His gracious beams would cheer my soul,
And make a spring throughout the year. (John Newton, 1725-1807)**

Sharing the Bread

The Word
³³For the bread of God is he who comes down from heaven and gives life to the world." ³⁴They said to him, "Sir, give us this bread always." ³⁵Jesus said to them, "I am the bread of life; whoever comes to me shall not hunger, and whoever believes in me shall never thirst.
John 6:33-35

Voice from the Church
"The Spirit beckons to people all around us, every day. The Spirit makes them aware of their need and their hunger. Our task is to meet them at their point of need and feed their hunger with the Bread of Life, the only food that satisfies." (Leighton Ford, b. 1930)*

Reflection
We do not always know where and when the providence of God will lead us to a needy soul. James and John were not granted prior knowledge that they would be instrumental in a man's healing at the Temple gate. Paul didn't know who would be present in the house of Cornelius when he traveled to Caesarea following a vision. Nor did Paul know that Lydia would be converted when he met with a few women for prayer on the banks of a Philippian river.

For those attuned to the Spirit, there are constant surprises. There will be occasions that we can only call "God-moments"—moments when God has ordered events in which our life will intersect some other life. It could be he has brought you to someone who needs the gospel message. Or possibly a person needs comfort or encouragement.

Before leaving the place of prayer each day, my habit is to ask God for a fresh filling of his Spirit. We need to be ready when God wishes to use us to bless a needy person.

Verse
I wonder how often I've failed
  to give fresh Bread to a hungry soul,
Because my own heart was so stale?
  I would feed on You, so not to fail.

"By this he condemned the world"

The Word

> By faith Noah, being warned by God concerning events
> as yet unseen, in reverent fear constructed an ark for the
> saving of his household. By this he condemned the world and
> became an heir of the righteousness that comes by faith.
> Hebrews 11:7

Voice from the Church

"Good examples will either convert sinners or condemn them. There is something very convincing in a life of strict holiness and regard to God; it commends itself to every man's conscience in the sight of God, and they are judged by it. This is the best way the people of God can take to condemn the wicked; not by harsh and censorious language, but by a holy exemplary behavior." (Matthew Henry, 1662-1714)*

Reflection

We are called by God to do good to people, when it is for their good and God's glory. Often when seeking to do good to people—and living a life of goodness before them—such good works will be rejected and sometimes mocked.

Noah was both a preacher of righteousness (2 Pet. 2:5) and lived a righteous life (Gen. 6:9). His preaching was rejected and by the world's standards, unsuccessful. Regardless, he kept preaching and walking with God, conducting himself before a watching world as a man who was pleasing to God, though rejected by man.

The Word says of Noah's faithful conduct, "he condemned the world." Not so much by what he said but by how he lived. The sacrifices he offered to the one and only true God, the ark that he was building, and, yes, the truth he proclaimed—condemned the ungodly.

Verse

Let the world despise and leave me,
They have left my Savior, too;
Human hearts and looks deceive me,
Thou art not, like man, untrue. (Henry F. Lyte, 1793-1847)**

Reaction to the Word

The Word
> [15]*For we are the aroma of Christ to God among those who*
> *are being saved and among those who are perishing,* [16]*to*
> *one a fragrance from death to death, to the other a fragrance*
> *from life to life. Who is sufficient for these things?*
> 2 Corinthians 2:15-16

Voice from the Church
"I find by happy experience, the more I am scorned, the more God delights to honour me in bringing home souls to Christ. And I write this for the encouragement of my fellow labourers, who have all manner of evil spoken against them falsely for Christ's sake. Let them not be afraid, but rejoice and be exceedingly glad, for the Spirit of God shall rest upon their souls." (George Whitefield, 1714-1770)*

Reflection
The Spirit of God uses the truth of God—always. God uses truth that is spoken and truth that is lived. Of his Word, God says, "it shall not return to me empty, but it shall accomplish that which I purpose, and shall succeed in the thing for which I sent it" (Isa. 55:11).

Because we don't always see a positive result from our witness for Christ, does not mean that God has not used his Word to accomplish his purposes. If people do not surrender to God's Word, he will often use that same Word to harden their hearts, as he did in the case of Pharaoh through Moses. Sadly, many who hear Christ preached, and preached in the power of the Spirit, will harden their hearts and will perish eternally.

God's witnesses must not lose heart because of those who reject God's Word. The vast majority who listened to the Lord Jesus, failed to heed his gracious words. The servant is not above his Lord.

Verse
The man of God went forth to sow;
* with tears the seed was planted.*
But not all gladly heard the Word;
* for this God's man lamented.*

As a Child

The Word

[1]At that time the disciples came to Jesus, saying, "Who is the greatest in the kingdom of heaven?" [2]And calling to him a child, he put him in the midst of them [3]and said, "Truly, I say to you, unless you turn and become like children, you will never enter the kingdom of heaven."

Matthew 18:1-3

Voice from the Church

"What we are to have inside is the childlike spirit; but the childlike spirit is not entirely concerned about what is inside. It is the first mark of possessing it that one is interested in what is outside. The most childlike thing about a child is his curiosity and his appetite and his power of wonder at the world" (G. K. Chesterton, 1874-1936)*

Reflection

The teachings of Christ always go to the *heart* of the matter—to the very core of our thoughts and intentions. Christ's words to the world and his disciples invariably and boldly strike us where it hurts; it hurts because of our innate fallenness.

Only the childlike can receive the words of Christ and the kingdom of heaven, according to Jesus. The arrogant and self-sufficient can't hear the words of Christ until the impervious soil of their hard hearts is broken in repentance. Once that fallow ground is broken by the penetrating and piercing Word and Spirit, the strong become weak and the high become low—like little children.

The childlike convert to Christ slowly turns his attention from himself to those around him. Childishness turns inward; childlikeness turns outward. Childishness competes with others; childlikeness cares for others. The mature in the faith are to remain childlike but never childish.

Verse

I would remain like a child—
Full of wonder, meek and mild,
Staying low at Jesus' feet,
Reaching out to all I meet.

Daring to Wait

The Word
Then David said in his heart, "Now I shall perish one day by the hand of Saul. There is nothing better for me than that I should escape to the land of the Philistines. Then Saul will despair of seeking me any longer within the borders of Israel, and I shall escape out of his hand."
1 Samuel 27:1

Voice from the Church
"When thou art most eager to act is the time when thou wilt make the most pitiable mistakes. Do not say in thine heart that thou wilt not do so and so; but wait upon God until he makes known his way. So long as that way is hidden, it is clear that there is no need for action, and that he accounts himself responsible for all the results of keeping thee where thou art." (F. B. Meyer, 1847-1929)*

Reflection
Many of us by nature are impatient people. We may not enjoy hearing it, but impatience is a childish disposition and can be a fleshly one as well.

King Saul's impatience precipitated his ultimate dethronement: he failed to wait for the prophet Samuel to offer sacrifice before going out to battle. Because Abraham became impatient with God's providence in giving Sarah a child, he opted to have his first a son through Hagar. And it was the impatience of Esau that caused him to sell his birthdate for a mess of pottage.

The psalmist David wrote more about waiting for God's timing before acting than any other biblical writer; however, even David failed to wait at times (see 1 Sam. 27).

Failing to wait for God's time often results in great pain, to ourselves and others. Let us learn to wait until God makes the way plain.

Verse
Silently now I wait for Thee,
Ready, my God, Thy will to see;
Open my eyes, illumine me,
* Spirit Divine!* (Clara H. Scott, 1841-1897)**

Our True Citizenship

The Word

[18] *For many, of whom I have often told you and now tell you even with tears, walk as enemies of the cross of Christ.* [19] *Their end is destruction, their god is their belly, and they glory in their shame, with minds set on earthly things.* [20] *But our citizenship is in heaven, and from it we await a Savior, the Lord Jesus Christ.*
Philippians 3:18-20

Voice from the Church

"While [Christians] dwell both in Greek and barbarian cities, each as his lot was cast, and follow the customs of the land in dress and food and other matters of living, they show the remarkable and admittedly strange order of their own citizenship. They live in fatherlands of their own, but as aliens. They share all things as citizens, and suffer all things as strangers.... They pass their days on earth, but they have their citizenship in heaven." (*The Letter to Diognetus 5*, Second Century)*

Reflection

There was a time when Christians in the Western World were more attune to eternal realities than temporal fancies. For many, the inverse is true today. The proverbial worldly camel has long since gotten his nose inside our shrinking tents (hearts).

If you are inclined to challenge this observation, permit me to ask: Do you miss a church service because of an entertainment event? Do you prefer watching TV instead of attending a prayer meeting? Do you find more enjoyment interacting on social media than you do reading the Word and spiritually profitable books? Is your heavenly citizenship easily recognized by others? Do you live each day to the glory of God and engage in good works in Jesus' name? How *Christian* are we?

Verse

If I gained the world, but lost the Savior,
Would my gain be worth the lifelong strife?
Are all earthly pleasures worth comparing
For a moment with a Christ-filled life? (Anna Olander, 1861-1939)**

Christ Building His Church Through You

The Word
⁶*And you became imitators of us and of the Lord, for you*
received the word in much affliction, with the joy of the Holy Spirit,
⁷*so that you became an example to all the believers in Macedonia*
and in Achaia. ⁸For not only has the word of the Lord sounded
forth from you in Macedonia and Achaia, but your faith in God
has gone forth everywhere, so that we need not say anything.
1 Thessalonians 1:6-8

Voice from the Church
"Oh, how thankful I felt to hear a Chinaman, of his own accord, telling his fellow-countrymen that God loved them; that they were sinners, but that Jesus died instead of them, and paid the penalty of their guilt. That one moment repaid me for all the trials we had passed through; and I felt that if the Lord should grant His Holy Spirit to change the heart of that man, we had not come in vain." (J. Hudson Taylor, 1832-1905)*

Reflection
One of the delights that brings great joy to a messenger of the gospel is to see his converts sharing the good news with others and making disciples of the Lord Jesus Christ. Through the years I have been privileged to meet some of my spiritual grandchildren, those who were converted through some of my own converts. What a joy!

This Christian progeny has continued from the first century forward: men and women faithfully sharing and living the gospel of Christ. On every continent and nation, from the east to the west and the north and south, in cities and villages, among the poor and wealthy, including every race—Christ has built his church. What a Day that will be when we meet those who are in Heaven because of our influence. Grace!

Verse
O thou whom thy Lord is sending,
Gather now the sheaves of gold;
Heav'nward then at evening wending,
Thou shalt come with joy untold. (James O. Thompson, 1834-1917)**

Loving Our Enemies

The Word

[43] *"You have heard that it was said, 'You shall love your neighbor and hate your enemy.'* [44]*But I say to you, Love your enemies and pray for those who persecute you,* [45]*so that you may be sons of your Father who is in heaven. For he makes his sun rise on the evil and on the good, and sends rain on the just and on the unjust.*

Matthew 5:43-45

Voice from the Church

"I have seen Christians in Communist prisons with fifty pounds of chains on their feet, tortured with red-hot iron pokers, in whose throats spoonsful of salt had been forced, being kept afterward without water, starving, whipped, suffering from cold—and praying with fervor for the Communists. This is humanly inexplicable! It is the love of Christ, which was poured out in our hearts." (Richard Wurmbrand, 1909-2001)*

Reflection

Undoubtedly most reading this meditation have never physically suffered at the hands of Christ's enemies. I know some who have. If you haven't endured physical abuse because of your Christian identity, possibly you have experienced verbal and emotional maltreatment.

My wife and I support a native missionary in Africa. Each time he goes on a mission into Muslim controlled territory, he solicits our prayers for the success of the gospel and physical protection.

I pastored a lady some years ago, who occasionally in arriving home after church faced a boarded door—her husband refusing to allow her to enter her own home.

Could it be that we (I) have fewer enemies because we are a little ashamed of Christ and some of his words? It makes me wonder.

Verse

Should persecution rage and flame,
Still trust in thy Redeemer's name;
In fiery trials thou shalt see,
That as thy days thy strength shall be. (John Fawcett, 1739-1817)**

Praying

The Word

[18]*Praying at all times in the Spirit, with all prayer and supplication. To that end, keep alert with all perseverance, making supplication for all the saints, [19]and also for me, that words may be given to me in opening my mouth boldly to proclaim the mystery of the gospel.*
Ephesians 6:18-19

Voice from the Church

"Believe me, prayer is our highest privilege, our gravest responsibility, and the greatest power God has put into our hands. Prayer, real prayer, is the noblest, the sublimest, the most stupendous act that any creature of God can perform. It is, as Coleridge declared, the very highest energy of which human nature is capable. To pray with all your heart and strength—that is the last, the greatest achievement of the Christian's warfare on earth." (Anonymous)*

Reflection

Our Adversary will fight us often in the place of prayer. For me, I have no difficulty in keeping my appointments with God; my problem lies, after getting there, to "shut the door" and keep it shut.

God has ordained that his kingdom moves forward, when God's people intercede for the saints, church leaders, family, sinners, and for every person he has placed on our hearts. I wonder if most of our prayers are centered on our respective families. What about our church leaders and missionaries? Do we pray for the spiritual maturation of new converts? Are we praying for the persecuted church? Are we praying against the onslaught of social evils and wicked philosophies? Are you praying that God will make you a bright shining light for Jesus?

"Lord, teach us to pray."

Verse

What various hindrances we meet
In coming to a mercy seat;
Yet who that knows the worth of prayer,
But wishes to be often there. (William Cowper, 1731-1800)**

Supplication

The Word

She [Hannah] was deeply distressed
and prayed to the Lord and wept bitterly.
1 Samuel 1:10

Voice from the Church

"Bring your cares to God by prayer in the morning and spread them before Him. Then make it appear all through the day, by the composure and cheerfulness of your spirits, that you left your cares with Him as Hannah did. For, when she had prayed, she "went her way, and did eat, and her countenance was no more sad" (1 Sam. 1:18). Commit your way to the Lord, and then submit to His arranging of it, though it may go against your expectations. Bear yourself up upon the assurances God has given you, that He will care for you as the tender father for the child." (Matthew Henry, 1662-1714)*

Reflection

As Christians, we should never forget that the God we bow our knees to is not only the Sovereign of the universe but also our Father in Heaven. And because he is our Father, he loves to listen to the heart-cries of his children and respond to their agonizing prayers, according to his and their best interests.

Remember, your supplications are made to "the throne of grace" (Heb. 4:16). Your Father sees every teardrop you shed and each burden you bear. We should never hesitate to take our needs and desires, our pains and our anxieties to him. Pour your soul out to your Father freely and fully; he cares for us more than we can imagine.

What is your need today? What is just now weighing down your soul and filling your mind with anxiety? Talk to your Father about it.

Verse

Is there a heart o'erbound by sorrow?
Is there a life weighed down by care?
Come to the cross, each burden bearing;
All your anxiety—leave it there. (Edward H. Joy, 1871-1949)**

Doing Good

The Word
And let our people learn to devote themselves to good works,
so as to help cases of urgent need, and not be unfruitful.
Titus 3:14

Voice from the Church
"Always keep your eyes open for the little task because it is the little task that is important to Jesus Christ. The future of the Kingdom of God does not depend on the enthusiasm of this or that powerful person; those great ones are necessary too, but it is equally necessary to have a great number of little people who will do a little thing in the service of Christ." (Albert Schweitzer, 1875-1965)*

Reflection
There are two ways to look at good works: one, to believe we are accepted by God because of the good we perform; two, to engage in good works because of our love for God and people. The one kind of good works is self-righteous; the other is Christ-centered and selfless. "For we are his workmanship, created in Christ Jesus for good works, which God prepared beforehand, that we should walk in them" (Eph. 2:10).

All my life I have been surrounded by good and godly people who were/are full of good works—beginning with my mother, who was constantly thinking of what she could do for other people.

I know people who would do anything for me—within their power—simply because of the love of God indwelling them. "By this we know love, that he laid down his life for us, and we ought to lay down our lives for the brothers" (1 John 3:16). Good works won't save us, but I'm not sure we will be saved without them either. "You see that a person is justified by works and not by faith alone" (James 2:24).

Verse
All works are good, and each is best
As most it pleases Thee;
Each worker pleases, when the rest
He serves in charity. (Thomas T. Lynch, 1818-1871)**

"The expulsive power of a new affection"

The Word

> *"I made known to them your name, and I will*
> *continue to make it known, that the love with which*
> *you have loved me may be in them, and I in them."*
> John 17:26

Voice from the Church

"Such is the grasping tendency of the human heart, that it must have something to lay hold of—and which, if wrested away without the substitution of another something in its place, would leave a void and a vacancy as painful to the mind, as hunger is to the natural system. It may be dispossessed of one object, or of any, but it cannot be desolated of all." (Thomas Chalmers, 1780-1847)*

Reflection

If we are to quit loving the world and its lusts, our attachment to earthly things must be displaced by a greater love. It is futile to say that we will simply make a fresh start, purpose to make some new resolutions, assert our will to quit certain sins, make new habits, and so forth.

While God must have the cooperation of our will to please him, he doesn't merely command us to leave off sin and begin a new life or break a bad habit. No, God replaces our love for lesser things and evil things with a greater love, a new love, his love. Thomas Chalmers (1780-1847) called it "the expulsive power of a new affection."

Without God's love cleansing, filling, permeating, and controlling our heart, the love of the world and the lusts of the flesh will inevitably overcome us. Thus, the necessity for daily renewal by the Holy Spirit, and a resolute habitual gaze upon our Lord and Savior.

Let us receive God's holy love today and every day.

Verse

If I am to love You with my all,
  I must have Your love within.
Pour Your love into my yearning heart;
  O God, a fresh work begin.

Don't Quit

The Word

[8]*For the word of the Lord has become for me reproach and derision all
day long.* [9]*If I say, "I will not mention him, or speak any more in his
name," there is in my heart as it were a burning fire shut up in
my bones, and I am weary with holding it in, and I cannot.*
Jeremiah 20:8-9

Voice from the Church

"The fire of God did so burn in my soul that I could not rest day or night
without doing something for my God and Saviour. Nor could I go with
satisfaction to sleep if I had not done something for His glory that day.
Time was so precious that I knew not how to improve it entirely to the
glory of God, and the good of others." (Howell Harris, 1714-1773)*

Reflection

As did the prophet Jeremiah, more than one preacher of the gospel has
vowed to quit preaching to an unwelcoming and resistant congregation.

A minister and friend of mine once told me of a discouraged evangelist. This preacher was powerful in the pulpit (I had heard him preach
several times) and appeared to be quite effective. He always received
more invitations to preach than he could fill. And, yet, he related to my
friend on one occasion, that he was prepared to quit preaching. If you
were not already aware of it, ministers often battle discouragement and
feel defeated.

However, as ministers, we are not ultimately serving people. On three
separate occasions the apostle Paul testified, "I was not disobedient to
the heavenly vision." And if any preacher had reasons to quit, Paul did.

If you are a preacher, take courage and keep encouraged. If you are a
layperson, pray faithfully for preachers of the gospel.

Verse

*He had grown discouraged,
And very tired became.
Then he went to his knees;
His heart was set aflame.*

Good Men Have Failed

The Word
> *David did what was right in the eyes of the Lord and did not
> turn aside from anything that he commanded him all the
> days of his life, except in the matter of Uriah the Hittite.*
> 1 Kings 15:5

Voice from the Church
"Let the Christian, whose hair is whitened by the sunlight of Heaven, tell his life-long story. He may have been one of the most upright and moral; but there will be one dark spot in his history, upon which he will shed the tear of penitence, because then he knew not the fear of the Lord. Let your heroic warrior of Jesus recount his deeds; but he, too, points to deep scars, the offspring of wounds received in the service of the evil one." (Charles Spurgeon, 1834-1892)*

Reflection
Of all the recorded narratives in the Old Testament, there are few prominent leaders mentioned who did not have some flaw. Noah drank excessively, following the flood. Lot made an unwise decision as to where he would reside and drank excessively, resulting in an incestuous relationship with his two daughters. To protect his own life, Abraham deceived two foreign leaders regarding Sarah his wife, saying she was his sister (a half-truth). Jacob, more than once, acted deceptively. Hezekiah paraded his wealth and possessions before envoys sent by the king of Babylon. And, of course, there was David.

We need reminded that God never approves of sin in any of his people, and that sin has its consequences. But we should remember as well, that he is a God of grace and with him there is mercy. Let us not be presumptuous when we sin; but neither let us despair.

Verse
Now incline me to repent,
Let me now my sins lament,
Now my foul revolt deplore,
Weep, believe, and sin no more. (Charles Wesley, 1707-1788)*

Sin and Repentance

The Word
David said to Nathan, "I have sinned against the Lord." And Nathan said to David, "The Lord also has put away your sin; you shall not die."
2 Samuel 12:13

Voice from the Church
"He who is in disobedience is in sin, and sin can never be atoned for or healed but by returning to God, and this is brought to pass by humble obedience. For so long as a man continueth in disobedience, his sin can never be blotted out; let him do what he will, it availeth him nothing. Let us be assured of this. For disobedience is itself sin. But when a man entereth into the obedience of the faith, all is healed, and blotted out and forgiven, and not else." (Martin Luther, 1483-1546)*

Reflection
The notable difference between King Saul and King David, after each had sinned, was that Saul sought God's forgiveness so that he would be spared great embarrassment in the eyes of his people. On the other hand, David's confession and repentance came from a truly broken heart: "For you will not delight in sacrifice, or I would give it; you will not be pleased with a burnt offering. The sacrifices of God are a broken spirit; a broken and contrite heart, O God, you will not despise" (Ps. 51:16-17).

When we have sinned, do we simply want God's forgiveness to soothe a guilty conscience, or does our repentance remind us who we have fundamentally sinned against, as in David's prayer? "Against you, you only, have I sinned and done what is evil in your sight" (Ps. 51:4).

What a relief it was to David when he heard the prophet announce: "The Lord also has put away your sin; you shall not die." That word is for us also. "He is the propitiation for our sins" (1 John 2:2).

Verse
For my pardon, this I see,
Nothing but the blood of Jesus;
For my cleansing this my plea,
Nothing but the blood of Jesus. (Robert Lowry, 1826-1899)**

The Wrong Kind of Tolerance

The Word

[20]*"But I have this against you, that you tolerate that woman Jezebel, who calls herself a prophetess and is teaching and seducing my servants to practice sexual immorality and to eat food sacrificed to idols. [21]I gave her time to repent, but she refuses to repent of her sexual immorality."*
Revelation 2:20-21

Voice from the Church

"Tolerance ... is the sin that believes in nothing, cares for nothing, seeks to know nothing, interferes with nothing, enjoys nothing, loves nothing, hates nothing, finds purpose in nothing, lives for nothing, and only remains alive because there is nothing to die for." (Dorothy Sayers, 1893-1957)*

Reflection

Before we tolerate sin in ourselves or in others, we must first redefine our view of Scripture. Those professing believers who embrace a brand of morality that is explicitly prohibited by the Word of God have adjusted the Word to fit their wicked and twisted views, instead of bowing to the God of the inspired authoritative Word. By first tolerating sin in their own life (which they don't consider it as *sin*), they find it easy to tolerate wickedness in other people, and for some, even advocating abominable conduct.

The apostle Paul rebuked the church at Corinth for tolerating sexual sin: "It is actually reported that there is sexual immorality among you, and of a kind that is not tolerated even among pagans, for a man has his father's wife" (1 Cor. 5:1).

Godly people guard against the smallest moral compromises. And godly shepherds warn their sheep against tolerating sin in themselves. Have you been tolerating any sin in yourself?

Verse

Run the straight race through God's good grace;
lift up thine eyes, and seek Christ's face.
Life with its way before us lies;
Christ is the path, and Christ the prize. (John S. B. Monsell, 1811-1875)**

The Object of Our Trust

The Word

"They shall besiege you in all your towns, until your high and fortified walls, in which you trusted, come down throughout all your land. And they shall besiege you in all your towns throughout all your land, which the Lord your God has given you."
Deuteronomy 28:52

Voice from the Church

"At the heart of all sin is the failure to trust God. Sin is our unwillingness to acknowledge our creatureliness and dependence upon the grace of God.... The effect of such sin is evil in the form of insensitivity, uncaringness, injustice, cruelty, and destruction aimed at our fellow creatures in this world. In short, sin is the failure to live up to Jesus' commandments to love God and love neighbor." (Ted Peters, b. 1941)*

Reflection

By nature, we either look to ourselves, others, or some material object to ultimately place our trust in. To sin is to exchange our trust in God for something else or someone else.

While Israel was armed with weapons of war, when going out to do battle with the enemy, God's people were never to solely rely upon their military prowess or equipment. The sweet psalmist of Israel knew this well: "Some trust in chariots and some in horses, but we trust in the name of the Lord our God" (Ps. 20:7). King David knew wherein Israel's strength lay: "The chariots of God are twice ten thousand, thousands upon thousands" (Ps. 68:17).

In whom are we placing our trust, our total reliance upon? Is it in the Lord God omnipotent who reigns for ever and ever, or is it in the arm of the flesh, which is destined to fail?

Verse

Cursed is the one who trusts in man,
Who leans on him for might.
He turns away from God the Lord;
His heart rejects what's right. (Susan H. Peterson, 1950-2004)**

Habits

The Word

> *"Oh that they had such a heart as this always, to fear me*
> *and to keep all my commandments, that it might go*
> *well with them and with their descendants forever!"*
> Deuteronomy 5:29

Voice from the Church

"Habit is one of the most powerful friends we can have, as well as our most potent enemy when our habits are wrong. Since so much of life flows from habit, special attention needs to be given to building godly habits based on biblical convictions." (Jerry White, b. 1937)*

Reflection

To do something *regularly* is to have formed a habit—whether a bad habit or a good one. Prior to our conversion to Christ, we had formed many bad habits. Following our conversion, the Spirit reprograms us in helping us to form good and godly habits. Good habits are important.

One of the first habits I began to form, following my conversion, was to daily have regular appointments with God, in prayer and Bible reading. I have faithfully kept this habit for almost 57 years (at this writing). This habit has served me well, by the grace of God.

Another habit I began to develop early was to "redeem the time." There are so many hours in a day; how we spend our time is important to God and should be to us. Time that is wasted can never be recovered. It is amazing how much can be accomplished by simply using our time well.

Someone once said, "Sow a thought, reap an action; sow an action, reap a habit; sow a habit, reap a character; sow a character, reap a destiny." Ask God to help you form good and godly habits.

Verse

If we fail to form good habits,
  when supple and young is the "twig,"
It will make our life much harder
  as the "tree" grows older and big.

Praise the Lord!

The Word
[1]Praise the Lord! Praise the Lord, O my soul! [2]I will praise the Lord as long as I live; I will sing praises to my God while I have my being.
Psalm 146:1-2

Voice from the Church
"I have found it quite remarkable that the one who has done so much to recover the praise-centeredness of the Psalms did so while *in the depths*. Claus Westermann was interned in a German prison camp during the Second Word War. He had with him only Luther's translation of the New Testament and the Book of Psalms. In his experience in a concentration camp, Westermann learned how to praise God." (Ronald B. Allen, b. 1941)*

Reflection
Of the 238 occurrences of the word "praise" in the Bible, 215 occur in the Old Testament, and the word is found in the Psalms 137 times. This should not surprise us, for the Psalter is a book of worship; and we cannot worship without giving praise to "the high and lofty One who inhabits eternity, whose name is holy" (Isa. 57:15 KJV).

How often and for what should we praise the Lord? "Seven times a day I praise you for your righteous rules" (Ps. 119:164). By what method should we praise the Lord? "Sing praises to the Lord, who sits enthroned in Zion! Tell among the peoples his deeds!" (Ps. 9:11). Where should we praise the Lord? "I will tell of your name to my brothers; in the midst of the congregation I will praise you" (Ps. 22:22). Who should praise the Lord? "You who fear the Lord, praise him! All you offspring of Jacob, glorify him, and stand in awe of him, all you offspring of Israel!" (Ps. 22:23). An on and on the Psalms repeat the word of praise.

Verse
Oh, praise him for his holiness,
His wisdom and his grace;
Sing praises for his precious blood
Which ransomed all our race. (Lelia Morris, 1862-1929)**

"You must therefore be perfect" (1)

The Word
"You therefore must be perfect, as your heavenly Father is perfect."
Matthew 5:48

Voice from the Church
"The wise and prudent must make a system and arrange things to his mind before he can say, *I believe*. The child sees, believes, obeys—and knows he must be perfect as his Father in heaven is perfect." (George MacDonald, 1824-1905)*

Reflection
When we read the words of our Lord in the above text, the natural man instinctively responds, *Impossible! That's ridiculous! Surely this is hyperbole! Jesus didn't mean what he said!* Really? Jesus didn't mean what he said?

Jesus' call for his followers to "be perfect" simply means—in the context of the Sermon on the Mount—that we are to love God with our all, to love our neighbors as ourselves, to obey God in all matters, and to trust God for and in all things. To "be perfect" means that we are called by God to be *complete* in our discipleship, that we must not allow for any pockets of resistance or disobedience, that God is to be our all in all and through all. It means our love for God is to be pure, flowing from a pure heart.

C. S. Lewis (1898-1963) once remarked on this text, "The command 'Be ye perfect' is not idealistic gas. Nor is it a command to do the impossible. He is going to make us into creatures that can obey that command."

We will either believe what Jesus said, or we will rationalize his words to excuse our own disobedience.

Verse
Am I to believe what Jesus said
and take Him at His word,
Or turn away in much self-conceit
and think our Lord absurd?

"If you would be perfect" (2)

The Word

> *Jesus said to him, "If you would be perfect, go, sell*
> *what you possess and give to the poor, and you will*
> *have treasure in heaven; and come, follow me."*
> Matthew 19:21

Voice from the Church

"He who hath given himself entirely unto God, will never think he doth too much for him." (Henry Scougal, 1650-1678)*

Reflection

Often it is one glaring thing that keeps us from a total surrender and abandonment of ourselves to the Lord Jesus. The wealthy young man, that came to Jesus, was very moral and upright in keeping God's commandments. Of the six commandments Jesus told him to keep (including five of the Ten Commandments and the one stated in Leviticus 19:18), the inquirer said he was faithfully keeping each one.

And, yet, the man knew he remained spiritually incomplete: "What do I still lack?" (Matt. 19:20). We can clearly deduce from this that a person can be a strict adherent to the letter of the Law of Moses and the moral law but remain incomplete in God's sight. Was the man a sincere seeker? We have no reason to believe otherwise.

God does not barter with us in matters of discipleship and his call to true holiness. We may have fulfilled many of our moral duties to our fellow man—not committing murder and adultery, not stealing and bearing false witness, honoring our parents, and loving our neighbor—but at the same time resist yielding that *one thing*. And that *one thing* will prevent us from owning Jesus as our "Lord." The Spirit says, "If you would be perfect, go _____ " (*fill in the blank*).

Verse

He seemed devout and upright,
* 'twas a good neighbor to all.*
Yet he lacked that one thing and
* rejected Christ's complete call.*

"Not that I ... am already perfect" (3)

The Word
Not that I have already obtained this or am already perfect, but I press on to make it my own, because Christ Jesus has made me his own.
Philippians 3:12

Voice from the Church
"In the present passage the apostle's ... complete repose in Christ as the righteousness of God for him, and then his deep nearness to his Lord as the power of God in him, alike seem not so much to banish as utterly to preclude any thought about himself but that of his own perfection." (H. C. G. Moule, 1841-1920)*

Reflection
The Christian will never be "perfect" in this life, in the sense that he will be incapable of sin. If our first parents, who were created by God pure and holy beings, fell in Eden's Garden, any believer is susceptible to the same. We can never expect to be "perfect" in an *absolute* sense, of course. The most mature Christian is always in need of the mercy of God and the atoning sacrifice of Christ. Why? Although we are called by God to love him with our all and our neighbor as ourselves, we still fail at times in doing so. Thus, we pray, "forgive us our debts" (Matt. 6:12), as our Lord taught us to pray. We incur a "debt" when we fail to give to God and others what we owe, which is to act in *agape* love.

The apostles never excused Christians for behaving contrary to the Law of God and teachings of Christ. The fact is, in the Epistles, Christians are often rebuked for sinful behavior. When Paul rejects any claim to personal perfection, we should not think he is making excuses for unacceptable behavior in himself. He is simply confessing that there is much room for growth, for example, in the nine-fold fruit of the Spirit.

Verse
When I look away to Christ,
then at myself look nearly,
I confess I fall far short,
yet abide in Him closely.

"Let us therefore, as many as are perfect" (4)

The Word
Let us therefore, as many as are perfect, have this attitude; and if in
anything you have a different attitude, God will reveal that also to you.
Philippians 3:15 NASB

Voice from the Church
"No word has been the occasion of so much stumbling and controversy
among Christians as this word 'perfect.' But the term is a spiritual one
and is used more frequently in the Bible than any other single term to set
forth Christian experience. It occurs more than 138 times in the Scripture, and in more than 50 of these instances it refers to human character
under the operations of grace." (Thomas Cook, 1867-1947)*

Reflection
In Philippians 3:12 the apostle rejected any claim to personal perfection,
in the sense that he had *arrived* at the pinnacle of Christian growth.
Three verses later, he speaks of those who "are perfect" (many Bible
versions translate the Greek word as "mature"). On the one hand, he
says he is not "perfect"; on the other hand, he refers to those who "are
perfect." Who are the "perfect" Paul is referring to?

We can be certain that what "perfect" does *not* refer to here is to those
who have been Christians for many years (mature). One can be old in
the faith and yet be an incomplete disciple of Christ. Nor does it refer to
those who no longer need to grow in the grace and knowledge of the
Lord Jesus Christ; this will be necessary as long as we live. Who are the
"perfect" Paul is speaking of? Those who are totally consecrated to God
and sanctified wholly by the Holy Spirit, and whose lives are characterized by love and righteousness and godliness. The "perfect" are those
whose love for God is unalloyed and whose heart is undivided.

Verse
Refining fire, go through my heart,
  illuminate my soul;
Scatter thy life through every part
  and sanctify the whole. (Charles Wesley, 1707-1788)**

"Let us therefore, as many as are perfect" (5)

The Word

Let us therefore, as many as are perfect, have this attitude; and if in anything you have a different attitude, God will reveal that also to you.
Philippians 3:15 NASB

Voice from the Church

"In regard to the doctrine of *sinless perfection* as a heresy, we regard contentment with *sinful imperfection* as a greater heresy." (A. J. Gordon, 1836-1895)*

Reflection

The "perfect" are those whose love for God is unalloyed and whose heart is undivided. The totality of Scripture underscores this call to total holiness.

No person should claim to be "perfect"—even in the biblical and evangelical sense of the word. However, all converts to Christ are exhorted by the Spirit to "present their bodies as a living sacrifice to God" (total consecration, Rom. 12:1); to "cleanse ourselves from every defilement of body and spirit, bringing holiness to completion in the fear of God" (total consecration, 2 Cor. 7:1); to receive from God a "love that issues from a pure heart" (1 Tim. 1:5); to be empowered and enabled by the Spirit to live a life that is characterized by walking in the Spirit and not in the flesh (power to please God, Gal. 5:16f).

Evangelical Christian perfection is no more and no less than "love that issues from a pure heart and a good conscience and a sincere faith" (1 Tim. 1:5); it is living out the call of Christ: "If anyone would come after me, let him deny himself and take up his cross and follow me" (Mark 8:34); it is to do justice, to love kindness, and to walk humbly with your God" (Micah 6:8); it is to humbly acknowledge our imperfections.

Verse

O God, Your call to a holy life
is without You impossible.
But since the Paraclete now abides,
there is hence no more obstacle.

Perfected through Suffering (6)

The Word

> After you have suffered for a little while, the God of
> all grace, who called you to His eternal glory in Christ,
> will Himself perfect, confirm, strengthen and establish you.
> 1 Peter 5:10 NASB

Voice from the Church

"All affliction is intended to drive one to God. It is intended to work a fuller submission, a greater beauty of spirit, a more selfless love toward both God and man. When it accomplishes this, then it may be classified as suffering with Christ and for His sake because it has enabled Him to achieve His end and purpose in that one." (Paul E. Billheimer, 1897-1984)*

Reflection

The perfecting grace that is given through affliction and personal suffering differs from the perfecting grace that results in a radical death to our sin-bent ego and a resultant pure heart.

Having walked with the Lord for a good many years now, I have been able to see God's perfecting grace in the lives of many suffering saints. These were men and women who walked with God, were fully consecrated disciples of the Lord Jesus, and lived sanctified lives. However, when they had undergone financial loss, or walked for several years through a terminal illness, or experienced sever domestic pain, or underwent an apparent ministry failure—I have observed in these saints a greater gentleness, deeper humility, a softer spirit; sharp edges had given way to a more tender heart. Their walk with God demonstrated a greater intimacy. A greater spiritual depth developed in these saints through suffering that God could not achieve otherwise. God uses suffering to perfect his human vessels.

Verse

Help me, Lord, when toil and trouble meeting,
E'er to take, as from a father's hand,
One by one, the days, the moments fleeting,
Till with Christ the Lord I stand. (Karolina Sandell-Berg, 1832-1903)**

Serving and Suffering

The Word
[8]*We are afflicted in every way, but not crushed; perplexed, but not driven to despair;* [9]*persecuted, but not forsaken; struck down, but not destroyed;* [10]*always carrying in the body the death of Jesus, so that the life of Jesus may also be manifested in our bodies.*
2 Corinthians 4:8-10

Voice from the Church
"Human happiness does not consist in avoiding adversity, suffering, sorrow, and bereavement, but in knowing that I am occupying a place in life which God intended for me and being permitted to do my work and make use of my talents in accordance with the will of God, whether it be in serving or in suffering." (Ole Hallesby, 1879-1961)*

Reflection
What default position do we resort to whenever we face troubles and trials, suffering and opposition? Do we instinctively ask God to remove the obstacle and difficulty? And this is not necessarily a bad thing to do. What is better is to seek what God may want to do in us and through us, during such times of testing.

Out constant mindset when facing life's troubles should be to seek the face of God, to ask how God might receive the greatest glory in my suffering. Would he receive greater glory in delivering me from this trial? Or would he receive greater glory in enabling me to walk through this valley, giving him praise all the way? We can serve God in health and when his kindness has showered us with a comfortable life. Can we not serve God in our sufferings as well, as many of the saints of old have done? Either way, we need God's grace—when the "clouds" hang low, or when the "sun" is clear and bright.

Verse
When the Lord brings into your life
a sorrow, trial, or deep pain,
You have a choice each time to make:
to praise or grumble and complain.

The Power of God (1)

The Word

*Once God has spoken; twice have I
heard this: that power belongs to God.*
Psalm 62:11

Voice from the Church

"God is almighty, and can do everything; with him nothing is impossible. All the powers of all the creatures are derived from him, depend upon him, and are used by him as he pleases. His is the power, and to him we must ascribe it. This is a good reason why we should trust in him at all times and live in a constant dependence upon him; for he is able to do all that for us which we trust in him for." (Matthew Henry,1662-1714)*

Reflection

The God of the Sacred Scriptures, who is the God of Abraham, Isaac, and Jacob, and the God and Father of our Lord Jesus Christ is God Almighty, the God of *power.*

The power God exercises is holy and infinite, eternal and sovereign, and is always compatible with his holiness and righteousness and his perfect knowledge and wisdom. God's power is never whimsical nor employed to entertain. God uses his power to create: "Let there be light" (Gen. 1:3); to preserve his creation: "he upholds the universe by the word of his power" (Heb. 1:3); to provide for his people: "he rained down on them manna to eat and gave them the grain of heaven" (Ps. 78:24); to form the plan of salvation: "his own arm brought him salvation" (Isa. 59:16); to guard the saints: "by God's power are being guarded through faith" (1 Pet. 1:5)—and so much more.

The God we serve is a God of power. Are you worshiping, trusting, and walking with this God today?

Verse

*Praise to the Lord, the Almighty, the King of creation!
O my soul, praise Him, for He is thy health and salvation!
All ye who hear, now to His temple draw near;
Sing now in glad adoration!* (Joachim Neander, 1650-1680)**

Power for the Weak and Waiting (2)

The Word

*²⁹He gives strength to the weary, and to him who lacks might He
increases power. ³⁰Though youths grow weary and tired, and vigorous
young men stumble badly, ³¹yet those who wait for the Lord will
gain new strength; they will mount up with wings like eagles, they
will run and not get tired, they will walk and not become weary.*
Isaiah 40:29-31 NASB

Voice from the Church

"To 'wait' on God is not simply to mark time; rather, it is to live in confident expectation of his action on our behalf. It is to refuse to run ahead of him in trying to solve our problems for ourselves. Thus, just as Isaiah called on the people of his own day to trust God to solve their problems, he calls on the exiles in the age to come to do the same thing." (John N. Oswalt, b. 1940)*

Reflection

We fallen creatures are most vulnerable to choosing a bypath in times of trial, temptation, discouragement, and distress. How often we suffer the consequences of poor choices, because we failed to wait on God during days of weakness. Satan's fiery arrows pierced our unguarded moments; we allowed the Adversary to triumph simply because we failed to rely on God and flee to him as a refuge in time of need.

God's mature saints have learned by experience that their weakest moments are divine appointments for God's power to be released on their behalf. To wait on and place our hope and expectations in God alone qualifies us for an outpouring of his mercy and grace. In failing to wait on God, we are left to depend on our own resources, which is futile. In waiting, we are assured of God's renewing power.

Verse

*When we deeply feel our weakness
 and all our strength is gone,
Let us trust God to renew us,
 waiting before His throne.*

Jesus and the Power of the Spirit (3)

The Word

¹⁴*And Jesus returned in the power of the Spirit to Galilee, and a report about him went out through all the surrounding country.* ¹⁵*And he taught in their synagogues, being glorified by all.*

Luke 4:14-15

Voice from the Church

"The wilderness was known as the home of Satan, the lodging of demons, the location of deadly dangers, the arena of evil forces, of the powers of darkness, of demonic activity, the habitation of wild beasts, poisonous serpents, etc." (Gerald F. Hawthorne, 1925-2010)*

Reflection

The human imagination is incapable of comprehending the depths of temptation our Lord faced in his Wilderness Temptations. The Son of Man was the object of Satan's fiercest and cruelest solicitations to evil man has ever experienced—and Jesus was a man, the God-Man.

But Jesus came through the forty days of unprecedented temptations victoriously not because he was the Son of God, but because he depended on the strength of God to enable him to resist each fiery arrow of the Enemy. Jesus entered the wilderness, being led of the Spirit; he triumphed in the wilderness by Word and Spirit; and he left the wilderness to minister in the power of the Spirit.

No person is qualified to minister to others who has not learned to overcome in the *wilderness*. The wilderness, the desert, is where God tests a person and Satan tempts. If we have not relied on God's might in the *wilderness*, we cannot be assured of God's help in life's *plains*, times of peace and rest. The same Spirit who enabled Jesus to overcome is the same Spirit given to you and me, that we might overcome.

Verse

Drink deeply in the desert;
  be refreshed and renewed.
Let his Spirit fill you fully,
  then go forth and be used.

Power and Proclamation (4)

The Word
> *"And behold, I am sending the promise of my Father upon you.*
> *But stay in the city until you are clothed with power from on high."*
> Luke 24:49

Voice from the Church
"The danger always lies in letting the form and content get in the way of what should be the single concern: the gospel proclaimed through human weakness but accompanied by the powerful work of the Spirit so that lives are changed through a divine-human encounter. That is hard to teach in a course in homiletics, but it stands as the true need in genuinely Christian preaching." (Gordon D. Fee, b. 1934)*

Reflection
Though the apostles of the Lord Jesus had followed him for three years, and heard his teachings in all kinds of venues, as well as observing the signs and miracles he performed, they were still unprepared to go to the ends of the earth proclaiming the gospel. Though these men had been present at Christ's crucifixion and were witnesses to his resurrection for some forty days, Jesus informed them that they were still unready to be his effective and fruitful witnesses.

What more was needed? What did the disciples lack? They lacked the mighty anointing, baptism, and fulness of the Spirit. "And behold, I am sending the promise of my Father upon you. But stay in the city until you are clothed with power from on high." And they did "stay."

Christ knew, and these men knew as well, their desperate inadequacy. It is one thing for the Spirit to *indwell* us; it is quite another matter for the Spirit to come *upon* us—in power, equipping us for service. Every servant of the Word falls short without this empowerment.

Verse
O God, clothe Your servants with power;
  may each be baptized with holy fire,
Until the gospel spreads far and wide
  and lives are changed and Christ glorified.

The Power of the Gospel (5)

The Word
For I am not ashamed of the gospel, for it is the power of God for salva-
tion to everyone who believes, to the Jew first and also to the Greek.
Romans 1:16

Voice from the Church
"He [Francis Schaeffer] was never ashamed of being a Christian or knowing God. One summer day, as he walked along the beach among the sunbathers, he mentioned to those with him, 'All these people are worshiping the wrong 'sun.' Then he began to sing softly for all to hear, 'Jesus loves me, this I know, for the Bible tells me so.'" (L. G. Parkhurst, Jr., b. 1946)*

Reflection
To combine an unashamed Christian with the spoken gospel of the Lord Jesus Christ is a powerful weapon in the hands of God. The apostle Paul was eager to share this gospel, and he strove to live-out its implications in his own life.

The gospel—the life, death, and resurrection of Jesus Christ, and all its associated factors—is God's word and method of saving sinners. There is no other word; there is no other method. It is the gospel that converts the Jew; it is the gospel that converts the Gentile. Yes, we are to *live* the gospel, but we must also *speak* the gospel: "And how are they to hear without someone preaching?" (Rom. 10:14). One need not be a vocationally ordained "preacher" to share the gospel. Every Christian can talk about Jesus to lost people. My dear godly mother took her accordion to the local courthouse square in the summer; she shared and sang the gospel to all who would listen. Are you ashamed of the gospel? When is the last time you shared Jesus with a sinner?

Verse
How sweet the name of Jesus sounds
  in a believer's ear!
It soothes our sorrows, heals our wounds,
  and drives away our fear. (John Newton, 1725-1807)**

The Power of Prayer (6)

The Word

> [16]The prayer of a righteous person has great power as it is working. [17]Elijah was a man with a nature like ours, and he prayed fervently that it might not rain, and for three years and six months it did not rain on the earth. [18]Then he prayed again, and heaven gave rain, and the earth bore its fruit.
>
> James 5:16-18

Voice from the Church

"We ask our heavenly Father for things because he has determined that many blessings will come to us only through prayer. Prayer is his ordained means of conveying his blessings to his people. That means we must pray according to his will, in line with his values, in conformity to his own character and purposes, claiming his own promises." (D. A. Carson, b. 1946)*

Reflection

Prayer is not eloquent speech. Prayer is more than simply talking to God. True prayer consists of sincerity, earnestness, faith, and submission. True prayer is offered by the child of God to his holy Father in heaven, who answers the prayers of his people in his own time and way. His answers always flow from his wisdom and goodness.

It appears that some of God's people are specially gifted in prayer. However, what appears as a gift may be no more a life lived in total surrender and obedience to the Father in heaven, to whom they make their requests. Thus, when these saints of God pray, "Heaven comes down [their] souls to greet, / And glory crowns the mercy seat." And God hears from on high; he responds to his faithful, persevering child. "Lord, teach us to pray."

Verse

While Moses stood with arms spread wide,
Success was found on Israel's side;
But when through weariness they fail'd,
That moment Amalek prevail'd. (William Cowper, 1731-1800)**

Desolation

The Word

> [17] *The seed shrivels under the clods; the storehouses are*
> *desolate; the granaries are torn down because the grain has*
> *dried up.* [18] *How the beasts groan! The herds of cattle are perplexed*
> *because there is no pasture for them; even the flocks of sheep suffer.*
> Joel 1:17-18

Voice from the Church

"There are towns and villages in this land [United Kingdom] which were once filled with praying, and praising, and glorying people, towns and villages which stand out in the annals of Christianity in this country once filled with the glory of God. But today they are desolate, they are deserted, they are forsaken." (Martyn Lloyd-Jones, 1899-1981)*

Reflection

In recent weeks, I've attended worship services in churches which were once both strong in numbers and faith. Today, these churches are but a shell of what they used to be. The reasons given by the remaining respective congregations for their desolation may be varied; however, let's be clear: When churches lie desolate, it is often because God has failed to be fully followed and honored. The churches lost their way because they departed from the Word and the Way.

In what was once a Dust Bowl in North America, there now exists thriving grasslands and fields of grain. How is that? Because farmers began to follow the natural laws (God's creation principles) in caring for the soil. Out of desolation sprang thriving vegetation. When God's people repent of their disobedience, lukewarmness, and carelessness, God pours out his life-giving Spirit, resulting in growth and fruitfulness. Will we ever learn?

Verse

From the emptiness of our parched souls,
  we repent of our many sins, O God.
From the soil that lies desolate and dry,
  with bitter tears we turn over the sod.

Making Every Effort

The Word

*And I will make every effort so that after my departure
you may be able at any time to recall these things.*
2 Peter 1:15

Voice from the Church

"Peter uses one of his favourite phrases to motivate us: we are to make every effort (2 Pet. 1:5, 10, 15) to be ready for our new home. This does not mean spending all day dreaming about it or trying to plot its arrival, but being ready in terms of ordinary, standard Christian living." (Dick Lucas & Christopher Green)*

Reflection

To live the Christian life requires the cooperation and exertion of our will. The Word makes clear that the Christian walk involves effort. How can we "follow" Christ without the engagement of the will? Of course, "apart from me, you can do nothing" (John 15:5). However, though we can do "nothing" apart from Christ, we are to do *everything* by engaging our will by his grace. There are four instances in 2 Peter where a word or phrase is used, where we are exhorted to exert our will. The word is translated by the ESV as "make every effort" and "diligent."

In 1:5 we are to "make every effort to supplement" our walk with God.

In 1:10 we are to be "diligent" to confirm our calling and election.

In 1:15 Peter says that he will "make every effort" to help God's people recall what he has written.

In 3:14 we are exhorted to "be diligent to be found by him without spot or blemish, and at peace."

Let us "make every effort" to cooperate with God, by his grace.

Verse

When Jesus says, "Come follow me,"
  He's appealing to my will.
When I say, "Lord, I will follow";
  He provides me with the will.

The Love of Christ

The Word

¹³For if we are beside ourselves, it is for God; if we are in our right mind, it is for you. ¹⁴For the love of Christ controls us, because we have concluded this: that one has died for all, therefore all have died; ¹⁵and he died for all, that those who live might no longer live for themselves but for him who for their sake died and was raised.
2 Corinthians 5:13-15

Voice from the Church

"Andrew Bonar wrote at the end of his sketch of Samuel Rutherford: 'Oh for his insatiable desires Christward! Oh for ten such men in Scotland to stand in the gap!—men who all day long find nothing but Christ to rest in, whose very sleep is pursuing after Christ in dreams.'" (John Stott, 1921-2011)*

Reflection

Agape love is more than affection—it is action. Before we can exercise love for Christ, we must experience the love of Christ. The apostle Paul knew this ... experientially. We cannot demonstrate God's love toward others, without our hearts being pervasively filled and controlled by God's love, as revealed in Christ.

Great saints are great lovers. They are great lovers because they are continually renewed in their spirit by the God of love. When the level of God's love runs low in our heart, our relationships with others are necessarily affected.

The Christian must seek daily to have his heart (the fountainhead of the will) replenished with the holy love of Jesus. This is our safeguard against sin and selfishness and motivates us toward humble and fruitful service.

Verse

My daily deep need is for Your love,
  O Christ, to continually control me.
Thus equipped by Your holy power,
  I can follow You hour-by-hour.

Living Well, Praying Well

The Word

The effective prayer of a righteous man can accomplish much.
[17]Elijah was a man with a nature like ours, and he prayed
earnestly that it would not rain, and it did not rain on the earth
for three years and six months. [18]Then he prayed again,
and the sky poured rain and the earth produced its fruit.
James 5:16b-18 NASB

Voice from the Church

"All things being equal, our prayers are only as powerful as our lives. In the long pull we pray only as well as we live." (A. W. Tozer, 1897-1963)*

Reflection

The prophet Elijah received answers to his prayers not because he was a prophet but because he was a righteous man. If our prayers are not accomplishing much, it may be because our lives do not measure up to our lips. Righteous conduct and answered prayers go hand in hand; where you find one, the other will always be present.

If when coming into the presence of God we sense a condemning heart, then we must clear the way before we can pray with confidence: "for whenever our heart condemns us, God is greater than our heart, and he knows everything. [21]Beloved, if our heart does not condemn us, we have confidence before God; [22] and whatever we ask we receive from him, because we keep his commandments and do what pleases him" (1 John 3:20-22). We must be on good "praying ground" before offering our petitions to a Father who loves to respond to the pleas of his children.

Verse

When I knelt before the throne today,
I thought of a brother whom I had
  thoughtlessly wronged.
Before I could pray any longer,
I confessed my sin,
  and resolved to correct my blunder.

Something More

The Word

> *He began to speak boldly in the synagogue, but when*
> *Priscilla and Aquila heard him, they took him aside and*
> *explained to him the way of God more accurately.*
> Acts 18:26

Voice from the Church

"There was something about [Daniel Whittle, an evangelist], some over-tone of power, some fragrance of Christ, some hovering Presence that melted the brilliant young Presbyterian minister [A, B. Simpson] like a vision of God. A thousand flaws appeared to him, galling, painful, Christ-dishonoring; and worst of all a constant gnawing emptiness within him, a desperate sense of spiritual suffocation. He must have more of God. He must be filled with the Spirit." (A. W. Tozer, 1897-1963)*

Reflection

More than one person, including ministers of the Word, have been found wanting when the light of God's Word and Spirit have uncovered a deep need in their heart. Often our theological background and religious prejudices cast shadows over some aspect of God's truth. But for those who have experienced God's regenerating grace, whenever the Spirit further enlightens the mind and convicts the conscience of previously undiscovered truth—about God's Word or a need of the heart—God will graciously lead such into a further blessing.

The apostle Peter needed a further understanding about God's future plan for the Gentiles; the Spirit graciously revealed himself to him. Apollos was lacking, so was A. B. Simpson; God graciously met their heart-needs. Because we are "in Christ," does not mean that we have complete understanding—doctrinally or experientially.

Verse

As they listened to the preacher, they knew God had more for him.
They took him quietly aside—what he lacked, explaining.
He humbly accepted God's further revelation to him,
And went forth to preach God's truth with a greater anointing.

Read Biographies

The Word

¹²Walk about Zion, go around her, number her towers, ¹³consider well her ramparts, go through her citadels, that you may tell the next generation ¹⁴that this is God, our God forever and ever. He will guide us forever.

Psalm 48:12-14

Voice from the Church

"Next to the Holy Scriptures, the greatest aid to the life of faith may be Christian biography. It is indeed notable that a large part of the Bible itself is given over to the life and labors of prophets, patriarchs and kings—who they were, what they did and said, how they prayed and toiled and suffered and triumphed at last." (A. W. Tozer, 1897-1963)*

Reflection

Many of my generation were readers. Then came the television, internet, social media, and a plethora of other distractions. Little by little we quit reading, or very little. And since we don't read much any longer, what we do read we read mostly for entertainment.

The Christian who takes God and his own spiritual growth seriously, will read and choose his reading carefully. One doesn't need to be a voracious reader to read profitably. After all, the farmer doesn't have as much time to read as the pastor. But if we are to grow in knowledge and grace, in addition to reading the Word, let us read Christian biography—and not those that are light and popular. Read the stories of men and women who made a mark for God. Let God stretch and encourage you as you read about the tests and temptations, the defeats and victories, that the saints of old experienced.

I thank God for those who have told their own story of faith, and for those who have told the stories of others. I'm the better for it.

Verse

For those who have fought the good fight,
And have persevered through fiery trials—
I have rejoiced, been blessed, and grown,
As I've read their stories over these miles.

Called "Christians"

The Word

> ^{25} So Barnabas went to Tarsus to look for Saul, ^{26} and when he
> had found him, he brought him to Antioch. For a whole year
> they met with the church and taught a great many people.
> And in Antioch the disciples were first called Christians.

Acts 11:25-26

Voice from the Church

"A traveler met an Englishman settled in business in one of the Black
Sea ports in Roumania. They conversed of spiritual things, and the Englishman related how he had been religious before coming to Roumania,
but now he had given it all up and was convinced that all who professed
to be Christians were hypocrites, 'but,' he added, correcting himself, 'I
have met with one genuine Christian, he used often to walk through the
place where I lived in Devonshire, his name was Robert Chapman.'" (E.
H. Broadbent, 1861-1945)*

Reflection

The word "Christian" appears three times on the pages of the New Testament (once in plural form, twice in the singular: Acts 11:26, 26:28; 1
Pet. 4:16). The above text reads, "And in Antioch the disciples were
first called Christians." The word "Christian" was possibly first used
derisively, by those opposed to this new sect. Or, it could be, it was a
word chosen by the disciples of Christ, identifying themselves as followers of the Lord Jesus. Either way, it eventually became the universal
term for true Christ-followers.

I once read a rather convicting and incisive question, which appeared
in a secular periodical; it asked, "If you were arrested for being a Christian, would there be sufficient evidence to convict you?"

Verse

Why do they call me a "Christian"?
Is it because to a church I belong?
Is it because I simply play along?
Or because they see Christ in me?

The Mind of Christ

The Word
³Do nothing from selfish ambition or conceit, but in humility count others more significant than yourselves. ⁴Let each of you look not only to his own interests, but also to the interests of others. ⁵Have this mind among yourselves, which is yours in Christ Jesus.
Philippians 2:3-5

Voice from the Church
"More than anything else, our world needs Christians to have the mind of Christ. If we don't, then we get in the middle of life's most difficult places, our witness will not be the same as his. There will be two voices instead of one, and one will be the voice of self-interest. If we let him bring us to the place where his will has become ours and his mind controls ours, then we will find that any witness we have is identical with his, and our world can see who Jesus Christ really is." (Dennis F. Kinlaw, 1992-2017)*

Reflection
We were born with both a propensity to sinning and an incurvature of our will. Our will is *naturally* bent inward—toward ourselves. Born of Adam, we came into this world and we walk through this world, with a mindset that is predominately self-centered. Since this is so, it requires the gracious act of God's regenerating grace, the cleansing blood of Christ, and the sanctifying ministry of the Holy Spirit, to transform us from selfish to selfless disciples of Christ.

The mind of Christ walks in humility before God and among others; it is neither conceited nor selfishly ambitious; another's interests are more important than its own; it seeks to serve rather than to be served.

How we (I) need the mind of Christ!

Verse
The mind of Christ—
  this my plea!
Let this mind
  be daily in me.

The Holy Spirit and Prayer

The Word

When the day of Pentecost arrived, they ...
were all filled with the Holy Spirit.
Acts 2:1, 4

Voice from the Church

"Edith, I wonder what would happen to most churches and Christian work if we awakened tomorrow, and everything concerning the work of the Holy Spirit, and everything concerning prayer, were removed from the Bible, I don't mean just ignored, but actually cut out—disappeared. I wonder how much difference it would make?" (Francis Schaeffer [1912-1984], speaking to his wife)*

Reflection

The Book of Acts would never have been written had the Spirit never descended. Jesus had been gloried (died, risen, ascended), but ... then what? The disciples would have had stories to tell—parables and principles taught, and miracles performed by the Lord—but they themselves were ill-prepared to minister. They needed a fiery cleansing and baptism; they needed power from on High.

Again, the Book of Acts would never have been written unless the Holy Spirit had descended, because Acts is a history of the acts of the Holy Spirit. From Acts 1:2 to Acts 28:25, the Holy Spirit is mentioned some 58 times. Moreover, without the Spirit, there would be no New Testament nor the Church itself, both products of the Spirit's creation.

Furthermore, if we excised the references to prayer in the Book of Acts, there would be no Book, for Acts is a record of praying saints.

The Holy Spirit gives birth to prayer. Where the Holy Spirit is present, authentic prayers are offered in Jesus' name.

Verse

They wondered how to grow the church;
Advice was offered, best plans laid.
But ... the Spirit was not present,
So Spirit-prayer was never made.

"Nail the colors to the mast!"

The Word

> *When he had gone through those regions and had given*
> *them much encouragement, he came to Greece.*
> Acts 20:2

Voice from the Church

"Nail the colors to the mast! That is the right thing to do, and, therefore, that is what we must do, and do it now. What colors? The colors of Christ, the work He has given us to do—the evangelization of all the unevangelized. Christ wants not nibblers of the possible, but grabbers of the impossible, by faith in the omnipotence, fidelity, and wisdom of the Almighty Savior Who gave the command. Is there a wall in our path? By our God we will leap over it! Are there lions and scorpions in our way? We will trample them under our feet! Does a mountain bar our progress? Saying, 'Be thou cast into the sea,' we will march on. Soldiers of Jesus! Never surrender! Nail the colors to the mast!" (C. T. Studd, 1860-1931)*

Reflection

Not everyone is called by God to leave their homeland to minister elsewhere. However, some are. The Son of God was sent from heaven into this world by the Father, to serve and save the lost. Paul was called by God to evangelize the Mediterranean regions. C. T. Studd left England to preach the gospel in Africa and other countries.

If God has not called you to "go" to other regions, you can pray that he would send laborers into the harvest fields (Luke 10:2) and pray for those who have gone. Furthermore, the Light of the World has charged each of us to be a light for Christ—wherever we live (Matt. 5:14).

Let's "Nail the colors to the mast!" Let's ask God to help us be Christ's witnesses—wherever we are.

Verse

There's surely somewhere a lowly place
In earth's harvest fields so wide
Where I may labor thro' life's short day
For Jesus, the Crucified. (Mary Brown & Charles Prior)**

Kingdom Essentials

The Word

> [16]So do not let what you regard as good be spoken of as evil. [17]For
> the kingdom of God is not a matter of eating and drinking but of
> righteousness and peace and joy in the Holy Spirit. [18]Whoever
> thus serves Christ is acceptable to God and approved by men.
> Romans 14:16-18

Voice from the Church

"The man ... who in these things serveth Christ—acts according to his
doctrine, is acceptable to God; for he has not only the form of godliness
in thus serving Christ, but he has the power, the very essence and spirit
of it, in having righteousness, and peace, and joy in the Holy
Ghost." (Adam Clarke, 1760-1832)*

Reflection

Undiscerning man is forever majoring in minors and minoring in ma-
jors. We quibble over the proverbial "gnats" while swallowing the proverbial "camels." It was so in the early church and it is so today.

We are slow learners when it comes to the truth addressed in Romans
14. It's a lot easier for us to construct a code of religious conduct on the
foundation of incidental and morally indifferent matters, than it is to
totally submit ourselves to the King of the Kingdom, allowing him to
produce within us kingdom essentials: "righteousness, peace, and joy in
the Holy Spirit.

Man-made religion—even man-made Christianity—exults in impos-
ing one's *personal* belief system on others. The kingdom of Christ begins in the heart, and the fruit of his kingdom is neither self-produced
nor imposed fruit—it is the fruit of the Spirit that results in true righteousness, true peace, and true joy. These are Kingdom essentials.

Verse

The kingdom of Christ is so hard,
Without the King within reigning.
When Christ is seated on the throne,
His is our will—enjoying.

Worship's Height

The Word

And Mary said, "Behold, I am the servant of the Lord; let it be to me according to your word." And the angel departed from her.
Luke 1:38
"Hallelujah! For the Lord our God the Almighty reigns.
Revelation 19:6

Voice from the Church

"The height of worship is expressed in the use of two words that have never been translated, which remain on the pages of the Holy Scriptures and in the common language of the church as they were in the language where they originated: 'Hallelujah' and 'Amen.' When I have learned to say those two words with all my mind and heart and soul and being, I have found the highest place of worship." (G. Campbell Morgan, 1863-1945)*

Reflection

When it comes to the worship of God—and all of life is to be continuous worship—we cannot improve upon the Virgin's response to the angel's announcement, that she would be God's choice to bear the Christ Child, and to the response of the angels, twenty-four elders, four living creatures, and the great multitude recorded in Revelation. What was Mary's response? "let it be to me according to your word." Essentially, she said, "Amen." What were the responses of those John saw in his vision, when they were ushered into the presence of God? "Hallelujah!"

We are prone to say "Amen" so casually. All our prayers conclude with an "Amen." But how often do we say, "Amen" when reading the sacred Scriptures, meaning, "Let it be so in my life"? Do we worship God with our own "Hallelujahs" ("praise to the LORD"), giving total praise to the God of all creation who is also our Redeemer?

Verse

God has spoken—
Amen!
God has redeemed us—
Hallelujah!

Christmas and the Cross

The Word

Therefore the Lord himself will give you a sign. Behold, the virgin shall conceive and bear a son, and shall call his name Immanuel.
Isaiah 7:14

Voice from the Church

"Christmas draws near again. In our thinking of it, we must never isolate Bethlehem from Golgotha, or the cradle from the Cross. Apart from the Incarnation there never *could* have been the Atonement; and apart from the Atonement there never *would* have been the Incarnation; and apart from the infinite love of God there neither could nor would have been either." (J. Sidlow Baxter, 1903-1999)*

Reflection

In one of Leonardo da Vinci's portraits, he depicts a portentous scene of the purpose of Messiah's birth. In setting paint to canvas, da Vinci reveals Mary holding the Christ-child, and the Christ-child staring at and gripping with both hands a yarn-winder, with its four spokes in the form of a cross. The master painter understood the ultimate purpose of the Incarnation. We should as well.

With all the festivities surrounding our celebration of Advent, our eyes should look beyond the Babe in the manger to the Christ on the Cross. The Lord Jesus knew well why he had come from the glories of heaven and his Father's side, to a fallen and sinful world; he often reminded his disciples why he had come. "And I, when I am lifted up from the earth, will draw all people to myself." He said this to show by what kind of death he was going to die" (John 12:32-33).

Let us joyfully celebrate Advent. But let us also remember there was a Cross overshadowing Bethlehem that Holy Night.

Verse

That You came as a Babe
  fills us with wonder, love and praise.
That You died on a Cross—
  we never cease to be amazed.

"He became poor"

The Word

For you know the grace of our Lord Jesus Christ,
that though he was rich, yet for your sake he became
poor, so that you by his poverty might become rich.
2 Corinthians 8:9

Voice from the Church

"Paul is saying that Christ was made poor because God deigned to be born as man, humbling the power of his might so that he might obtain for men the riches of divinity and thus share in the divine nature, as Peter says. He was made man in order to take humanity right into the Godhead. Therefore Christ was made poor, not for his sake but for our." (Ambrosiaster, d. 397)*

Reflection

That the eternal Son of God became the lowly Son of Man is simply incomprehensible to the finite mind. He, through whom the universe was created in the beginning—"All things were made through him, and without him was not any thing made that was made" (John 1:3)— "became poor." Humankind has never known such poverty. The Son of God stooped lower than any person has ever stooped, when the *seed* of God was implanted in the womb of Mary.

The Son, who had from eternity past, had always been at his Father's side, left the glories of heaven, making the Great Descent into a fallen world. We must never think of Christ's incarnational *poverty* in material terms; his poverty consisted of his laying aside his innate credentials as Son—all to make us "rich" through his atoning death and resurrection. "Thanks be to God for his inexpressible gift!" (2 Cor. 9:15). Let us offer thanks today and each day, that Christ "became poor" for you and me.

Verse

O how I love Him! How I adore Him!
My breath, my sunshine, my all in all!
The great Creator became my Savior,
And all God's fulness dwelleth in Him. (William E. Booth-Clibborn, 1893-1969)**

Name Above All Names

The Word
⁹Therefore God has highly exalted him and bestowed on him the name that is above every name, ¹⁰so that at the name of Jesus every knee should bow, in heaven and on earth and under the earth, ¹¹and every tongue confess that Jesus Christ is Lord, to the glory of God the Father.
Philippians 2:9-11

Voice from the Church
"The theme of Wilson's preaching and teaching was always Jesus Christ. When he quarreled with any scheme of doctrine, it was always because it took from Christ the honor due his name. The name of Jesus was in every sermon Daniel Wilson preached and every prayer he prayed." (Roger Steer, b. 1945)*

Reflection
The disciple of Jesus—at every level in the church—faces the ongoing challenge of keeping the Lord of the church at the very core of one's life and teaching. The theology of the church is to be *Christological*; the confession of the church must be *Jesus is Lord*; the ministry of the church is always to be done as *servants of Christ*; the prayers of the church are to be offered *in Jesus' name*; the hope of the church is *the coming of Christ*; the future of the church is *with Christ*. The insidious tendency for us is to elevate a doctrine, a message, a mission, or a man above the Savior and the Man at God's right hand.

Since it was Christ who came, taught, died, arose, ascended, intercedes, returns, prepares a place for us, and before whom we will cast our trophies of grace, let us spend our days exalting the Father's beloved Son in all that we say and do, thus we will honor the Father who sent him and the Spirit who empowered Christ during his earthly ministry.

Verse
There is no other worthy name,
Deserving our high praise.
Let us exalt the Father's Son,
Walking in all His ways.

Is God's Home *in* You?

The Word

[22]Judas (not Iscariot) said to him, "Lord, how is it that you will mani-fest yourself to us, and not to the world?" [23]Jesus answered him, "If anyone loves me, he will keep my word, and my Father will love him, and we will come to him and make our home with him."
John 14:22-23

Voice from the Church

"Then there came the quiet, gentle response of God's voice: 'My Spirit is imparted in plenitude to the one prepared to obey me. Your love for me is demonstrated, not by emotion, but by your readiness to comply with my wishes, to do my will. Are you ready to give me your will?'" (W. Phillip Keller, 1920-1997)*

Reflection

Too many of us are driven by our emotions in our walk with God, in-stead of devoted love for God which influences our will. If we don't *feel* like doing the right thing, we don't do it.

We all enjoy *feeling* good, but how do we act when our feelings are something other than good? The faithful husband gets out of bed each morning and goes to work, whether he feels like it or not. The devoted wife and mother fulfills her daily chores, whether she feels like it or not. Someone once asked a noted Bible scholar and writer, "How do you write as much as you do?" His answer: "I apply the seat of my pants to the seat of my chair every morning, whether I feel like it or not."

To love God is to obey God—irrespective of our feelings. The more we repetitively obey our Lord, the easier obedience becomes. It's to those whose lives are characterized by obedience, that the Father and Son, through the Spirit, come to make their home.

Verse

I once served You with fits and starts;
My will was weak, my heart many parts.
Then I cried out, "Make my heart one!"
You came with fire and said, "It is done."

God's Plaintive Plea

The Word

> ^{13} *"Oh, that my people would listen to me, that Israel*
> *would walk in my ways! ^{14}I would soon subdue*
> *their enemies and turn my hand against their foes."*
> Psalm 81:13-14

Voice from the Church

"We are apt to say, 'If such a method had been taken, such an instrument employed, we should soon have subdued our enemies:' But we mistake; if we had hearkened to God, and kept to our duty, the thing would have been done, but it is sin that makes our troubles long and salvation slow. And this is that which God himself complains of, and wishes it had been otherwise. Note, Therefore God would have us do our duty to him, that we may be qualified to receive favour from him. He delights in our serving him, not because he is the better for it, but because we shall be." (Matthew Henry, 1662-1714)*

Reflection

Just as Israel was a privileged people, so are we. But just as Israel often turned from following their true Shepherd, too many of the people of God fail to follow their Deliverer with a whole heart.

To be unfaithful is to be disobedient. We are ravished by our Adversary because we fail simply to listen to the voice of the Good Shepherd. There is no obstacle and enemy of our soul that cannot be conquered through grace, if we would but listen. To "listen" is more than to read the Bible and hear a good sermon. To listen is to obey, to hearken to our Shepherd's voice. God wants more than our offerings of religious platitudes; the Shepherd of Israel demands that we walk in his ways. Only a heart purified by love is intent on listening and walking with God.

Verse

I would be faithful through each passing moment;
I would be constantly in touch with God;
I would be strong to follow where He leads me;
I would have faith to keep the path Christ trod. (Howard Walter, 1883-1918)**

Finishing Well

The Word

⁷I have fought the good fight, I have finished the race, I have kept the faith. ⁸Henceforth there is laid up for me the crown of righteousness, which the Lord, the righteous judge, will award to me on that day, and not only to me but also to all who have loved his appearing.
1 Timothy 4:7-8

Voice from the Church

"I am now an old man [Wesley died 13 months later at age 87], decayed from head to foot. My eyes are dim; my right hand shakes much; my mouth is hot and dry every morning; I have a lingering fever almost every day; my motion is weak and slow. However, blessed be God, I do not slack my labor: I can preach and write still." (John Wesley, 1703-1791)*

Reflection

To begin the Christian race with a good start is necessary and must not be minimized. After all, there is no beginning in this race without true repentance and a saving faith in God through our Lord Jesus Christ. However, not all who begin the Christian pilgrimage finish well, or finish the race at all; our Lord's parable of the seed and the sower are reminders of this sad truth. Furthermore, there are many exhortations given by the apostles throughout the New Testament for believers to persevere to the end in their walk with God.

The apostle reminds us that the Christian life is a "fight" and a "race." We are engaged in an ongoing battle against the world, the flesh, demonic forces, and the god of this world—Satan himself. We fight this race while running. Through the merits of the shed blood of Christ, and the indwelling strength of the Holy Spirit, we can finish this race well—to the praise and glory of the Lord Jesus Christ. I pray you shall.

Verse

True, 'tis a strait and thorny road,
And mortal spirits tire and faint;
But they forget the mighty God,
That feeds the strength of every saint. (Isaac Watts, 1674-1748)**

Goodness and Mercy

The Word

Surely goodness and mercy shall follow me all the days of my life, and I shall dwell in the house of the Lord forever.
Psalm 23:6

Voice from the Church

"The goodness of God is that which disposes Him to be kind, cordial, benevolent, and full of good will toward men.... As judgment is God's justice confronting moral inequity, so mercy is the goodness of God confronting human suffering and guilt. Were there no guilt in the world, no pain and no tears, God would yet be infinitely merciful; but His mercy might well remain hidden in His heart, unknown to the created universe." (A. W. Tozer, 1897-1963)*

Reflection

Of all the Old Testament texts, Psalm 23 is undoubtedly the one Christians are most familiar, with many having memorized it. We don't know when David, the sweet psalmist of Israel, penned this song. Was it while caring for his father's sheep? Or, more likely, was it after walking with the Good Shepherd of Israel for many years? Whenever it was that he composed the words that were to become the favorite psalm of God's people across the centuries, David had become convinced of two indisputable facts: the goodness and mercy of God would always accompany his steps, until he entered the very dwelling place of God.

To walk with and to know God is to experience his goodness. To have sinned (and repented)—as David had—is to know God's mercy. It is because God is love, that he demonstrates his goodness. It is because God is kind, that he extends his mercy, especially toward the penitent. For these twin attributes of God, let us always be grateful.

Verse

When all Thy mercies, O my God,
My rising soul surveys,
Transported with the view, I'm lost
In wonder, love, and praise. (Joseph Addison, 1672-1719**

Staying Thirsty

The Word

> [1] As the deer pants for the water brooks,
> So my soul pants for You, O God.
> [2] My soul thirsts for God, for the living God;
> When shall I come and appear before God?
> Psalm 42:1-2 NASB

Voice from the Church

"We'll find no rest outside of his presence. We know that, yet we have this horrible habit of looking for him in all the wrong places. No creed will satisfy, no nicely formulated idea about God, no relic or symbol. What we need is the living water—not brackish, swampy stuff either. We need water that tumbles and leaps and rushes, water that is alive." (Abraham Kuyper, 1837-1920)*

Reflection

As finite beings who serve an infinite all-knowing God, we may end this year and begin the next confident that he who led us thus far will be with us every moment into our future. There is no past that God cannot heal; there is no future where God cannot lead.

Regardless of the twists and turns that lie before each of us, let us purpose to tend to those things that ultimately matter. Water is the most precious natural resource God has given his creatures. Christ is the water of life, through whom God chooses to channel and supply our every spiritual longing. The Holy Spirit is God's agent on earth, creating in us a longing for God, an intense desire for Reality.

The only way and the only One who can quench soul-thirst is the One who made us in his own likeness. True thirst leads us to Christ; continual thirst will cause us to follow Christ. Drink deeply, my friend!

Verse

I wasn't sure what made me so thirsty,
Until I found Him who gave me a drink.
I discovered one drink insufficient;
I keep drinking; this Well is so deep.

Endnotes

January 1 *Our Daily Bread, January 9, 2016.

January 2 *Bud Robinson, Sunshine and Smiles, pp. 43-44.
       **From "Satisfied" by Clara T. Williams.

January 3 *A. J. Gordon, The Ministry of the Spirit, p. 32.

January 4 *Charles Spurgeon, "The New Park Street Pulpit," Sermon 279.
       **From "Ho, Every One That is Thirsty!" by Lucy J. Meyer.

January 5 *C. S. Lewis, Surprised by Joy, p. 237.
       **From "Hidden Peace" by John S. Brown.

January 6 *Wayne Grudem, Systematic Theology, p. 33.
       **From "Open My Eyes, That I May See" by Clara H. Scott.

January 7 *Edward Griffin, PuritanSermons.com.

January 8 *Dennis F. Kinlaw, Let's Start with Jesus, p. 147.
       **From "Breathe on Me, Breath of God" by Edwin Hatch.

January 9 *Gregory Nazianzen, Letters XLI, NPNF 2 7:450.
       **From "Only Believe" by Paul Rader.

January 10 *John Paton, John Paton: Missionary to the New Hebrides, p. 14.
       **From "What Various Hindrances We Meet" by William Cowper.

January 11 *Fritz Rienecker, A Linguistic Key to the Greek New Testament, Forward.

January 12 *George Whitefield, George Whitefield's Journals, March 28, 1739).

January 13 *W. E. Sangster, The Path to Perfection, p. 193.

January 14 *Jeremy Taylor, Holy Living, p. 17.

January 15 *Frederick D. Bruner, The Christbook, p. 174.

January 16 *Oswald Chambers, My Utmost for His Highest, September 30.

January 17 *George Whitefield in George Whitefield's Journals by Ian Murray, Preface.
       **From "Outwitted" by Edwin Markham. Markham's poem reads "wit to win." I took the liberty to sanctify

his verse!

January 18   *Sinclair B. Ferguson, banneroftruth.org.

January 19   *Dietrich Bonhoeffer, *Discipleship*, p. 181.

January 20   *Francis de Sales, *Living Love*, p. 126.

January 21   *Gordon Fee, *God's Empowering Presence*, p. 901.
               **From "How Great Thou Art" by Carl Gustav Bob-
               erg; translated by Stuart K. Hine.

January 22   *V. Raymond Edman, *The Disciplines of Life*, p. 69.
               **From "Must Jesus Bear the Cross Alone" by Thomas
               Shepherd.

January 23   *Gary M. Burge, *Interpreting the Gospel of John*, p.
               180.

January 24   *John Wesley, *The Journals of John Wesley*, May 24,
               1738.

January 25   *Purkiser, Taylor & Taylor, *God, Man, & Salvation*, p.
               456.

January 26   *Martin Luther, quoted in James M. Kittleson, *Luther
               the Reformer*, p. 270.
               **From "A Mighty Fortress is Our God" by Martin
               Luther.

January 27   *H. C. G. Moule, quoted in W. H. Griffith Thomas, *The
               Holy Spirit of God*, p. 272.
               **From "Fill Me Now" by Elwood H. Stokes.

January 28   *Harold J. Ockenga, *Power Through Pentecost*, p. 43.
               **From "Alas! And Did My Savior Bleed?" by Isaac
               Watts.

January 29   *Donald G. Bloesch, *The Holy Spirit: Works & Gifts*, p.
               338.

January 30   *Madam Guyon, *Experiencing the Depths of Jesus
               Christ*, p. 303.

January 31   *A. J. Gordon, *Ecce Venit: Behold He Cometh*, p. 30.
               **From "If Christ Should Come Tonight" by Harriet E.
               Jones.

February 1   *Leon Morris, *The Apostolic Preaching of the Cross*, p.
               249.
               **From "Arise, My Soul, Arise" by Charles Wesley.

February 2   *Henry B. Swete, *The Holy Spirit in the Ancient
               Church*, p. 15.

**From "In the Cross of Christ I Glory" by John Browning.

February 3   *Duncan Campbell, *Heart Purity*, theoldtimegospel.org.

February 4   *Marva J. Dawn, *The Sense of the Call*, p. 16.

February 5   *J. Sidlow Baxter, *The Master Theme of the Bible*, p. 92.
**From "Love Divine, All Loves Excelling" by Charles Wesley.

February 6   *Murray J. Harris, *Slave for Christ*, p. 18.

February 7   *Andrew Bonar, *Andrew Bonar: Diary and Life*, January 21, 1878.
**From "I Am Thine, O Lord" by Fanny Crosby.

February 8   *Diogenes Allen, *Spiritual Theology*, p. 35.

February 9   *Jean-Pierre de Caussade, *The Joy of Full Surrender*, p. 175.

February 10   *John Owen, *The Holy Spirit*, p. 208.

February 11   *William Barclay, *The Letter to the Hebrews, The Daily Study Bible Series*, rev., p. 29

February 12   *Richard of Chichester, original source unknown.
**From "My Faith Looks Up to Thee" by Ray Palmer.

February 13   *Frances de Sales, *Living Love*, pp. 69-70.
**From "More Love to Thee, O Christ" by Elizabeth P. Prentiss.

February 14   *Dennis F. Kinlaw, *This Day With the Master*, January 25.

February 15   *Charles H. Spurgeon, *Spurgeon's Expository Encyclopedia*, p. 286.

February 16   *John Owen, *Hebrews: The Epistle of Warning*, p. 235.
**From "Turn Your Eyes Upon Jesus" by Helen H. Lemmel.

February 17   *George H. Morrison, quoted in *Take Heart; Daily Devotions with the Church's Great Preachers*, ed. by Diana Wallis, p. 117.
**Original source unknown.

February 18   *J. I. Packer, *A Quest For Godliness*, p. 36.
**From "Search Me, O God" by J. Edwin Orr.

February 19   *Wesley Duewel, *Touch the World Through Prayer*, p. 12.

**From "Rescue the Perishing" by Fanny Crosby.

February 20   *F. F. Bruce, *The Epistle to the Hebrews*, p. 7.

February 21   *Kari Torjesen Malcolm, *We Signed Our Lives Away*, p. 18.

**From "Faith of Our Brothers" by Susan H. Peterson.

February 22   *Josh McDowell, *The Resurrection Factor*, p. 6.

February 23   *David Livingstone, quoted by Rob Mackenzie, *David Livingstone: The Truth Behind the Legend*, p. 109.

February 24   *Philip G. Ryken, *Art for God's Sake*, p. 24.

**From "Give of Your Best to the Master" by Howard B. Grose.

February 25   *W. Phillip Keller, *Thank You, Father*, p. 154.

February 26   *Quoted by Leonard Ravenhill in *Revival Praying*, 175.

**From "Children of the Heavenly Father" by Karolina W. Sandell-Berg, translated by Ernst W. Olson.

February 27   *Elisabeth Elliot, *A Chance to Die: The Life and Legacy of Amy Carmichael*, p. 73.

February 28   *A. W. Tozer, *The Knowledge of the Holy*, p. 12.

**From "Praise to the Lord, the Almighty" by Joachim Neander, translated by Catherine Winkworth.

March 1   *F. F. Bruce, *The Gospel & Epistles of John*, p. 111.

March 2   *Thomas C. Oden, *Life in the Spirit: Systematic Theology*, 3:470.

March 3   *Richard Collier, *The General Next to God: The Story of William Booth and the Salvation Army*, p. 44.

March 4   *Oswald Chambers, *My Utmost for His Highest*, February 15.

March 5   *Robertson McQuilkin, *Life in the Spirit*, p. 144.

**From "Stepping in the Light" by Eliza E. Hewitt.

March 6   *Thomas à Kempis, *Imitation of Christ*, p. 53.

March 7   *Watchman Nee, *Love Not the World*, p. 16.

**From "Desire of God" by Frederick W. Faber.

March 8   *Andreas J. Köstenberger, *John: Baker Exegetical Commentary on the New Testament*, p. 495.

**From "Moment by Moment" by Daniel W. Whittle.

March 9   *J. Sidlow Baxter, *Majesty: The God You Should Know*, p. 117.

March 10	*Aristides, cited by Charles Colson, *Loving God*, p. 173.
March 11	*Harry E. Jessop, *I Met a Man with a Shining Face*, pp. 11-12.
March 12	*Martin Luther, *Martin Luther: Weimarer Ausgabe Edition*, 2:618.
March 13	*N. T. Wright, *Simply Christian: Why Christianity Makes Sense*, p. 122.
March 14	*Henry Drummond, *The Greatest Thing in the World*, p. 17.
March 15	*D. A. Carson, *A Call to Spiritual Reformation*, p. 126.
March 16	*Marvin Vincent, *Word Studies in the New Testament*, Vol. III, p. 418.
March 17	*Richard Owen Roberts, from a sermon preached April, 2006 at The Cove, Ashville, North Carolina.
March 18	*Thomas Cook, *New Testament Holiness*, p. 7.
March 19	*D. A. Carson, *A Call to Spiritual Reformation, p.* 136.
March 20	*J. Sidlow Baxter, *A New Call to Holiness*, p. 241.
March 21	*John Owen, *The Holy Spirit*, p. 135.
March 22	*Paul S. Rees, *Triumphant in Trouble: Studies in 1 Peter*, p. 39.
March 23	*Ignatius Loyola, quoted by *Eerdmans Handbook to the History of Christianity*, p. 411.
	**From "All for Jesus" by Mary D. James.
March 24	*G. Campbell Morgan, *The Spirit of God*, p. 149.
March 25	*Frederick D. Bruner, *The Christbook*, p. 163.
March 26	*Paul E. Billheimer, *Don't Waste Your Sorrows*, p. 99.
	**From "Much Fruit" by Annie Johnson Flint.
March 27	*Vance Havner, *Why Not Just Be Christians?*, p. 13.
	**From "Indwelt" by Beatrice Clelland.
March 28	*Adolph Saphir, *The Hidden Life*, p. 150.
March 29	*Francis A. Schaeffer, *The Mark of the Christian*, p. 13.
March 30	*Roy Hession, *My Calvary Road*, p. 161.
March 31	*From "On a Hill Far Away" by George Bennard.
	**From "In the Cross of Christ I Glory" by John Bowring.
April 1	*Adam Clark, *Clarke's Commentaries*, 4:203.
April 2	*John F. Walvoord, *Jesus Christ is Lord*, p. 82.

April 3	*Matthew Henry, *A Commentary on the Whole Bible,* Isaiah 53:3.
	**From "Man of Sorrows, What a Name" by Philip P. Bliss.
April 4	*R. C. Sproul, *The Consequences of Ideas*, p. 153.
	**From "When I Survey the Wondrous Cross" by Isaac Watts.
April 5	*John R. W. Stott, *The Cross of Christ, p.* 147.
	**From "Alas! and Did My Saviour Bleed" by Isaac Watts.
April 6	*George Steinberger, *In the Footprints of the Lamb*, p. 57.
	**From "Majestic Sweetness Sits Enthroned" by Samuel Stennett."
April 7	*Kenneth L. Barker & John Kohlenberger, Zondervan *NIV Bible Commentary*, 1:1132.
	**From "Majestic Sweetness Sits Enthroned" by Samuel Stennett."
April 8	*John N. Oswalt, *The NIV Application Commentary: Isaiah*, p. 586.
	**From "There is a Green Hill Far Away" by Cecil F. Alexander.
April 9	*John N. Oswalt, *The NIV Application Commentary: Isaiah*, p. 586.
	**From "There is a Green Hill Far Away" by C. Frances Alexander.
April 10	*J. Sidlow Baxter, *The Master Theme of the Bible*, p. 280.
	**From "Man of Sorrows, What a Name" by Philip P. Bliss.
April 11	*John Bunyan, *The Acceptable Sacrifice*, p. 87.
April 12	*J. B. Phillips, *Your God is Too Small*, p. 119.
April 13	*The Scots Confession*, chapter 18, p. 1560.
April 14	*Dallas Willard, *Divine Conspiracy*, p. 111.
April 15	*Guy Davies, exiledpreacher.blogspot.com.
April 16	*Ted Peters, *Sin: Radical Evil in Soul and Society*, p. 124.
April 17	*John Webster, *Holiness*, p. 88.
April 18	*F. F. Bruce, *Jesus: Lord & Savior*, pp. 204-205.

April 19	*Eugene H. Peterson, *Subversive Spirituality*, p. 207.
April 20	*François Fénelon, *Meditations on the Heart of God*, p. 10.
April 21	*John Wesley, *John Wesley's Journal*, March 26, 1790.
April 22	*Ole Hallesby, *Prayer*, p. 24.
	**From "What a Friend We Have in Jesus" by Joseph M. Scriven.
April 23	*Adam Clarke, *Clarke's Commentary*, 1:122.
	**From "Father of Jesus Christ, My Lord," by Charles Wesley.
April 24	*Simon Chan, *Spiritual Theology*, p. 110.
April 25	*Wayne Grudem, *Systematic Theology*, p. 78.
	**From "The Word of God" by Ken Bible.
April 26	*Glenn R. Phillips, quoted by Lettie Cowman in *Springs in the Valley*, p. 354.
April 27	*William Burkitt, Burkitt's Notes on the New Testament, 1:516.
April 28	*Charles Spurgeon quoted by Arnold A. Dallimore, *Spurgeon: A Biography*, p. 18.
	**From "Look and Live" by William A. Ogden
April 29	*"Yes, I Know!", cyberhymnal.org.
	**From "Yes, I Know" by Anna W. Waterman.
April 30	*St. John Chrysostom, *Ancient Christian Writers*, 31:780.
	**From "I Shall Know Him" by Fanny Crosby.
May 1	*F. F. Bruce, *Paul: Apostle of the Heart Set Free*, p. 329.
May 2	*F. W. Grosheide, *Commentary on The First Epistle to the Corinthians*, p. 53.
May 3	*W. T. Purkiser, Richard S. Taylor, Willard H. Taylor, *God, Man, & Salvation*, p. 55.
May 4	*William Barclay, *The Letter to the Corinthians, The Daily Study Bible Series*, rev., pp. 22-23.
May 5	*D. Martyn Lloyd-Jones, *God's Ultimate Purpose: An Exposition of Ephesians 1:1-2:23*, pp. 161-162.
	**From "Redeemed, How I Love to Proclaim It!" by Fanny Crosby.
May 6	*Martin Israel, *Smoldering Fire*, p. 117.

May 7   *Jonathan Edwards, *Religious Affections*, abridged and updated by E. Sanna, p. 309.

May 8   *Dietrich Bonhoeffer, *Life Together*, p. 86.
          ** From "What Various Hindrances We Meet" by William Cowper.

May 9   *Charles G. Trumbull, quoted by V. Raymond Edman in *They Found the Secret*, p. 149.

May 10   *F. B. Meyer, *The Christ-Life for the Self-Life*, p. 41.

May 11   *Dennis F. Kinlaw, This *Day with the Master: 365 Daily Meditations*, December 4.

May 12   *Matthew Henry, *A Commentary on the Whole Bible*, Colossians 3:1-2.

May 13   *Adam Clarke, *Clarke's Commentary*, 6:520.
          From "Higher Ground" by Johnson Oatman, Jr.

May 14   *Myron S. Augsburger, *Convicted & Transformed*, p. 1.

May 15   *Evangelist speaking to "Christian" in John Bunyan, *The Pilgrim's Progress*, p. 99.
          **From "Awake, Our Souls; Away, Our Fears" by Isaac Watts.

May 16   *Thomas C. Oden, *Life in the Spirit: Systematic Theology*, 3:160.

May 17   *J. Nieboer, *Practical Exposition of James*, p. 82.

May 18   *Alister McGrath, *Knowing Christ*, p. 11.
          **From "Ye Must Be Born Again" by William T. Sleeper.

May 19   *E. Stanley Jones, *A Song of Ascents: A Spiritual Autobiography*, p. 35.
          **From "And Can It Be That I Should Gain?" by Charles Wesley.

May 20   *W. Phillip Keller, *Wonder O' the Wind*, p. 232.
          **From "O Thou God of My Salvation" by Thomas Olivers.

May 21   *Martyn Lloyd-Jones, *The Love of God: Studies in 1 John*, p. 45.

May 22   *Robert Law, *The Tests of Life: A Study of the First Epistle of John*, pp. 261-262.

May 23   *Cyprian, Bishop of Carthage, quoted by Robert E Coleman in *Songs of Heaven*, p. 118.

	**From "Faith is the Victory" by John H. Yates.
May 24	*William Law, *A Serious Call to a Devout and Holy Life*, p. 67.
	**From "Sun of My Soul, Thou Savior Dear" by John Keble.
May 25	*Gordon F. Fee, *Gospel and Spirit: Issues in New Testament Hermeneutics*, p. 80.
May 26	*F. F. Bruce, *The Epistle to the Hebrews*, p. 416.
May 27	*Armin Gesswein, "Billy Graham Center Archives, Wheaton College," Collection 517.
May 28	*Peter Kreeft, *Christianity for Modern Pagans: Pascal's Penesées Edited, Outlined and Explained*, p. 161.
May 29	*E. Stanley Jones, *A Song of Ascents: A Spiritual Autobiography*, p. 73.
May 30	*I. Howard Marshall, quoted by Dallas Willard, *The Divine Conspiracy: Discovering Our Hidden Life in God*, p. 59.
May 31	*Abraham Kuyper, *Near Unto God: Daily Meditations, Adapted for Contemporary Christians* by James C. Schaap, p.162.
June 1	*Murray J. Harris, *Slave of Christ: A New Testament Metaphor for Total Devotion to Christ*, p. 171.
June 2	*J. C. Ryle, *Holiness*, p. 36.
June 3	*Iain H. Murray, *Heroes*, p. x.
June 4	*Erich Sauer, *In the Arena of Faith*, p. 82.
	**From "Nothing Between" by Charles A. Tindley.
June 5	*Steven Barabas, quoted by Helen Roseveare, *Living Holiness*, p. 171.
June 6	*F. F. Bruce, *Commentary on the Book of Acts*, p. 337.
	**From "Joy Unspeakable" by Barney E. Warren.
June 7	*G. Campbell Morgan, *The Crises of the Christ*, pp. 206-207.
June 8	*Sir Walter Scott, *The Monastery*, Kindle Edition.
	**From "Come, Ye Disconsolate" by Thomas Moore.
June 9	*Paul Tournier, *The Healing of Persons*, p. 107.
June 10	*James Stewart, *Heralds of God*, p. 209.
June 11	*George & Donald Sweeting, *The Acts of God*, pp. 28-29.
June 12	*Scott Larsen, *Indelible Ink*, p. 116.

June 13	*James Stewart, *The Strong Name*, p. 123. **From "In Heavenly Love Abiding" by Anna L. Waring.
June 14	*Donald G. Bloesch, *Spirituality Old & New: Recovering Authentic Spiritual Life*, p. 142.
June 15	*R. Kent Hughes, *Mark: Jesus, Servant and Savior*, 1:182. **From "O Love of God, How Strong and True" by Horatius Bonar.
June 16	*Francis A. Schaeffer, *No Little People*, p. 25.
June 17	*John Julian, *A Dictionary of Hymnology*, cited by wholesomewords.org. **From "O for a Thousand Tongues to Sing" by Charles Wesley.
June 18	*Frederick Dale Bruner, *The Christbook*, pp. 426-427.
June 19	*Murray J. Harris, *Slave of Christ*, pp. 155-156. **From "By Thy Blessed Word Obeying" by Daniel S. Warner.
June 20	*Handley C. G. Moule, *Letters and Poems of Bishop Moule*, p. 48.
June 21	*E. M. Bounds, quoted by Lyle W. Dorsett in *E. M. Bounds: Man of Prayer*, pp. 151-152.
June 22	*Robert Law, *The Tests of Life*, p.60.
June 23	*Martyn Lloyd-Jones, quoted by Iain H. Murray, *Lloyd-Jones: Messenger of Grace*, p. 101.
June 24	*Edmund Clowney, *The Message of 1 Peter*, p. 212. **From "All Your Anxiety" by Edward. H. Joy.
June 25	*W. Phillip Keller, *Taming Tension*, p. 91. **From "Leave It There" by Charles A. Tindley.
June 26	*W. E. Sangster, *Methodism Can Be Born Again*, p. 116.
June 27	*Jim Petersen, *Evangelism As a Lifestyle*, p. 97. **From "Rescue the Perishing" by Fanny Crosby.
June 28	*E. M. Bounds, *Purpose in Prayer*, p. 23. **From "Tell It to Jesus" by Jeremiah E. Rankin.
June 29	John Stott, *Life in Christ*, p. 128. **From "Joy in the Presence of Jesus" by John Newton.
June 30	*Francis Schaeffer, *No Little People*, p. 21.

July 1   *Matthew Henry, *A Commentary on the Whole Bible*,
                Matthew 13:45-46.
                **From "Jesus, Priceless Treasure" by Johann Franck.

July 2   *Edith Schaeffer, *The Life of Prayer*, p. 26.

July 3   *Adam Clarke, *Clarke's Commentary*, 5:470.

July 4   *Andrew Murray, *The Holiest of All*, p. 502.

July 5   *Gordon D. Fee, *Gospel and Spirit*, p. 111.

July 6   *William Barclay, *The Gospel of Matthew*, 1:145.

July 7   *A. J. Gordon, *The Ministry of the Spirit*, p. 145.

July 8   *S. D. Gordon, *Evangelical Saints*, edited and reprinted
                by Ralph I. Tilley, p. 33.

July 9   *A. W. Tozer, *Life in the Spirit*, p. 90.

July 10   *John G. Paton, *Thirty Years with South Sea Canni-
                bals: Autobiography of Dr. John G. Paton*, p. 14.
                **From "O My Heart Sings Today" by Haldor Lillenas.

July 11   *Herbert M. Carson, *The Epistles of Paul to the Colos-
                sians and Philemon*, pp. 96-97.

July 12   *C. S. Lewis, *Letters to an American Lady*, p. 11.
                **From "Blest Be the Tie That Binds" by John Faw-
                cett.

July 13   *John Newton, quoted by Iain H. Murray in *Heroes*, p.
                95.
                **From "Wherewith, O Lord, Shall I Draw Near?" by
                Charles Wesley.

July 14   *Peter Kreeft, *Christianity for Modern Pagans: Pas-
                cal's Penseés Edited, Outlined and Explained*, p. 63.

July 15   *John R. W. Stott, *The Cross of Christ*, p. 294.
                **From "When I Survey the Cross" by Isaac Watts.

July 16   *William Wilberforce, *Real Christianity*, ed. by James
                M. Houston, p. 123.

July 17   *Matthew Henry, biblestudytools.com/commentaries/
                matthew-henry-complete/isaiah/.

July 18   *George Steinberger, *In the Footprints of the Lamb*, p.
                57.
                **From "Stand Up! Stand Up for Jesus" by George
                Duffield.

July 19   *Kenneth N. Taylor, *My Life: A Guided Tour*, p. 352.

July 20   *Michael Green, *The Second Epistle of Peter and the

Epistle of Jude, p. 181.

July 21   *Samuel Chadwick, *The Way to Pentecost*, p. 67.

July 22   *A. W. Tozer, *God Tells the Man Who Cares*, p. 141.

July 23   *Eugene Peterson, *The Wisdom of Each Other*, p. 106.
           **From "All the Way My Savior Leads Me" by Fanny
           Crosby.

July 24   *Carl F. H. Henry, *God, Revelation and Authority*, Vol.
           VI, Part Two, p. 398.

July 25   *Charles W. Colson, *Born Again*, p. 117.

July 26   *William Burkitt, *Burkitt's Notes on the New Testa-
           ment*, p. 5.

July 27   *F. B. Meyer, *David: Shepherd, Psalmist, King*, p. 160.
           **From "God Leads Us Along" by George A. Young.

July 28   *Brother Lawrence, *The Practice of the Presence of
           God*, p. 63.

July 29   *C. S. Lewis, *The Four Loves*, p. 120.

July 30   *Michael Horton, *Christless Christianity*, pp. 256-257.
           **From "The Church's One Foundation" by S. J.
           Stone.

July 31   *Dietrich Bonhoeffer, *The Cost of Discipleship*, p. 11.
           **From "In Christ There is No East or West" by Wil-
           liam A. Dunkerley.

August 1   *Timothy George, "The Word Became Flesh," beeson-
           divinity.com.

August 2   *James Houston, *The Transforming Power of Prayer*,
           p. 36.
           **From "Himself" by A. B. Simpson.

August 3   *John Wesley, *Wesley's Works*, June 14, 1739.

August 4   *Francis A. Schaeffer, *The Mark of a Christian*, p. 21.

August 5   *Samuel Brengle, *Helps to Holiness*, p. 69.
           **James Montgomery quoted in *When the Spirit Came*
           by John Greenfield, p. 26.

August 6   *J. I. Packer & Carolynn Nystrom, *Praying*, p. 265.

August 7   *Rienecker & Rogers, *Linguistic Key to the Greek N.
           T.*, pp. 786-787.
           **From "I Love Thee, I Love Thee, author unknown.

August 8   *George Eldon Ladd, *The Blessed Hope*, p. 115.
           **From "Will Jesus Find Us Watching?" by Fanny

Crosby.

August 9   *William Barclay, *The Daily Study Bible Series, The Gospel of Luke*, rev. ed., p.167.
**From "My Soul, Be on Thy Guard" by George Heath.

August 10   *George Steinberger, *In the Footprints of the Lamb*, edited and reprinted by Ralph I. Tilley, p. 57.

August 11   *David F. Wells, *God the Evangelist*, p. 58.
**From "So Let Our Lips and Lives Express" by Isaac Watts.

August 12   *G. K. Chesterton, *Orthodoxy*, p. 165.

August 13   *Downloaded 12/16/08 from Ravi Zacharias, Christianity.com.

August 14   *Matthew Henry, *Matthew Henry's Commentary*, Psalm 16:8.
**From "Be Thou My Vision" by Dallan Forgaill, translated by Mary E. Byrne.

August 15   *Thomas à Kempis, *Imitation of Christ*, p. 15.
**From "Stand Up, Stand Up for Jesus" by George Duffield.

August 16   *Frederick D. Bruner, *The Christbook*, p. 457.
**From "Holy, Holy, Holy! Lord God Almighty" by Reginald Heber.

August 17   *J. C. Ryle, *Holiness*, p. 172.

August 18   *F. W. Robertson, from a sermon preached October 28, 1849.

August 19   *Oswald Chambers, *Workmen of God*, p. 88.

August 20   *John G. Paton, *John G. Paton: Missionary to the New Hebrides*, p.496.
**From "Jesus Saves" by Priscilla J. Owens.

August 21   *William Burkitt, *Burkitt's Notes on the New Testament*, p. 5.
**From "Thy Word Have I Hid in My Heart" by Ernest O. Sellers.

August 22   *C. F. Keil & F. Delitzsch, *Commentary on the Old Testament*, 1:231-232.
**From "Prayer is the Soul's Sincere Desire" by James Montgomery.

August 23   *Timothy George, "Delighted by Doctrine," beesondivinity.com.

August 24	*A. J. Gordon, *The Ministry of the Spirit*, pp. 116-117.
	**From "Search Me, O God" by James E. Orr.
August 25	*Robert Murray M'Cheyne, quoted by Andrew Bonar in *The Life of Robert Murray M'Cheyne*, p. 174.
August 26	*George Whitefield, *George Whitefield's Journals*, November 29, 1739.
	**From "God Leads Us Along" by G. A. Young.
August 27	*David & Kim Butts, *Revolution on Our Knees*, p. 66.
August 28	*J. Sidlow Baxter, *Going Deeper*, p. 133.
August 29	*Gilbert Meilaender, "First Things," 2:29.
August 30	*Charles Finney, *Charles G. Finney: An Autobiography*, p. 97.
August 31	*Ole Hallesby, *Why I am a Christian*, p. 132.
September 1	*Paul Brand, *The Forever Feast*, p. 91.
	**From "Depth of Mercy" by Charles Wesley.
September 2	*Tim Chester, "You Can Change" in *Revive*, 42:1.
	**From "More Like the Master" by Charles H. Gabriel.
September 3	*P. Kluepfel, *The Holy Spirit in the Life and Teaching of Jesus and the Early Church*, pp. 122-123.
	** Ibid., p. 137.
September 4	*James M. Houston, "Principles," religionandculture.org.
September 5	*Bakht Singh, quoted by Leonard Ravenhill in *Revival Praying*, p. 41.
	** Quoted by George Sayer in *Jack: A Life of C. S. Lewis,* p. 411.
	***From "Be Thou My Vision," author unknown, translated by Mary E. Byrne.
September 6	*Andrew Murray, quoted in *Andrew Murray* by William Lindner, Jr., p. 123.
	**From "Higher Ground" by Johnson Oatman, Jr.
September 7	*Robert E. Coleman, *Dry Bones Can Live Again*, p. 36.
September 8	*Excerpt from a letter to Evan Roberts from R. A. Torrey, quoted in *Invasion of Wales by the Spirit* by James A. Stewart, pp. 76-77.
	**From "My Soul, Be on Thy Guard" by George Heath.

September 9   *Jonathan Goforth, *By My Spirit*, p. 21.
             **From "O the Deep, Deep Love of Jesus" by S. Trevor Francis.
September 10 *Festo Kivengere, *When God Moves in Revival*, pp. 31-32.
September 11 *George MacDonald, *Knowing the Heart of God*, p. 183.
             **From "There's a Wideness in God's Mercy" by Frederick W. Faber.
September 12 *Duncan Campbell, *The Price and Power of Revival*, p. 58.
             **From "There's a Wideness in God's Mercy" by Frederick W. Faber.
September 13 *Arthur Wallis, *In the Day of Thy Power*, p. 130.
             **From "Whiter Than Snow" by James L. Nicholson.
September 14 *Ian Macpherson, *Like a Dove Descending*, p.78.
             **From "Rejoice in God's Saints" by Fred Pratt Green.
September 15 *J. Gregory Mantle, *Beyond Humiliation: The Way of the Cross,* p. 63.
             **From "I Surrender All" by Judson W. Van DeVenter.
September 16 *John M. Drescher, *Spirit Fruit*, p. 276.
             **From "Shall I, for Fear of Feeble Man" by Johann J. Winkler
September 17 *Elisabeth Elliot, *Discipline: The Glad Surrender*, p. 75.
             **From "Father of Light, Conduct My Feet" by Christopher Smart.
September 18 *Oswald Chambers, *If Ye Shall Ask*, p. 31.
September 19 *Martin Luther in a letter to Philip Melanchthon, quoted by Eric Metaxas in *Martin Luther*, p. 383.
             **From "My Hope is Built" by Edward Mote.
             ***Ibid.
September 20 *James O. Fraser; quoted in *Mountain Rain: A Biography of James O. Fraser* by Eileen Fraser Crossman, p. 105.
             **From "Great is Thy Faithfulness" by Thomas O. Chisholm.
September 21 *C. S. Lewis, *The Great Divorce*, p. 71.

September 22   *Malcolm Muggeridge, *Jesus Rediscovered*, pp. 48-49.
                **From "God Omniscient" by Daniel O. Teasley.

September 23   *Ravi Zacharias, *The Grand Weaver*, pp. 148-149.
                **From "Before Thy Throne, O God, We Kneel" by William B. Carpenter.

September 24   *Martyn Lloyd-Jones, *Walking with God*, p. 53.
                **From "Love Divine, All Loves Excelling" by Charles Wesley.

September 25   *Lee Strobel, *The Case for Christ*, p. 269.
                **From "Wonderful, Wonderful" by Haldor Lillinas.

September 26   *Leon Morris, *The Cross of Jesus*, pp. 103-104.
                **From "A Charge to Keep I Have" by Charles Wesley.

September 27   *Thomas C. Oden, *The Transforming Power of Grace*, p. 17.
                **From "At Calvary" by William R. Newell.

September 28   *Henry Scougal, *The Life of God in the Soul of Man*, Kindle Edition.

September 29   *Jim Elliot, quoted by Elisabeth Elliot in *The Journals of Jim Elliot*, pp.461-462.
                **From "Oh, Be Careful Little Eyes What You See" by Unknown Author.

September 30   *Charles Simeon, quoted in *Henry Venn and His Ministry*, Kindle Edition.
                **From "Indwelt" by Beatrice Clelland.

October 1   *Watchman Nee, *Not I But Christ*, p. 75.
              **From "Joy Unspeakable" by Barney E. Warren.

October 2   *Andrew Murray, *Absolute Surrender*, p. 119.
              **From "Abide in Christ—This Highest Blessing Gain." Author unknown.

October 3   *Kurt Koch, *The Coming One*, p. 78.
              **From "How Firm a Foundation" by George Keith.

October 4   *Warren Wiersbe, *Be Myself*, p. 322.
              **From "You Servants of God, Your Master Proclaim" by Charles Wesley.

October 5   *John Newton, quoted by Arthur Fawcett in *The Cambuslang Revival*, pp. 222-223.

October 6   *John Stott, *Evangelical Truth*, p. 54.

October 7   *E. Stanley Jones, *A Song of Ascents: A Spiritual Auto-biography*, pp. 32-33.
             **From "Happy the Church, Thou Sacred Place" by Isaac Watts.

October 8   *Charles Colson, *Life Sentence*, p. 274.

October 9   *Richard C. Halverson, quoted by V. Raymond Edman in *They Found the Secret*, p. 67.

October 10   *Joe Brice, *Pentecost*, p. 92.

October 11   *Dennis Kinlaw, *We Live as Christ*, p. 64.
             **From "Arise, My Soul, Arise" by Charles Wesley.

October 12   *George MacDonald, quoted by C. S. Lewis in *George MacDonald: An Anthology*, p.106.

October 13   *Mrs. Charles E. Cowman, *Springs in the Valley*, January 22.
             **From "Blessed Quietness" by Manie P. Ferguson.

October 14   *Adam Clarke, *Clarke's Theology*, p. 154.
             **From "Blessed Assurance" by Fanny Crosby.

October 15   *W. Phillip Keller, *Wonder O' the Wind*, pp. 40-41.

October 16   *John Fischer, *On a Hill Too Far Away*, p. 173.
             **From "At Calvary" by William R. Newell.

October 17   *David Livingstone, quoted in *David Livingstone: The Truth Behind the Legend* by Rob Mackenzie, p. 271.
             **From "We'll Work till Jesus Comes" by Elizabeth K. Mills.

October 18   *Dr. Paul Brand and Philip Yancy, *In His Image*, p. 245.
             **From "I Stand Amazed in the Presence" by Charles H. Gabriel.

October 19   *Gerald F. Hawthorne, *The Presence & the Power*, p. 239.

October 20   *Dietrich Bonhoeffer, quoted in *A Third Testament* by Malcolm Muggeridge, p. 148.
             **From "Others" by Charles D. Meigs.

October 21   *J. C. Ryle, *Walking with God*, p. 77.

October 22   *Sheldon Vanauken, *A Severe Mercy*, p. 229.
             **From "Friendship with Jesus" by Joseph C. Ludgate.

October 23   *Charles R. Swindoll, *Living Above the Level of Mediocrity*, p. 254.
             **From "When I Survey the Wondrous Cross" by Isaac

Watts.

October 24   *Raymond C. Ortlund, Jr., *Whoredom: God's Unfaithful Wife in Biblical Theology*, p. 30.
**From "I Surrender All" by Judson W. Van de Venter.

October 25   *George E. Ladd, *The Blessed Hope,* p. 146.
**From "At the Lamb's High Feast We Sing" by Robert Campbell (translator).

October 26   *David F. Wells, *No Place for Truth*, p. 183.
**From "Deeper and Deeper" by Oswald J. Smith.

October 27   *Charles Colson and Nancy Pearcey, *How Now Shall We Live?* p. 487.
**From "I'll Live for Him" by Ralph E. Hudson .

October 28   *Harry Blamires, *The Christian Mind*, p. 44.

October 29   *Os Guinness, *The Last Christian on Earth*, p. 11.

October 30   *Paul C. Vitz, *Psychology as Religion: The Cult of Self-Worship*, p. 100.
**From "The Love of God" by Frederick M. Lehman.

October 31   *James M. Kittelson, *Luther the Reformer: The Story of the Man and His Career*, p. 100.
**From "Not All the Blood of Beasts" by Isaac Watts.

November 1   *John Bunyan, *The Acceptable Sacrifice*, p. 45.

November 2   *Vallance Cook, *Thomas Cook: Evangelist-Saint*, p. 109.
**From "All That I Was" by Horatius Bonar.

November 3   *D. L. Moody, *The Overcoming Life*, p. 116.

November 4   *Sinclair Ferguson, *Devoted to God*, p. 40.
**From "All for Jesus" by Mary D. James.

November 5   *John R. W. Stott, *The Message of Romans*, 375.
**Rupert Meldenius is considered a *non de plume* used by Richard Baxter.

November 6   *Richard Collier, *The General Next to God: The Story of William Booth and the Salvation Army*, p. 44.
**From "Bring Them In" by William A. Ogden.

November 7   *Jonathan Aitken, *John Newton: From Disgrace to Amazing Grace*, p. 222.
**From "Love Each Other" by William J. Henry.

November 8   *Michael Green, *The Empty Cross of Jesus*, p. 213.

November 9   *James Stewart, *The Strong Name*, p. 156.

**From "That Man No Guard or Weapons Needs" by John Newton.

November 10 *Leighton Ford, *The Power of Story*, p. 163.

November 11 *Matthew Henry, *A Commentary on the Whole Bible*, *Hebrews* 11:7.
**From "Jesus, I My Cross Have Taken" by Henry F. Lyte.

November 12 *George Whitefield, *George Whitefield's Journals*, April 18, 1739.

November 13 *G. K. Chesterton, *A Year with G. K. Chesterton: 365 Days of Wisdom, Wit, and Wonder,* Kindle Edition, p. 41.

November 14 *F. B. Meyer, *David, Shepherd, Psalmist, King*, p. 135.
**From "Open My Eyes That I May See" by Clara H. Scott.

November 15 *"The Letter to Diognetus 5," quoted by William Barclay in *Education Ideals in the Ancient World*, p. 196.
**From "If I Gained the World, but Lost the Savior" by Anna Olander.

November 16 *J. Hudson Taylor, *The Autobiography of Hudson Taylor: Missionary to China*, Kindle Edition, p. 43.
**From "Far and Near the Fields Are Teeming" by James O. Thompson.

November 17 *Richard Wurmbrand, *Tortured for Christ*, Kindle Edition.
**From "Afflicted Saint, to Christ Draw Near" by John Fawcett.

November 18 *Anonymous, *The Kneeling Christian*, Kindle Edition.
**From "What Various Hindrances We Meet" by William Cowper.

November 19 *Matthew Henry, *Experiencing God's Presence*, Kindle Edition.
**From "All Your Anxiety" by Edward H. Joy.

November 20 *Albert Schweitzer, quoted by Ken Gire in *Answering the Call: The Doctor Who Made Africa His Life*, Kindle Edition, p. 193.
**From "Dismiss Me Not Thy Service, Lord" by Thomas T. Lynch.

November 21 *Thomas Chalmers, *The Expulsive Power of a New*

Affection, Kindle Edition.

November 22 *Howell Harris, *Howell Harris: His Own Story*, Kindle Edition.

November 23 *Charles Spurgeon, *An Autobiography*, Kindle Edition.
**From "Depth of Mercy" by Charles Wesley.

November 24 *Martin Luther, *The Theologia Germanica of Martin Luther*, Kindle Edition.
**From "Nothing But the Blood" by Robert Lowry.

November 25 *Dorothy Sayers, *Creed or Chaos*, p. 108.
**From "Fight the Good Fight of Faith" by John S. B. Monsell.

November 26 *Ted Peters, *Sin: Radical Evil in Soul and Society*, p. 8.
**From "Cursed is the One Who Trusts in Man" by Susan H. Peterson.

November 27 *Jerry White, *Honesty, Morality & Conscience*, p. 238.

November 28 *Ronald B. Allen, *And I Will Praise Him*, p. 57.
**From "Let All the People Praise Thee" by Lelia Morris.

November 29 *George MacDonald, *Creation in Christ*, edited by Rolland Hein, p. 186.

November 30 *Henry Scougal, *The Life of God in the Soul of Man*, Kindle Edition.

December 1 *H. C. G. Moule, *Philippian Studies* p. 120.

December 2 *Thomas Cook, *New Testament Holiness*, p. 57.
**From "Jesus, Thine All-Victorious Love" by Charles Wesley.

December 3 *A. J. Gordon, *The Ministry of the Spirit*, p. 116.

December 4 *Paul E. Billheimer, *Don't Waste Your Sorrows*, pp. 59-60.
**From "Day by Day" by Karolina Sandell-Berg.

December 5 *Ole Hallesby, *God's Word for Today*, November, 5.

December 6 *Matthew Henry, *A Commentary on the Whole Bible*, Psalm 62:11.
**From "Praise to the Lord, the Almighty" by Joa-chimNeander, translated by Catherine Winkworth.

December 7 *John N. Oswalt, *Isaiah: The NIV Application Commentary*, p. 448.

December 8 *Gerald F. Hawthorne, *The Presence & the Power*, p.

137.

December 9   *Gordon D. Fee, *God's Empowering Presence*, p. 890.

December 10   *L. G. Parkhurst, *Francis & Edith Schaeffer*, p. 76.
    **From "How Sweet the Name of Jesus Sounds" by John Newton.

December 11   *D. A. Carson, *A Call to Spiritual Reformation*, p. 32.
    **From "Exhortation to Prayer" by William Cowper.

December 12   *Martyn Lloyd-Jones, *Revival*, p. 253.

December 13   *Dick Lucas & Christopher Green, *The Message of 2 Peter & Jude*, p. 48.

December 14   *John Stott, *Life in Christ*, p. 128.

December 15   *A. W. Tozer, *The Root of the Righteous*, p. 80.

December 16   *A. W. Tozer, *Wingspread: Albert B. Simpson—A Study in Spiritual Altitude*, p. 49.

December 17   *A. W. Tozer, in *Let My People Go: The Life of Robert A. Jeffray*, p. 1.

December 18   *E. H. Broadbent, *The Pilgrim Church*, p. 386.

December 19   *Dennis F. Kinlaw, Cricket Albertson, ed., *Malchus' Ear and Other Sermons*, p.122.

December 20   *Francis Schaffer, quoted in L. G. Parkhurst, Jr., *Francis & Edith Schaeffer*, p. 77.

December 21   *C. T. Studd quoted by Norman Grubb in *C. T. Studd*, pp. 164-165.
    **From "I'll Go Where You Want Me to Go" by Mary Brown and Charles Prior.

December 22   *Adam Clarke, *Clarke's Commentaries*, 6:153.

December 23   *G. Campbell Morgan, quoted by Diana Wallis in *Take Heart: Daily Devotions with the Church's Great Preachers*, p. 82.

December 24   *J. Sidlow Baxter, *Awake My Heart*, p. 352.

December 25   *Ambrosiaster, quoted in *Ancient Christian Commentary on Scripture*, Thomas C. Oden, editor, 7:269.
    **From "Down From His Glory" by William E. Booth-Clibborn.

December 26   *Roger Steer, *Guarding the Holy Fire*, p. 184.

December 27   *W. Phillip Keller, *Wonder O' the Wind*, p. 231.
    **From "I Walked a Mile with Pleasure" by Robert Browning Hamilton.

December 28   *Matthew Henry, *A Commentary on the Whole Bible*,

Psalm 81:13-14.

**From "I Would Be True" by Howard A. Walter.

December 29   *John Wesley, *The Works of John Wesley*, Vol. IV,
January 1, 1790.

**From "Awake Our Souls; Away, Our Fears" by Isaac
Watts.

December 30   *A. W. Tozer, *The Knowledge of the Holy*, pp. 88, 97.

**From "When All Thy Mercies, O My God" by Joseph Addison.

December 31   *Abraham Kuyper, *Near Unto God*, p. 235.

More Books by Ralph I. Tilley . . .
(available in paperback and Kindle)

Books Authored by Ralph I. Tilley
Thirsting for God: Poetry, Meditations, Prayers
Letters from Noah (historical fiction)
Breath of God: Experiencing Life in the Spirit
A Passion for Christ: A Walk into Christlikeness
Christ in You: Living the Christ-Life
Renewed by the Spirit: 365 Daily Meditations
Wellspring: 365 Daily Readings

Anthologies Compiled & Edited by Ralph I. Tilley
The Christian's Vital Breath: An Anthology on Prayer
How Christ Came to Church: An Anthology
of the Works of *A. J. Gordon*
Called to Be Saints: An Anthology on Holiness

Books Edited and Reprinted by Ralph I. Tilley
The Mind of Christ / *John D. MacDuff* (Christian Classic)
The Bow in the Cloud / *John D. MacDuff* (Christian Classic)
In the Footprints of the Lamb / *George Steinberger* (Christian Classic)
Not Peace But a Sword: How Revival Came
to Riverby Memorial Church / *Vance Havner* (fiction)
Convicted & Transformed: The Christian's
Relationship to the Holy Spirit / *Myron S. Augsburger*
Evangelical Saints: 47 Biographical Sketches / *Ernest Gordon*

Made in the USA
Lexington, KY
15 November 2018